Jack the Ripper

JACK THE RIPPER

THE DEFINITIVE HISTORY

PAUL BEGG

Longman

An imprint of **Pearson Education**

London · New York · Toronto · Sydney · Tokyo · Singapore · Hong Kong · Cape Town
Madrid · Paris · Amsterdam · Munich · Milan

PEARSON EDUCATION LIMITED

Head Office:
Edinburgh Gate
Harlow CM20 2JE
Tel: +44 (0)1279 623623
Fax: +44 (0)1279 431059

London Office:
128 Long Acre
London WC2E 9AN
Tel: +44 (0)20 7447 2000
Fax: +44 (0)20 7447 2170
Website: www.history-minds.com

First published in Great Britain in 2003

ISBN 0 582 50631 X

British Library Cataloguing in Publication Data
A CIP catalogue record for this book can be obtained from the British Library

Library of Congress Cataloging in Publication Data
A CIP catalog record for this book can be obtained from the Library of Congress

10 9 8 7 6 5 4 3 2 1

Typeset by Fakenham Photosetting Ltd, Fakenham, Norfolk, NR21 8NN
Printed and bound in Great Britain by Bookcraft Ltd, Midsomer Norton

The Publishers' policy is to use paper manufactured from sustainable forests.

for
Martin Fido and Keith Skinner

*in the sincere hope that they will find some merit in this
effort to set the crimes in their historical context*

ACKNOWLEDGEMENTS

There are many people who have, over the years, assisted with my research into the Jack the Ripper mystery and many have become good and very valued friends. Not only would it be impossible to thank them all, but I am sure I would unintentionally insult someone to whom I owe a great debt by omitting their name. I will do no one a disservice, however, if I express my sincerest gratitude to my wife Judy and daughter Sioban, whose support and encouragement is and has been unstinting and is deeply and genuinely appreciated. My thanks, of course, also go to Josh.

Permission for 'Mitre Square' granted by Royal London Hospital Archives. Please can you include the following copyright line/ acknowledgement under the image:

© Royal London Hospital Archives. Reproduced by permission of Royal London Hospital Archives and Museum.

Permission for the photographs of Catherine Eddowes and Mary Kelly is still outstanding so could you please just include the source below these photographs.

CONTENTS

INTRODUCTION

Why does Jack the Ripper exert such fascination?

The quick and easy answer is that the mystery of his identity taunts the curiosity and inspires the imagination of the armchair detective. But such a simple answer, although true, dodges the question. There are lots of unsolved crimes, but none has the allure of Jack the Ripper. Being unsolved doesn't explain the continuing fascination with the case. The horrific brutality of the murders is even less of an answer. It is difficult to imagine how a murderer could be more brutal than Jack the Ripper, yet recent history has produced killers whose sickening depravity has far exceeded the Ripper's post-mortem mutilations – so the shock and horror of the crimes don't explain Jack the Ripper's notoriety either. As Jack the Ripper observes in Nicholas Mayer's 1979 movie, *Time After Time,* 'Ninety years ago I was a freak. Now I'm an amateur'.

It should also be observed that the 'Great Victorian Mystery', as the Jack the Ripper murders have been dubbed, hasn't always received the profound interest and detailed study it does today. The bookshelf of an enthusiast of the Ripper mystery could easily contain over eighty non-fiction books, almost all of them propounding a theory about the killer's identity, but more and more of them being highly factual reference titles. What would be noticeable, though, is that nearly every one has been published since 1960. The question about Jack the Ripper's appeal would therefore seem to have not only to do with what happened way back then but also to do with what happened in or about 1960 to ignite a mini-publishing boom that has lasted for forty years and shows no sign of dying out.

In late 1959 the pioneering television journalist and broadcaster Daniel Farson[1] was making a series called 'Farson's Guide to the British' and was introduced to Lady Aberconway, the youngest daughter of Sir Melville Macnaghten, one time Assistant Commissioner CID, Scotland Yard. She possessed some of her father's papers, amongst them a transcript of a memorandum he had written in February 1894 in which he named three men who were suspected of being Jack the Ripper, including the man he considered the most likely suspect. Farson's programme was broadcast on 12 November 1959. Macnaghten's suspect was identified only by the initials 'MJD' – who was revealed as Montague John Druitt by American-born author Tom Cullen in 1965,[2] Farson published his own investigations in 1972.[3] For the first time it seemed possible that the mysterious Jack the Ripper might be given a face – and interest in the mystery began to increase.

Interest was heightened on the publication of an article by Dr. Thomas Eldon Stowell, 'Jack the Ripper – A Solution?' in *The Criminologist* in November 1970. Stowell maintained that he had seen in the papers of Sir William Gull that Jack the Ripper was Prince Albert Victor,[4] the grandson of Queen Victoria. Despite the relative obscurity of *The Criminologist*, the story made headlines in newspapers around the world. People who had never before had an interest in the Ripper, who had never even heard of Jack the Ripper, suddenly became fascinated and the story spawned further tales. In 1973 a BBC Television series called 'Jack the Ripper' featured Joseph Sickert telling a story about how the marriage between Prince Albert Victor and a Catholic shop girl named Annie Crook had been witnessed by Mary Kelly, who later, with other prostitutes, began blackmailing the government. The Prime Minister, Lord Salisbury, turned to the Freemasons for help and Sir William Gull sought out and murdered the conspirators. This story was picked up by other writers, notably Stephen Knight in his book *Jack the Ripper: The Final Solution*, Frank Spiering's *Prince Jack*, Melvyn Fairclough's *The Ripper and the Royals* and Jean Overton Fuller's *Sickert and the Ripper Crimes*. Purists fulminate against such highly imaginative theorising, but the fact is that such sensational tales introduced people to the mystery of the Ripper, in turn creating an audience for the plethora of books published since then, including the more serious theories and growing number of specialist books.[5]

But of course the Ripper *was* remembered before 1960. He was remembered differently though. For reasons which in essence are the *raison d'être* of this book, very soon after the murders stopped – and probably even as they were being committed – Jack the Ripper passed through a strange transformation from real life murderer to bugaboo of nightmare. It is said that mothers warned their children to 'be good or Jack the Ripper will get you!'. Jack the Ripper became the ultimate representation of human evil, a 'lurker in the shadows', the personification of the feared and unknown. The image is reflected in numerous stories going back to Frank Wedekind's turn of the century *Lulu*, in which the predatory Lulu ends up a victim of the predator Jack the Ripper. References can also be found in diverse offerings like *The Longest Day* (1962), a panoramic movie about the D-Day landings of World War II. In one scene two soldiers are complaining about their commanding officer, Lieutenant Colonel Benjamin Vandervoort (John Wayne), and in mitigation one soldier says, 'But at least he knows his job'. Unimpressed, the other soldier replies, 'So did Jack the Ripper'. It isn't a great moment of cinema history, but it illustrates how Jack the Ripper had passed into the common language as an icon of evil. It wasn't necessary to say who Jack the Ripper was, what he did, or when he did it. People didn't have to know even that Jack the Ripper really existed. People understood because they knew what Jack the Ripper represented. The question, however, is why? Why did Jack the Ripper develop this almost mythic status? What distinguished Jack the Ripper from other murderers of the day?

That's the question that this book attempts to address and the argument being advanced in these pages is that Jack the Ripper would probably have been forgotten had he murdered somewhere else, at some other time, or murdered upper-class women rather than the lowest prostitute. But Jack the Ripper murdered in the East End of London, a stage already primed for something sensational to happen. This book explains what primed it. Whether it succeeds or not is something you will have to decide, but in combining the murders with key historical events that formed a backdrop to the crimes, I hope readers will have an opportunity to see the bigger picture of time and place.

Notes

1. Daniel Farson (1927–97) played himself in 'The Angry Silence' (1960) and shortly before his death made a cameo appearance in the Derek Jacobi movie 'Love is the Devil' (1998), inspired by Farson's 1993 memoir, *The Guilded Gutter Life of Francis Bacon* published in New York by Pantheon Books.
2. Cullen, Tom (1965) *Autumn of Terror: Jack the Ripper His Crimes and Times.* London: Bodley Head.
3. Farson, Daniel (1972) *Jack the Ripper.* London: Michael Joseph.
4. Stowell called him 'S', but the veil was thin and easily seen through.

5. Titles that simply wouldn't have had a market 20 or more years ago include Begg, P., Fido, M. and Skinner, K. (1990) *The Jack the Ripper A to Z*. London: Headline; Evans, Stewart P. and Skinner, Keith (2000) *The Ultimate Jack the Ripper Sourcebook*. London: Robinson; Curtis, Jr, L. Perry (2001) *Jack the Ripper and the London Press*. New Haven and London: Yale University Press; and Chisholm, Alexander, DiGrazia, Christopher-Michael and Yost, Dave (2002) *The News from Whitechapel. Jack the Ripper in The Daily Telegraph*. Jefferson, North Carolina: McFarland and Co.

chapter one

THE EAST END

... An evil plexus of slums that hide human creeping things; where filthy men and women live on penn'orths of gin, where collars and clean shirts are decencies unknown, where every citizen wears a black eye, and none ever combs his hair.[1]

I have seen the Polynesian savage in his primitive condition, before the missionary or the blackbirder or the beach-comber got at him. With all his savagery, he was not half so savage, so unclean, so irreclaimable, as the tenant of a tenement in an East London slum.[2]

During the 1880s the East End became the focus of a great many general anxieties about unemployment, overcrowding, slum dwellings, disease and gross immorality. It was feared that the unwashed masses would tumble out of their dark alleys and bleak hovels, sweep beyond their geographical containment and submerge civilised society. A working class uprising and revolution was an imagined reality that waited just around the corner. Jack the Ripper gave those fears substance and form, flesh and bone, because Jack the Ripper was a product of 'the nethworld'[3] who could – and in one case fractionally did – move out of the warren of hovels and alleys into the civilised city. And if Jack the Ripper could do it, so could the diseased savages themselves, espousing socialism, demanding employment and fair wages, education and acceptable housing, and bringing an end to the world as the Victorian middle classes knew it.

This isn't an exaggeration or an attempt to give Jack the Ripper greater importance than he deserves. Many saw the hand of the social reformer in the Ripper crimes, most famously George Bernard Shaw, whose letter to *The Star* newspaper is often quoted:

SIR, – Will you allow me to make a comment on the success of the Whitechapel murderer in calling attention for a moment to the social question? Less than a year ago the West-end press, headed by the *St. James's Gazette*, the *Times*, and the *Saturday Review*, were literally clamouring for the blood of the people – hounding on Sir Charles Warren to thrash and muzzle the scum who dared to complain that they were starving – heaping insult and reckless calumny on those who interceded for the victims – applauding to the skies the open class bias of those magistrates and judges who zealously did their very worst in the criminal proceedings which followed – behaving, in short as the proprietary class always does behave when the workers throw it into a frenzy of terror by venturing to show their teeth. Quite lost on these journals and their patrons were indignant remonstrances, argument, speeches, and sacrifices, appeals to history, philosophy, biology, economics, and statistics; references to the reports of inspectors, registrar generals, city missionaries, Parliamentary commissions, and newspapers; collections of evidence by the five senses at every turn; and house-to-house investigations into the condition of the unemployed, all unanswered and unanswerable, and all pointing the same way. The *Saturday Review* was still frankly for hanging the appellants; and the *Times* denounced them as 'pests of society'. This was still the tone of the class Press as lately as the strike of the Bryant and May girls. Now all is changed. Private enterprise has succeeded where Socialism failed. Whilst we conventional Social Democrats were wasting our time on education, agitation, and organisation, some independent genius has taken the matter in hand, and by simply murdering and disembowelling four women, converted the proprietary press to an inept sort of communism. The moral is a pretty one, and the Insurrectionists, the Dynamitards, the Invincibles, and the extreme left of the Anarchist party will not be slow to draw it. 'Humanity, political science, economics, and religion', they will say, 'are all rot; the one argument that touches your lady and gentleman is the knife'. That is so pleasant for the party of Hope and Perseverance in their toughening struggle with the party of Desperation and Death![4]

The Ripper wasn't a social reformer, nor did Bernard Shaw mean to suggest that he was. However, it was recognised then, as it has been recognised since, that the crimes provoked a horrified response from those who had hitherto disregarded or ignored the appeals of traditional reformers and for a short time brought a clamouring for change that would in its small way bring about both social changes and changes to the very fabric of the area, such as hastening the destruction of notorious slums. As Jerry White has written:

Within six years, then, Jack the Ripper had done more to destroy the Flower and Dean St. rookery than fifty years of road building, slum clearance and unabated pressure from police, Poor Law Guardians, vestries and sanitary officers.[5]

England in the 1880s was in transition, shedding the skin of Victorianism and moving towards a more modern age. Winston Churchill described the 1880s as:

> the end of an epoch. The long dominion of the middle classes, which had begun in 1832, had come to its close and with it the almost equal reign of Liberalism. The great victories had been won. All sorts of lumbering tyrannies had been toppled over. Authority was everywhere broken. Slaves were free. Conscience was free. Trade was free. But hunger and squalor and cold were also free and the people demanded something more than liberty . . .[6]

Society was undergoing fundamental and far-reaching changes to its social, political and economic structure, and as with anything new and different it was frightening, especially for those who by nature or desire abhorred change. By the end of the decade people genuinely felt that revolution was in the air and that there would be an uprising of the masses – as Basil Thompson, Assistant Commissioner CID from 1913 recalled: 'unless there was a European war to divert the current, we were heading for something very much like revolution'.[7] And the social evils of London as a whole, and the country beyond, came to be embodied by the poor, the destitute and the unemployed of the East End. As Peter Ackroyd observed in his remarkable and monumental *London: The Biography*: 'All the anxiety about the City in general then became attached to the East End in particular, as if in some peculiar sense it had become a microcosm of London's own dark life'. And Jack the Ripper came to represent the East End and so to represent all the anxieties of the age, again as Peter Ackroyd perceptively observed,

> . . . the defining sensation which for ever marked the 'East End', and created its public identity, was the series of murders ascribed to Jack the Ripper between the late summer and early autumn of 1888. The scale of the sudden and brutal killings effectively marked out the area as one of incomparable violence and depravity . . . The fact that the killer was never captured seemed only to confirm the impression that the bloodshed was created by the foul streets themselves; that the East End was the true Ripper.

It can therefore be fairly said that had Jack the Ripper killed anywhere else or killed at any other time he would today be a footnote in criminal history, a mere idle curiosity, the subject of a book here and there. But that didn't happen. By accident – it is unlikely to have been by design – Jack the Ripper committed his crimes in an area that had come to represent the dangerous and threatening underbelly of Victorian society. His notoriety for generations to come was thus assured. But what was so special about the East End? Why was it perceived as representing the evils of society? How did it come to be the way it was? We shall be exploring some of these issues in the coming chapters, but the East End itself is a special place, perhaps even a magical place for those with the gift to feel and sense it. It has a distinct character and a colourful and vibrant history, but it is not a single entity, it did not even exist in the sense of a place defined by the use of capital letters – East End – until the 1880s, when the phrase was first coined.[8] What the East End is and how it came to be the way it is forms the backdrop to this story and much is down to local geography and the Romans.

The Thames, with marshes stretching from its north and south banks, and the tidal River Lea flowing into it at what is now Poplar, created frontiers and natural barriers and isolated the East End from the surrounding areas like the houses in a cul-de-sac. The area never seems to have enjoyed any concentration of population. About ten thousand years ago some Maglemosean people left a few traces of their habitation in Hackney. This evidence and signs of a pre-Roman trackway running north of the Thames along the line of the modern Bethnal Green Road to a crossing of the Lea at Old Ford are pretty much the only evidence we have of pre-Roman settlement. London itself seems to have been a Roman foundation, although 'Londinium' is not a wholly Roman name. Indeed, it may not be Roman at all, but derived from a pre-Roman place-name of considerable antiquity.[9] Little remains in legend beyond a few stories, perhaps the best known being that of King Lud,[10] who was king of a territory with its capital at London, called Caer Lud, later corrupted into Caer Lundein and then London, and who is today remembered in the place-name 'Ludgate'. However, there remains little or no archaeological evidence to support significant pre-Roman habitation.

London developed essentially as a Roman city and it appears to have become a rather important trading centre, rather than a place of political or military significance. The Roman historian Tacitus, describing the uprising of a British tribe called the Iceni under the leadership of Queen Boudica in AD60 said that London 'undistinguished by the name of a colony, was much frequented by a number of merchants and trading vessels'.[11] The Boudican revolt[12] was a disaster for Roman Britain: Dio Cassius says that 'eighty thousand of the Romans and of their allies perished' and London was razed along with St. Albans (Verulamium) and Colchester (Camulodunum). Following Boudica's eventual defeat London was rebuilt, expanded, and provided with a forum, basilica, public baths and a palace for the provincial governor. By AD200 it had acquired considerable status and the Romans built a protective wall around the 330 acres that the city then occupied. This wall was about 21 feet (6.4m) high, ran for about 2 miles (3.2km) around the perimeter and probably used about 86,000 tonnes of stone. The wall essentially defined the City of London, what would become known as the square mile, the financial and commercial heartland. The City was entered and exited through one of five large gates that opened onto superbly constructed roads linking London with several nearby towns, and beyond them across the country. These gates have not survived, the last gates to the City and surrounding walls being demolished between 1760 and 1766, but the locations are preserved in London place-names. Newgate and Ludgate converged outside the city perimeter and ran westwards to Silchester, Hampshire. Aldersgate led out to the famous Roman road called Watling Street, then ran north-west towards St. Albans in Hertfordshire. From Bishopsgate the road led north to Godmanchester, Cambridgeshire. And from Aldgate the road ran north-east to Colchester. This was the east gate (Aldgate perhaps derived from the Saxon *Æstgeat*) and that part of London within the wall by Aldgate would have been the original East End.

The gates were grand affairs. We don't know what the original Aldgate looked like, but it was reconstructed in the late 1500s and a description has been left us by Don Manoel Gonzales in 1731:

> Upon the top of it, to the eastward, is placed a golden sphere; and on the upper battlements, the figures of two soldiers as sentinels: beneath, in a large square, King James I, is represented standing in gilt armour, at whose feet are a lion and unicorn, both couchant, the first the supporter of England, and the other for Scotland. On the west side of the gate is the figure of Fortune, finely gilded and carved, with a prosperous sail over her

head, standing on a globe, overlooking the city. Beneath it is the King's arms, with the usual motto, *Dieu et mon droit*, and under it, *Vivat rex*. A little lower, on one side, is the figure of a woman, being the emblem of peace, with a dove in one hand, and a gilded wreath or garland in the other; and on the other side is the figure of charity, with a child at her breast, and another in her hand; and over the arch of the gate is this inscription, viz., *Senatus populusque Londinensis fecit*, 1609, and under it, Humphrey Weld, Mayor, in whose mayoralty it was finished.[13]

Roman cemeteries have been found outside the City walls at Minories and Trinity Square. Three other cemeteries further out have suggested small communities, although the Romans did bury their dead along roadways. One cemetery was found at Old Ford, which was a place where roads met to cross the River Lea, an unsurprising place for a community to have developed. Another has been found at Shadwell, which is where access to the Thames is easier than at any place between the City and Blackwall, so a community may have grown up there. But the Roman cemetery discovered in Spitalfields is more difficult to explain.

In 407 the Roman troops in Britain elevated to emperor a soldier named Constantine and in 409 he withdrew the garrisons to Boulogne to seize and secure Gaul. He enjoyed success until betrayed, after which his campaign collapsed and he was captured and executed at Ravenna in 411. Constantine had not abandoned Britain, but intended to return. Troops would therefore have been deployed, albeit in seriously depleted numbers, and the political, administrative and commercial machinery would have remained in place, strong enough after three hundred years of Roman rule to survive Constantine's collapse, although officials appointed by Constantine probably changed sides, fled, or quietly retired. There is even a vague suggestion that the Britons rose against and ruthlessly slaughtered Constantine's appointees.[14] Whatever happened, by 410 someone had acquired sufficient power that they could communicate on behalf of the country and pledge the allegiance of the *civitas* (cities) of Britain to Emperor Honorius. London is unlikely to have been abandoned and left to decay and collapse, as is the impression most often received. We know that a leader called Vortigern (it's a title meaning 'High King', not a personal name) acted on behalf of an organisation known as the Council of Britons, and from what meagre evidence exists, Britain seems to have been settled, prosperous, and intellectually active. We know that the Britons adopted a heretical teaching called Pelagianism (which denied original sin – the hereditary stain inherited from Adam – and Christian grace) and that the Pope and the bishops of Gaul became so alarmed that in 429 they sent an important cleric named Germanus to Britain to confront the Pelagian leaders. The fact that a religious heresy could have gained such a foothold and cause such concern suggests that despotic leaders, civil wars, foreign invasion or major strife did not trouble Britain at that time. Germanus, we know, confronted the Pelagian leaders in a major debate and it has been plausibly argued that this took place in London. E.A. Thompson has surmised that the pope and Gallic bishops would have been little concerned had the heresy merely contaminated an out of the way town, but from London the heresy could 'vomit its poison'[15] across Britain, 'London, we need not doubt, was still by far the largest centre of population in Britain. The road system of the entire island was based on it . . .'[16]

Eventually Romano-Britain suffered a severe blow. Vortigern had followed the Roman practice of hiring mercenaries to protect vulnerable areas from attack in return for lands on which they could settle, but a mercenary army settled in Kent, under the leadership of two brothers called Hengest and Horsa, rebelled. As one chronicler described it

> All the major towns were laid low by the repeated battering of enemy rams . . . swords glinted all round as the flames crackled. It was a sad sight. In the middle of the squares the foundation stones of high walls and towers that had been torn from their lofty base, holy alters, fragments of corpses, covered with a purple crust of congealed blood, looked as though they had been mixed up in some dreadful wine-press. There was no burial to be had except in the ruins of houses or the bellies of beasts and birds.[17]

Whether or not London was one of the 'major towns' isn't known, but it probably was not.[18] Archaeological investigations suggest that the Roman way of life continued in London into the fifth century, and the lack of Saxon burials anywhere close to London suggests that someone was strong enough to protect it. There is some slight textual evidence to support the view as well.

What is curious, however, is the almost complete dominance of Saxon place-names in the area. An assimilation of Romano-British and Saxon culture would have given us a mixture of Celtic, Romano-British and Saxon names. The dominance of Saxon names doesn't suggest a gradual collapse of what went before, but a complete and sudden end, as in the case of a massive slaughter or, perhaps more likely, an evacuation following a formal cessation of territory. Whatever happened, the Roman city of London within the walls was almost completely abandoned. Eventually a Saxon trading settlement called Lundenwic established west of the city walls, in the area that is now the Strand and Charing Cross, was by the middle 600s a thriving 'market for many peoples coming by land and sea'.[19]

Whatever happened to London and its immediate environs, the Roman influence appears to have been almost completely obliterated. The influence in the East End is almost completely Saxon. The names of villages are Saxon. The names of fields are Saxon. 'The disappearance of earlier traditions is apparent in the English names given to all the natural features peculiar to the locality save the Thames and the Lea. The only names of wells, springs and steep slopes which ante-date the Norman Conquest are English; none retains the least accent of the Celt, not one recalls the terseness of the Latin tongue'.[20] Here the place-names derive from early settlers: Stibba (Stepney), Waeppa (Wapping), Blida (Bethnal), Deorlof (Dalston), Haca (Hackney), Hunberth (Homerton) and Lull (Lollsworth).

The first named place in the area of which we have a record is Stepney, mentioned in a document dated about 1000 and called Stybbanhythe. This was originally the name of the landing place of a Saxon named Stibba or Stebbe and probably referred to modern-day Ratcliff, a natural landing place on the north bank of the Thames between the marshes of Wapping and the Isle of Dogs. Stepney church, St. Dunstan's,[21] is of great antiquity and until the thirteenth century was the only church for the whole of Stepney.[22] In medieval times the parish of Stepney was huge, extending from the City to the River Lea and from Hackney to the River Thames, and it is known that from at least the reign of Edward the Confessor the lands (which then included Hackney) were held by the Bishop of London.

> The origin of the Bishop of London's estate in Stepney is unknown. Some would have it that the episcopal estates, lying as they did in 1086 in a semi-circle round London from Stepney on the east to Fulham on the west, dated from a time when the bishop had assumed or had had laid upon him the duty of protecting the City from the barbarians without. There is no evidence other than the disposition of the estates to support this view but that disposition, while it may be due to chance, is certainly arresting.[23]

Stepney is the only place in the eastern marshes of London mentioned in the Domesday Survey. The area appears to have been a well-established farming community with some landowners and peasant households. There was arable land with good meadows, rich pastures and woodlands; mills were on the Lea,[24] perhaps for milling grain destined for London, which had a population estimated to be 10,000–15,000. There were 183 peasant households consisting of 74 villeins, 52 borders and 57 cottars, and on the standard estimate of five people per household, this would have given the area a population of about 900. We know nothing about any of them.

London grew. The area within the walls was eventually rebuilt and the city grew and prospered. William the Conqueror granted London special rights and privileges and built the Tower of London, thus protecting London's population and trade. The walls around London were rebuilt and repaired several times. Roger of Wendover recounted how in 1215, the year the Magna Carta was signed, the barons entered the city by Aldgate and robbed the Jews of what money they possessed and broke their houses, afterwards repairing the walls and gates of the city with stone taken from the Jews' houses, in particular Aldgate. Another chronicler, Matthew Paris, records that Henry III ordered further repairs to Aldgate in 1257. In 1282, however, Robert Kilwarby, Archbishop of Canterbury, wanted to extend Blackfriar's Church and Edward I gave him permission to take down part of the wall for the necessary bricks. Fortunately, Edward IV permitted Ralph Joceline, mayor of London, to repair the wall between Aldgate and Aldersgate.

Beyond the walls roads radiated out and hamlets developed along their route and at river crossings; or around institutions such as hospitals such as St. Mary Spittal and Bethlehem. The East End was a quiet rural retreat, comprising fields and farmland, some cottages scattered here and there, and as time passed some grand country houses built by the affluent and influential. It would have taken a significant leap of the imagination to foresee how this idyllic rural landscape would become a *terra incognita* populated by savages.[25]

How the East End turned into that *terra incognita* – and how Jack the Ripper helped to transform that landscape – is the story of rapid development, fascinating for anyone interested in knowing the origin of the places so closely associated with Jack the Ripper and his victims. Defining the East End, however, is another matter. Strictly speaking, the East End was that part of the walled City near the eastern gate, Aldgate, and that is the view taken by the *Encyclopedia Britannica*, which declares that the East End began at a place called the Aldgate Pump, 'a stone fountain constructed beside a well at the confluence of Fenchurch Street and Leadenhall Street; the existing pump lies a few yards to the west of the original'.[26] Others have argued that the real East End begins at the point where Whitechapel Road and Commercial Road meet, for long known as Gardiner's Corner after a large and now demolished department store that dominated the area. But the real problem is defining where the East End ended and what land it encompassed, because not only do the boundaries seem to expand and contract almost at the whim of the authority consulted, the East End for many has more than just a geographical context. Some commentators[27] include Bermondsey and Rotherhithe on the south side of the river, others thought with some justification, socially but not geographically, that it exclusively denoted the riverside districts on the north of the Thames,[28] and others included West Ham and East Ham in Essex.[29] Such diversity explains why each area had its own 'peculiar flavour'. As William Booth put it, 'One seems to be conscious of it in the streets. It may be in the faces of the people . . . or it may lie in the sounds one hears or in the character *of the people*'.[30] But as a widely accepted[31] rule of thumb the East End is the area of land bounded to the east by the River Lea, which joins the Thames at Poplar and formerly marked the boundary between Middlesex and Essex, to the west by the city wall, to the north by Clapton Common and to the south the Thames.[32] To all intents and purposes it includes the three old Metropolitan Boroughs of Stepney, Poplar and Bethnal Green and is essentially the area of Tower Hamlets. It must be said, however, that the real East End is the community just within and just beyond the eastern gates, primarily Spitalfields and Whitechapel, the heartland of Jack the Ripper.

From the Roman walled City three roads ran vaguely eastwards. The most important was Ermine Street, which ran from Bishopsgate through Spitalfields and Shoreditch to Kingsland and Stamford Hill and then to the north. A second road ran from Aldgate, inclined north and crossed the River Lea at Old Ford, continuing on to Stratford Langthorne, then splitting into two branches, one going into Essex and the other turning north-eastwards towards East Anglia and Colchester. Its precise route is not known, although an early map shows a road diverging from the Essex road at Mile End

Gate and then proceeding westward to Old Ford. The third road left a picket-gate near the site of the future Tower of London and followed a route similar to the modern Ratcliffe Highway towards Shadwell.

Aldgate opened onto what is today Aldgate High Street, which has various name changes as it runs towards Whitechapel – from which the Jack the Ripper murders derived their early name of the Whitechapel Murders – and on through Mile End to Bow and the River Lea. Whitechapel itself takes its name from the lime-washed chapel dedicated to St. Mary Matfelon (the derivation of *Matfelon* is uncertain but may be the name of a founder) that gave the district its name. The chapel was built in the thirteenth century and in about 1338 became the parish church of St. Mary Whitechapel. It was rebuilt several times over the succeeding years and in most recent times was noted both for an open-air pulpit from which preachers could either harangue pedestrians or, more often, preach to crowds too large to all get into the church itself, and for a clock that overhung Whitechapel Road. During World War II the church was badly damaged by German bombing and had to be demolished. The area is now a small park.

Beyond Whitechapel was Mile End, which retained its ruralness throughout the Middle Ages, a favourite place of recreation for Londoners and a convenient place close to the City for people to gather, it was where the men of Essex met Richard II during the Peasants' Revolt (1381) and where in 1299 a parliament was held in the home of Henry de Waleis, Lord Mayor of London, to confirm Magna Carta. By the end of the sixteenth century Stow was complaining that 'this common field, being sometime the beauty of this city on that part is so encroached upon by building of filthy cottages, and with other purpressors, inclosures and lay stalls, that in some places [Mile End Road] scarce remaineth a sufficient highway for the meeting of carriages and droves of cattle'. It developed very rapidly, the western part, being named Mile End New Town, becoming little more than an extension of Spitalfields.

Mile End, Whitechapel and Spitalfields were all victims of the growth and expansion of London. People moved beyond the City walls and they moved west. Both the river and the prevailing winds went from west to east. This meant that the Thames, the main source for the disposal of effluent, provided comparatively clean water in the West and carried the effluent to the East. The winds did the same with smoke and all manner of noxious fumes from thousands of homes and businesses. This had two profound effects. Those who could avoid it lived in the healthier and more sanitary west and only the poorest lived in the east; and the east was accordingly a good place to locate the most noxious of trades, such as tanning, glue-making and brewing, all of which produced odours that hung heavy over the surrounding district. Thus it was that the stink industries moved east, along with the poorest of people, who in turn needed basic housing. The east was unfashionable for homes, the locale of unpleasant, malodorous and sometimes dangerous jobs, and dominated by the poor and deprived. It was a 'nether world', its inhabitants perceived as troglodytes, barely aware of the civilised standards and morals of the West End. Mile End was home to a large dye-house, extensive warehouses for Trueman's brewery, metalworks, a sugar refinery, saw mill, timber yards and a fish-curing factory. Between 1802 and 1901 the population increased from 5,000 to 18,000.

The Priory of the Holy Trinity at Aldgate was founded in 1108. It applied for, and was granted ownership of, the lands immediately beyond the City wall – what would in future be called Portsoken Ward. In the middle of the twelfth century it gave land to the east of the Tower for a hospital for the poor, which later took the name of the Royal Hospital of St. Katherine and enjoyed the patronage of all the Queens of England throughout the Middle Ages. For this reason it was not dissolved by Henry VIII, and survived until the site was required for docks in the 1820s, when it was demolished. Walter Besant in his book *London*[33] exclaimed: 'Poor East London! It had one – only one – ancient and venerable foundation, and they have wantonly and uselessly destroyed it'.

From the Royal Hospital of St. Katherine to Aldgate ran a road called the Minories that took its name from the Convent of the Sisters of St. Clare, the sisters being known variously as 'Poor Clares', 'Little Sisters' or 'Minoresses'. The convent was founded in 1293 by Edmund, Earl of Lancaster, Leicester and Derby (brother to Edward I), probably on behalf of his wife Blanche d'Artois, queen of Navarre. It survived until surrendered to Henry VIII in 1539 by Dame Elizabeth Salvage, the last abbess. Thereafter, as London chronicler John Stow recalled,

> In place of this house of nuns is now built divers fair and large storehouses for armour and habiliments of war, with divers workhouses, serving to the

same purpose: there is a small parish church for inhabitants of the close, called St. Trinities.

Near adjoining to this abbey, on the south side thereof, was sometime a farm belonging to the said nunnery; at the which farm I myself in my youth have fetched many a halfpenny worth of milk, and never had less than three ale pints for a halfpenny in summer, nor less than one ale quart for a halfpenny in the winter, always hot from the kine, as the same was milked and strained. One Trolop, and afterwards Goodman, were the farmers there, and had thirty or forty kine to the pail. Goodman's son, being heir to his father's purchase, let out the ground first for grazing of horses, and then for garden-plots, and lived like a gentleman thereby.[34]

By the 1890s it was a place of general trade but the church of the Holy Trinity of the Minoresses was destroyed in 1940.

At Aldgate, almost opposite Minories, was a street called Hogge Lane which connected with Bishopsgate Street. Another road, Houndsditch, also ran north from Aldgate, but it wasn't a street until the mid-1500s. Prior to that time it was a moat or ditch that bounded the City wall and according to John Stow derived its name because it was used by the City to dump rubbish 'especially dead dogges'. Another and perhaps more reasonable suggestion is that it was the location of the kennels for the dogs for the City hunt. The chronicler Richard of Cirencester[35] says that King Edmund Ironside's (c.980–1016) murderer, the traitorous Edric, was slowly roasted to death in the flames of torches and his body then flung into Houndsditch, but Richard of Cirencester is an unreliable source and it is likely that Edmund Ironside died of natural causes. John Stow claimed that in his youth there was a field next to Houndsditch owned by the Holy Trinity Priory where sick people had cottages and where every Friday people gave them alms. By the time he wrote in the 1590s, however, the ditch had been filled in and levelled and carpenters' yards and large houses built on it. It eventually became the location of an old clothes sellers' market and was notorious for pickpockets, visitors in the nineteenth century being advised to leave their valuables at home and not take offence at what was called 'Bishopsgate Banter'.

Hogge or Hog Lane was known at least by the end of the 1500s as Peticote or Petticoat Lane, so named, it is popularly said, because of the increasingly fashionable clothes dealers who carried on business in the area. It wasn't until after 1665, when the Great Plague drove out the fashionable folk, that Huguenot weavers and Jewish traders moved in – and by the 1750s it was a well-established trading centre. The name was changed to Middlesex Street in about 1830, though it never successfully threw off the name Petticoat Lane, and in the Ripper's day, as today, it formed the boundary between the City of London and Tower Hamlets.

Hog Lane joined Bishopsgate and led to the Priory of St. Mary Spital, of which more shortly.

The Bishop's Gate which stood at the northern end of modern day Camomile Street led out onto Ermine Street, which ran north to Lincoln and York. Being a major road – one of the most important roads in Roman Britain – it was quickly lined with buildings, among the first being the Priory of St. Mary Spital. The Priory of St. Mary Bethlehem was another establishment, founded in 1247 by Sheriff Simon Fitz Mary. By 1377 a hospital attached to this priory was being used for the care of 'distracted people', although 'care' meant being chained to a wall, or when violent, ducked in water or whipped. The Priory itself was bought from the King at the time of the Dissolution and converted into a lunatic asylum, when it was known as 'Bedlam'. The hospital was relocated in 1675 and the site is now occupied by Liverpool Street Station.

According to John Stow, in his day a large inn called the Dolphin stood at the junction of Houndsditch and Bishopsgate Street, and a short distance away was a large and sumptuous house where Stow says Queen Elizabeth once stayed. It was so overwhelmingly grand that it was known mockingly as Fisher's folly. Stow wrote:

> From Fisher's folly up to the west end of Berward's Lane, of old time so-called, but now Hogge lane, because it meeteth with Hogge lane, which commeth from the bars without Aldgate, as is afore showed, is a continual building of tenements, with alleys of cottages, pestered, etc. There is there a large close called Tasel close, sometime for that there were tassels planted for use of cloth-workers, since letten to the cross-bow makers wherein they used to shoot for games at the popinjay: now the same being enclosed with a brick wall, serveth to be an artillery yard, whereunto the gunners of the tower do weekly repair namely, every Thursday; and there levelling certain brass pieces of great artillery against a butt of earth, made for that purpose, they discharge them for their exercise.

A map of the area dating from before 1600 clearly shows how the area of Spitalfields was an idyllic country retreat. Buildings line the main arteries, but behind them are fields in which animals are shown grazing, archers are practising, a few cottages scattered here and there, and the dominating hospital of St. Mary Spital with large formal gardens and orchards beyond. A far cry from the slum it became in Jack the Ripper's day. Along the riverside, however, there was a different story.

The natural landing place of Ratcliff had been used as a docks for shipbuilding in the 1300s, but increasingly it was an area for repairing, fitting out and victualling ships, including many ships engaged in the sixteenth century voyages of discovery. But in the first half of the 1500s Wapping Marsh was drained by a Dutchman, Cornelius Vanderdelft, and the waterfront began to be developed, the hamlets there expanding into peculiarly narrow and serpentine shapes as they followed the line of the river. By the end of the 1500s the area was becoming slumland and Stow described Wapping High Street as 'a continual street, or filthy straight passage, with alleys of small tenements or cottages, built, inhabited by sailors' victuallers'. By Charles II's day the area was mainly populated by seamen of the royal navy and Pepys often described the disturbances they made. In 1688 the notorious Judge Jeffreys was captured at the Red Cow, one of many alehouses in Wapping, whilst trying to escape to France. Dr. Johnson recommended Wapping as a colourful place to visit, but Boswell was unimpressed. It was at Wapping that pirates were hanged at what was called Execution Dock, their bodies left to hang until covered by three tides. Captain Kidd and one of his companions, Darby Mullins, were hanged here on 23 May 1701.

Nowhere really suffered from misreporting – or invention – more than Limehouse, a primarily Chinese quarter that developed a terrible and sinister reputation for opium dens and villainous orientals. Sax Rohmer[36] created Limehouse-based Dr. Fu Manchu – 'a brow like Shakespeare and a face like Satan ... the yellow peril incarnate' bent on world domination. Thomas Burke wrote several stories based here, collected most notably in *Limehouse Nights* and *The Pleasantries of Old Quong*, which feature innocent young girls and dope-driven deviant orientals. Rohmer had never been to Limehouse and Burke admitted in his autobiography *Son of London* that he knew nothing at all about the Chinese and was 'thus able to write those stories with the peculiar assurance a man has who knows nothing of what he is writing or talking about'.

Apart from the docks, it was in the area of Spitalfields that expansion began, spreading beyond to Whitechapel and Mile End in one direction and Bethnal Green in the other. This would be Jack the Ripper's territory, a land of extreme poverty and vice.

Spitalfields derived its name from the Priory of St. Mary Spital, a religious house founded by Walter and Rosia Brune in 1197 and refounded as a hospital in 1235, eventually becoming the largest hospital in medieval London. Surrounded by open space, a cemetery, a farm, gardens and an orchard, its existence meant that the area remained largely rural until the priory was dissolved in 1538 and it became courtiers' residences, as Stow recorded: 'In place of this hospital, and near adjoining, are now many fair houses built for receipt and lodging of worshipful persons'. Much of the land was bought from the king by Stephen Vaughan, although he didn't buy it all in one go, but acquired it over time, and on his death the estate was inherited by his son, also named Stephen, among whose prominent tenants was the French Ambassador, Charles de Foix.

Vaughan's estate did not include the area known as Lollesworth Field. Records from as early as 1276 refer to *Lolsworth* Fields and probably recall an owner or tenant named Loll; but by the late twelfth century the area was known as *Spittellond* (in records of 1399) and by 1561 as *Spyttlefieldes*, at which time they were sold to a man named Christopher Campion, whose heirs allowed much of Lolesworth Field to be dug for brickearth in 1576. According to John Stow:

> On the east side of this churchyard lieth a large field, of old time called Lolesworth, now Spittle field; which about the year 1576 was broken up for clay to make brick; in the digging wherof many earthen pots, called urnæ, were found full of ashes and burnt bones of men, to wit, of the Romans that inhabited here ... Every one these pots had in them with the ashes of the dead one piece of copper money, with the inscription of the Emperor then reigning: some of them were of Claudius, some of Vespasian, some of Nero, of Anthoninus Pius, of Trajanus and others.

Other items were found including jars of various sorts containing, or once containing, oils and waters, and stone coffins which Stow supposed to be of important Britons or Saxons, plus the bones of people buried in long-rotten wooden coffins.

The ownership of Spitalfield passed through several hands, Campion's heirs selling it in 1581 to Richard Celye, who sold it to Ralph Bott in 1590, who in turn sold it to a London goldsmith named

Richard Hanbery in 1594. Hanbery bequeathed the land to his son-in-law, Sir Edmund Wheler, another London goldsmith, who lived in the village of Datchet in Buckinghamshire and was Sheriff in 1602. He expanded the estate with other purchases until it was divided in 1649, the northern part of the estate, roughly that which extended along the line of Lamb Street and Hanbury Street towards Shoreditch, going to Sir William Wheler of Westbury, and the southern part placed in the care of Edward Nicholas and George Cook, trustees of the seven daughters of Sir William Wheler of Datchet. Sir William Wheler of Westbury began to lay out streets on his property in the 1650s and 1660s, most notably Wheler Street which ran north-south and was a main thoroughfare almost completely obliterated when a more modern street, Commercial Street, was built. The remains of Wheler Street can be seen today running up the side of the Commercial Tavern.

The southern part contained the Spitalfield. Daniel Defoe could remember it as 'a field of grass with cows feeding on it' and it was crossed by footpaths from Losesworth Lane (later Browns Lane and then Hanbury Street[37]) to Vine Court (formerly on the north side of Lamb Street); from the 'Red Lion' (an inn on the corner of Puma Court, which is a small passage breaking the block of buildings between Hanbury Street and Fournier Street) to Smock Alley; and from the 'George' to Smock Alley (today's Artillery Passage). Nicholas and Cook built the western side of Crispin Street and petitioned to close the footpaths crossing Spitalfield. The permission was granted in June 1673, but only on condition that they replaced them with a road, which the authorities stipulated must be about 40 feet long and 24 feet wide. Nicholas and Cook complied and the result was Datchet Street, which was of the stated dimensions. Datchet Street became corrupted to Dorset Street and in due course it would become one of the most notorious and reputedly one of the most dangerous streets in the neighbourhood. Jack the Ripper's last victim was horribly butchered here. It was at this time that the neighbouring street, New Fashion Street (later White's Row[38]), and Paternoster Row (the eastern end of Brushfield Street) were built.

In 1679 a man named John Balch, a silk thrower probably of Somerset origin, married Katherine Wheler, one of the seven Wheler daughters, and bought out the shares in Spitalfield of three other sisters (Frances Wheler, spinster; Anne Pitcarne, widow; and Mary, wife

of Martin Vandenancker). He then applied for the right to hold a
market on the land, which was granted on 29 July 1682, market days
being restricted to Thursdays and Saturdays. The market was for
both vegetables and meat and it grew in importance, by 1770 being
described as 'of great reputation for all sorts of provisions'. It was in
1875 that the leasehold interest in the market together with the
market franchise was sold to Robert Horner, who had begun his
working life as a porter in the market, and the building was completely rebuilt. The plaster panel over the arched entrance in the
south range is inscribed 'Spitalfields Market rebuilt by Robert
Horner during the year of Queen Victoria's Jubilee 1887'. On the
Lamb Street corner is a plaster panel inscribed, 'This market was finished rebuilding by R. Horner 1893'. In 1920 it was bought by the
Corporation of London, who over the next seven years extended
the market, in the process acquiring property on the north side of
Lamb Street, the south side of Brushfield Street and also in the area
of the Old Artillery Ground. Enlargements to the market caused the
destruction of the northern part of Crispin Street and one side of
Dorset Street.

Apart from Spitalfields market – the foremost fruit and vegetable
market in London (and now entirely relocated) – the most dominant
feature of the area is the magnificent Christ Church. At a meeting in
1710 it was decided that Spitalfields should become a Parish and an
organisation known as The Commissioners For Building Fifty New
Churches in London and Westminster and the Suburbs[39] decided that
the parish church would be designed by their surveyor, Nicholas
Hawksmoor, a pupil of Sir Christopher Wren. The foundations were
dug in 1714, the foundation stone laid the following year, and the
church, completed at a cost of £40,000, was consecrated in 1729. It
still stands, an imposing structure that would once have looked far
grander, being set back off the road (before the present Commercial
Street was built). It was struck by lightning in 1841 and some fairly
nasty alterations were carried out, but it remains one of Hawksmoor's
masterpieces. By the 1880s it reflected the general dilapidation of the
area and the churchyard was commonly known as 'Itchy Park' because
of the number of bug-infested and scratching homeless people who
gathered there. Even at the turn of the century Jack London described
it as 'a welter of rags and filth, of all manner of loathsome skin diseases,
open sores, bruises, grossness, indecency, leering monstrosities and
bestial faces'.[40]

Christ Church stands today on the corner of Commercial Street, which was laid out in 1849, many buildings being demolished in the process, including several buildings at the Market end of Church Street (present Fournier Street). It was therefore some distance down the street that a carpenter named Joseph Drew built three houses and, in March 1758, a 'messuage ... and wharehouses thereunto adjoining' was built on Joseph Drew's instruction by John Sabatier. In due course it would become a public house named Ten Bells, after the number of bells then in the Church, and with the construction of Commercial Street would become a corner pub. It was the last place in which a Ripper victim named Mary Kelly was seen drinking and some two hundred years later an enterprising landlord renamed the pub the 'Jack the Ripper'. Although it reverted back to its original name in the late 1980s, it remains a mecca for Ripperphiles and tourists.

Fournier Street itself contains some fine examples of Georgian houses built at a time when the area was the largely prosperous home of silk weavers known as Huguenots, the French Protestant followers of John Calvin. When, in 1685, Louis XIV revoked the 1598 Edict of Nantes, so ending their freedom to worship, over 200,000 Huguenots fled France. About 50,000 settled in England, some in Soho and Wandsworth, but most in Spitalfields. They quickly established a silk weaving industry that was hugely successful, employing a large number of people and proving highly profitable. Many people made large fortunes, as some of the fine houses in the East End today reveal, but in 1860 the Government introduced a free-trade policy that allowed the duty-free import of French material. The effect on the British silk industry was catastrophic: in 1854 50,000 people in East London were employed in the silk industry; by 1880 the figure had shrunk to just 3,300. The knock-on effect was poverty, unemployment and a deterioration of social conditions.

Roughs inhabited some of the streets in the area and crime was beginning to increase. Some infamous characters in Whitechapel during the 1700s included the thug Dick Turpin, who was made unjustly famous as a highwayman by Harrison Ainsworth in his novel *Rookwood*. Born in Essex in 1705, Turpin was apprenticed to a butcher in Whitechapel until he was discharged 'for the brutality of his manners'. He turned to crime, including highway robbery, teaming up sometime after 1735 with Matthew King and operating largely in the East End, until ambushed by the law when drinking in an inn called the Old Red Lion[41] on Whitechapel High Street. King was mortally wounded, possibly shot in the back by Turpin to create a diversion, but Turpin escaped and fled to York (his horse wasn't called Black Bess and he didn't complete the journey in a single fifteen hour ride), where he was eventually discovered and executed on 7 April 1739.

But the worst of the slums to emerge from all this building had its origins in 1642 when Lewis and Thomas Fossan acquired land in the area and began to lay out the streets. By 1654 they had built Fossan Street (which over time became corrupted into Fashion Street), George Street (now Lolseworth Street) and part of Thrall Street (corrupted to Thrawl Street). Then in August 1655 the Fossans leased two plots south of Fashion Street to John Flower and Gowan Dean, bricklayers of Whitechapel, who built Flower and Dean Street. The houses originally built were not high quality and ceased to be maintained, and additional building was of the lowest standard. About 1676 the northern and eastern parts of the Fossan Estate were owned by George Keate, described as a merchant of St. Bartholomew's Exchange, London. The property was passed down through Keate's family, who did much building: Upper Keate Street (the western part of Thrawl Street) and Lower Keate Street (which ran south from Flower and Dean Street and no longer exists). The quality of the houses erected was appalling, so bad in fact that in 1854 the fronts of five houses were so ruinous that they had to be demolished. A line of men named George Keete came to own the property. Of them, one was a man of note and distinction,[42] being a writer, artist and antiquarian who moved in elevated circles and counted Voltaire among his friends. He did some rebuilding but 'without any very deliberate policy of development or improvement'[43] and on his death the properties passed via his wife to their daughter Georgiana[44] and her husband John Henderson.[45] None of these people did anything to the buildings they owned, but left them to deteriorate. The majority became common lodging houses of the most disreputable kind, offering a bed for the night, often shared, for a few pence. By 1805 Georgiana and her husband John Henderson owned 250 dilapidated houses that brought in an annual rental of £700. F.H.W. Sheppard comments:

> That these lodging houses made a profit for their owners seems incredible in view of the tenants' poverty but ... it was done. A proprietor of six houses in Thrawl Street, who had 'a country house in Hampstead'

installed in each house a 'deputy' on whom he calls every week to collect his dues.[46]

Seventy years later, in 1877, it was reported that the registered common lodging houses of the Flower and Dean Street area contained in all 123 rooms with accommodation for 757 occupants. At 4d a night per person, this would have generated an annual income of £4,368 – not a bad profit from some crumbling old houses. The area had become notorious, James Greenwood in 1885 describing the 27 courts, streets and alleys packed into the square quarter mile area collectively known as, and centred on, the Flower and Dean Street rookery, as 'what is perhaps the foulest and most dangerous street in the whole metropolis'.

Some effort was made to clear away the rookeries, not because anyone was really much concerned about the brutalising lives the people living there suffered, but because they feared the squalid conditions may provoke action which would spew out from its East End confinement and confront respectable London – 'What concerned the middle classes were street crime, prostitution, the threat of revolt, expensive pauperism, infectious disease spreading to respectable London . . .'.[47] Perhaps the most significant measure, as we shall see, was the building of Commercial Street. For a long time nothing was built on the road, some sites remaining undeveloped as late as 1870. It was during this time that many buildings were erected, among them the Commercial Tavern at the junction of the old main thoroughfare of Wheler Street and the new one, Commercial Street, which was built about this time by Abraham Keymer of the Norfolk Arms in Bethnal Green on a site leased to him in February 1865. The H Division police station in Commercial Road, the scene of so much activity during the Ripper scare, was built in 1874–75 by Messrs Lathey Brothers to the design of Frederick H. Caiger, Surveyor for the Metropolitan Police. At that time it had a three storey frontage, the top storey and Elder Street wing not being added until 1906.

This, then, was Jack the Ripper's East End. A place of noble origins – fields and streams, grazing land, rural inns, the finest strawberries and cream – that fast became a gigantic slum. Most of the buildings are long gone, but a few remain, now renovated, restored and expensive, but when walking the Ripper's East End, as thousands of people do every year, or merely returning from the comfort of one's armchair to those streets of carboniferous fogs, gas lamps and hansom cabs, it is valuable and instructive to know a little of its history, to know how it got that way.

Commercial Street connected Whitechapel with another noted slum district, Shoreditch, which has a long history stretching back to Roman times. In 1576 James Burbage founded the Theatre, the first playhouse in England, which was dismantled in 1598 and moved across the river to Southwark, where re-erected it became The Globe. The area began to undergo considerable development and very soon established for itself the reputation of being 'a disreputable place, frequented by courtesans'. By the mid-nineteenth century it was perhaps best known for its violent street gangs, particularly one known as the Old Nichol Gang after their notorious place of origin, the Nicol, to be immortalised in literature as the Jago. These gangs roamed the district and caused considerable trouble. They were even suspected of committing the Jack the Ripper murders.

Notes

1. Morrison, Arthur (1894) *Tales of Mean Streets*. London: Methuen.
2. Huxley, T.E. quoted in Besant, Walter (1901) *East London*. London: Chatto and Windus.
3. Gissing, George (1889) *The Netherworld*. London: Smith Edler.
4. Shaw, George Bernard (1888) 'Blood Money To Whitechapel', *The Star*, 24 September.
5. White, Jerry (1980) *Rothschild Buildings: Life In An East End Tenement Block 1887–1920*. London: Routledge and Kegan Paul, pp.29–30.
6. Churchill, Winston Spencer (1906) *Lord Randolph Churchill*. New York: Macmillan.
7. Thompson, Basil (1922) *Queer People*. London: Hodder and Stoughton.
8. Barnett, Samuel (1886) 'Sensationalism and Social Reform', *Nineteenth Century*, xix, no. 2, February.
9. See for discussion Rivet, A.L.F. and Smith, Colin (1979) *The Place Names of Roman Britain*. London: B.T. Batsford.
10. Lud may be a fictional figure with his origins in mythic pre-Christian beliefs, but the chronicler Geoffrey of Monmouth portrays him in his audacious *History of the Kings of Britain* as the elder brother of Cassivellaunus and father of Tenuantius, two genuine historical figures. Cassivellaunus was the overlord of a confederation of several tribes collectively known as the Catuvallauni which opposed Julius Caesar in his second expedition to Britain in 54BC. Caesar said that Cassivelaunus's territories 'are divided from the maritime states by the river called Tamesis, about eighty miles from the sea' (Caesar De Bello Gallico v.11) and went on to say that he 'led his army into the borders of Cassivellaunus as far as the River Thames, which can be crossed at one

place only on foot, and that with difficulty . . .' (Caesar De Bello Gallico v.18). But it is Tenuantius who is utterly fascinating because his name is derived from Tasciovanus, who ruled the Catuvallauni from c.20BC–c.AD10 and is known to us only from coins uncovered by archaeologists. That Geoffrey of Monmouth knew about Tasciovanus is seen as evidence supporting his claim to have possessed '. . . a certain very ancient book written in the British language' brought for him from Brittany by Walter, Archdeacon of Oxford. Geoffrey of Monmouth's history might therefore have a factual foundation insofar as many of its characters are concerned, albeit that their lives are largely Geoffrey's invention.

11. Tacitus, *Annales* xiv, 33.
12. Prasutagus, the king of one of the native tribes of Britain called the Iceni, had voluntarily placed his people under the rule of the Romans in the belief that they would be treated honourably, but on his death the Romans behaved as if the Iceni had been defeated in war; property was plundered, Prasutagus's widow, Boudica, was scourged, and his daughters raped. As a result the Iceni rose against the Romans and under the leadership of Boudica, described by the Roman writer Dio Cassius as 'very tall, in appearance most terrifying, in the glance of her eye most fierce, and her voice was harsh; a great mass of the tawniest hair fell to her hips', rebelled with great and considerable violence.
13. Gronzales, Don Manoel (1888) *London in 1731*. London: Cassell and Co.
14. *De Vita Christiana*, c.411.
15. Gildas (1978) *De Excidio et Conquesti et Britanium* (*On The Ruin and Conquest of Britain*) 24: 3–4. Edited and translated by Michael Winterbottom. Chichester, Sussex: Phillimore.
16. Thompson, E.A. (1984) *Saint Germanus of Auxerre and the End of Roman Britain*. Woodbridge, Suffolk: The Boydell Press.
17. Gildas, *ibid*.
18. The *Anglo-Saxon Chronicle* for 456 records that the Saxon leaders Hengest and Æsc defeated the Britons at Crayford in Kent and that the Britons fled to London 'in great terror', presumably because the fortified city not only still stood, but afforded protection. From *The Anglo-Saxon Chronicle* (1972). Translated by G.N. Garmonsway. London: J.M. Dent.
19. Bede (1982) *A History of the English Church and People*. London: Penguin.
20. McDonnell, Kevin (1978) *Medieval London Suburbs*. Chichester: Phillimore, p.9.
21. Allegedly rebuilt in the tenth century by St. Dunstan, Bishop of London 959–60, but this is highly unlikely.
22. Some 67 parishes would be created in this extensive area, the first of which was Whitechapel.
23. McDonnell, *ibid*. and Madge, S.J. (1938) *Early Records Of Harringay alias Hornsey*. Hornsey: Public Libraries Committee, pp. 45–57.
24. The bishop had four; Hugh de Berners one, Aluuin, son of Britmar, one, Edmurd, son of Algot, one, possibly at Old Ford.

25. East Enders were often compared to assorted 'savages'. Salvation Army founder William Booth likened them to 'African pygmies', scientist T.H. Huxley to 'Polynesian savages'.

26. Ackroyd, Peter (2000) *London: The Biography*. London: Chatto and Windus, p.676.

27. Fletcher, Geoffrey (1965) *Pearly Kingdom*. London: Hutchinson, p.10. Fletcher argues that the East End had expanded beyond its traditional confines to embrace East Ham, West Ham and Stratford, and that Bermondsey and Deptford south of the river 'are as unmistakably East End as Whitechapel', which indeed they might be, but are they east London?

28. Smith, Ashley (1961) *The East-Enders*. London: Secker and Warburg, p.34. Smith paints a personal view, but one shared by other commentators who feel that the docklands provided the East End with a character and many may associate that character with the East End as a whole, but it was the character of docklands, that spread out from docklands, and was not the unique character of the East End that grew up beyond Aldgate.

29. Sinclair, Robert (1950) *East London. The East and North East Boroughs*. London: Robert Hale, pp.32–6. Sinclair, who carries with him considerable authority, rejects the view (held by the current author) that the real East End is the 3 square mile area just beyond Aldgate and Bishopsgate and he does so passionately, seeing it as defined solely by a state of mind. 'I see no reason to use the phrase "East End" unless very exceptionally to indicate the state of somebody's mind. The social assumptions are now obsolete which prevailed when the phrase became fashionable: its use has always been patronising, and its overtones are offensive to any ear that has not been dulled by custom'. But this seems to focus too closely on the conditions of poverty that marked out that area, rather than the historical expansion that began there.

30. Booth, General (1890) *In Darkest England and the Way Out*. London: Salvation Army.

31. Burke, Thomas (1932) *The Real East End*. London: Constable, p.4 and Cox, Jane (1994) *London's East End: Life and Traditions*. London: Weidenfeld and Nicolson.

32. Rose, Millicent (1951) *The East End of London*. London: Cresset Press, p.v. This book is now horribly out of date but probably remains the most authoritative history of the area.

33. Besant, Walter (1894) *London*. London: Chatto and Windus.

34. Stow, John (1987) *The Survey of London*. London: J.M. Dent.

35. Richard of Cirencester (1863–69) *Speculum Historiale de Gestis Regum Angliae*. Edited in two volumes by John E.B. Mayor. London: Longman.

36. Sax Rohmer's real name was Arthur Henry Ward.

37. Hanbury Street seems to have been built about 1648, for at that time it was described as 'newly named' Lolesworth Lane, but it took the name Browns Lane very soon afterwards, after a tenant named William Brown, who owned a cow house and pasturage in the area. Corbet's Court, which runs off Hanbury Street, was the destination of one of the men who, en

route to work there, discovered the body of Jack the Ripper's first victim. The Ripper's second victim was found in Hanbury Street, and it was the location of the Salvation Army's first refuge for 'fallen women'. Rebecca Jarret, a central figure in the 'Maiden Tribute' scandal, briefly stayed there.

38. Jack Sheppard, famed for his daring escapes from prison and less so for his girlfriends – 'Edgeworth Bess' (real name Elizabeth Lyon) and the superbly named 'Poll Maggot' – was born in White's Row in March 1702. After a short but celebrated criminal career he was brought to justice by the corrupt Jonathan Wild and executed at Tyburn in 1724.

39. The newly-elected High Church Tory Government celebrated its victory with a decision to built fifty new churches and in 1711 the appropriate act of parliament – the Fifty New Churches Act – was passed, the money being raised by a tax on coal.

40. London, Jack (1903) *The People of the Abyss*. London: Macmillan.

41. The Old Red Lion, which was located near the south exit of Aldgate East underground station, was demolished at the end of the 19th century and rebuilt, but for many years stood empty and forlorn and was demolished during the writing of this book.

42. Descended from Catherine Seymour, sister of Lady Jane Grey, George Keate was born at Trowbridge, Wiltshire, on 30 November 1729. Although he was called to the bar in 1753 and made bencher of Middle Temple in 1791, he never practised. He lived abroad, notably in Geneva and Rome, before returning to England and devoting himself to literature – mainly poetry – art and archaeology and antiquities. He produced a volume a year for many years, exhibited six pictures at the Society of Artists and thirty at the Royal Academy. He was elected F.S.A. and F.R.S. in 1766. In his later years his health declined markedly and he died suddenly on 28 June 1797. He was survived by his wife Jane Catharine (née Hudson), whom he'd married in February 1769, and by one child, Georgiana Jane (1770–1850). His best known book was probably *An Account of the Pelew Islands*.

43. Sheppard, F.H.W. (1979) *Survey of London. Vol. XXVII. Spitalfields and Mile End New Town. The Parishes of Christ Church and All Saints and the Liberties of Norton Folgate and the Old Artillery Ground*. London: The Athlone Press. University of London. L.C.C., p.248.

44. Georgiana Jane (1770–1850) exhibited four pictures at the Society of Artists in 1791 and painted from memory a portrait of Prince Lee Boo, 15 months after his death, for her father's account of the Pelew islands. She married John Henderson, B.C.L. (1764–1843) on 9 June 1796. She died on 8 January 1850, and was buried in her husband's grave at Kensal Green.

45. John Henderson, B.C.L. (1764–1843), one of the early patrons of Thomas Girtin and J.M.W. Turner – who frequently worked together in his house – and himself an amateur artist of great merit. Their children were two sons, John Henderson and Charles Cooper Henderson, and three daughters who died unmarried. John (1797–1878) was a collector of works of art and an

archaeologist. Charles Cooper Henderson (1803–77) was a very prolific artist and extremely skilled in drawing horses and coaching and road scenes. His paintings are acknowledged as the most accurate and authentic pictures of nineteenth century carriages and mail and stage coaches. He married in 1828 and fathered seven sons, among them Colonel Kennett Gregg Henderson, C.B., and two daughters. He died at Lower Halliford-on-Thames on 21 August 1877, and was buried in the catacombs at Kensal Green. There is a book of his paintings: Lane, Charles (1984) *Cooper Henderson and the Open Road: The Life and Works of Charles Cooper Henderson*. London: J.A. Allen and Co. Ltd.

46. Sheppard, *ibid*, p.248.
47. White, Jerry (1980) *Rothschild Buildings: Life In An East End Tenement Block 1887–1920*. London: Routledge and Kegan Paul, p.7.

chapter two

EMMA ELIZABETH SMITH

A t the time of her death in 1888 Emma Elizabeth Smith was 45 years old, 5ft 2in, of fair complexion, with light brown hair and an identifying scar on her right temple. She claimed to have been a country girl, but apparently hadn't returned home for ten years or more. The widowed[1] mother of two children, a boy and a girl who at the time of her death were living in the Finsbury Park area, she had for some eighteen months been living in a common lodging house at 18 George Street, paying 4d for her bed. She was noted for leaving the house between 6pm and 7pm and returning at various times, usually drunk. She evidently didn't hold her drink well and Mrs. Mary Russell, deputy keeper at the lodging house in George Street, who said that she had known the deceased for about two years, revealed that when Emma had had drink she acted like a madwoman, she had often come home with black eyes that men had given her, and on one occasion had returned home and said that she had been thrown out of a window.[2]

Walter Dew, who would achieve fame as the detective who raced across the Atlantic in time to arrest Dr. Crippen for the murder of his wife Belle Elmore, was assigned to Whitechapel at the time of the Ripper crimes. In his autobiography, he wrote:

> Emma, a woman of more than forty, was something of a mystery. Her past was a closed book even to her most intimate friends. All that she had ever told anyone about herself was that she was a widow who more than ten years before had left her husband and broken away from all her early associations.
>
> There was something about Emma Smith which suggested that there had been a time when the comforts of life had not been denied her. There was a touch of culture in her speech unusual in her class.
>
> Once when Emma was asked why she had broken away so completely from her old life she replied, a little wistfully: 'They would not understand now any more than they understood then. I must live somehow.'[3]

On the night of Easter Monday, 3 April, she seems to have stuck to her routine. She was seen by Margaret Hayes,[4] a fellow lodger at 18 George Street, at 12.15am near Farrant Street, Burdett Road, talking to a man dressed in dark clothes and a white scarf. Interestingly this witness said that she had been assaulted herself only a few minutes before by two men, one of whom had stopped her by asking her the time, the other then striking her on the mouth. Both had then run away and the witness had seen Smith when she was getting away from the neighbourhood 'where there had been some rough work that night'. This witness said that she had been hurt by men just before Christmas 1887[5] and had been two weeks in the infirmary. Testimony to the roughness of the area, although the witness's observation that 'there had been some rough work that night' might indicate that the night Emma Smith was murdered was exceptional.

One and a quarter hours after this sighting Emma Smith was making her way down Whitechapel Road. Ahead of her, near Whitechapel Church, were some men and she crossed the road to avoid them. They followed. She turned into Osborne Street and opposite 10 Brick Lane, about 300 yards from 18 George Street, the men had assaulted her, robbed her of all the money she had, and then rammed something into her. There were two or three men, she would later say, one of them looking like a youth aged about 19.

Somehow she had managed to get back to her lodgings – though the reports suggest that she returned there between 4am and 5am, which if true give some indication of the pain she must have been in if it took her two hours or more to cover 300 yards. At the lodging house she saw several lodgers, among them Margaret Hames and Annie Lee, as well as Mary Russell, the deputy. Russell and Lee saw that Emma Smith's face was bleeding, that her ear was cut and that she was in distress and took her to the London Hospital in Whitechapel Road, some half a mile away. Emma reportedly went to the hospital reluctantly. The locals feared the hospital, as they did the workhouse – as Frederick Treves, an intern there in 1888, explained:

> The hospital in the days of which I speak was anathema. The poor people hated it. They dreaded it. They looked upon it primarily as a place where people died. It was a matter of difficulty to induce a patient to enter the wards. They feared an operation and with good cause, for an operation then was a dubious matter. There were stories afloat of things that happened in the hospital, and it could not be gainsaid that certain of these stories were true.[6]

The three women walked the half mile to the hospital and en route Smith pointed out the spot close to Taylor Bros. cocoa factory where she had been assaulted. Mary Russell said Smith had seemed unwilling to go into details and this may have been because of the pain she was in, but Inspector Edmund Reid noted in his report that 'She would have passed a number of PCs en route but none was informed of the incident or asked to render assistance'. Perhaps this reluctance to involve the police was because she knew her assailants and knew the punishment they would later exact if she had talked.

At the London Hospital she was attended by a doctor.[7] She was able to talk about what had happened to her and although the doctor thought she had been drinking, she was sober and aware of what was happening, but there was little that could be done. Peritonitis set in, from which Emma Smith died at 9am on 4 April.

The first the police knew of the attack was on Friday 6 April when the office of the Coroner for East Middlesex, Wynne E. Baxter, reported that the inquest would be held the next day at the London Hospital. Police attended. The verdict was 'wilful murder'.

Only Walter Dew ever seems to have believed that Emma Smith was a victim of Jack the Ripper, writing in his autobiography, 'I have always held that Emma Smith was the first to meet her death at the hands of Jack the Ripper',[8] but Dew's memory of the crime is clearly in error over detail and it is otherwise quite clear that she was the victim of a brutal attack by several men. It was with her murder, however, that the police opened the Whitechapel Murders file, a file that remained open until completion of the investigation into the murder of Frances Coles in February 1891. The file embraced the Jack the Ripper murders, but not all the murders were attributed to the Ripper and there was and is a degree of disagreement about which were and which were not his work. Emma Smith, though, was clearly the victim of a brutal assault, just one of what we can assume to have been several on the streets that night.

Given Margaret Hayes' report of an attack on her that same night it is possible that there may have been some gang trouble on the streets – which is odd, given that no policeman seems to have mentioned it. None of the PCs in the area had heard or seen anything at all and the streets were said to be quiet at the time.

The police suspected that the crime was committed by one of the gangs that inhabited the area. Some of these gangs, such as the Blind Beggar Mob, who took their name from the Blind Beggar Pub (which achieved lasting notoriety when Ron Kray shot and killed George Cornell there in the 1960s), based themselves in Whitechapel but operated as pickpockets elsewhere. There were fighting gangs, such as the Green Gate Gang who took their name from a road of the same name. They had been involved in a riot in Bethnal Green in late 1881 and again made the news in 1882 when about 20 of them attacked Frederick Willmore and another man, beating them so severely that Willmore had died from his injuries. One of the gang, Thomas Galliers, was tried at the Old Bailey and received a sentence of ten years for manslaughter.[9] Another gang was the Old Nichol Gang, who operated out of The Nichol, a close-knit community of some 6,000 people[10] who lived in the squalid area bounded by High Street, Shoreditch, Hackney Road to the north and Spitalfields to the south. It was a place of evil reputation, though it is somewhat unclear just how much this reputation was deserved and how much derived from the writings of Arthur Morrison,[11] who called it 'The Jago', and Rev. A. Osborne Jay,[12] who was the source of much of Morrison's information and is portrayed, albeit rather glamorously, in Morrison's famous *A Child of the Jago*, as Father Sturt. Perhaps exaggerated by Morrison, it was nevertheless an area noted for decades as a place of extreme deprevation:

> ... the earnest visitor has only to cross the road and turn up Nichols-row, to find himself in as foul a neighbourhood as can be discovered in the civilised world (savage life has nothing to compare to it), and amongst a population depressed almost to the last stage of human endurance ... This district of Friars-mount, which is nominally represented by Nichols-street, Old Nichols-street, and Half Nichols-street, including, perhaps most obviously, the greater part of the vice and debauchery of the district, and the limits of a single article would be insufficient to give any detailed description of even a day's visit. There is nothing picturesque in such misery; it is but one painful and monotonous round of vice, filth, and poverty, huddled in dark cellars, ruined garrets, bare and blackened rooms, teeming with disease and death, and without the means, even if there were the inclination, for the most ordinary observations of decency or cleanliness.[13]

Gangs like the Old Nichol operated as ponces, street robbers, extortionists, protection racketeers, and generally as bullies and thugs, and their like would dominate the East End for years to come. Other notable gangs included the Hoxton Mob or Hoxton High Rips, who were also suspected of committing the Ripper murders; The Coons, run by a Jewish man named Isaac Bogard, known by the very un-PC nickname 'Darky the Coon' because he was swarthy skinned; the Vendetta Mob, run by Arthur Harding; The Titanics; and immigrant gangs of notoriety such as the Bessarabians and their rivals the Odessians.

Whether Emma Smith was the victim of a gang is uncertain. Her reaction of crossing the road to avoid the men who attacked her may indicate that she knew who they were, or they may simply have seemed threatening. Her silence about her attacker may have been caused by fear of retribution or simply because she honestly did not take notice of them during her brutalisation. On the whole, it seems most likely that she happened to be in the wrong place at the wrong time.

Notes

1. The newspapers (*East London Advertiser*, 14 April 1888, for example) state that she was a widow, but the London Hospital admission registers state that she was married and gave her occupation as charwoman. London Hospital, Patient Admission Register, 1888, RLHAM.
2. Mary Russell's inquest testimony reported in *Walthamstow and Leyton Guardian*, 14 April 1888.
3. Dew, Walter (1938) *I Caught Crippen: Memoirs of Ex-Chief Inspector Walter Dew CID*. London: Blackie and Son, p.92. Dew must be reciting information received at second hand because he doesn't hint that he knew Emma Smith. And it should be noted that his account is otherwise faulty, for although he recalls much that is accurate, such as the location of the assault, he incorrectly says that a man found her there lying unconscious and bleeding to death. This is not impossible because Emma Smith was somewhere for the hour or more between the attack and reaching her lodging.
4. *The Times*, 14 April 1888.
5. It has been suggested that this is the origin of the story of Fairy Fay. Terence Robinson, writing in *Reynolds News*, 29 October 1950, gives this name to a woman who was supposedly murdered on 26 December 1887, but nothing has been found to support the story. A woman nicknamed 'Tottie Fay' was committed to Broadmoor in February 1894 suffering from maniacal fits.
6. Sir Frederick Treves (1923) *The Elephant Man and Other Reminiscences*. London: Cassell, pp.54–5; reprinted London: Star Books, 1980.
7. He is called Mr. George Haslip in Inspector Reid's report, Dr. Hellier in *Lloyd's Weekly News*, Sunday 8 April 1888 and Dr. G.H. Hillier in *Morning Advertiser*, Monday 9 April 1888.
8. Dew, *ibid*. p.92.
9. PRO CRIM 1/13/6.
10. According to an estimate made by the London County Council at a time of redevelopment in 1895. See Greater London Record Office, *A Description of the Boundary Street Scheme . . . 1896.*
11. Arthur Morrison was an East End born journalist, author of *Tales of the Mean*

Streets (1894), which inspired Rev. Jay to contact him and say that the Nichol was rougher and the hardships greater than in the East End portrayed. He also wrote a series of early detective novels around the character of Martin Hewitt which were illustrated by Sidney Paget and begin with Morrison, Arthur (1895) *Martin Hewitt Investigator.* London: Ward, Lock and Bowden Ltd.

12. Rev. Arthur Osborne Jay (1867?–1945) was the vicar of Holy Trinity from 1886 until 1921. An Anglican, he began his ministry in a loft over some stables, and thereafter preached from a variety of accommodations that included a club room, gymnasium and lodging house. He was an extraordinary publicist who managed to stay friends with his parishioners while at the same time portraying them to the outside world as violent and of bad reputation. His writings on the area include *Life In Darkest London, a Hint to General Booth* (1891), *The Social Problem, Its Possible Solution* (1893), and *A Story of Shoreditch* (1896). A short essay on Jay and his father is to be found in Hall Caine's *Father and Son: A Study in Heredity* and Mee, Arthur in 'A Transformation in Slumland, The Remarkable Story of a London Clergyman', *Temple Magazine*, vol. 21, no. 181.

13. *The Illustrated London News*, 24 October 1863. See also 'More Revelations of Bethnal Green', *The Builder*, vol. XXX1, no. 1082, 31 October 1863.

chapter three

THE BITTER CRY

The brutal and barbarous death of poor Emma Elizabeth Smith would probably have passed almost unremarked and certainly unremembered, her birth a minor statistic of no importance and her life of no consequence – just one of the many creatures who inhabited the *terra incognita* of the slums. But her death was the prologue to a drama that would soon unfold and would ensure her a kind of immortality.

It was widely believed that Emma Smith had been attacked by members of the Old Nichol Mob, a gang of roughs and thugs centred on an area between Shoreditch High Street and Brick Lane known as The Nichol, a 'Shoreditch parish of 8,000 people with a death rate four times that of the rest of London, with 17 public houses and no church of any kind at all, a parish with a record of criminality which none could surpass or even equal, a parish which was described in the newspaper, as "the sink of London" worse than barbarian.'[1]

It was one of the oldest parts of Spitalfields/Shoreditch, the area already half built over by the time of the Gascoyne map of 1703, but within a hundred years the houses had decayed badly and by the nineteenth century it was 'a territory inhabited by clans of roughs, who lived partly by casual labour and partly by petty crime. Life within the island of old building was harsh and reckless ... street fighting was endemic, and every man carried a cosh'.[2] The housing here was appalling, living conditions literally indescribable, some people living in underground cellars, as at 59 Nichol Street:

> But as regards the cellar, in all our experience of London destitution and awful conditions, we have seen nothing so harrowing as what there met the view. Through the narrow space of the window that is left open there came a glimmering light, which fell upon two figures, on a broken truckle, seemingly naked, with the exception of some black rags which passed across the

middle of their bodies; but the greater part of the room, small as it is, was in total darkness. Mr. Price said that there were more figures visible; and on asking if any were there, a female voice replied, 'Yes; here are two of us. Mother is out'; and gradually, as the eye became accustomed to the gloom two other figures were to be seen lying in a corner upon rags . . . The height of the room, all of which is below the surface, is not quite 6 feet. The window would not open; the ceiling was ready to fall; and the walls, so far as the light showed, were damp and mildewed. The inmates here were a widow and her four children: one a girl twenty years of age, another girl eighteen, a boy of fourteen, and a boy of twelve.[3]

The room cost 2s–3s a week. Two adjoining houses of six rooms each contained 48 persons. The only water was supplied by a small tap at the back of one of the houses that was turned on for 10 or 12 minutes each day, except Sunday. Infant mortality was high. One woman interviewed by a journalist for *The Builder* said that she had four children living, although one was ill and according to the doctor would die, and five who had died. A companion said she had two living and had lost three. Apart from the dirt, vermin, disease, human and other waste ('house refuse had not been removed for fourteen years'), the buildings were in immediate danger of collapse. As far as *The Builder* was concerned, the houses contravened the law and should be forcibly shut up and demolished. 'It is no answer to say the inhabitants prefer to live, or (more truly) to die, in such rooms rather than meet the difficulty of finding a better room elsewhere. They must not be allowed to do so.'[4]

Whitechapel was almost as bad, as Henrietta Barnett recorded:

None of these courts had roads. In some the houses were three storeys high and hardly six feet apart, the sanitary accommodation being pits in the cellars; in other courts the houses were lower, wooden and dilapidated, a stand pipe at the end providing the only water. Each chamber was the home of a family who sometimes owned their indescribable furniture, but in most cases the rooms were let out furnished for 8d a night. In many instances broken windows had been repaired with paper and rags, the banisters had been used for firewood, and the paper hung from the walls which were the residence of countless vermin.[5]

Despite appeals like those made by *The Builder*, few people cared about the slums of London, except when the effects spilled across into respectable neighbourhoods, as when there was a cholera epidemic. It was not until the mid-1800s that attitudes changed, largely due to a pamphlet called *The Bitter Cry of Outcast London*, which pricked the social conscience. The lesson *The Bitter Cry* taught was underlined by Jack the Ripper in a unique and horrible way. As Jerry White observed:

> Among the innumerable cures for these ills with which the leader columns were filled and correspondence pages bombarded during those few fever-ish weeks [of the Ripper scare], were practical solutions for the Spitalfields problem. Besides the pleas for more clergymen, more policemen, more middle-class 'slummers', more night shelters where poor women could sleep and laundries where they could work, one theme was consistently stated. How could housing problems be improved?[6]

As we have seen, during the 1500s the distinction between the indus-trial district east of London and the affluent areas to the west had begun to show itself.[7] John Stow complained that in the 1540s there were no houses from St. Katherine's eastwards along the river, but by his own day there was 'a continual street or filthy strait passage with alleys of small tenements or cottages built, inhabited by sailors' vict-uallers, almost to Ratcliffe'. He also complained with a plaintive voice familiar to many modern opponents to the endless encroachment of urbanisation on rural communities, that the road from Aldgate to Whitechapel Church was built up:

> both sides of the street be pestered with cottages and alleys, even up to Whitechapel church, and almost half a mile beyond it, into the common field; all which ought to be open and free from all men. But this common field, I say, being sometime the beauty of this city on that part, is so encroached upon by building of filthy cottages, and with other purpressors, inclosures, and laystalls (notwithstanding all proclamations and acts of par-liament made to the contrary), that in some places it scarce remaineth a suf-ficient highway for the meeting of carriages and drives of cattle; much less is there any fair, pleasant, or wholesome way for people to walk on foot; which is no small blemish to so famous a city to have so unsavoury and unseemly an entrance or passage thereunto.[8]

The road from St. Mary Spital to Shoreditch (which Stow originally called Sewers Ditch), he similarly complained 'is all along a continual building of small and base tenements, for the most part lately erected'.

Writing about 1780, Johann William von Archenholtz (1743–1812) commented on the distinction between west and east London:

> the East end, especially along the shores of the Thames, consists of old houses, the streets there are narrow, dark and ill-paved; inhabited by sailors and other workmen who are employed in the construction of ships and by a great part of the Jews. The contrast between this and the West end is

astonishing: the houses here are mostly new and elegant; the squares are superb, the streets straight and open . . .[9]

As Stow indicates, many of the buildings were erected illegally – 'notwithstanding all proclamations and acts of parliament made to the contrary' – and there was therefore little reason to invest in good craftsmanship or quality building materials when it was not known whether or not they would be quickly torn down by the authorities. There was also often uncertainty about the ownership of the land leased for building, meaning that a builder could find that he had no claim to houses he had erected on land leased from an owner who it turned out didn't own it. When such uncertainty existed or was suspected there was again no incentive to invest in decent workmanship or materials. Other factors leading to jerry-built housing included short-term leases, meaning that the builder would quickly lose right to the properties built and therefore lacked any incentive to build anything that would survive the term of the lease, and the acquisition of leases by individuals whose lack of funds meant that they hired the cheapest labour and materials. Another factor, after the Great Fire of 1666, was the desperate need to re-house those made homeless in the destruction, which caused many buildings to be thrown up, there being no intention that they should be other than temporary, on land of uncertain ownership. By the eighteenth century one of the most conspicuous features of London was the number of old ruinous houses, horrendously unsafe and liable to collapse. This they often did – 'falling houses thunder on your head', as Samuel Johnson remarked in 1738.

Other factors played a part in the erection and continued use of substandard properties, not the least being the increase in the population. When an Act of Parliament in 1740 granted Spitalfields the status of a parish it was estimated that it contained 1,800 houses and a population of 15,000. By 1841 it was estimated that it contained 12,000 houses and a population of 74,000. In the nineteenth century London's population as a whole grew considerably, almost doubling between 1821 and 1851 and doubling again by the end of the century.[10] Other factors as well as population growth combined to further reduce the availability of decent housing.

In the 1850s and early 1860s Shoreditch, Bethnal Green and Whitechapel were among several parts of London particularly hit when housing was demolished to make way for railway extensions. As many as 23,000 people were displaced – as were a further 13,176 between 1867 and 1875.

> People have been driven from the dwellings destroyed in Holborn, Clerkenwell and Spitalfields, and they have been thrust on the other population; huddled in any hole and corner they could put their head into – not from poverty, but from sheer want of any dwelling within reach of their work . . .[11]

Amongst the properties demolished in this second phase were several houses in Bucks Row, Whitechapel. They were replaced by gates leading to the vacant lot (used for stabling) in which Jack the Ripper's first canonical[12] victim was found.

Meanwhile, between 1800 and 1805 1,300 houses along the riverside were demolished for the building of the London Docks. The creation of St. Katherine's Dock in 1828 caused the loss of a further 1,033. This led to a large number of people moving into Whitechapel and, as John Liddle, the Medical Officer for Whitechapel, observed, 'crowding themselves into those houses which were formerly occupied by respectable tradesmen and mechanics, and which are now let out into tenements'.[13] Similarly, as the Charity Organisation Society reported in 1881, people were displaced by the conversion of living accommodation into workshops, pointing to displacement along both Commercial Road and Commercial Street.

The resulting need for accommodation meant not only that houses were quickly erected on any available patch of land, this 'infill' building creating a warren of streets and courts and alleys and passages, but that the hovels of the seventeenth and eighteenth centuries were cheerfully and profitably pressed into commission. These decaying, patched together and sometimes empty and derelict houses of uncertain ownership were converted into common lodging houses or brothels.

There are some references from the late 1500s to common lodging housing, so named because anyone with the asking price could use them, and they were a very profitable business in the 1700s. For example, the *Annual Register* in 1765 recorded the death of a Mrs. Farrel, who from letting two-penny lodgings was found on her death to be worth £6,000. Lodging houses had already become a cause for concern, not because people were so poor that they had to use them, but because unsanitary overcrowding caused alarm in neighbouring, more prosperous communities – as in 1721 when the plague raging at

Marseilles pricked the London authorities into denouncing the conditions of such housing:

> It is now become a common practice in the extreme parts of the town, to receive into their houses persons unknown, without distinction of sex or age on their paying one penny or more per night for lying in such houses without beds or covering, and ... it is frequent in such houses for fifteen or twenty or more to lie in a small room.[14]

Areas where there were large numbers of poor quality, hastily erected buildings developed lots of common lodging houses. Sometimes, as in the case of Flower and Dean Street, the whole street was rented out, either as a common lodging or, even more frequently, converted into tenements – homes formerly occupied by one family being rented out by the room, often to whole families. Converted into brothels or rooms used for prostitution, places of sanctuary for assorted criminals, sinks of vice, and verminous homes to squalor and disease, these scenes of dereliction were noted as dangerous places, and even in the 17th century included Ratcliffe Highway and, along the river, Goodman's Fields, Houndsditch, Whitechapel – Rosemary Lane and Petticoat Lane in particular – Shoreditch and Bethnal Green.

These areas of common lodging houses and rented tenements were considered to be home to the 'dangerous classes', the loci of cholera[15] and crime, dirt and disease, and social dissidents from Chartists to Radicals and every shade and persuasion in between. Morals had withered and all but died, civilised society had been crushed by vice and immorality, the hand of God weakened by sin and alcohol. The horror of such places was such that it sometimes left people uttering almost comical middle-class banalities: a Dr. Willan couldn't conceal his distaste when he wrote: 'It will scarcely appear credible, though it is precisely true, that persons of the lowest class do not put clean sheets on their beds three times a year'.[16]

That such places existed, and the fear their existence generated, led to occasional bursts of ruthless slum clearance, as when Commercial Street was built in Whitechapel, thousands of people being forced from their homes, diseased and dangerous hovels though they may have been. It has been estimated that 'altogether street clearance accounted for the displacement of not far short of 100,000 persons between 1830 and 1880'.[17] And unsurprisingly, except to the authorities, those displaced did not leave the district, but stayed near to their work, where they were known and where they had friends, and would pile into any vacant space they could find. The overcrowding became worse and the knock-on effects pushed the infrastructure to the point of collapse.

Efforts were made to change things. Two Acts introduced by Lord Shaftesbury in 1851 empowered local authorities to supervise common lodging houses and the Torrens Act of 1866 enabled them to compel the owners to put them in proper condition. By the 1870s the work of Octavia Hill had grabbed the public imagination.

Born in Wisbech, Cambridgeshire, in 1852, Octavia Hill went to London to work at the Ladies' Guild, a Christian-Socialist co-operative association managed by her mother. Her work there and at Frederick Maurice's Working Men's College, where she was Secretary of the women's classes, along with her teaching of slum children, impressed upon her the need for improved housing for the poor. In 1864 John Ruskin lent her sufficient money to purchase three houses in Paradise Place, Marylebone. She rented the properties on the principle that the investors in their purchase would make 5 per cent profit, other monies earned being ploughed back into repairs and improvements, and the tenants were expected to look after the properties they rented. She founded the Charity Organisation Society to administer the properties and the experiment was so successful that the scheme spread, other properties were bought and other organisations adopted her principles, including several in the East End. From 1884 she was appointed by the Church Commissioners to manage their property in Southwark and elsewhere. Having no political leanings she refused to join the Royal Commission on Housing in 1889, but did serve with the young Beatrice Webb on the Poor Law Commission (1905–08).

The year 1875 was one of social legislation, called Disraeli's *annus mirabilis* of social reform. Richard Asherton Cross, one of the very greatest Home Secretaries ever to hold office, spearheaded several important Acts, notably two relating to employment and trade unionism, a Sale of Food and Drugs Act and the Artisans' Dwellings Act – which became known as the Cross Act – which enabled local authorities of 87 towns in England and Wales to condemn, demolish and reconstruct whole areas. A second Cross Act and a second Torrens Act were both passed in 1879, but although these Acts were implemented, most notably by Joseph Chamberlain, then Mayor of Birmingham, who cleared a massive 40 or 50 acres of slums, they gave powers to local government but without any requirement that they use them. By 1881 only ten of the 87 local authorities had actually used these powers[18] and a select committee of the House of Commons was set up to investigate, another Act following in 1882. The publicity given to the horrors of slum dwelling, be it reports of Parliament or the large number of articles that appeared in both the popular and specialist press, including a series of brilliant articles in the *Pictorial World* by George R. Sims (the 'Dante of the London Slums' as he was called), can have left no literate or moderately intelligent person unaware of the problems. Indeed, there were so many articles on the subject that by 1880 one author felt moved to apologise for adding to the pile, writing 'it appears superfluous at the present time to enlarge upon it or to enter into distressing details now so widely known and so deeply deplored'.[19] And yet the subject failed to arouse much interest, concern or sympathy. The fact that people were forced to live in such appalling conditions that parents had to stay awake all night to ensure that their baby was not eaten alive by rats seemed not to matter – unless disease, crime, immorality or one of the associated evils that knew no social boundaries, spilled into respectable areas. But in the middle of October 1883 this changed.

The London Congregational Union, one of the dissenting churches, published a small penny pamphlet that contained little that was original and drew extensively on the work of others, notably George R. Sims, yet in common with Jack the Ripper it appeared at precisely the right time and it had a provocative name. The pamphlet was called *The Bitter Cry of Outcast London*.

It was published anonymously and its authorship was the subject of a lot of speculation, it having been ascribed variously to Rev. William C. Preston,[20] Arnold White, G.R. Sims[21] and W.T. Stead amongst others. But in December 1883, in the introduction to an article published in the *Contemporary Review*, Rev. Andrew Mearns, Secretary of the London Congregational Union, claimed authorship:

> I ought to explain that I have no wish to be described as the author of 'The Bitter Cry of Outcast London', but having seen printed statements to the effect that two others who acted as my assistants are credited with the pamphlet, it seems necessary that I should say that the inception was entirely mine, the investigation was carried out under my direction, and the pamphlet was prepared according to my instructions and subject to my revision. I was ably helped in the investigation by the Rev. James Munro, formerly of Limerick, and in the literary work by the Rev. W.C. Preston, formerly of Hull, and acknowledge my indebtedness to both. Others helped, but to a less degree.[22]

It was a claim William Preston would contest, and with some justification – he did *write* it – but he certainly couldn't lay the same claims
as Mearns' to intellectual ownership.[23] He does deserve the credit for
the title, to which much of the success of *The Bitter Cry* is attributa-
ble, and may even, with Mearns, have been responsible for the journalistic 'shock' approach. This avoided the dangers of ruinous houses,
vermin infestation, the risk of disease spreading to better class districts
and most of the appeals to the public conscience that marked the tracts
of other housing activists. Instead it concentrated on the religious
apathy of slum dwellers, the dramatic lack of moral values and other
abominations that, out of regard for his readers' feelings he was compelled to leave undescribed – though his admission that 'incest is
common' was sufficient to genuinely shock the nation and leave them
wondering what the other abominations could conceivably be. A
Royal Commission on the Housing of the Working Classes tried to
find out, with some disappointment.[24] Nevertheless, 'that sins condemned in savages were being committed in the centre of the Empire
came as a great shock to many Victorians and spurred them to reform
activity'.[25]

It has to be said, however, that although *The Bitter Cry* may have
spread its seed in the social conscience, it sprouted, grew and flowered
in the hands of W.T. Stead, the flamboyant pioneer of New Journalism
and editor of the campaigning *Pall Mall Gazette*. The widespread
immorality in the overcrowded slums where the rich exploited the
poor and defenceless was the perfect combination of sensation, sex
and social commentary, and 'if a date can be singled out for the inception of Stead's brand of New Journalism, perhaps it was Tuesday,
October 16, 1883'[26] when Stead echoed the *Cry* by publishing an
abridgement of Mearns' pamphlet stripped of all its evangelicalism and
accompanying it with a strongly worded editorial condemning landlords, the Church, the wealthy, the intellectuals and the politicians.
Stead's article caused a sensation, reached many influential readers
and, so cynics would point out, increased the circulation of his newspaper. Stead also put the thumbscrews on the landlords of these properties, writing that, 'These fever dens are said to be the best-paying
property in London, and owners who, if justice were done, would be
on the treadmill, are drawing 50 to 60 per cent on investments in
tenement property in the slums'. As early as 1892 it was recognised
that Stead was responsible for bringing about changes to the East End:
one contemporary asked the question, 'How much regenerating social

activity would have gone into the East London if [Stead's] articles had not been written, and the tract had reached only readers of such things?'[27] But if Stead attached the thumbscrews to slum landlords, a few years later Jack the Ripper tightened them, notably on the Henderson family who owned the Flower and Dean Street rookeries.

The *Pall Mall Gazette* led the way, the *Daily News* and the *Daily Telegraph* followed, and *The Times* disapproved, observing that the slums were the subject of fervent rhetoric from 'everybody who can write or speak a few consecutive sentences'.[28] Which was unintentioned good news for housing reform campaigners. Over 50 years of almost continuous agitation against slum housing had failed to do much more than gently prick the social or political conscience, but Mearns' pamphlet proved a battering ram that drove the 'housing question' to the forefront of the minds of the highest and lowest in the land. On 2 January 1884 the *Pall Mall Gazette* reported that *The Bitter Cry* had been 'echoing from one end of England to the other . . . We shall have to go back a long time to discover an agitation on any social question in England which has produced so prompt, so widespread, and, as we believe, so enduring an effect'. The *Lancet* also observed that previous reformers had 'preached almost to deaf ears [and] till very lately scarcely ruffled the conscience of political men'.[29] Although an exaggeration, there was some justification for one of the leading papers asserting that, 'it was not until *The Bitter Cry* stirred the nation that the slums came to be regarded as unpleasant abodes . . .'.

Queen Victoria was deeply moved by the plight of the slum dwellers and as early as 30 October 1883 she wrote from Balmoral to Gladstone demanding that he 'obtain more precise information as to the true state of affairs in these overcrowded, unhealthy, and squalid abodes'. Gladstone had no interest in the subject, unenthusiastically referred to past improvements and avoided discussing possible new ones – 'his old-fashioned Liberalism in home affairs had not caught up with the needs of the 'eighties'. Therefore the Queen petitioned Sir Richard Cross, who told her that the *Cry* was somewhat exaggerated, Sir William Harcourt, who said complacently that the London poor were no worse off than they had ever been, and radical housing expert Sir Charles Dilke, who produced the Rev. Harry Jones. He had worked in the East End and told her that although the poor lived utterly dismal lives their misery had not turned them against the upper classes. As a personal response to the sufferings of the poor, Queen Victoria banned mutton from gracing the Palace dining tables.

'Letters of thanks poured in. The ban was lifted two or three weeks later to the relief of the Household, especially Lord Sydney who greatly missed his *cotelettes à l'agneau aux points d'asperge*'.[30]

But others were profoundly affected by the *Cry*. James Adderley[31] recalled that 'whereas up to the year 1883 you could count on your fingers the names of men like Edward Denison who had studied the social question', after the publication of the *Cry*, whose author Adderley thought was worthy of being canonised, it was common for the upper classes to go down to the East End.[32] It was called slumming and the editor of *The Christian World* remarked that as a result of *The Bitter Cry* 'slumming [became] fashionable in the early 'eighties'. The idea that Jack the Ripper was a 'toff' wasn't far-fetched, at least inasmuch as the middle and upper classes did venture into the East End, be it legitimately or as sensation seeking slummers. One recent biographer of the East End has echoed Bernard Shaw's tongue-in-cheek suggestion that Jack the Ripper was a philanthropist and suggested that the Ripper was a slummer:

> More likely he was a fanatical slummer whose wrath burst through the seals of reason when he perceived around him the moral corruption of which Sims and Mearns had written. It is significant that the murders took place in the furthest west, and already much publicised blackspot of the East End.[33]

The Church was moved, smarting perhaps from the mild slapping delivered by Stead, who said the Church did nothing to abate the evils of the slums, but involved itself instead in petty quarrels that turned Christianity into a mockery. Several clergymen, particularly those with parishes in slum districts, felt moved to respond. Rev. C. Carruthers swung the bludgeon at the landlords, arguing that 'if the owners of house property were *really* Christians, they could never consent to enrich themselves at the expense of the comfort and health of their poorer brethren . . .'.[34] One additional effect on the East End was that the East End university settlement Toynbee Hall found itself more favourably looked upon: 'The settlement movement had its beginnings . . . well before Mearns wrote his pamphlet, but not until the great agitation over the London slums began, were the various elements necessary for the settlement movement synthesised'.[35]

The settlement movement was the idea that if better off and better educated people moved into deprived areas then they would raise the level of life around them. A number of sincere Oxford graduates took this notion to heart and chose to live in the East End, among them

John Richard Green – a future Librarian at Lambeth Palace and author of the *Short History of the English People*, who for nine years was a curate in Stepney – and Edward Denison, who took lodging in Philpot Street, Whitechapel. Other undergraduates were welcomed by Rev. Samuel Barnett, the vicar of St. Judes. Barnett – 'a diminutive body clothed in shabby and badly assorted garments ... small black eyes set close together, sallow complexion, and a thin and patchy pretence of a beard'[36] – was sent to Whitechapel in 1872 at the age of 28 to become vicar of the derelict church of St. Jude's, no doubt wondering how he would fare in what his Bishop had unencouragingly told him was 'the worst parish in the diocese, inhabited mainly by a criminal population'.[37] He found out soon enough when on arrival in Whitechapel he was knocked down and had his watch stolen. Of diminutive stature, Barnett was a giant in other respects and was also married to the energetic and highly intelligent Henrietta Octavia Barnett (d.1939), who would stand beside him steadfastly. Her account of his life remains the definitive biography and her influence should never be underestimated: Archbishop Lang is said to have once remarked of Samuel Barnett that 'Samuel was but the mouthpiece of Henrietta and had the courage of her opinions'.

Both Barnetts were close friends of Octavia Hill and played a prominent role in the early activities of the Charity Organisation Society. Barnett became increasingly concerned with the Whitechapel slums. Having always welcomed to St. Jude's the 'slummers' from Oxford University, he utilised the publicity associated with *The Bitter Cry* to petition for a Universities Settlement in the East End – a university which would bring educated young people into the area, who would lodge among the poor and whose education it was hoped would rub off on them. It was opened in a disused boys' school in Commercial Street in June 1884 and named after Arnold Toynbee (1852–81), the Balliol historian who was deeply committed to providing adult education opportunities for the working class. It was the first university settlement and became a model for those that followed. From an original 16 settlers, Barnett developed a social welfare and education programme that included adult education, youth work, social work, health provision, economic development and, not unsurprisingly, housing. On this last issue Barnett, though very enthusiastic, 'was among the over-zealous muddle-heads'.[38] He was so anxious to rid the area of the terrible slums that he gave little thought to where the occupants would be re-housed and didn't appreciate that the majority wouldn't be able to afford even the low rents being asked for rooms in the charitable dwellings with which the slums were replaced.

The 'housing question' also tapped into the growing fear in the 1880s of revolution – the fear that savage and heathen population of the slums would push through the crust of decency and civilisation like magma bursting from a volcano and would flow out to destroy all that stood before it. As journalist Frank Harris observed, recalling the warning of Danton, 'If you suffer the poor to grow up as animals they may change to become wild beasts and rend you', and he argued that housing reform could be seen as an insurance policy protecting the property of the rich. As the *Cry* grew louder, from the Queen down and from the Press up, the politicians, caught between a rock and a hard place, had to act. And the action was taken, surprisingly, by Lord Salisbury. Salisbury's motives have long been questioned. Did he step into the fray because he had a genuine concern about working class housing? Because he was genuinely moved by *The Bitter Cry*? Or because he saw it as an opportunity to attract working class votes to the Tories? It appears not to have been mere political manoeuvring. He had made speeches about the need for housing reform before the publication of *The Bitter Cry*, his daughter wrote in her four volume biography of her father that slum housing was a subject about which he had 'always felt strongly',[39] and an article on housing reform he wrote for the *National Review* that was published on 5 November 1883 must have been started some time before Mearns' pamphlet appeared. Whether or not *The Bitter Cry* materially influenced him, Salisbury urged Parliament to appoint a Royal Commission on housing and 'his thoughtful speech is one of the most important in the history of nineteenth-century housing reform'.[40]

The Royal Commission met in February 1884, much to the pleasure of Queen Victoria, and concluded that overcrowding was increasing, that good accommodation was not affordable even by the decent, hard-working and sober artisan, let alone the casual labourer, that the local vestries were at best lethargic and at worst corrupt, and that the housing needed to be near the occupant's place of work. The Commission led to legislation, the Housing Act of 1885, but it was not until 1890 that the relevant housing legislation was consolidated in another Act.

Flower and Dean Street in Spitalfields – 'the foulest and most dangerous street in the whole metropolis',[41] was one of the reasons why Whitechapel had more assaults on police than anywhere else in the city.[42] It was also notable for the number of prostitutes who lived there. All but one of Jack the Ripper's canonical victims lived in, or close to, Flower and Dean Street: Polly Nichols was living at 56 Flower and Dean Street; Elizabeth Stride was staying at 32 Flower and Dean Street; Catharine Eddowes lived at 55 Flower and Dean Street; and Mary Kelly had lived in neighbouring Thrawl Street. Some effort was made to literally and figuratively ventilate the Spitalfields rookeries in the 1830s, when Commercial Street was built and about 1,300 people were made homeless in the process.[43] The majority of people affected simply moved to houses within the locality, increasing the overcrowding and doing nothing whatsoever to alleviate the social and moral pressures. The rookery remained.

But Flower and Dean Street was also the lodging house centre of Spitalfields – and this, curiously, afforded it some protection. This the Whitechapel Board of Guardians discovered when on 25 January 1876 they sought under the provisions of the Cross Act the demolition of the whole area from Fashion Street to Whitechapel High Street, home to an estimated 4,354 people, on the grounds that it was an area 'fruitful of sickness, misery, pauperism and crime within Whitechapel Union'.[44] This, it transpired, was insufficient reason for the Medical Officer of Health to sanction the demolition. He was afforded authority only if the property was unfit for habitation and lodging houses had since 1851 been subject to police supervision and could be closed down if they did not meet the minimum standards of cleanliness and repair. Eventually an improvement scheme was approved on 14 May 1877, but nothing was done, largely because 13,000 people would have been displaced. It was not until 1883 that a quarter of Flower and Dean Street was demolished, along with several other streets, courts and alleys. The land remained a vacant area until sold to the Four Per Cent Industrial Dwellings Company, a group headed by Nathan Mayer Rothschild and dedicated to providing accommodation for working class Jews. A tenement was designed by N.S. Joseph and called Charlotte de Rothschild Dwellings in honour of Lord Rothschild's mother. It opened on 2 April 1887.

Much of the rookery remained, however, including the majority of the common lodging houses. Nothing, it seemed, could shift them. Nothing bar Jack the Ripper. As Jerry White observed,

> Large-scale redevelopment was Jack the Ripper's most important legacy to the Flower and Dean Street neighbourhood.[45]

The Jack the Ripper murders, or perhaps more correctly the Whitechapel murders, drew attention to the surviving slums of the Old Nichol, the surviving Flower and Dean Street rookery and other such areas in the East End. Although a few conservative journals argued that the Ripper's victims 'preferred the excess of degradation to entering the workhouse'[46] and suggested that the national conscience should not be worried by the social and moral mores the investigation of their deaths had revealed, the majority of people were worried and their attention became focused on the slum owners. *The Times* urged that their names be printed. Canon Barnet spoke out against the owners too: 'My hope is that, as they realise that the rents are the profits of vice, they will either themselves take direct action to improve this disgraceful condition of things, or sell their property to those who will undertake its responsibility'.[47]

The owners did nothing immediately after the murders, but gradually plots of land did come up for sale. First to be sold was land on the north side of Wentworth Street, at the rear of Lolesworth Buildings, which was bought by the East End Dwellings Company, who built Strafford Houses there in 1889. The bulk of the north side of Flower and Dean Street was put on sale about 1890 and was bought by the Four Per Cent Dwelling Company for £4,500 – probably something like £2 million today. With a display of true charity they evicted about 500 people into bitterly cold weather at Christmas 1891, an unknown man dying of exposure or starvation on Boxing Day in nearby Lolesworth Street.[48] Nathanial Dwellings, a barrack-like block of 170 flats, was constructed in its place. In 1893–94 the Hendersons demolished houses located between Flower and Dean Street and Thrawl Street, which included the east side of Lolesworth Street. A local 'philanthropic' builder erected flats there between 1895 and 1897. All that remained of the old Flower and Dean Street were three houses on the north side and five on the south. Strangely enough, among the houses that survived was number 56, where Polly Nichols had lodged.

By the turn of the century a man named Jimmy Smith had bought the eight remaining houses and he became extremely wealthy from the rent he earned. According to Arthur Harding, a local villain who hailed from the Nichol, 'Jimmy Smith was ... the governor around Brick Lane'. He died in the 1920s and left his second wife £60,000. Smith's stepson, Benny Hall, took over the lodging houses and sidelined in supplying guns to the local gangsters. In the end German aircraft dropped bombs on Flower and Dean Street during a raid on 13 June 1917 and the houses were eventually all demolished in the 1920s.

Notes

1. Jay, Rev. A. Osborne (1896) *A Story of Shoreditch.* London: p. 5.
2. Rose, Millicent (1951) *The East End of London.* London: Cresset Press, p.265.
3. *The Builder*, vol. XXI, no. 1082, 31 October 1863.
4. *The Builder*, vol. XXI, no. 1082, 31 October 1863. It was certainly no answer that the people preferred to live in such conditions, but it was nevertheless a fact that many of those made homeless by the eventual destruction of the Nichol did not move into the flats that replaced them but, as Arthur Morrison observed in *A Child of the Jago*, 'had gone to infect the neighbourhoods across the border, and to crowd the people a little closer ... And so another Jago, teeming and villainous as the one displaced, was slowly growing ...'. *The Builder*'s journalist was horrified by what he saw, and rightly so, but wholesale destruction of the hovels wasn't the answer.
5. Barnett, H.O. (1918) *Barnett, Canon Barnett: His Life, Works and Friends.* London: John Murray, vol. 1, pp.73–4.
6. White, Jerry (1980) *Rothschild Buildings: Life In An East End Tenement Block 1887–1920.* London: Routledge and Kegan Paul, p.26.
7. Which was not to say that the west didn't have poverty. It did, and some of the foulest rookeries were located there.
8. Stow, John (1912) *The Survey of London.* London: J.M. Dent. Everyman edition with a new introduction by Valerie Pearl. London: J.M. Dent, 1987, p.376.
9. von Archenholtz, Johann William (1797) *A Picture Of England: Containing A Description Of The Laws, Customs, And Manners Of England. Intersperced with Curious and Interesting Anecdotes Of Many Eminent Persons.* London.
10. Jones, Gareth Stedman (1971) *Outcast London: A Study in the Relationships between Classes in Victorian Society.* Oxford: Oxford University Press. Harmondsworth, Middlesex: Penguin Books, 1976, p.160.
11. It has been widely accepted, largely on the assertion of Sir Melville Macnaghten, later Deputy Commissioner, CID at Scotland Yard, that Jack the Ripper killed five women – Mary Nichols, Annie Chapman, Elizabeth Stride, Catharine Eddowes and Mary Kelly. These are generally referred to as the canonical victims.
12. Godwin, George (1859) *Town Swamps and Social Bridges*, p.20. Leicester: Leicester University Press, 1972.
13. Quoted in Denton, William (1861) *Observations on the Displacement of the Poor by Metropolitan Railways and other Public Improvements*, p.6.
14. George, M. Dorothy (1925) *London Life in the Eighteenth Century.* London:

Kegan Paul, Trench, Trubner and Co. Ltd. London: Peregrin Books, 1966. p.97, quoting *Middlesex Records, Orders of Court*, cal., p.153.

15. There were four major epidemics of cholera in London, in 1831–32 (6,536 people died), 1848–49 (14,137), 1853–54 (10,738) and 1866 (5,596). The last of these epidemics was confined to the East End between Aldgate and Bow and was due to the contamination, through gross negligence, of the reservoirs of the East London water company and the company's failure to comply with the requirements of the 1851 and 1852 Metropolis Water Acts. The only benefit was that it became beyond doubt that cholera was primarily water-borne. For a full account of the cleaning of London see Halliday, Stephen (1999) *The Great Stink of London: Sir Joseph Bazalgette and the Cleansing of the Victorian Metropolis*. Stroud, Gloucestershire: Sutton.

16. Willan, Dr. (1805) *Diseases in London*, p.255.

17. Jones, Gareth Stedman *op. cit.*, p.169.

18. Rubinstein, W.D. (1998) *Britain's Century: A Political and Social History 1815–1905*. London: Arnold, p.173.

19. Rivington, F. (1880) *A New Proposal for Providing Improved Dwellings for the Poor* . . . London, p.1.

20. Fishman, William J. (1988) *East End 1888: A Year in a London Borough Among the Laboring Poor*. London: Duckworth. London: Hanbury, 2001.

21. Ensor, Sir Robert (1936) *England 1870–1914*. Oxford: Oxford University Press, p.127.

22. Mearns, Andrew (1883) 'The Outcast Poor. II. Outcast London'. *Contemporary Review*, XLIV, December, p.933.

23. William Preston was an experienced journalist and novelist and an ordained Congregationalist minister who in a letter to the *Daily News* on 8 April 1884 said that he was solely responsible for selecting the facts, arranging them, coming up with the startling subject headings and the winning title, and for physically writing the pamphlet. Mearns firmly denied Preston's claim, saying that he had conceived the idea, that he and others had researched the content, that Preston had written no more than a first draft according to close instructions, often at dictation and always after close consultation, and that he, Mearns, had edited and revised the script. In fairness, Mearns probably has the greater claim to the intellectual property, though Preston, the penman whose melodramatic style seeps out despite Mearns' editing, was no doubt responsible for many of the features that created the *Bitter Cry* sensation.

24. Mearns was forced to explain that he didn't mean 'very frequent' when he said 'common'. He said, 'You do meet with it and frequently meet with it, but not very frequently'.

25. Wohl, Anthony S. (1970) *The Bitter Cry of Outcast London with leading articles from the Pall Mall Gazette of October 1883 and articles by Lord Salisbury, Joseph Chamberlain and Forster Crozier*. London: Leicester University Press, p.17.

26. Schults, Raymond L. (1972) *Crusader In Babylon: W.T. Stead and the Pall Mall Gazette*. Lincoln, Nebraska: University of Nebraska Press, p.50.

27. Woods, R. (1892) *English Social Movements*. New York: Charles Scribner's Sons, p.173.
28. *The Times*, 26 November 1883.
29. *The Lancet*, 15 December 1883, p.1050.
30. Longford, Elizabeth (1964) *Victoria R.I.* London: Weidenfeld and Nicolson, London: Abacus, 2000, pp.504–5.
31. James Adderley was the head of the Oxford House Mission, established in the East End soon after Toynbee Hall.
32. Adderley, James (1916) *In Slums and Society*. London: Dutton, pp.16–17.
33. Palmer, Alan (2000) *The East End: Four Centuries of London Life*. London: John Murray, p.94.
34. Carruthers, Rev. C. (1883) *The Root of the Matter, or the Only Cure for the Bitter Cry of Outcast London and Other Similar Evils of the Present Day*. London, p.11.
35. Wohl, Anthony S. *op. cit.*, p.23.
36. Webb, Beatrice (1926) *My Apprenticeship*. London: Longmans, Green and Co. London: Penguin, 1939; Cambridge: Cambridge University Press, 1979, p.219.
37. Barnett, Henrietta Octavia (1918) *Canon Barnett: His Life, Work and Friends*. London: John Murray, p.68.
38. Palmer, Alan, *op. cit.*, p.82.
39. Cecil, Lady Gwendolen (1921–32) *Life of Robert, Marquis of Salisbury*. London: Hodder and Stoughton. vol. iii, p.77.
40. Wohl, Anthony S., *op. cit.*, p.33.
41. Greenwood, James (1883) *In Strange Company*. London, p.158; *Tower Hamlets Independent*, 19 November 1881.
42. *Report of the Commissioner of Police of the Metropolis*, 1870, p.34.
43. The *Fourth Report of the Commissioners ... [for] improving the Metropolis*, 23 April 1845, p.7, acknowledged that Commercial Road was built to achieve 'the destruction of a neighbourhood inhabited by persons addicted to vices and immorality of the worst description'.
44. *Whitechapel Board of Guardians*, Minutes, 25 January 1876.
45. Quoted in White, Jerry (1980) *Rothschild Buildings: Life In An East End Tenement Block 1887–1920*. London: Routledge and Kegan Paul, 1980.
46. White, Jerry, *op. cit.*
47. *Daily Telegraph*, 16 November 1888.
48. *East London Advertiser*, 2 January 1892.

chapter four

MARTHA TABRAM

On Bank Holiday Monday, 6 August 1888 Martha Tabram[1] – also sometimes known as 'Emma' and also as Martha Turner after the surname of the second man with whom she co-habited after her drinking caused her separation from her first husband, Henry Tabram – and Mary Ann Connolly, a tall, masculine-looking woman nicknamed 'Pearly Poll', entered a pub with a corporal and a private. They moved on to a pub called the White Swann in Whitechapel Road and separated at about 11.45, Tabram going off with the private.

The Bank Holiday slipped away into Tuesday 7 August. At 1.40am Joseph Mahony returned with his wife Elizabeth to the flat they occupied in a tenement block in George Yard called George Yard Buildings, which was 'inhabited by people of the poorest description'.[2] George Yard was a narrow street connecting Wentworth Street at the north end and Whitechapel High Street to the south, from where it was entered through a covered archway next to a pub called The White Hart. George Yard Buildings, which were commonly referred to as Model Dwellings, had been built about 13 years earlier, the venture of a local philanthropist named Crowther, and had been visited a couple of years later by Princess Alice.[3] George Street itself was described as 'one of the most dangerous streets in the locality, and that street, together with others, has for years been a regular rendezvous and hiding place for deserters'.[4]

About five minutes later Mrs. Mahony left their accommodation to purchase some supper from a chandler's shop in Thrawl Street. It didn't take her long and within ten minutes she was back. She noticed nothing suspicious, although she said that the stairs were unlit and the staircase was very wide, so that it was possible that a body could have been there and been unnoticed by her. At 3.30am a young man in his early twenties named Alfred George Crow went up the same stairs as

Mrs. Mahony and saw a body on the first floor landing, but the area being a very poor one, people often slept anywhere that offered shelter and he had regularly seen people sleeping on the landing, so he thought nothing about it. It was not until 4.50am that John Saunders Reeves left his room and began his descent of the stairs. On the first floor landing he saw the same 'sleeping' figure, but in the early dawn light he saw that it was laying on its back in a pool of blood. Reeves ran for a policeman, returning a short while later with PC Thomas Barrett, who immediately sent him off to fetch Dr. Timothy Killeen from his home at 68 Brick Lane. Killeen examined the body and determined that Martha Tabram had died about 3.30am – the time at which Alfred Crow had returned home. Martha Tabram had been stabbed 39 times, her breasts, stomach, abdomen and vagina having been the target of the killer's frenzied attack with what appeared to have been an ordinary penknife. One wound, which had penetrated the sternum, could have been made with a dagger or sword bayonet. Death, according to Dr. Killeen, was due to haemorrhage and loss of blood.

The murder, it seems, had been committed in total silence. The superintendent of the dwellings, Francis Hewitt, and his wife occupied a room which, as he measured for a journalist, was exactly 12 feet from the murder scene. 'And we never heard a cry', remarked Mr. Hewitt. Mrs. Hewitt claimed that early in the evening she did hear a single cry of 'Murder!'. It echoed through the building, but did not emanate from there. 'But', explained Mr. and Mrs. Hewitt, in a breath, 'the district round there is rather rough, and cries of "Murder!" are of frequent, if not nightly, occurrence in the district'.[5]

The body was removed to the mortuary on a police ambulance and was photographed. The photograph is still extant and shows a pleasant if slightly podgy face with a slight double chin and swept back hair that was dark in colour. Martha Tabram was only 5ft 3in tall.

The police investigation, supervised by Detective Inspector Edmund Reid, was focused on the soldier with whom Tabram had left the White Swann. PC Barrett, who had been brought to the body by John Reeves, said that at 2.00am he had seen a Grenadier guardsman loitering in Wentworth Street near the junction with George Yard. He had spoken with the man, who explained that he 'was waiting for a mate who had gone with a girl'. PC Barrett was able to provide a good description of the man and Inspector Reid organised an identity parade. All the Grenadier guardsmen with leave on 6 August were lined up and Inspector Reid instructed PC Barrett to walk along the line and, if the man he had seen was there, to touch him. Barrett did so and touched a private soldier. He returned to Reid, who asked him to repeat the process and this time Barrett touched a different man. The first man, Barrett explained, had been wearing medals but the man he had seen had not been. The second man, who was named John Leary, was released when he was able to show that he had spent his leave in the pubs of Brixton with another soldier.

On 9 August Mary Ann Connolly appeared at the Commercial Street Police Station and recited her activities with Martha on the night of the murder. Arrangements were made for her to attend an identity parade the following day at the Tower of London, but Connolly didn't turn up. Instead – and for reasons never really clarified, at least in the extant records – she had gone to stay with her cousin near Drury Lane. Eventually tracked down by Sergeant Caunter, who had the nickname 'Tommy Roundhead', she promised to be at the Tower for another parade, which took place on 13 August. She looked at the Grenadier guards assembled there and when asked if she recognised the men she 'placed her arms akimbo, glanced at the men with the air of an inspecting officer, and shook her head. This indication of a negative was not sufficient. "Can you identify anyone?" she was asked. "Pearly Poll" exclaimed, with a good deal of feminine emphasis, "He ain't here"'.[6] Poll then explained that the men she and Martha Tabram had been with had white bands around their caps. This meant they were Coldstream and not Grenadier guards. Two days later the Coldstream guardsmen on leave on 6 August were paraded before Pearly Poll at Wellington Barracks. Without hesitation she picked out two privates, George and Skipper, one of whom had three good conduct stripes which Poll thought made him a corporal. Both had solid alibis.

Meanwhile the newspapers had been reporting the case with a verbosity typical of a time when it was customary not to use a single word when a great many would do. The *East London Observer* remarked that, 'Another fearful murder has been committed under circumstances which, it is to be feared, are too mysterious to admit of a hope that the avenging hand of justice will overtake the villain or villains concerned in the murderous outrage'.[7] Many people visited George Yard Buildings to view the murder scene, where it was reported, 'there is still a large surface of the stone flags crimson stained. It is at the spot where the blood oozed from the poor creature's heart'.[8]

The inquest into the death of Martha Tabram had opened at the Working Lads' Institute in Whitechapel Road, near the present Whitechapel underground station. There, in the Alexandra Room, a lecture room and library, the deputy coroner of the South Eastern Division of Middlesex, George Collier, presided over the proceedings in some magnificence, seated beneath a painting by Louis Fleischmann of the Princess of Wales and surrounded by what was described as a profusion of other portraits of the royal family and of landscape pictures around the walls of the room. To Mr. Collier's left sat the jurymen, a Mr. Geary their elected foreman, and to his right were Dr. Keleen, Sergeant Green and Inspector Reid. The latter was described as 'a smart looking man, dressed in blue serge, who, without taking so much as a note, seemed to be absorbing all the material points'.[9] In front of the coroner was a woman who had identified the deceased as Martha Turner (the name by which Tabram was also known). She had a baby in her arms and was accompanied by a woman who was apparently the witness's mother. Several witnesses testified to the finding of the body and when an unusually animated Mr. Collier concluded the proceedings for the day, adjourning the inquiry for a fortnight, he observed that the case was 'one of the most terrible cases that anyone can possibly imagine. The man must have been a perfect savage to have attacked the woman in that way'.

When the inquest resumed on Thursday 23 August, there was a small crowd gathered outside the Working Lads' Institute, but no public were allowed inside. The witnesses included Henry Samuel Tabram and William Turner.[10] In describing these men the press intentionally or otherwise reflected the 'before and after' aspects of Martha Tabram's life: the former, in the shape of Henry Tabram, who was described as a short, well-dressed foreman packer in a furniture warehouse; and the latter, represented by William Turner, who was described as a short, slovenly dressed street hawker, somewhat dirty in appearance. The greatest interest was reserved for Mary Ann Connelly. Inspector Reid requested that she be cautioned and deputy coroner Collier patiently explained that she need not answer any question, but what she did say would be taken down, and could be used in evidence against her. When sworn in, the 'big woman' stated 'in a husky low voice'[11] that she had for the past two months lived at Crossingham's Lodging House, in Dorset Street (where the Ripper's second canonical victim lived and opposite where the last canonical victim was murdered). She repeated the details of the identification parade, but nothing new was forthcoming. After a brief summing up, 'the jury's foreman, Mr. F.W. Hunt, stood up and said they found a unanimous verdict that the deceased had been feloniously and wilfully murdered by some person or persons unknown, but the jury wished to add a rider to the effect that they thought it was a wrong thing to allow the passages of these model lodging-houses to remain unlighted at night time. This verdict was then accepted by the coroner, the jurymen were dismissed, and the proceedings terminated'.[12]

The police came in for immediate criticism. The *Eastern Post* reported with meaningful nod-and-wink inverted commas: 'A considerable amount of mystery surrounds the whole affair, which the police have entirely failed to unravel, and the evidence they have been able to obtain has been very meagre indeed. No arrest has been made, and it would seem that as usual the "clever" detective officers have been relying upon some of the same miserable class of the wretched victim to "give them the clue"'.[13]

As far as Walter Dew was concerned, the criticism 'was grossly unfair'. He went on to explain that,

> It would be impossible to recount here all that was done, the hundreds of inquiries that were made, the scores of statements taken and the long, long hours put in by us all. No clue was turned down as too trivial for investigation.
>
> We all had heartbreaking experiences, several times I got on to something which looked like a clue, followed it up day and night, only to find in the end it led nowhere.[14]

But this criticism of the police was merely a warning shot. The main salvo had yet to come. It would be far worse.

Whether or not Martha Tabram was murdered by Jack the Ripper is now debated, but it was undeniably accepted by the majority of investigators at the time[15] and although Martha Tabram hadn't been disembowelled or mutilated, a cut in the abdomen 3 inches long and 1 inch deep may have been an attempt at 'ripping' and the frenzy of the attack took it well beyond the league of 'normal' murder. The coroner concluded that the murder of Martha Tabram 'was one of the most horrible crimes that had been committed for certainly some time past. The details were very revolting ... and the person who had inflicted the injuries could have been nothing less than a fiend'.[16] Young constable Dew, looking back with the benefit of perhaps more than just a modicum of hindsight, recalled 'Already I had formed the view that we were up against the greatest police problem of the century. A third heinous crime shortly afterwards proved how right this theory was'.[17]

Notes

1. She was born Martha White, the daughter of Charles White and his wife on 10 May 1849, the youngest of their five children.
2. *East London Observer*, 11 August 1888.
3. Princess Alice Maud Mary (1843–78), the second daughter of Queen Victoria; she died from diptheria.
4. *East London Advertiser*, 18 August 1888.
5. *Weekly Herald*, 17 August 1888.
6. *Weekly Herald*, 17 August 1888.
7. *East London Observer*, 11 August 1888.
8. *Weekly Herald*, 17 August 1888.
9. *East London Observer*, 11 August 1888.
10. Not William Turner Carpenter, as reported in some newspapers (see *Eastern Post*, 25 August 1888), the mistake being a misreading of William Turner, carpenter.
11. *East London Advertiser*, 25 August 1888.
12. *East London Advertiser*, 25 August 1888.
13. *Eastern Post*, 25 August 1888.
14. Dew, Walter (1938) *I Caught Crippen: Memoirs of Ex-Chief Inspector Walter Dew CID*. London: Blackie and Son, pp.101, 103.
15. Inspector Abberline told a journalist that poisoner George Chapman, who Abberline for a while at least believed to have been the Ripper, 'occupied a lodging in George-yard, Whitechapel-road, where the first murder was committed' (*Pall Mall Gazette*, 24 March 1903). Sir Robert Anderson stated in his autobiography that the night before he took charge of the CID from James Monro 'the second of the crimes known as the Whitechapel murders was committed ...' (Anderson, Sir Robert (1910) *The Lighter Side of My Official Life*. London: Hodder and Stoughton, p.135). Walter Dew wrote, 'Whatever may be said about the death of Emma Smith there can be no doubt that the August Bank Holiday murder, which took place in George Yard Buildings, less than a hundred yards from the spot where the first victim died, was the handiwork of the dread Ripper' (Dew, *op. cit.*, p.97).
16. *East London Advertiser*, 25 August 1888.
17. Dew, *op. cit.*, p.104.

chapter five

FLOUNDER AND FUMBLE, AND 'CATCH WHOM YOU CAN!'[1]

O ne of the reasons why the Whitechapel murders are remembered today is because they focused attention on the deficiencies and inadequacies of the police. The police, already the subject of considerable press criticism, particularly from the liberal and radical press, and were widely believed to be incompetent, inefficient, interfered with – and dominated by a Commissioner more interested in polished boots and buckles and enforcing military discipline, particularly, and inappropriately, on the detective force. Police investigation of the Whitechapel crimes was very soon under close scrutiny, particularly from W.T. Stead and the crusading *Pall Mall Gazette*. E.G. Jenkinson, a civil servant who had been appointed Assistant Under Secretary at Dublin Castle with a special responsibility for crime and the police, thus working closely with Scotland Yard, complained of, 'just about everything from the dinginess of Scotland Yard's premises to corruption (drunkenness and immoral living) in its higher ranks'.[2] The failure of the police to bring the culprit to justice – or come anywhere near to identifying him[3] – naturally, if unfairly, added weight to the criticisms.

Crucial to any understanding of the crimes in a historical context is a broad general knowledge of the policemen involved and the view they had of the case overall. Chief Inspector John Littlechild who headed the 'Secret Department' (subsequently the Special Branch) from 1883 until his retirement in 1893[4] wrote in his memoirs:

Apart from the dynamite conspiracies, and explosions, and the Whitechapel murders, perhaps no matter has been regarded of such great importance at Scotland Yard as the discovery of the Great Turf Frauds of 1876.[5]

This passing reference to the Whitechapel murders provide a singular insight into the importance of the crimes. There is no question that the wave of terrorist Fenian[6] bombings in London were extremely serious crimes, but they also embarrassingly focused considerable press and public attention on the competence of the police and were thus given a double importance. This Great Turf Frauds better illustrate the distinction. This was one of the names given to an elaborate but otherwise unremarkable con trick in which people were encouraged to gamble on horse races that never took place. It was not an especially heinous or dramatic crime, but the men running the con, Harry Benson and William Kerr, always seemed to be one step ahead of the police and were proving very difficult to catch. Eventually it was shown that the four senior officers of the Detective Department – Inspector John Meiklejohn, Chief Inspector Clarke, Chief Inspector Druscovitch and Chief Inspector Palmer – were in the pay of Benson and Kerr or had by other means been duped or blackmailed into doing their bidding.[7] The resulting court case and scandal rocked Scotland Yard to its very core and the result was a thorough reorganisation of the Detective Department and a change in name to the Criminal Investigation Department (CID). As a crime the Turf Frauds were relatively insignificant, but as a scandal its effect was hugely influential. When the context of the Fenian bombings and the Great Turf Frauds is understood, the Whitechapel crimes can be seen as being listed because they too exposed the police to public scrutiny and widespread criticism. Indeed, what is remarkable and little realised is that the Whitechapel murders very nearly brought about the collapse of the government, effectively drove the final nail into the coffin of the Home Secretary's political career and were instrumental in bringing an end to the tenure of office of the Commissioner of Police.[8]

Public confidence in the police had been severely shaken by a number of events in the first half of the 1880s and not the least by the official response to demonstrations by the unemployed. These incidents are discussed in greater depth in a later chapter, but the first incident, known as 'Black Monday' – 6 February 1886 – was a fiasco in which a faction broke away from an assembly of unemployed people in Trafalgar Square and 'rioted' in Pall Mall, St James's and Oxford Street, whilst police reserves were sent in the confusion to 'the Mall' instead of Pall Mall and were completely useless. Colonel Sir Edmund Henderson, the Commissioner of the Metropolitan Police since 1869, was the scapegoat and resigned following severe censure by the Home Secretary, Hugh Childers[9] – 'never a figure of great popularity or charm'[10] – to whom the Prime Minister Gladstone seemed peculiarly attached. Childers then sent a telegraph inviting Sir Charles Warren to accept the post of Commissioner.

Sir Charles Warren was a remarkable man to whom fate certainly dealt two cruel cards. The first was his appointment as Commissioner of the Metropolitan Police, which severely tarnished his reputation; the second was his position of authority in the battle of Spion Kop – a massacre of British troops on 24 January 1900 during the Boer War – which turned the tarnish black. In both cases the fault wasn't altogether Warren's, although in the case of the latter, whilst it is impossible to absolve him of responsibility[11] – and he has been described as 'arguably the most incompetent British commander of the whole Second Boer War of 1899–1902'[12] – officers at the time were critical of the overall commander, General Sir Redvers Buller.[13] So strong is the long-held view that Warren was a lousy Commissioner[14] that it is difficult to buck the trend. However, history *has* dealt unfairly with Warren who was the right man for the right job at the wrong time and surrounded by the wrong people. He faced a press intolerant of misjudgement and in some cases actually seeking the blood of officials. Nobody could have emerged unscathed and hardly anyone did, except, perhaps, Sir Robert Anderson.

Warren was born on 7 February 1840 in Bangor, North Wales, the fifth of six children born to Major General Charles Warren, and was educated in Shropshire, Cheltenham College, Sandhurst and at the Royal Military Academy, Woolwich. In 1857 he was commissioned and served with the Royal Engineers. From 1859 to 1865 he was employed on the Gibraltar survey, and in the latter year became assistant instructor in surveying at the school of military engineering at Chatham. In 1867, as a Captain, he was selected for special service in Palestine and on behalf of the Palestine Exploration Fund undertook a reconnaissance of Philistia, the Jordan valley and Gilead, and also excavated extensively in Jerusalem, shedding considerable light on the topography of ancient Jerusalem and the archaeology of the Temple Mount/Haram al-Sherif. He published three books on these experiences, *The Recovery of Jerusalem* (1871), *Underground Jerusalem* (1874) and *The Temple or the Tomb* (1880). Ill health forced him to return to England, where from 1871 to 1872 he held command at Dover and from 1872 to 1876 held an appointment at the school of gunnery at Shoeburyness.

In 1876 he was sent out to South Africa as a special commissioner to survey the boundary between the Orange Free State and Griqualand

West, which he completed in 1877, receiving the CMG as reward for his efforts. From 1877 to 1878 he commanded the Diamond Fields Horse during the Kafir War and saw action, being severely wounded at Perie Bush. He was mentioned in dispatches three times, received the medal and clasp and was promoted to lieutenant colonel. He was afterwards appointed special commissioner to investigate native questions in Bechuanaland, and in 1879 became administrator and commander-in-chief of Griqualand West. Returning to England in 1880 he spent the next four years as chief instructor in surveying at the school of military engineering at Chatham, but was sent to Egypt for special duty under the Admiralty. The orientalist Edward Henry Palmer had been sent on a secret-service mission in June 1882, but had vanished during the night of 10–11 August. Warren, accompanied by Lieutenants Haynes and Burton, R.E., were sent out to find Palmer and his party. Following a minute and intricate inquiry, they discovered that the party had been ambushed and driven about a mile to the Wady Sudr. Forced to stand in a row on the edge of a gully with a 60 feet fall before them, they were shot by the Arabs, Palmer falling with the first shot. The murderers were tracked down, caught and following a trial, executed. The fragmentary remains of Palmer and two of his team, Flag lieutenant Harold Charrington and Captain William John Gill, were brought home and buried in the crypt of St. Paul's Cathedral on 6 April 1883. For this sterling work and example of detective prowess, Warren received the KCMG medal, bronze star and third class Medjidie, and in 1883 he was created a knight of justice of the Order of St. John of Jerusalem. Back in England, in 1885 he sought an entry into politics by standing as the Liberal candidate for the Hallam Division of Sheffield, and was narrowly defeated by the Conservative candidate C.B. Stuart-Wortley. In January 1886 he was posted to Sudan to take command of a garrison on the Red Sea port of Suakim, but his stay there was short-lived and he was recalled to serve as Commissioner of the Metropolitan Police.

Warren would rejoin the army on leaving the police and take command of troops in Singapore. In 1895 he returned to England to the command of the Thames district, where he took responsibility for the important but routine completion of the Thames defence schemes. At the outbreak of war in South Africa, Warren was given the command of the fifth division and sailed for the Cape. He was promoted to lieutenant general in 1897, and with the fifth division joined Sir Redvers Buller in Natal on 21 December 1899, finding himself in command of the disastrous assault on a hill called Spion Kop. Later, however, he forced a crossing of the Tugela River and won Pieters Hill, paving the way for the relief of Ladysmith. Warren returned to England in August 1900, was promoted to general in 1904 and colonel commandant of the Royal Engineers in 1905. He retired the following year.

Warren was a very keen freemason and Founding Master of Quatuor Coronati Lodge No. 2076, in 1884. After his retirement he took a keen interest in the Church Lads' Brigade and was a pioneering Scoutmaster in the movement founded by his boyhood friend and military colleague, Lord Baden-Powell in 1908, running the 1st Ramsgate – 'Sir Charles Warren's Own' – Boy Scout Troop. During this time he wrote extensively on religious questions, produced a volume of reminiscences called *On the Veldt in the Seventies* and devoted a great deal of time to Masonic research. He died at Weston-super-Mare on 21 January 1927, leaving two sons and two daughters, his wife having predeceased him.

At first Warren's appointment was greeted with satisfaction:

> Childers knew quite well what sort of man was needed as Police Chief at this juncture, and, turning aside more than 400 candidates for the post, he deliberately appointed Warren. Parliament, the public and the press formed a consensus of opinion which was, almost unanimously, strongly in favour of the appointment ... The *Pall Mall Gazette* ... expressed the hope 'that having selected as Colonel Henderson's successor the man who of all others left to us is the most like General Gordon[15] in conviction, in temper, and in impatience of being meddled with, Mr. Childers will avoid the fatal precedent of the Soudan, allow his Chief Commissioner a free hand, and back him up like a man who sets to work to make a clean sweep of the Augean stable of Scotland Yard'.[16]

Warren's skills were right for the job, as *The Times* observed:

> In many essential respects, Sir Charles Warren is precisely the man whom sensible Londoners would have chosen to preside over the Police Force of the Metropolis. Though he is in the prime of life (he is only forty-six), there are few officials in Her Majesty's service who have had more varied experience. He is at once a man of science and a man of action; and for nearly twenty years he has been engaged in work of the kind most likely to develop the administrative faculties.[17]

The *Pall Mall Gazette* was happy; Warren lacked 'gaiety of spirit and genial humour' and had a 'deep religious conviction' and stern views on prostitution and drink.

What all this meant was that it was generally believed that the police lacked proper discipline and needed a firm hand on the tiller. Warren was selected and was generally thought to be an excellent choice for the job, but as the *Pall Mall Gazette* observed, Warren worked best without interference. And for a while Childers did give Warren a free hand, but Gladstone's government was not long for power and on 7 June 1886 it was defeated in an election. Lord Salisbury returned to the premiership, appointing Henry Matthews (later Lord Llandaff) Home Secretary.

Matthews was born in 1826 in Ceylon, where his father was a puisne judge. He was educated at the University of Paris and London University and called to the bar at Lincoln's Inn, where he enjoyed a successful practice and was a skilled cross-examiner who played a part in some notable trials, the best known today probably being Lyon v. Home (1868), an action brought against a spiritualist; the Tichborne case (1869); and most famously Crawford v. Crawford and Dilke (1886), which brought about the political downfall of Sir Charles Dilke.

Matthews entered politics in 1868, but lost his seat in 1874 and did not find a constituency until 1886 when, as a protégé of the self-destructive Lord Randolph Churchill, who leant his substantial popular support to Matthews' campaign, he stood for and won the marginal seat of East Birmingham. However, having Churchill's patronage was a double-edged sword, as he was not particularly popular. When Lord Salisbury made Churchill Leader of the House and Chancellor of the Exchequer, it was an appointment opposed by Queen Victoria who described Churchill as 'so mad and odd'. Lord Salisbury himself, when appointing Churchill in 1886, likened him to the Mahdi, who 'pretends to be mad and is very sane in reality'.[18] Perhaps unsurprisingly Churchill has been advanced as a Ripper suspect.[19]

Churchill was also disliked by a variety of Conservative politicians, a few of whom had objected to being called 'Marshalls and Snelgroves' by Lord Randolph, who was referring to the staid and perhaps dowdy London department store. Others were victims of his 'offensive and often pointless rudeness'.[20] Making enemies did not help Lord Randoph's political career and at the end of 1886, when he tendered his resignation, apparently as a card in a political reshuffle and without any expectation that it would be accepted, Lord Salisbury – 'not a man to resist the suicide of a nuisance' – accepted it. Eight years later Lord Randolph Churchill was dead. 'He was the chief mourner at his own protracted funeral', said Lord Salisbury's successor as Prime Minister, Lord Rosebery – the final analysis of his short-lived political career being that it consisted of a lot of noise and of little achievement.

It may have been at Churchill's request that Lord Salisbury appointed Matthews, a relatively new and inexperienced political newcomer, as Home Secretary, the first Roman Catholic to serve in the Cabinet since the reign of James II. Apparently Queen Victoria urged Salisbury to appoint Matthews. Her reaction, on being told of his religion, is recorded by the *Dublin Review*: '"What of that?" snapped the old Queen, who disliked the Liberal party more than she did the Pope'.[21] Whoever's idea it was, in retrospect it was a serious mistake. Matthews was witty, charming, generous, played 'a prominent part in the festivities of the bar mess' and possessed a fine legal brain. However, notwithstanding the praise of people like Lord Chief Justice Coleridge, who considered Matthews the best home secretary he had known,[22] Matthews managed to be unpopular with all political persuasions, with the press and with the people. As A.J. Balfour put it, he was 'the member of the Govt. whom everyone wishes to turn out!'[23], his 'Minesterial career was a complete failure'[24] and 'He did more, perhaps, to render the government unpopular than any other minister'.[25]

As Home Secretary he was unlucky to have not only the Ripper case to deal with, which did much to bring about his delayed but ultimate downfall, but also those of Lipski (1887), Miss Cass (1887), Mrs. Maybrick (1889)[26] and the Davies brothers (1890).[27] Interestingly, in the case of Miss Cass a vote for adjournment was carried against the government and Matthews tendered his resignation, which Lord Salisbury refused to accept. The reason was that Matthews was fortunate to have won a marginal seat which Salisbury's government could not afford to put at risk. Resignation and outright dismissal for incompetence were therefore impossible (and in any event incompetence could not be admitted), and quiet removal would have generated all sorts of speculation and rumours and created the problem of with whom Matthews could have been replaced. Lord Salisbury entertained reservations about both leading contenders, Lord Knutsford, who was 'so amiable, he would hang nobody' and Michael Hicks Beach 'on the other hand, would make a very good Home Secretary, and would hang everybody'.[28] So it was that for the time being Matthews – whose political star had never really risen and had, if anything, sunk well below the horizon after the 'Bloody Sunday' riots and who, as a Churchillite, had a precarious political future – had to stay in office. The Ripper crimes didn't force the Home Secretary's resignation but they did effectively lower Henry Matthews' political coffin into the ground and shovel soil onto the lid.

Lord Salisbury had already concluded that Matthews was not the right man to be Home Secretary, but his perceived mismanagement of the Ripper reinforced that conclusion, especially when the Queen wrote to Salisbury on 28 October 1888, after three more women had been murdered, to complain that the Home Secretary's 'general want of sympathy with the feelings of the *people* are doing the *Government* harm'.[29] Salisbury admitted that Matthews had not been a success, telling her, 'There is an innocence of the ways of the world which no one could have expected to find in a criminal lawyer of sixty',[30] and expressed his desperation in his flirtation with the idea of promoting Matthews to a Lord Justice of Appeal and shifting C.T. Ritchie into the Home Office. As relieved as Queen Victoria would no doubt have been to see Matthews' departure, she dissuaded Lord Salisbury on the not unreasonable grounds that Matthews was blatantly unqualified for the position. It was therefore thought by all the big political players of the day – Salisbury, Goschen, Smith and Balfour – that Matthews should stay *in situ* until the general election. He could then be quietly shuffled off with a title in appreciation of services rendered. As Viscount Llandaff he thereafter played little part in public life. He travelled – always a great passion of his – but never visited America because, he said, he did not understand it,[31] and he died, after suffering for several years with rheumatism, in 1913.[32]

Warren was a man who *believed* himself to have full and complete authority over the police, and Matthews was a man who possessed full and complete authority over the police and insisted on exercising it. Relations between the two men predictably hit very choppy waters and by the end of 1888 would reach such implacability that Warren resigned. Opinion is divided as to who was responsible. The general judgement of history is that, 'Warren was a man noted for his tactlessness and peppery temper; there was a stiff pride about Sir Charles too which made it difficult for him to act in a subordinate capacity . . .'[33] Other voices lay the blame elsewhere. Evelyn Ruggles-Brise, Private Secretary to four Home Secretaries, including Matthews, sympathised with Warren, saying that Matthews was 'quite incapable of dealing with men; he was a regular Gallio in his attitude to Warren's complaints. Later on he quarrelled with Bradford, and if you couldn't get on with Bradford you could get on with nobody'.[34] Sir Robert Anderson likewise laid the blame with the Home Office, however he clearly and firmly placed the responsibility at the doorstep of Godfrey Lushington,[35] with whom he used to play lawn tennis, and whose personality he described as an irritant 'blister' when a 'plaister' was needed. Anderson was probably correct.[36] The reality seems to be that Warren believed, probably rightly, that he had been appointed by Hugh Childers to reorganise a demoralised police force and had been given a free hand in how he achieved it. Matthews evidently understood the situation differently or did not agree with the arrangement, began to impose his authority over Warren, and Warren objected. The result was hostility.

Warren also came into conflict with the Assistant Commissioner CID, James Monro, who had succeeded Sir Howard Vincent in 1884 when the latter had embarked on a long and successful political career as Conservative MP for Central Sheffield. Sir Robert Anderson, who shared Monro's committed millenniarist religious beliefs and was a close personal friend until something damaged their relationship irreparably shortly before Monro resigned in 1890, observed that Monro's 'appointment marked an epoch in Police administration in London; but the good which ought to have resulted from it was largely hindered by the bickerings which, after a time, began between him and the Chief Commissioner. And those bickerings were aggravated by Sir Charles Warren's relations with the Home Office'.

Born in 1838 in Edinburgh, the son of a solicitor, James Monro, who suffered infantile paralysis that left him lame, entered the Bengal Civil Service in 1857, starting as an Assistant Magistrate and finishing as Commissioner of the Presidency Division. Blessed 'with the instinct of a born detective ... his name became a word of terror to the subtlest native conspirators'[37] and when by chance he happened to be in London he applied for the vacant position of Assistant Commissioner CID. To his surprise he was appointed. He would resign as Assistant Commissioner in 1888, but was retained as an advisor to the Home Office until succeeding Sir Charles Warren as Commissioner. His relationship with Matthews was equally difficult as his predecessor's and they disagreed especially over the same issue of police pensions which had caused the final clash between Warren and Matthews. In 1890 he tendered his resignation and returned to India where he founded the Ranaghat Medical Mission. He retired to Cheltenham in 1905 and died in 1920.

Warren's 'bickerings' with Monro reflected an irreconcilable difference of opinion about the purpose of police work and the relative
responsibilities of the uniformed and detective police. This difference
of opinion might not have prevented the two men from working
together in harmony, but unfortunately Monro had a second function,
running the 'Secret Department', for which he was not answerable to
Warren and did not have to consult him. Monro therefore embodied
Warren's resentments about not having complete responsibility for the
force. Furthermore, with regard to Warren's feelings, Monro seems to
have acted with an extraordinary lack of tact.

Monro also came into conflict with a man named Edward Jenkinson
who was working for the Home Office in their anti-Fenian activities.
According to Monro's unpublished memoirs,

> When I joined the Met. Police, I found that there was a kind of Central
> Bureau of Intelligence ... At the Home Office Mr. E.G. Jenkinson was the
> Head of this department. His business was to collect all information from
> many countries, especially America, regarding the dynamiters, and to give
> to the various police forces concerned any information which concerned
> people under their jurisdiction, so that any necessary police action might
> be taken by them. Mr. Jenkinson's functions were entirely those of an intel-
> ligence department; he was not a member of any police force; he had no
> police authority anywhere; all that he had to do was to keep the police gen-
> erally acquainted with any information which, from his various agents, he
> acquired, suggesting any course of action which he might think desirable.
> But the responsibility for police action, taken or not taken, lay of course
> with the police forces concerned, and not with Mr Jenkinson ...[38]

This was clearly a blueprint for disaster. Childers had hired Sir Charles
Warren and given him a free hand to reorganise the police force, and
Jenkinson had been hired and given an equally free hand to counter
Fenian terrorists. Both were not left alone to get on with their
respective job and in several ways this would impact on the Ripper
investigation.

The Fenian-obsessed Sir William Vernon Harcourt,[39] Home
Secretary from April 1880 to June 1885, was hugely influential in
determining police policy over the first half of the 1880s and after. A
bit of a 'stage-door-Johnny' in his youth, and at one point close to
the great French actress and courtesan Rachel, with whom he
exchanged mementoes, he was twice married but seems to have preferred the company of men and has been described as 'the ultimate
male chauvinist'.[40] He was an imposing man who stood 6 feet 3½

inches tall and possessed 'a high facility of comprehension and expression, without much subtlety or originality'.[41] He sometimes exhibited a strange eccentricity, as when Lady Beaconsfield was on her deathbed and he sent her a consignment of full-strength Trinity Audit Ale. He was renowned for his luncheon and dinner parties and as an 'enthusiastic partaker of the copious food and drink he provided',[42] which in time added to his imposing presence. But he is chiefly noted for his exceedingly fiery temper: 'Harcourt was notorious for the hottest temper in politics. But he was generous, warm-hearted and quick to forgive and even apologise';[43] he was 'one of the late-Victorian Liberal party's two rogue elephants' and people were forever upset by the 'strong personal antagonism and irritations his abrasive manner provoked'.[44]

His temperamental outbursts and intemperate criticism of his colleagues – his official biographer pointed out that 'he could not be content with beating a man but wanted to roll him in the dust as well'[45] – made him enemies. Occasional discomfitures were greeted with greater glee than they might otherwise have done, as when at a speech in Burton-on-Trent he announced that he felt ready for 'a bit of ducking' and was reported in *The Times* with an 'f' substituted for the 'd'. Copies of the newspaper apparently exchanged hands for the equivalent of £50 and cost him the premiership. A potential successor to Gladstone, at the most crucial moment in his career he lacked support and 'had no Cabinet allies'.[46] Gladstone was succeeded by Lord Rosebery.

Harcourt over-reacted to the Fenian threat, deferring most of the day-to-day business of Home Secretary across to Dilke at the Local Government Board, saying that he had little time for anything but police business. He had an instinctive dislike of the Irish and discovered a liking for cloak and dagger secret policing. Dilke remarked that 'Harcourt fancied himself as a Fouché (Napoleon's chief of police) . . .'. In Ireland the Queen's representative as head of the British administration was the Lord Lieutenant and on 11 December 1868, when Gladstone formed his first administration, John Poyntz Spencer, the fifth Earl Spencer,[47] was appointed to that position – 'the latest of a succession of noblemen, usually of impressive lineage and inoffensive character, sent out to ape the functions of monarchy at Dublin Castle'.[48] Earl Spencer held office during Gladstone's administrations and was reappointed on 3 May 1882, being sworn in at Dublin Castle on 6 May, with Lord Frederick Cavendish sworn in as Chief Secretary. That evening Spencer rode to the Viceregal Lodge in the Phoenix Park, and Cavendish and Under Secretary Thomas Burke followed on foot. In the Park Cavendish and Burke were set upon and knifed to death by a gang calling themselves the 'Invincibles'. For a while the police seemed to be at a loss and Earl Spencer sought assistance from London, being sent a Colonel Brackenbury. Edward Jenkinson was appointed Assistant Under Secretary with a special responsibility for crime and police. Eventually the murderers were caught and executed, but Spencer and Sir George Trevelyan (Cavendish's replacement) were in 'daily even hourly danger of their lives'.[49] Spencer was hated, described as of 'cruel, narrow, and dogged nature', and dubbed the 'Red Earl'. By 1885, however, he was a supporter of home rule, partly simply out of support for Gladstone, and he took an active part in the framing of the first home rule bill. When this was rejected on the second reading, Gladstone immediately dissolved parliament but was heavily defeated at the polls. One effect of Gladstone's action was to push W.T. Stead into his 'Maiden Tribute To Modern Babylon' articles (see Chapter 7).

When the Fenian problem developed in England, Home Secretary Harcourt borrowed Edward Jenkinson from Spencer and brought him to London, promising him authority over all Britain's mainland anti-Fenian agencies. It was a rash promise and one that Harcourt could not keep, so Jenkinson found himself obliged to hand his information over to the Metropolitan Police for them to do with as they saw fit. This understandably enraged Jenkinson, who patiently collected information from agents whose lives were in some cases at risk and then had to hand it over to men who treated it cavalierly, endangered his agents, and to cap it off, didn't act on the information correctly. Jenkinson accordingly lost all respect for the Yard, whose officers he considered to be grossly inefficient – often unable to trace suspects he was able to find without difficulty – and riddled with corruption: 'There is hardly a man among them who does not take money', he wrote to Earl Spencer in Ireland. Jenkinson's way of working around the problem was to refuse to share his information. However, according to Monro's memoirs, Jenkinson,

> . . . not only collected intelligence regarding London, but he acted upon it, without any reference to the London police, by means of a number of Irish police who he had, without any authority whatever, stationed in London . . .[50]

James Monro had been chief of police in Bengal, which made him experienced in political policing – meaning the policing of political crime such as secret societies, terrorist organisations and so forth.[51] The Indian police were armed 'and deliberately distanced from their communities, amongst whom they had a reputation for corruption and oppression'.[52] Jenkinson regarded Monro as 'a very good man in his way', but – perhaps unsurprisingly, given his low opinion of almost everyone – with 'little energy or originality'.

It has to be said that Jenkinson's opinion that everyone at Scotland Yard was hopelessly inept was harsh, as he sometimes mistook Scotland Yard policy for ineptitude. This was something Monro seems to have understood, despite his years in India, but that Jenkinson, well versed in political policing, did not. For example, Jenkinson thought the Yard inept because they did not cultivate informants – yet it was Scotland Yard policy to accept information provided by somebody who chose to inform them, but to frown upon actively cultivating informants. Jenkinson also thought it was ineptitude when criminals were warned off committing a crime instead of being arrested in the process of committing it. But preventive policing was policy – and not a policy necessarily always endorsed by Monro. Unfortunately, though understandably, Jenkinson thought it prudent to withhold information for as long as it was possible to do so, but Monro seriously objected to this (yet curiously seemed to show no understanding on Warren's position when he complained about Monro doing the same thing). By mid May 1885 the hostility between the two men was palpable and lit the fuse to Harcourt's powder-keg temper. He laid into Jenkinson, telling him that his protection of his information was 'all jealousy, nothing but jealousy'. The next day Harcourt apologised for his outburst, but he had made up his mind to side with Monro; Jenkinson was told that he had no legal authority and everything he did had to be done through and by the police. A month later Harcourt brought Jenkinson and Monro together in his office and effectively ordered Jenkinson to make his information known to Monro, but the animosity continued, reaching a point where Monro could stand it no longer and tendered his resignation. But, as Monro wrote,

In the Autumn of '86 I was sent for by Mr. Matthews, the new Secretary of State, and had an interview with him which lasted for more than three hours. I laid the whole of the circumstances before him and told him very plainly that I could not consent any longer to work with Mr. Jenkinson. He had constantly interfered with police action and to me personally on more than one occasion he had lied in such a disgraceful manner that I declined to have any dealings with him.

Briefly the end was, after a short time, that Mr. Jenkinson was dismissed.

According to Monro, after replacements had been considered and rejected,

> at the urgent request of the Government. I consented to act as Chief of the Secret Department as regards intelligence, and at the same time retain my office as Asst. Commissioner.[53]

The so-called Secret Department, known as 'Section D', was the forerunner of the modern Special Branch (which is commonly but erroneously believed to have evolved from the Irish Branch, 'Section B'). It was financed out of Imperial Funds, not Metropolitan Police Funds, and its brief was to keep covert surveillance on all subversives (groups such as anarchists, Fenians and assorted revolutionaries). Although the detectives working for the Secret Department were not to be outwardly distinguished from other detectives, they and the department were not under the authority of the Commissioner but were directly responsible to Henry Matthews, the Home Secretary. The policemen employed in the Secret Department were Chief Inspector Littlechild and Inspectors Pope, Melville and Burke.

Anything Monro did that was connected with the work of 'Section D' was reported directly to the Home Secretary, not to Sir Charles Warren, which meant that Warren had a subordinate officer engaged in police work over whom and partly over which he had no authority or influence and about which he was not even consulted. It is easy to understand how galling this must have been for Warren, plagued as he already was by the Home Secretary's interference. A firmer hand than Matthews' might have resolved the differences between the two men, and Monro, if he had any comprehension of Warren's position, could have behaved with greater tact and sensitivity.

But Monro was extraordinarily insensitive and in November 1887 he complained to Warren that he was overworked and requested the creation of a new post of Assistant Chief Constable to relieve the strain on his senior officers and himself. The complaint was probably justified, one senior officer, Frederick 'Dolly' Williamson, having become ill through overwork, but Warren instead suggested that Monro shed some of his responsibilities, clearly meaning the Secret Department work. He wrote that the only reason Monro was able to undertake his Secret Department work was 'due to the efficiency of the Criminal

Investigation Department' and argued,

> that the Assistant Commissioner should be allowed to devote his time and
> energy to his legitimate work, and that he should not be burdened with the
> care and anxiety of duties which previously occupied the whole of the
> attention of an officer of undoubted experience and ability at a very high
> salary.[54]

Monro rather lamely replied that the secret agent work never
detracted from his CID work because, 'If there is pressure the special
work suffers first'. If that was intended to calm Warren, then it may
not have calmed the government so much.[55]

Matthews vacillated. Monro recommended that Sir Melville
Macnaghten be appointed Assistant Chief Constable, saying, 'I saw his
way of managing men when I was an official in India and was struck
by it, for he had a most turbulent set of natives to deal with, and he
dealt with them firmly and justly'.[56] The Home Office agreed to the
appointment. But Warren was less than impressed, pointing out that
Macnaghten had provoked some apparently mild-mannered natives
into attacking him. Macnaghten was, said Warren, 'the one man in
India who has been beaten by Hindoos', and he argued that there
were in any case men better qualified for the job.[57] This time the
Home Secretary sided with Warren, and Macnaghten was turned
down. This created an awkward situation for Monro because he had
already told Macnaghten that the job was in the bag.[58]

Behind all this 'bickering' was a very serious philosophical issue that
has reached down the decades to the police force today, namely the
questions of visible policing and the relative importance of crime prevention and crime detection – in simple terms whether the uniformed
or detective police were the most important. Warren believed that
policing should be visible and open to inspection, that the police
should adhere to accepted standards of moral behaviour, and that the
principal responsibility of the police was to be an active and visible
deterrent to crime. Monro, perhaps less rightly but more realistically,
believed that criminals acted secretly, would not be caught by men visible and open to inspection, and that certain crimes would only be
solved through intelligence gathering before the crime and detective
work after the crime. In simple terms Monro believed that you could
not catch sewer rats by staying out of the sewer. On the surface this
difference of concept took shape in an argument about whether or not
the plain-clothed CID and crime detection was secondary to the

uniformed police and crime prevention. Warren did not conceal his opinion:

> The whole safety and security of London depends, in great measure, upon the efficiency of the uniform police constable acting with the support of the citizen ... And it cannot be too strongly impressed upon the mind, at a time when the detective efficiency of the police is being called into question, that it has always been held as a police maxim that 'the primary object of an efficient police is the prevention of crime. The next that of detection and punishment of offenders if crime is committed ...[59]

Relations between the two men continued to deteriorate and eventually Monro bitterly declared that Warren had imposed such restrictions on the functioning of the CID that, 'I must in justice to myself disclaim all responsibility meanwhile for any unfavourable results, to which the system now initiated will lead'.[60] Nothing changed and eventually Monro felt that he could take no more. In his unpublished memoirs Monro wrote,

> Commissioner, Sir C. Warren made life so intolerable for me that I resigned. What the Home Secretary thought of the merits of the matter at issue between us may be gathered from the fact that he retained me as Chief of the Secret Department ...[61]

For five East End prostitutes these shenanigans in the corridors of Scotland Yard and the Home Office, had they known about them, would no doubt have seemed as far removed from their own lives as it was possible to get. Yet, as Bernard Porter observed in his book *The Origins of the Vigilant State*, this clash 'was really a hoary old dilemma of the British police since its earliest days: how to reconcile purity with results. Warren and Monro represented Scylla and Cherybdis between which the Metropolitan force had tried to steer for years. In the 1880s it steered on to both of them; with the result that several poor women in Whitechapel got drowned'.[62]

Monro had resigned as head of the CID, but Matthews didn't dispense with his services. Instead he shifted him across to an office at the Home Office, where he continued his duties as head of the Secret Department and, it seems, acted as Matthews' consultant on CID matters. He was replaced as Assistant Commissioner CID by Robert Anderson, who later wrote,

> I may here say at once that, though I was warned by many, including officers who had served under him in South Africa, that 'I could never get on with Warren', my relations with Sir Charles were always easy and pleasant

... I always found him perfectly frank and open, and he treated me as a colleague, leaving me quite unfettered in the control of my department; and
when his imperious temper could no longer brook the nagging Home
Office ways of that period, and he decided to resign his office, I felt sincere
regret at his going'.[63]

Sir Charles Warren had by 1888 won the support of the uniformed
police, but according to Anderson the officers of the CID were
demoralised, the more so because of Monro's resignation and initial
uncertainty about his replacement, but some stability was restored
when it was announced that Robert Anderson was to succeed him.
Just how much stability was restored remains to be seen, as we only
have Anderson's side of things – and it is unlikely that much stability was immediately restored because Anderson had barely dusted
his office chair with the seat of his trousers before he took sick leave
in Switzerland, apparently suffering from exhaustion and a throat
infection. He was therefore on leave when all but one of the Ripper
crimes took place. He is nevertheless an immensely important figure
in the Ripper story because he is the only senior officer at Scotland
Yard to have categorically stated that the Police knew the identity of
the Ripper. And as Assistant Commissioner he was in a position to
know!

Born in Dublin, Ireland, the son of Crown Solicitor Matthew
Anderson, he was educated at Trinity College, Dublin, took his BA in
1862 and in 1863 was called to the Bar at King's Inn, Dublin. In
1866 his elder brother Samuel, Solicitor General in the vice-regal
administration, secured him work at Dublin Castle providing the
Secretary General Lord Mayo[64] with a précis of known Fenian
activity. His services were again requested by the Attorney General
following 'the Fenian Rising' of March 1867, and for a third time in
the autumn of 1867. In December of that year an explosion in
Clerkenwell, London, determined Anderson's future career. A prominent Irish-American Fenian named Richard O'Sullivan Burke had
been sent to Clerkenwell prison. On 11 December Scotland Yard
received a letter from Superintendent Daniel Ryan of the Dublin
Metropolitan Police:

I have to report that I have information from a reliable source to the effect
that the rescue of Richard Burke from prison in London is contemplated.
The plan is to blow up the exercise wall by means of gunpowder – the hour
between 3 and 4 pm and the signal for all right, a white ball thrown up outside when he is at exercise.

On 12 December a policeman in Corporation Row, which was bounded by the prison wall, saw some men bring up a barrel and insert and light a fuse, but the fuse was damp and the men took the barrel away. The next day they returned and again watched by the police lit the fuse. The terrible explosion destroyed about 60 yards of prison wall as well as several houses opposite, and windows over a wide area were shattered. Six people were killed outright, another six subsequently died from injuries sustained, and 120 people, mainly women and children, were injured. A week later several of the conspirators were identified, but only Michael Barrett, who was identified as the man who lit the fuse, was convicted. On 26 May 1868, he was executed outside Newgate prison, the last person to be publicly executed in England. The Metropolitan Police Commissioner, Sir Richard Mayne, tendered his resignation, but the Prime Minister refused to accept it and the Home Secretary told the House of Commons on 9 March 1868 that the authorities had been misled by the wording of Superintendent Ryan's warning: 'they thought it (the prison wall) would probably be blown up from underneath, and had no conception that it would be blown down . . .'.

The government was panicked by the explosion – or perhaps they were unnerved by the breathtaking incompetence displayed by the authorities – and with pretty much a knee-jerk reaction the Cabinet set about finding ways of improving intelligence. It initially decided against setting up a specialist Fenian department at Scotland Yard, preferring instead to create a temporary anti-Fenian Secret Service Department attached to the Home Office. Colonel the Hon. William Fielding was appointed as its head and, on the recommendation of Lord Mayo, Robert Anderson was appointed to assist him. Anderson took up his new duties in London on 19 December 1867. After three months the department was closed, Fielding went off to perform other duties and Anderson was retained with the title Home Office Advisor on Political Crime.

Following the Invincibles' brutal murder of Lord Frederick Cavendish and Thomas Burke the British government was very shaken. This was a personal loss for Prime Minister Gladstone, Cavendish being his nephew by marriage and thought of almost as a son. It perhaps also halted in its tracks the possibility of a united Ireland, for it was rumoured that Charles Stewart Parnell knew of the assassination plot. Parnell in fact denounced the outrage with conviction and a parliamentary commission appointed to investigate the

charges exonerated him, but he lost considerable trust. Another consequence of the murders was that the failings of the Irish police were
exposed and it was decided to send someone over from England to
undertake a thorough reorganisation. The man chosen for the job was
a very reluctant Colonel Henry Brackenbury, who received substantial
funding to organise an intelligence network aimed at destroying
Fenianism in Ireland, America and mainland Britain. According to
Anderson, 'he appealed to me to represent his department in London.
I twice refused in the most definite way to accept his overtures; but at
last, under pressure from Sir William Harcourt, I had to comply'.[65]

The reluctant Brackenbury was to all intents and purposes fired a
short time after his appointment, following a huge row when it was
discovered that he was seeking active service in Egypt instead of applying himself to the hunt for Fenians. He was succeeded by his second-
in-command, a one-time Indian civil servant named Edward
Jenkinson,[66] who proved enormously successful and soon had tabs on
pretty much everything that the Fenians were doing in Ireland. The
weak link was Britain, where Fenianism seemed to flourish despite the
efforts of 16 RIC men stationed in London, Liverpool, Birmingham
and Glasgow, and the informants run by Anderson, whose main agent
was a man named Thomas Billis Beach, who had infiltrated the
Fenians in America under the name Henry Le Caron and for over 20
years fed Anderson quality information. Home Secretary Harcourt
asked Earl Spencer, the Lord Lieutenant of Ireland, for the loan of
Jenkinson to oversee Fenian intelligence gathering on mainland
Britain. Meanwhile, he arranged for the formation of an Irish Bureau
at Scotland Yard under the command of Chief Superintendent
Williamson.

Jenkinson had a poor opinion of the set up in England. He
suggested that instead of re-vamping the existing set up the Home
Office should create a replica of his own office in Ireland. In other
words a Home Office department should be formed with a head to
whom all other services, including Williamson's Irish Branch, was
answerable and who in turn would be given extensive freedom of
action according to his own discretion and would be answerable
directly to the Home Secretary. Jenkinson suggested that Major
Nicholas Gosselin, a resident magistrate in Ireland, be its head, and he
was duly appointed and given the task of overseeing Fenian intelligence gathering in the North of England and Glasgow. Gosselin may
have been considerably over-confident because he soon began to run

into problems as his sources of information dried up. Harcourt, clearly desperate, requested the return of Jenkinson, who duly left Dublin on 7 March 1884 for a troubled three year stint in London, during which time he complained bitterly that Scotland Yard was unable to keep a secret, was hopelessly inefficient and 'worse than useless' in intelligence work.

Anderson had effectively been replaced by Gosselin, but was given such a dressing down by Harcourt at the beginning of 1884 that a lesser – or wealthier – man would have resigned. Instead he was relieved 'entirely for the present of all my responsibilities & duties relative to Fenianism in London' – apart, presumably, from his function as Le Caron's postman. He was appointed to the Royal Commission on Loss of Life at Sea.

In May 1883 Anderson was deprived of his right to receive intelligence from Williamson and the RIC, but was kept on at the Home Office on the condition that he expand his network of informers in the North of England and in America. In September, Jenkinson reported that Anderson had still not 'found a single agent'.[67] His main value was the line of intelligence he had with Le Caron, who would report to no one else. But by November Jenkinson's information started drying up and despite Gosselin's claim in January 1884 that he knew 'every Fenian leader of importance from the Tweed to Birmingham and could put my hand on them tomorrow',[68] his sources began to dry too.

In the meantime trouble with Jenkinson had been brewing, largely because 'Liberalism in Britain may have been stretched and strained by some of the things that hit it in the 1880s, but it remained pure enough for political policing and espionage on the Irish pattern still to appear incongruous',[69] but also because the politicians, as ever the ones to put a problem out of mind when it ceased to be of immediate concern, were becoming slightly complacent in the absence of terrorist activity. Jenkinson resigned in January 1887 and was replaced by James Monro and his department replaced by 'Section D', the Secret Department. Monro had, despite objections raised by the under secretary, Godfrey Lushington,[70] recalled Robert Anderson from the cold and appointed him his assistant at a salary of £400 per annum.

Anderson would in turn succeed Monro as head of the CID. Jenkinson, now long-gone from the Home Office, perhaps predictably deplored the appointment: 'what an infamously bad appointment it is! Anderson is not the 19th part of a man, and if it were known what kind of man he is, there would be a howl all over London'.[71] Jenkinson's views were coloured, of course, by the fact that Anderson was staunchly anti-Home Rule, whereas Jenkinson, like Earl Spencer, was pro-Home Rule, and Anderson played by the rules (to the extent that he was a survivor, whilst Warren, Jenkinson, Monro and even Matthews all fell on the bloody battlefield of office politics). Anderson, in fact, is a difficult man to assess. Deeply religious, a millenniarist – a believer in 'the second coming of Christ, with attendant Last Judgement etc.'[72] – and the author of 16 religious books, some of which remain in print and enjoy considerable respect, 'Anderson was no doubt an irritating and opinionated man, inclined – as pious people are – to maintain that an action was morally justified because his principles debarred him from committing an immoral one'.[73] He was 'very unwilling to give up an opinion once he had formed it. He was self-satisfied, and at times, in his theological and penological ideas, original to the point of eccentricity. At the same time he had a peculiarly scrupulous regard for the truth and would never have lied directly, though when he thought anti-social criminals were involved he was prepared to mislead with half-truths or mental reservation (as he did before the Parnell Commission)'.[74] But Anderson was also 'a man who set great store by moral probity'.[75]

Anderson has been accused of being garrulous – he reportedly 'could not keep quiet about his secret work'[76] – and he came in for some particularly offensive criticism following revelations in the serialisation of his autobiography in 1910.[77] As J.A. Cole has observed, often Anderson 'was publicly attacked by men who were actually aiming at a larger target' and this must have rankled; Sir William Harcourt had openly criticised him, 'then written him a placatory letter'. Criticism of Anderson – as with criticism of anyone else involved – must be assessed as part of a wider historical and political context: Harcourt, Jenkinson, Warren, Anderson, Monro and Matthews were all severely criticised, disliked, had career problems and had genuine enemies. Most of these people were dealing with political crime. There were serious and almost irreconcilable differences of opinion and policy, serious and sometimes debilitating office politics and strong personalities clashing with one another. There also seems to have been an awful lot of 'shifting of responsibility' going on, as well as back watching. However, Anderson, like Monro, did not believe that secrecy should be maintained after the need for secrecy had passed; indeed they both believed that it was to the public benefit to know about things once the danger had passed. Anderson also had a singular sense of history and justified some of his disclosures by saying that they were historical events about which future generations deserved to know. To suggest that Anderson was garrulous is therefore imprecise and gives the wrong impression; when he recognised the need for secrecy, he was silent. Harcourt once said of him that his 'idea of secrecy is not to tell the Secretary of State'[78] and Henri Le Caron, the spy who would only work for Anderson, declared that for 21 years Anderson 'never wavered or grew lax in his care ... ever watchful' and he expressed the opinion that had his safety been entrusted to others then he would have been dead'.[79] Perhaps the final word is best left to Anderson's friend Major Arthur Griffiths:

> he is the most discreet, the most silent and reserved of all public functionaries. Some one once said he was a mystery even to himself. This to him inestimable quality of reticence is not unaided by a slight but perhaps convenient deafness, which Mr Anderson cultivates and parades on occasions. If he is asked an embarrassing question, he quickly puts up his hand and says the enquiry has been addressed to his deaf ear ... he has achieved greater success than any detective of his time ...[80]

This was the man who stepped into James Monro's shoes as Assistant Commissioner CID. Unfortunately, as Anderson says, he was unable to take immediate command:

> ... I was at that time physically unfit to enter on the duties of my new post. For some time past I had not had an adequate holiday, and the strain of long and anxious work was telling on me ... Dr. Gilbart Smith, of Harley Street, insisted that I must have two months' complete rest, and he added that he would probably give me a certificate for a further two months' 'sick leave'. This, of course, was out of the question. But I told Mr. Matthews, greatly to his distress, that I could not take up my new duties until I had had a month's holiday in Switzerland. And so, after one week at Scotland Yard, I crossed the Channel.
>
> But this was not all. The second of the crimes known as the Whitechapel murders was committed the night before I took office, and the third occurred the night of the day on which I left London.[81]

Notes

1. 'Blind Man's Buff' from *Punch,* 22 September 1888.
2. Porter, Bernard (1987) *The Origins of the Vigilant State: The London Metropolitan Police Special Branch before the First World War.* London:

Weidenfeld and Nicolson, p.81. Jenkinson may not have been too far from the truth: Supt. John Shore, one of the most senior policemen at Scotland Yard, was 'a notorious womaniser and frequenter of London's brothels', described by the American detective William Pinkerton as 'in the habit of what we would call in this country "chasing chippies"; that is running after girls of a low order', and he was particularly fond of a brothel run by an American madam known as one-legged Nellie Coffey in the Borough. Coffey was also an informer who used to meet Shore in private rooms above a pub called the Rising Sun at the head of Fleet Street. (Macintyre, Ben (1997) *The Napoleon of Crime: The Life and Times of Adam Worth, the Real Moriarty*. London: HarperCollins, p.129.)

3. The police never publicly identified the Ripper. Almost as soon as he was free of some of the restrictions imposed by his office, Sir Robert Anderson implied that the identity of the Ripper was known. In *The Nineteenth Century*, February 1901, Anderson wrote that women in London outside the 'limited district of the East End' were as safe during the weeks of the murders as they were before they began 'or after he had been safely caged in an asylum'. Anderson, as we shall see in a later chapter, repeated this claim several times in the years following 1901.

4. On his retirement he became a private inquiry agent and is noted as having been hired by the prosecution to gather more evidence against Oscar Wilde.

5. Littlechild, John G. (1894) *The Reminiscences of Chief-Inspector Littlechild*. London: The Leadenhall Press, p.45.

6. The Fenian movement was an Irish revolutionary organisation born out of the famine of the 1840s which focused Irish discontent with English rule and led to a quickly quelled uprising in 1848. John O'Mahony was among the revolutionists and he afterwards emigrated to the United States where he organised a movement which he called the Fenian Brotherhood after a band of warriors led by the legendary Gaelic hero Finn Mac Cool. In Ireland the movement was led by James Stephens (1825–1901) who had formed a Dublin-based secret society known as the Irish Republican Brotherhood and began publishing *Irish People*, the party organ, which was suppressed by the government. Stephens was arrested but managed to escape to America, where arms and considerable money had been accumulated by the organisation. The Fenian movement diminished following World War I and its influence was absorbed by Sinn Féin and other organisations.

7. Inspector John Meiklejohn was the most corrupt of the quartet; Clarke was blackmailed; Druscovitch was encouraged to borrow from Kerr to pay a debt of his brother's for which he had become responsible and could not otherwise pay; and Palmer was duped into joining his colleagues. Clarke was acquitted and promptly resigned from the Force, but the others went to prison for two years. Druscovitch died prematurely, Palmer became a publican and the corrupted Meiklejohn became a private detective. A book about the case, sometimes known as 'The Madame de Goncourt case' was written: Dilnot, George (1928): *The Trial of the Detectives*. London: Geoffrey Bless.

8. Sir Charles Warren, the Commissioner, resigned as a consequence of a dispute with the Home Secretary about the publication of a magazine article, but there had been long-standing differences of opinion that had hardened during the Ripper investigation and Warren's resignation was accepted when previously it had been rejected. Home Secretary Matthews' willingness to accept the resignation was therefore arguably influenced by disagreements during the Ripper inquiry.

9. Hugh Culling Eardley Childers, 1827–96.

10. Jenkins, Roy (1995) *Gladstone*. London: Macmillan. New York: Random House, 1997, p.544.

11. Warren himself published an anonymous defence of his actions. 'Defender' (1902) *Sir Charles Warren and Spion Kop A Vindication*. London: Smith Elder and Co.

12. David, Saul (1997) *Military Blunders*. London: Constable Robinson, p.35.

13. 'The chief fault lay in the disinclination of the officer in supreme command to assert his authority and see that what he thought best was done.' Quoted in Symons, J. (1963) *Buller's Campaign*. London: Cresset Press, p.568.

14. That Warren was an autocrat who wanted everything done his own way, rather than a leader brought in to enforce discipline who then had his hands tied by a vacillating Home Secretary, is an image that has succeeded in obscuring the truth. Belton Cobb, a commentator who should have known better, called Warren 'an autocratic, eldery soldier who wanted to run every-thing his own way – the military way'. (Cobb, Belton (1956) *Critical Years At The Yard*. London: Faber and Faber, p.226.)

15. Others also drew comparisons between Warren and General Gordon. Roy Jenkins refers in his excellent biography of Winston Churchill to Lord Salisbury's observation that Mahdi 'pretends to be half mad and is very sane in reality'. Mr. Jenkins wryly observes that 'the same remark, either way round for that matter, might have been applied' to Gordon.

16. Williams, Watkin Wynn (1941) *The Life of General Sir Charles Warren: By His Grandson*. Oxford: Blackwell, pp.196–7.

17. *The Times*, 20 March 1886.

18. Foster, R.F. (1981) *Lord Randolph Churchill, A Political Life*. Oxford: Clarendon Press, p.150, citing a letter from Salisbury to Lady John Manners.

19. Fairclough, Melvyn (2002) *The Ripper and the Royals*. London: Duckworth.

20. Jenkins, Roy (2002) *Churchill*. London: Macmillan.

21. Leslie, Shane (1921) 'Henry Matthews Lord Llandaff' *The Dublin Review*, vol. 168, January, p.6.

22. Coleridge to Matthews, 13 July 1892, quoted in Leslie, Shane, *op. cit.*

23. William, R.H. (1988) *The Salisbury-Balfour Correspondence 1869–1892*. Hitchen: Hertfordshire Record Soc.

24. James, Robert Rhodes (1959) *Lord Randolph Churchill*. London: Weidenfeld and Nicolson, p.245. In fairness, it should be pointed out that Matthews never asked for the office of Home Secretary and 'He was so flabbergasted by

the offer of a Secretaryship of State that he left Arlington House under the impression that he had declined, but, finding himself gazetted Home Secretary the next day accepted his fate'. (Leslie, Shane, *op. cit.*)

25. Ensor, Sir Robert (1936) *England 1870–1914.* Oxford: Oxford University Press.
26. A 'diary' purporting to have been written by James Maybrick claims that he was inflamed by his wife's infidelity and driven to commit the Jack the Ripper crimes. Despite two best-selling books arguing in favour of the 'diary's' genuineness, it is widely regarded to be a forgery, although who forged it is the subject of considerable and often over-heated debate. James Maybrick's wife, Florence was accused of his murder and convicted, largely on the evidence of a mentally unstable judge, and the conviction was passed to Matthews, who was called upon to exercise mercy and who commuted the death sentence to life imprisonment. This caused considerable uproar, particularly from W.T. Stead, editor of the *Pall Mall Gazette*, who had supported Mrs. Maybrick's innocence.
27. Two boys convicted of murdering their father because of his ill-treatment of their mother; Matthews allowed the elder to be executed.
28. Matthews privately objected to the death penalty and suffered agonies when called upon to review cases such as that of Mrs. Maybrick, accused of poisoning her husband and convicted largely on the summing up by an unstable judge. He would quote St. Augustine: 'I hasten not his death but leave the criminal time for repentance'.
29. The full import of this may be judged when one realises that Matthews had been 'a great favourite of the Queen'. (Leslie, Shane, *op. cit.*)
30. Roberts, Andrew (1999) *Salisbury: Victorian Titan.* London: Weidenfeld and Nicolson, pp.506–7.
31. Leslie, Shane, *op. cit.*
32. There is an unpublished biography of Henry Matthews by W.S. Lilly.
33. Ransford, Oliver (1969) *The Battle of Spion Kop.* London: John Murray, p.33.
34. Williams, Watkin Wynn, *op. cit.*, p.220. 'Bradford' was Sir Edward Bradford, Commissioner 1890–1903.
35. Anderson, Sir Robert (1910) *The Lighter Side of My Official Life.* London: Hodder and Stoughton, p.126.
36. Leslie, Shane, *op. cit.* places much emphasis on how Matthews 'kept officials at a distance through his secretaries'. George Dilnot refers to 'the friction that notoriously existed between Sir Godfrey Lushington and the high officials of the police.' (Dilnot, George (1930) *The Story of Scotland Yard.* London: Geoffrey Bless, p.97.)
37. *The Penny Illustrated Paper* 8 December 1888 and *Illustrated Times,* 8 December 1888.
38. James Monro's memoirs, unpublished and discovered by Keith Skinner, copy in the author's collection.
39. At Cambridge he was one of the radical chic known as the Apostles, or the Society (of twelve), who featured in a Ripper theory advanced by Howells,

Martin and Skinner, Keith (1987) *The Ripper Legacy*. London: Sidgwick and Jackson.

40. Jenkins, Roy (1998) *The Chancellors*. London: Macmillan, p.47.

41. *Ibid.*, p.40.

42. *Ibid.*, p.46.

43. *Ibid.*, p.46.

44. Porter, Bernard *op. cit.*, p.36.

45. Jenkins, Roy (1998) *The Chancellors*. London: Macmillan, p.49.

46. *Ibid.*, p.61.

47. When the fifth Earl Spencer died he was succeeded to the title by his half brother, Charles Robert Spencer, who was the great-grandfather of Lady Diana Spencer, Princess of Wales.

48. Corfe, Tom (1968) *The Phoenix Park Murders: Conflict, Compromise and Tragedy in Ireland, 1879–1882*. London: Hodder and Stoughton, p.21.

49. Lady Frederick Cavendish in *The Times*, 18 August 1910.

50. James Monro's memoirs, unpublished and discovered by Keith Skinner, copy in the author's collection.

51. As Sir William Harcourt wrote to Queen Victoria on 25 June 1884, the police in India 'had to deal largely with secret societies'. (Harcourt papers, box 692, folio 69.)

52. Porter, Bernard, *op. cit.*, p.17.

53. James Monro's memoirs, unpublished and discovered by Keith Skinner, copy in the author's collection.

54. Porter, Bernard, *op. cit.*, p.87

55. Porter, Bernard, *op. cit.*, p.87.

56. Monro to Warren, 19 March 1888. HO144/190/A46472B, sub. 6.

57. See HO144/190/A46472B, subs. 7 and 9 and MEPO 1/48 and 1/55 pp.211–12.

58. HO144/190/A46472B sub. 9 and MEPO4/487.

59. Warren, Charles (1888) 'The Police of the Metropolis', *Murray's Magazine*, Vol. 4, November.

60. Monro to Home under-secretary, 11 June 1888: HO144/190/A46472B, sub. 9.

61. James Monro's memoirs, unpublished and discovered by Keith Skinner, copy in the author's collection.

62. Porter, Bernard, *op. cit.*, p.84.

63. Anderson, Sir Robert, *op. cit.*, p.129.

64. Richard Southwell Bourke, sixth Earl of Mayo 1822–72, was appointed Chief Secretary for Ireland in Lord Derby's short-lived administration of 1858–59 and again during the administration of 1866–69, when he was appointed viceroy and governor-general of India. He was murdered, whilst visiting the penal settlement of Port Blair on 8 February 1872, by a Pathan from Afghanistan named Shere Ali, a former Punjab Mounted Policeman who had murdered an old enemy during a blood feud and been sentenced to death, the sentence being commuted to a prison sentence. 'In this case, however, the

penal system had misjudged its criminal. Shere Ali apparently felt that killing a feuding enemy was no crime at all, and in his dying confession he asserted that he had resented his transportation sufficiently to want to kill "some European of high rank".' (Sen, Satadru (2000) *Disciplining Punishment: Colonialism and Convict Society in the Andaman Islands.* Oxford: Oxford University Press, p.68.)

65. Anderson, Sir Robert, *op. cit.*, p.108.

66. Jenkinson was described as a 'mutiny magistrate trained in the despotic school of Indian officialdom, furnished with all the powers of "spymaster general" in Ireland', by Irish MP Frank Hugh O'Donnell. (*Hansard*, 2 August 1882.)

67. Jenkinson to Harcourt, 4 September 1883, Harcourt's papers, box 103, ff.117.

68. Gosselin to Harcourt, 7 January 1884, Harcourt's papers, box 105, ff.109–10.

69. Porter, Bernard, *op. cit.* In the summer of 1884 Harcourt had written to the Queen: 'there is such a violent prejudice against this *espionage* which can alone remark these secret plots that the task of detection is very difficult'.

70. Troup memorandum, 8 April 1910: HO144/926/A49962, sub. 7. This may explain the blame Anderson laid at Lushington's door over the problems Warren had with Matthews, assuming Anderson ever knew of Lushington's objections.

71. Jenkinson to Spencer, 24 September 1888.

72. Fido, Martin (2001) 'Anderson's Quirkiness', *Ripperologist*, no. 34, April, pp.27–8.

73. Cole, J.A. (1984) *Prince of Spies: Henri Le Caron.* London: Faber and Faber, p.207.

74. Begg, Paul, Fido, Martin and Skinner, Keith (1996) *The Jack the Ripper A to Z.* London: Headline, pp.21–2.

75. Porter, Bernard, *op. cit.*, p.70.

76. Cole, J.A., *op. cit.*, p.207.

77. Winston Churchill described Anderson's memoirs as 'the garrulous and inaccurate indiscretion of advancing years', but Anderson rightly called his treatment 'sneers and insults' and declined to notice them. Anderson had revealed in his memoirs that the organiser of a Fenian plot to assassinate Queen Victoria at the time of her Jubilee in 1887 was a British informer, and he had also revealed that he had authored some anti-Parnell articles published in *The Times* called 'Behind the Scenes in America'. Irish Nationalist MPs were outraged by the latter and there were questions in the House of Commons. The government, however, didn't want the Irish MPs inquiring too deeply into the Jubilee Plot because, according to Christy Campbell, the plot had been engineered by the British government to discredit Parnell. The Home Secretary in 1910, Winston Churchill, at the direction of his civil servants, was happy, therefore, to hang Anderson out to dry. (Campbell, Christy (2002) *Fenian Fire: The British Government Plot to Assassinate Queen Victoria.* London: HarperCollins.)

78. Harcourt quoted in Short, K.R.M. (1979) *The Dyamite War*. Dublin: Gill and Macmillan Ltd.

79. Le Caron, Major Henri (1895) *Twenty-Five Years in The Secret Service: The Recollections of a Spy*. London: William Heinemann, p.271.

80. Griffiths, Major Arthur (1895) 'The Detective in Real Life', *The Windsor Magazine*, vol. 1, Jan.–Jun., pp.506–7. Sir John Moylan said that 'the period 1890 to 1900 proved to be one during which there was an almost continuous decrease in crime ... the CID built up in the nineties a world-wide reputation for efficiency in crime detection ...". (Moylan, Sir John (1929) *Scotland Yard and the Metropolitan Police*. London: Putnam, p.52.) Not a bad epitaph to a career.

81. Anderson, Sir Robert, *op. cit.*, pp.134–5. Anderson was referring to the murder of Martha Tabram and Mary Ann Nichols.

chapter six

MARY ANN NICHOLS

As Robert Anderson slept soundly in his bed in the early hours of Friday 30 September 1888, exhausted in body and mind and looking forward to a recuperative break in the fresh air of Switzerland, a prostitute named Mary Ann Nichols was warming herself in the humble communal kitchen of a lodging house at 18 Thrawl Street. The deputy lodging house keeper asked her for the fourpence (4d) she needed for a bed and she replied that she had no money. She was asked to leave and did so with slightly tipsy good humour. 'I'll soon get my doss money. See what a jolly bonnet I've got now', she said indicating a worse for wear black bonnet that was obviously a recent acquisition with which she was pleased. The time was 1.20am.

The summer of 1888 had been one of the coldest and wettest on record. On the night of 30 August there was a storm, the rain was sharp and frequent and was accompanied by peals of thunder and flashes of lightning. The drama of the evening was increased by a dull red glow in the night sky caused by a terrible fire in the London docks. Shortly before 8.30pm a smell of burning was noticed and shortly afterwards there was an immense burst of flames from the top of one of the huge South Quay warehouses. Whitechapel Fire Station did not receive the alarm until after 9.00pm and the response was immediate, not just from Whitechapel but from every district in London, but by this time the fire was extremely fierce, raging through the upper floors of a building 150 yards long and half as broad. As the *East London Advertiser* reported:

> The flames could not have broken out in a more dangerous part of the docks than the site of this fire. They were crammed with colonial produce in the upper floors, and brandy and gin in the lower floors. Through the great iron-barred windows the fire could be seen raging like a furnace, and the enormous tongues of bluish and yellowish flames which constantly

burst up with great roars pointed to the fact that spirits were aiding the progress of the flames.[1]

It was an exciting spectacle, visible for miles and it drew people from across London. An enormous crowd had gathered around the dock-yard gates to watch as firemen, policemen and dock officers battled to extinguish the blaze. By 11.00pm the fierceness of the fire diminished, but by midnight the firemen were still at work and it was some hours before the fire would be extinguished.

The clock of Whitechapel Church was striking 2.30am when Mary Ann Nichols was seen by her friend Mrs. Emily Holland outside a grocer's shop on the corner of Whitechapel Road and Osborn Street, opposite Whitechapel Church. Nichols was leaning against a wall and was very drunk. Holland stopped to talk for six or seven minutes and tried to persuade her friend to return to the lodging house, but Nichols refused, saying, 'I've had my lodging money three times today and I've spent it. It won't be long before I'm back'. And with that optimism she staggered off into the night.

Mary Nichols was 5ft 2in tall, her hair was greying and she had grey eyes and small delicate features with high cheekbones. A small scar on her forehead was a reminder of a childhood accident, and her front teeth were slightly discoloured,[2] four of them missing. She was in her mid forties, but had a youthful appearance – remarkable given the privations she must have undergone and the abuse she had suffered, self-inflicted through the bottle as well as possible others we need only imagine. A journalist viewing her body estimated her age as between 30 and 35[3] but at her inquest her father said that 'she was nearly 44 years of age, but it must be owned that she looked ten years younger'.[4] Emily Holland described Mary Ann as 'a very clean woman' who always seemed to keep herself to herself.[5]

She was born on 26 August 1845 in Shoe Lane off Fleet Street,[6] the daughter of a blacksmith named Edward Walker and his wife Caroline. She married William Nicols, a printer from Oxford, on 16 January 1864 at St. Bride's Parish Church. The couple had five children – Edward, Percy, Alice, Eliza and Henry, the last born in 1879 – but the marriage was marked by a series of separations and in 1880 or 1881 the couple separated for good. William Nichols claimed that the separation had been caused by Mary Ann's heavy drinking, but her father, whilst acknowledging that she drank heavily,[7] alleged that William Nichols had taken up with the woman who had nursed Mary Ann through her last confinement.

Poor Mary Ann's life over the next few years is recorded in various workhouse records. Apart from a short time between late March and the end of May 1883, when she lived with her father, she was resident at Lambeth Workhouse. Then in June 1886 she began living with a man named Thomas Stewart Drew, a blacksmith with a shop at 15 York Street, Walworth. Later that month, respectably dressed, she had attended the funeral of her brother (presumably Henry Alfred) who had been burned to death when a paraffin lamp exploded. Her father had seen her at the funeral, but he had not spoken with her. 'He was not friendly with her', he said.[8] The relationship with Drew ended in 1887 and Mary Ann appears in the workhouse records again, at St. Giles Workhouse and the Strand Workhouse, Edmonton. By the end of the year she was sleeping rough in Trafalgar Square, but when the vagrants were cleared from there in mid December she was revealed to the authorities to be destitute and without means of subsistence. She was accordingly re-admitted to the Lambeth Workhouse, where she spent Christmas 1887. In the fateful new year she spent until early April at Mitcham Workhouse and from mid April until early May was back at Lambeth, where she met Mary Ann Monk, described as a young woman with a 'haughty air and flushed face', who would identify Mary's body for the police. Another friend in the Lambeth Workhouse was a Mrs. Scorer, the separated wife of James Scorer, an assistant salesman in Spitalfields Market.

Perhaps with help from the workhouse authorities, Mary Ann Nichols secured employment as a servant for Samuel and Sarah Cowdry at 'Inglseside', Rose Hill Road, Wandsworth. Samuel was the Clerk of Works in the Police Department. Mary wrote to her father on 17 April 1888:

I just write to say you will be glad to know that I am settled in my new place, and going on all right up to now. My people went out yesterday, and have not returned, so I am left in charge. It is a grand place inside, with trees and gardens back and front. All has been newly done up. They are tee-totallers, and religious, so I ought to get on. They are very nice people, and I have not too much to do. I hope you are all right and the boy has work. So goodbye for the present. From yours truly,

Polly

Answer soon, please, and let me know how you are.[9]

Mr. Walker had sent a nice, conciliatory letter back, but did not receive a reply and had no further contact with his daughter. Mary's silence was probably because she had stolen clothing from her employers and absconded.

In August 1888 Mary Ann Nichols was living in a lodging house at 18 Thrawl Street. For 4d a night she shared a room with four other women, one of them being 50-year-old Emily Holland.[10] She moved from there on 24 August to a lodging house known as the White House at 56 Flower and Dean Street.

At the rear of Whitechapel tube station there was a short thoroughfare known as Buck's Row. It was a quiet, rather nondescript street, although at one end was the grim and imposing structure of a board school and almost opposite was a slightly grand structure called Essex Wharf, as was spelt out along its side in ornate brickwork. It was described by Leonard Matters in 1929 when he visited the area while researching his book *The Mystery of Jack the Ripper*:

Buck's Row cannot have changed much in character since its name was altered.[11] It is a narrow, cobbled, mean street, having on one side the same houses – possibly tenanted by the same people – which stood there in 1888. They are shabby, dirty little houses of two storeys, and only a three-feet pavement separates them from the road, which is no more than twenty feet from wall to wall.

On the opposite side are the high walls of warehouses which at night would shadow the dirty street in a far deeper gloom than its own character in broad daylight suggests.

All Durward Street is not so drab and mean, for by some accident in the planning of the locality – if ever it was planned – quite two thirds of the thoroughfare is very wide and open.

The street lies east and west along the London and Northern Railway Line. It is approached from the west by Vallance Street, formerly Baker's Row. On the left are fine modern tall warehouses. I was interested to note that one of them belongs to Messrs. Kearly and Tongue, Ltd. in front of whose premises in Mitre Square another murder was committed on September 30th. On the left side of the street is a small wall guarding the railway line, which lies at a depth of some twenty feet below ground level. Two narrow bridge roads lead across the railway to Whitechapel Road. The first was called Thomas Street in 1888, but now is Fullbourne Street. The other is Court Street. By either of these two lanes, no more than two hundred and fifty yards long, the busy main artery of the Whitechapel area can be reached from the relatively secluded Buck's Row.

Going still further east, an abandoned London County Council school building breaks the wide and open Durward Street into narrow lanes or alleys. The left hand land retains the name of Durward Street 'late Buck's

Row', and the other is Winthrop Street. Both are equally dirty and seemingly disreputable . . .[12]

Leonard Matters painted a rather depressing picture of Buck's Row as it was when he visited it, but *The Times* in 1888 reported that the short row of houses were tenanted by a 'respectable class of people superior in many ways to many of the surrounding streets'.

As Matters wrote, the eastern end of the road as entered from Vallance Road is very wide, but at the board school divides into Winthrop Street on the right and Buck's Row on the left. Passing the board school into Buck's Row, there were some gates on the right leading to a stables owned by a Mr. Brown. Next to the gates was the first in a short row of houses that led down to the intersection with Brady Street, on the corner of which was a pub called The Roebuck. The house next to the gates was a more recent structure than the rest of the street, having been built after a number of the cottages had been demolished when the East London Railway had been put in in 1875–76. This house was called New Cottage and it was demolished along with the neighbouring house sometime before 1948 and replaced by a garage-like structure (now also demolished, but which appears in some of the more recent surviving photographs of the street). In 1888 it was occupied by a widow, Mrs. Emma Green, her two sons and a daughter. One of the sons had retired to bed at 9.00pm, the other at 9.45pm, and Mrs. Green and her daughter, who shared a room at the front of the house, had gone to bed at 11.00pm. She claimed to be a light sleeper and said that she had not been disturbed by any unusual sounds. Opposite New Cottage was Essex Wharf. Walter Purkiss, the manager of the wharf, lived here with his wife, children and servant. He and his wife had their bedroom on the second floor, at the front of the building. They had retired about 11.00–11.15pm and slept fitfully. Awake at various times during the night, they had heard nothing.

In Winthrop Street, which ran adjacent to Buck's Row, was Barber's Yard, a slaughteryard owned by a Mr. Barber. At midnight two workers, Harry Tomkins and Charles Britten, left the yard and walked to the end of the street. Apparently they were away for about an hour, so presumably they walked on a bit further, stopped for a smoke and a chat, or perhaps nipped to the Roebuck for a drink. Neither saw or heard anything unusual. As they returned to their work, Walter Purkiss in Essex Wharf woke up and heard nothing. Buck's Row, he said, was unusually quiet.

This said, several newspapers, among them *The Star* and *East London Advertiser*, carried accounts of a reported disturbance that night: 'Several persons in the neighbourhood state that an affray occurred shortly after midnight, but no screams were heard, nor anything beyond what might have been considered evidence of an ordinary brawl'.[13] The *New York Times* carried a more detailed story which shifted the time of the assault to about 3.00am and portrayed a far more serious disturbance:

> The victim was a woman, who, at 3 o'clock, was knocked down by some man, unknown, and attacked with a knife. She attempted to get up, and ran a hundred yards, her cries for help being heard by several persons in the adjacent houses. No attention was paid to her cries, however, and when found at daybreak she was lying dead in another street, several hundred yards from the scene of the attack.[14]

The fact that this story didn't get wider coverage suggests it was either a fiction or the woman concerned wasn't Nichols. Nichols' body was reportedly warm when discovered, so she had only recently been murdered. We do not know if anyone ever came forward and identified themselves as the person attacked, but it wouldn't necessarily have been reported in the press or been mentioned in the severely depleted police case papers.

At 3.20am Charles Cross[15] left his home at 22 Doveton Street, off the Cambridge Heath Road, and began walking to work at hauliers Pickford and Co. in Broad Street. Twenty-five minutes later he turned into Buck's Row and walked up the warehouse-lined north side of the street. In the gloom he saw across the road something lying against the gates leading to the stables next to New Cottage. He later told the inquest:

> I could not tell in the dark what it was at first; it looked to me like a tarpaulin sheet, but stepping into the road, I saw it was the body of a woman. Just then I heard a man – about 40 yards off – approaching from the direction that I myself had come from. I waited for the man, who started to one side as if afraid that I meant to knock him down. I said, 'Come and look over here, there's a woman'.

The other man was Robert Paul. It was very dark and the two men couldn't see much, though they noted that the woman's clothes were raised almost to her stomach. Cross felt her hands, which were cold and limp. 'I believe she's dead', he said. Paul had felt her face and found it warm. Trying to find a heartbeat, he detected a faint movement. 'I think she's breathing', he said, 'But it's very little if she is'. He suggested that they try to sit her up, but Cross objected and the two men decided to head off in the direction of work and see if they could find a policeman on the way.

Perhaps within seconds of their leaving Buck's Row, PC Neil entered the street on his beat and walking up the south, cottage-lined side of the street he found the body as Cross and Paul had left it. He shone the light of his bullseye lamp onto her face and her open, life-less eyes gazed back. He also saw, as Cross and Paul in the darkness had not, that blood had oozed from a wound in her throat. Lying by the right side of the body was a bonnet, the one of which Mary Ann Nichols had been so proud only a few hours before.

Within four or five minutes of leaving the body Cross and Paul met PC G. Mizen, 56 H, at the corner of Hanbury Street and Baker's Row, 300 yards from Buck's Row. PC Mizen[16] headed for Buck's Row and Cross and Paul continued on their way to work, parting company at the Commercial Street end of Hanbury Street, where Paul turned into Corbett's Court and Cross walked on alone to Broad Street.

At 3.47am PC Thain, on his beat along Brady Street, passed the entrance of Buck's Row and was heard by PC Neil, who signalled with his lamp. Thain went down to his colleague, who said, 'For God's sake, Jack, go fetch a doctor'. Or so PC Thain said. PC Neil recalled that his actual words were, 'Here's a woman has cut her throat. Run at once for Dr. Llewellyn'. Whatever the precise words, PC Thain immediately went to the surgery of Dr. Rees Ralph Llewellyn[17] at 152 Whitechapel Road (going via the slaughter yard to retrieve his cape and telling Harry Tomkins about the murdered woman while doing so).[18] Harry Tomkins went with another slaughterman named James Mumford to view the body, later being joined by Charles Britten. They remained there until the body was taken away and for a while they would be suspects and subjected to long and detailed interviews by the police, but were able to account for themselves.[19] They were soon after joined by Patrick Mulshaw, a night porter employed by the Whitechapel District Board of Works at some sewage works 70 yards or so from the slaughter yard in Winthrop Street, who had been told by a passing man: 'Watchman, old man. I believe somebody is mur-dered down the street'. Mulshaw immediately went round the corner into Buck's Row.[20]

In the meantime, PC Mizen, having arrived in Buck's Row, had been sent by PC Neil to fetch an ambulance. PC Thain returned with Dr. Llewellyn, who made a very cursory examination of the body, pronounced the woman dead and directed that the body be taken to the mortuary in Old Montague Street. PC Mizen arrived with the ambulance – basically a hand-cart – and together with PC Neil lifted the body onto it. PC Thain noticed that there was a lot of blood on the back of the body and assumed that this had run down from the neck. When he assisted in lifting the body aboard the ambulance he got a lot of blood on his hands. He also noticed a spot of congealed blood about 6 inches in diameter underneath the body that had begun to run towards the gutter.

Inspector John Spratling, J Division, heard about the murder when in the Hackney Road and he hastened to the murder scene, arriving there just after the body had been removed to the mortuary. PC Thain pointed out the spot where the body had been found, then the two men went together to the mortuary, which was locked, the body still on the ambulance in the mortuary yard. The keys to the mortuary had been sent for, and whilst he waited for them Spratling began taking down a description of the body, pausing when the mortuary attendant, a pauper inmate of the Whitechapel Workhouse named Robert Mann, arrived with the keys and the body was moved indoors. Continuing to take down the description, Spratling discovered that Nichols had suffered severe injuries to the abdomen and sent for Dr. Llewellyn.

At 6.30am James Hatfield and another inmate of the Whitechapel Workhouse arrived at the mortuary and – despite instructions from Detective Sergeant Enright not to touch the body – Hatfield and Robert Mann stripped it and washed it down, dumping Nichols' clothing in the yard. Returning to the mortuary, Inspector Spratling noticed that Nichols' petticoats bore a stencil stamp of the Lambeth Workhouse. The Workhouse matron was immediately summoned to view the body, but was unable to identify it and said that the petticoats might have been issued any time during the past two or three years.[21]

At 10.00am Dr. Llewellyn made a full post-mortem examination of the body. His description of the injuries given at the subsequent inquest makes grim reading:

> He deposed that on Friday morning about four o'clock he was called up by a policeman, with whom he went to Buck's-row. He there found the deceased lying on her back with her throat deeply cut; there was very little blood on the ground. She had apparently been dead about half-an-hour. He was quite certain that the injury to her throat was not self-inflicted. There was no mark of any struggle either on the body or near where it was found. About an hour afterwards he was sent for again by the police, and going to

the mortuary, to which the body had been carried, found most extensive injuries on the abdomen. At ten o'clock that (Saturday) morning, in the presence of his assistant, he began a post-mortem examination. On the right side of the face was a recent and strongly-marked bruise, which was scarcely perceptible when he first saw the body. It might have been caused either by a blow from a fist or by pressure of the thumb. On the left side of the face was a circular bruise, which might have been produced in the same way. A small bruise was on the left side of the neck, and an abrasion on the right. All must have been done at the same time. There were two cuts in the throat, one four inches long and the other eight, and both reaching to the vertebrae, which had also been penetrated. The wounds must have been inflicted with a strong-bladed knife, moderately sharp, and used with great violence. It appeared to have been held in the left hand of the person who had used it. No blood at all was found on the front of the woman's clothes. The body was fairly well nourished, and there was no smell of alcohol in the stomach. On the abdomen were some severe cuts and stabs, which the witness described in detail. Nearly all the blood had drained out of the arteries and veins, and collected to a large extent in the loose tissues. The deceased's wounds were sufficient to cause instantaneous death.

Questioned by jurymen, the witness said the deceased was a strong woman. The murderer must have had some rough anatomical knowledge, for he seemed to have attacked all the vital parts. It was impossible to say whether the wounds were inflicted by a clasp knife or a butcher's knife, but the instrument must have been a strong one. When he first saw the body, life had not been out of it for more than half-an-hour. The murder might have occupied four or five minutes. It could have been committed by one man so far as the wounds were concerned.[22]

Later recalled, Dr. Llewellyn added that 'no part of the viscera was missing'.[23] A slightly more detailed account of Dr. Llewellyn's initial opinions was reported in *The Times*:

The weapon used would scarcely have been a sailor's jack knife, but a pointed weapon with a stout back – such as a cork-cutter's or shoemaker's knife. In his opinion it was not an exceptionally long-bladed weapon. He does not believe that the woman was seized from behind and her throat cut, but thinks that a hand was held across her mouth and the knife then used, possibly by a left-handed man, as the bruising on the face of the deceased is such as would result from the mouth being covered with the right hand. He made a second examination of the body in the mortuary, and on that based his conclusion.[24]

The important points in Dr. Llewellyn's testimony were that the knife appeared to have been held in the murderer's left hand, that the murderer 'must have had some rough anatomical knowledge', and that it had taken no more than four or five minutes for the injuries to have been inflicted.

Not mentioned by Dr. Llewellyn but widely reported in the press on 1 September was that one of Mary Ann Nichols' fingers bore the impression of a ring which was missing, apparently removed. It is not known whether Nichols was wearing a ring on the night of the murder or whether she or her murderer had removed it, but the next victim of the Whitechapel Murderer, Annie Chapman, had worn two cheap brass rings that appeared to have been forcibly removed from her fingers.

A journalist working for *The Star* newspaper was allowed into the mortuary to view the body of Mary Ann Nichols and at 11.30am filed a story:

> The body appeared to be that of a woman of 35. It was 5ft. 3in. in height and fairly plump. The eyes were brown, the hair brown, and the two centre upper front teeth missing, those on either side being widely separated. This peculiarity may serve to identify the deceased, of whom at present writing nothing is known. Her clothing consisted of a well-worn brown ulster, a brown linsey skirt, and jacket, a gray linsey petticoat, a flannel petticoat, dark-blue ribbed stockings, braid garters, and side spring shoes. Her bonnet was black and rusty, and faced with black velvet. Her whole outfit was that of a person in poor circumstances, and this appearance was borne out by the mark 'LAMBETH WORKHOUSE, P.R.', which was found on the petticoat bands. The two marks were cut off and sent to the Lambeth institution to discover if possible the identity of the deceased. The brutality of the murder is beyond conception and beyond description. The throat is cut in two gashes, the instrument having been a sharp one, but used in a most ferocious and reckless way. There is a gash under the left ear, reaching nearly to the centre of the throat. Along half its length, however, it is accompanied by another one which reaches around under the other ear, making a wide and horrible hole, and nearly severing the head from the body.[25]

Another journalist gave the following account:

> The Whitechapel Mortuary is a little brick building situated to the right of the large yard used by the Board of Works for the storage of their material. Accompanied by Mr. Edmunds, the keeper, our reporter visited the temporary resting place of the victim on Friday morning. The first evidence seen of the tragedy on arriving in the yard was a bundle of what were little more than rags, of which the woman had been divested, and which were

lying on the flagstones just outside the mortuary. They consisted of a dull red cloak already mentioned, together with a dark bodice and brown skirt, a check flannel petticoat which bore the mark of the Lambeth Workhouse, a pair of dark stockings, and an old pair of dilapidated-looking spring-side boots, together with the little and sadly battered black straw bonnet, minus either ribbons or trimmings. Contrary to anticipation, beyond the flannel petticoat, and with the exception of a few bloodstains on the cloak, the other clothing was scarcely marked. The petticoat, however, was completely saturated with blood, and altogether presented a sickening spectacle. Entering the deadhouse, with its rows of black coffins, the keeper turned to the one immediately to the right of the door, and lying parallel with the wall. Opening the lid, he exposed the face of the poor victim. The features were apparently those of a woman of about thirty or thirty-five years, whose hair was still dark. The features were small and delicate, the cheek-bones high, the eyes grey, and the partly opened mouth disclosed a set of teeth which were a little discoloured. The expression on the face was a deeply painful one, and was evidently the result of an agonising death. The gash across the neck was situated very slightly above the breastbone; it was at least six inches in length, over an inch in width, and was clean cut. The hands were still tightly clenched. The lower portion of the body, however, presented the most sickening spectacle of all. Commencing from the lower portion of the abdomen, a terrible gash extended nearly as far as the diaphragm – a gash from which the bowels protruded ... The body, with the exception of the face was covered with a white sheet and a blanket.[26]

Apart from the small bundle of clothing, Mary Ann Nichols' only other possessions were a comb and a piece of a looking glass found in her pockets.[27]

The petticoats had born the identity 'Lambeth Workhouse P.R.' This indicated the workhouse at Princess Road. It had been abandoned as the main Lambeth Workhouse for some years, but in 1887–88 it was used for the construction of a new 'test' workhouse for 200 men and 150 women. The aged and infirm were left at the workhouse in Renfrew Road, whilst the able bodied moved to Princess Road where they were required to endure a particularly strict regime and perform work such as stone-breaking and oakum-picking in order to receive relief. Each sex was segregated into three classes, according to their previous known conduct and character. Those classified as being of bad character performed their work in isolation from one another. The workhouses were joyless places which most people tried hard to avoid.[28]

Lambeth Workhouse achieved fame because in 1895 Charles Chaplin (then aged 7) became an inmate together with his mother and his younger brother Sydney. The two children were later transferred to Hanwell School for Orphans and Destitute Children, while Charlie's mother, who had suffered a mental breakdown, was sent to the Cane Hill Lunatic Asylum. In 1922, the workhouse and infirmary were amalgamated and renamed Lambeth Hospital and in 1930 its administration was taken over by the London County Council. The infirmary and most of the workhouse have now been demolished.

As the day wore on and news of the murder spread numerous women visited the mortuary to view the body, which was eventually recognised as that of a woman who had lodged at 18 Thrawl Street and was known as Polly. People from the lodging house were summoned and among those who turned up was Emily Holland, who told about her meeting with 'Polly' at 2.30am. It was not until 7.30pm, however, that Mary Ann Monk, an inmate of Lambeth Workhouse, came to the mortuary and identified the body as that of Mary Ann Nichols, otherwise known as Polly.

By the end of the day two theories were given wide circulation. One was that the murder had been committed by one of the gangs known to operate in the area and extort money from the local prostitutes. Little is known about these gangs, although one which achieved notoriety was the 'Old Nichol gang' who hailed from an area known as the Old Nichol in Bethnal Green. This idea had been dismissed very quickly, however, and both Inspector Helson and Inspector Abberline were reported as expressing the opinion that a single perpetrator was responsible.

The other idea which is still current among theorists today[29] is that the murder was not committed in Buck's Row. *The Times* reported:

> Viewing the spot where the body was found, it seems difficult to believe that the woman received her death wounds there ... if the woman was murdered on the spot where the body was found, it is almost impossible to believe that she would not have aroused the neighbourhood by her screams.[30]

However, Inspector Helson reported that there 'was no doubt but that the murder was committed where the body was found'.[31]

By the early hours of Saturday afternoon Mary Ann Nichols' husband had been contacted and with one of his sons taken to the mortuary, where he was greatly distressed by the sight of his wife. 'I forgive you, as you are, for what you have been to me', he said.

In the afternoon the inquest was opened before Wynne E. Baxter, coroner for the South-Eastern Division of Middlesex, at the Working Lads' Institute in Whitechapel Road. Detective Inspectors Abberline and Helson and Sergeants Enright and Godley watched the case on behalf of the Criminal Investigation Department. The Foreman of the Jury, Mr Horey, and the jury members were sworn in, then taken by Mr. Banks, the Coroner's Assistant, to view the body. On their return the proceedings opened. Wynne Baxter was seated at the head of a long table, around him assorted documents and sheets of paper onto which to write the witnesses' depositions.

On the afternoon of Thursday 6 September, Mary Ann Nichols was buried:

> The arrangements were of a very simple character. The time at which the *cortège* was to start was kept a profound secret, and a rouse was perpetrated in order to get the body out of the mortuary where it has lain since the day of the murder. A pair-horsed closed hearse was observed making its way down Hanbury-street and the crowds, which numbered some thousands, made way for it to go along Old Montague-street, but instead of doing so it passed on into the Whitechapel-road, and, doubling back, entered the mortuary by the back gate, which is situated in Chapman's-court. Not a soul was near other than the undertaker[32] and his men, when the remains, placed in a polished elm coffin, bearing a plate with the inscription, 'Mary Ann Nichols, aged 42; died August 31, 1888' were removed to the hearse, and driven to Hanbury-street, there to await the mourners. These were late in arriving, and the two coaches were kept waiting some time in a side street. By this time the news had spread that the body was in the hearse, and people flocked round to see the coffin, and examine the plate. In this they were, however, frustrated, for a body of police, under Inspector Allisdon, of the H Division, surrounded the hearse and prevented their approaching too near. At last the *cortège* started towards Ilford, where the last scene in this unfortunate drama took place. The mourners were Mr. Edward Walker, the father of the deceased, and his grandson, together with two of the deceased's children. The procession proceeded along Baker's-row and passed the corner of Buck's-row into the main-road, where police were stationed every few yards. The houses in the neighbourhood had the blinds drawn, and much sympathy was expressed for the relatives.[33]

The funeral took place on Thursday, when the polished elm coffin was deposited in a hearse supplied by Mr. H. Smith, of Hanbury-street, and driven to Ilford Cemetery, in company with two mourning coaches containing the father of the deceased and his grandson, together with two of the deceased's children. There was a very large number of spectators present, who evinced the greatest sympathy.[34]

The police investigation stalled very quickly, perhaps unsurprisingly as random murders are very difficult to detect, but the idea that the Whitechapel Murders had been committed by a gang seems to have been quickly abandoned, or so most of the newspapers reported on 1 September, saying that similarities in the crimes had caused the police to believe that they were the work of one individual,[35] 'a maniac haunting Whitechapel'.[36] The *Manchester Guardian* reported that by the evening of 4 September the police believed they had a clue to the perpetrators of the crime and were maintaining surveillance on 'certain persons',[37] the use of the plural perhaps suggesting that belief in a single perpetrator may not have been universally held.

The following day there were hints of reticence by the police: 'Whatever information may be in possession of the police they deem it necessary to keep secret, but considerable activity is being exercised in keeping a watch on suspected persons. It is believed that their attention is particularly directed to two individuals, one a notorious character known as "Leather Apron", and the other a seafaring man'.[38]

The mysterious Leather Apron was very well described and very well known,

> Of this individual the following description is given:– He is 5ft. 4in. or 5ft. 5in. in height, and wears a dark close-fitting cap. He is thickset, and has an unusually thick neck. His hair is black, and closely clipped, his age being about 38 or 40. He has a small black moustache. The distinguishing feature of his costume is a leather apron, which he always wears, and from which he gets his nickname. His expression is sinister, and seems to be full of terror for the women who describe it. His eyes are small and glittering. His lips are usually parted in a grin, which is not only not reassuring, but excessively repellent. He is a slippermaker by trade, but does not work. His business is blackmailing women late at night. A number of men in Whitechapel follow this interesting profession. He has never cut anybody, so far as is known, but always carries a leather knife, presumably as sharp as leather knives are wont to be. This knife a number of the women have seen. His name nobody knows, but all are united in the belief that he is a Jew or of Jewish parentage, his face being of a marked Hebrew type. But the most singular characteristic of the man is the universal statement that in moving about he never makes any noise. What he wears on his feet the women do not know, but they agree that he moves noiselessly. His uncanny peculiarity to them is that they never see him or know of his presence until he is close by them. 'Leather Apron' never by any chance attacks a man. He runs

away on the slightest appearance of rescue. One woman whom he assailed some time ago boldly prosecuted him for it, and he was sent up for seven days. He has no settled place of residence, but has slept oftenest in a four penny lodging-house of the lowest kind in a disreputable lane leading from Brick Lane. The people at this lodging house denied that he had been there, and appeared disposed to shield him. 'Leather Apron's' pal, 'Mickeldy Joe', was in the house at the time, and his presence doubtless had something to do with the unwillingness to give information. 'Leather Apron' was last at this house some weeks ago, though this account may be untrue. He ranges all over London, and rarely assails the same woman twice. He has lately been seen in Leather Lane, which is in the Holborn district.[39]

But the reality was that there was absolutely no evidence against him. Leather Apron who was identified as John or Jack Pizer, who prostitutes alleged extorted money from them. According to a report made by Inspector Helson:

> The inquiry has revealed the fact that a man named Jack Pizer, alias Leather Apron, has, for some considerable period been in the habit of ill-using prostitutes in this, and other parts of the Metropolis, and careful search has been, and is continued to be made to find this man in order that his movements may be accounted for on the night in question, although at present there is no evidence whatsoever against him.[40]

But the mysterious Leather Apron achieved wide circulation and was sensationally reported, especially in US newspapers:

> The crime, committed last Friday night, has shocked the whole of England, and is generally charged to a short, thickset, half crazy creature, with fiendish black eyes, and known as 'Leather Apron'. He frequented the dark alleys, and like a veritable imp haunted the gloom of the halls and passage ways of Whitechapel, and lived by robbing the female Arabs who roamed the streets after nightfall. Of powerful muscle, carrying a knife which he brandished over his victims, the London murder fiend was too terrible an assailant for the victim that cowered beneath the glitter of cold steel.[41]

In the London press, however, it was early wondered whether Leather Apron was 'a mythical outgrowth of the reporter's fancy':[42]

> a theory exists that 'Leather Apron' is more or less a mythical personage, and that he is not responsible for the terrible crimes with which his name has been associated. All the same, the details of his appearance have been widely circulated with a view to his early apprehension, and all the police in the vicinity are on the look-out for him.[43]

The week passed, then Jack the Ripper struck again.

Notes

1. *East London Advertiser*, 1 September 1888.
2. *East London Observer*, 1 September 1888.
3. *East London Observer*, 1 September 1888.
4. *East London Observer*, 8 September 1888.
5. *East London Observer*, 8 September 1888.
6. Rumbelow, Donald (1975) *The Complete Jack the Ripper*. London: W. H. Allen, p.41. Rumbelow cites a statement made by Nichols to the authorities at Mitcham Workhouse that she was born in August 1851 and married William Nichols on 16 January 1864 – when she would have been only 12.
7. Inquest testimony. For a short time in 1883 Mary Ann Nichols had lived with her father. He said that although she was not in the habit of staying out late at night and not, he thought, 'fast' with men, she had been a heavy drinker and this had led to friction and they'd had an argument. The following morning Mary had left.
8. Inquest testimony, *East London Observer*, Saturday 8 September 1888.
9. Extensively cited in the press: *East London Observer*, Saturday 8 September 1888; *Woodford Times* (Essex), Friday 7 September 1888. Edward Walker confirmed that the handwriting was his daughter's and it is interesting that Mary Ann was literate.
10. Emily Holland had two convictions at the Thames Magistrate Court for being drunk and disorderly. Some newspapers gave her name as Jane Oram (see *The Times*, 4 September 1888) and Jane Hodden (see the *Manchester Guardian*, 4 September 1888) and Inspector Abberline calls her Ellen Holland (MEPO 3/140 fol.246). She was described as the lodging house keeper at 18 Thrawl Street in the *Woodford Times*, Friday 7 September 1888.
11. Bucks Row had been renamed Durward Street by the time Leonard Matters wrote.
12. Matters, Leonard (1929) *The Mystery of Jack the Ripper*. London: Hutchinson.
13. *The Star*, 31 August 1888; *East London Advertiser*, 1 September 1888; *Weekly Herald*, 7 September 1888.
14. *New York Times*, 1 September 1888. Also reported in *British Daily Whig* (Canada) on 1 September 1888.
15. Charles Cross's name is erroneously given as George Cross in *The Times* and this has been followed by several writers. Others have called him William Cross. Other accounts, notably that given by Donald McCormick are entirely fictional, including details that did not and could not have happened, and entirely fictional narratives. Such literary embellishments were acceptable literary conventions at the time. (McCormick, Donald (1959) *The Identity of Jack the Ripper*. London: Jarrolds.)
16. There is some confusion over this incident. At the inquest PC Mizen said that

he had been approached by two men who told him, 'You are wanted in Buck's Row by a policeman; a woman is lying there'. He denied that either man had said the woman was dead. Cross and Paul, however, said that Cross had said the woman 'looks to me to be either dead or drunk', Paul adding, 'I think she's dead'. Cross was asked at the inquest if he'd told Mizen he was wanted by a policeman, and had replied, 'No, because I did not see a policeman in Buck's Row'. There seems no reason to disbelieve Cross.

17. Dr. Llewellyn (1851–1921) was a local physician who died aged 70 at Toxteth Lodge, 108 Stamford Hill, Middlesex, on 17 June 1921.

18. It is curious how the same event can be reported differently in the newspapers. *The Times* (18 September 1888), calling PC Thain PC Phail, reported that 'he did not take his cape to the slaughterer's but sent it by a brother constable'.

19. Report by Inspector Abberline dated 19 September 1888, MEPO 3.140 fol.249.

20. The expression 'old man' is common enough not to elicit any real suspicion, but it is interesting to note that Matthew Packer, who claimed to have sold some fruit to a later Ripper victim named Elizabeth Stride, said that a man had addressed him: 'Well, what's the price of the black grapes, old man?' And on being told, had replied, 'Well, then, old man, give us a half a pound of the black'.

21. *The Times,* 1 September 1888.

22. *The Times,* 8 September 1888.

23. *The Times,* 18 September 1888.

24. *The Times,* 1 September 1888.

25. *East London Advertiser*, Saturday 1 September 1888.

26. *East London Observer*, 1 September 1888.

27. *The Times,* 1 September 1888.

28. The workhouses were rather notorious establishments, particularly in the early part of the century. *The London Medical Gazette* records the inquest held at Norwood in Surrey on 26 January 1838 on a boy named Henry Bailey who had been flogged to death at Lambeth Workhouse. The boy, whose age is not stated, had been flogged by a Mr. Rowe to a degree where the back, thighs, legs and arms were nearly covered with black marks and there was also a bruise on the forehead. Still alive, he had then been taken from the workhouse to the House of Industry at Norwood, used for the infant poor of the Parish of Lambeth – where he died six days later. Mr. Rowe, in a manner unstated, apparently died on the morning the boy was taken to Norwood and was thus beyond punishment. But what was remarkable was that the inquest set about debating whether the boy had died from the severity of the whipping or from a disease of the lungs discovered during the *post-mortem* examination. Or whether death was caused by the latter exacerbated by the former. A 'very nice legal point', observed Mr. W. Street, a surgeon giving evidence, with some sarcasm. (*The London Medical Gazette*, Vol. 21, 1837–38, p.1053.)

29. It is integral to the Royal conspiracy theory presented by Stephen Knight in *Jack the Ripper: the Final Solution* and reiterated in several books and movies since then, most notably *Murder By Decree* (1979), *Jack the Ripper* (1988) and *From Hell* (2000).
30. *The Times*, 1 September 1888.
31. Inspector Helson's report dated 7 September 1888 is in MEPO 3/140 fol.237.
32. The undertaker was a Mr. H. Smith of Hanbury Street according to the *East London Observer*, 8 September 1888.
33. *East London Advertiser*, Saturday 8 September 1888.
34. *East London Observer*, Saturday 8 September 1888.
35. *The Times*, 1 September 1888.
36. *The Star*, 31 August 1888.
37. *Manchester Guardian*, 5 September 1888.
38. *Manchester Guardian*, 6 September 1888.
39. *Manchester Guardian*, 10 September 1888.
40. MEPO 3/140, ff.235–8 – report from Inspector Helson, Local Inspector, CID, J Division, to Scotland Yard, 7 September 1888.
41. *Austin Statesman*, 5 September 1888. An interesting article that drew a comparison with 'the servant girl murderers in Austin in 1885, which latter remains a mystery as profound and unravelled as that of Whitechapel. All were perpetrated in the same mysterious and impenetrable silence, and what makes the coincidence more singular is that the Austin murder fiend, who was seen on one occasion, was, like "Leather Apron", a short, heavy set personage'.
42. *Leytonstone Express and Independent*, Saturday 8 September 1888.
43. *Manchester Guardian*, 10 September 1988.

chapter seven

THE MAIDEN TRIBUTE

Victorian society appeared to be respectable, controlled and above the vices prevalent on the continent, and this view existed into the mid twentieth century, enabling the distinguished historian Sir Robert Ensor to write as late as 1934 in his authoritative *England 1870–1914*, 'it is very significant that when well-to-do Victorians gave way to vice they commonly went to Paris to indulge it'.[1] It was widely believed that the Empire was built upon the hard work and clear-eyed vision of men who channelled their sex drive into other things, a view again echoed by Sir Robert Ensor:

> A school of recent writers, concerned to paint the Victorians as hypocrites, has suggested that behind a façade of continence their men were in fact profligate and over-sexed. Religious restraints, it argues, did not really check physical impulse. The view may, like any other, be backed by particular instances. But as a generalisation it misunderstands the age. The religion-ruled Englishmen then dominant in the governing, directing, professional, and business classes spent, there can be little doubt, far less of their time and thought on sex interests than either their continental contemporaries or their twentieth century successors; and to this saving their extraordinary surplus of energy in other spheres must reasonably be in part ascribed.

He went on to state that, 'Probably at the bottom of society there was a greater amount of coarse prostitution than now, just as there was of drunkenness, of physical squalor, and of ruffianly crime'.

It was rather more than a probability.

It is well known that an open sewer of vice and sexual exploitation lay barely hidden behind those pillars of middle-class Victorian respectability – the sanctity of the family, moral virtue, a strong Protestant work ethic, thrift, a deep commitment to religious belief, prudishness to the point of repressiveness, and restraint or preferably abstinence in the use of stimulants; 'duty, industry, morality and domesticity ...' as Lytton Strachey put it.[2] The question still debated by historians is whether middle-class respectable Victorians were aware of the sewer beneath this façade and hypocritically chose to pretend it wasn't there; or whether vice, like Father Brown's postman, was so visible that it passed unnoticed. Certainly the extent of prostitution was not realised, nor were its causes and effects. Prostitutes, like paupers, were moral failures, self-made degenerates undeserving of help, charity or understanding, who preferred to walk the streets in their paint and ragged finery rather than embrace work, thrift and self-improvement. They were consequently of no greater interest or worthy of attention than are the ants scurrying about their business underfoot on the pavement. And, of course, prostitution wasn't a subject suitable for discussion. In polite circles it did not exist.

But during the first half of the nineteenth century eyes began to be opened, at first to the dangers of prostitution and later to the suffering and shame with which it was associated. From the 1850s onwards prostitution became the subject of fierce debate in the highest political circles and down through all strata of society, except perhaps in the lowest where it was a daily reality rather than a subject for shocked and outraged discussion. In 1885 a series of articles about child prostitution, called 'A Maiden Tribute to Modern Babylon', in the ever-campaigning *Pall Mall Gazette,* shook the nation. The articles painted a horrifying picture of children and young women being enticed or forcibly abducted into brothels at home and abroad, to be used, exploited and discarded by the debauched rich who used their influence in government and law to protect the procurers and the brothel keepers from justice.

Moral degeneracy in the slums was portrayed as having reached such a level that a mother would sell her child for prostitution in a foreign land. The articles were shocking, appalling, broke the conventions of journalism, caused a sensation, stimulated discussion, opened eyes, horrified minds, and focused attention on the slum areas that had hitherto been largely ignored.[3] It obviously wasn't intentional, but the campaigns against prostitution and the 'Maiden Tribute' articles highlighted the poverty ridden, prostitute-filled and slum-ridden East End streets. When Jack the Ripper struck against the very class of woman whose existence had been the subject of moral, social and political clamour, and when the police failed to catch the killer, it seemed to confirm that the police weren't interested in protecting poverty-stricken East End prostitutes, that the lower orders didn't matter.

The East End and prostitution seem to go hand in hand and neither has ever been far removed from scandal. As far back as 1303 two local women, Alice la Faleyse and Matilda the wife of Thomas Bat, had houses within the precinct of St. Mary Spital and were suspected of running brothels visited by the canons and perhaps run by the Prior, Robert de Cerne.[4] Just over 500 years later the East End was still noted as the primary location of low lodging houses that acted as brothels. Henry Mayhew noted, 'In order to find these low houses it is necessary to journey eastwards, and leave the artificial glamour of the West End, where vice is pampered and caressed. Whitechapel, Wapping, Ratcliffe Highway, and analogous districts, are prolific in the production of the infamies'.[5] Here were women recorded for posterity by Mayhew with colourful names such as China Emma, Lushing Loo, Cocoa Bet and Salmony-faced Mary Anne.

Prostitution was available across London, from the East End to the West End, and was equally available in other British cities, but it was invisible to all but the eyes of those who wanted to see it and it simply wasn't discussed. Religious organisations had campaigned against prostitution, as they campaigned against all kinds of fornication and almost any kind of entertainment, but the extent of prostitution was unknown – partly because it was often impossible to distinguish between regular prostitutes and woman who accepted gifts and money in return for sexual favours. There was a fine but clearly drawn distinction: women who acknowledged that they supplied sex for money did not consider themselves prostitutes, especially if they did not regard the money as their primary source of income, and even if it was their only source of income. The problem of prostitution began to be quietly discussed from the 1830s onwards and a few organisations sprang up like the Society for the Suppression of Vice (otherwise the London Society for the Protection of Young Females and Prevention of Prostitution). Several important books were also written. In 1839 Michael Ryan, in *Prostitution in London*, drew attention to the extent of prostitution – he estimated that one in five women in London between the ages of 15 and 50 was a prostitute, estimated that £8 million was spent on prostitution, and warned of the danger such wanton degeneracy had on young men. Further publications tried in various ways to engender public support for the suppression of prostitution. These included *Magdalenism* by William Tait, a survey of prostitution in Edinburgh in 1842, *Lectures on Female Prostitution* by Ralph Wardlaw in 1842 and *The Miseries of Prostitution* by J.B. Talbot in 1844. But it was the publication in 1850 in the *Westminster Review* of an article by William Rathbone Greg (republished as a pamphlet in 1853 entitled *The Great Sin of Great Cities*) that proved enormously shocking and volunteered a radical concept with far-reaching implications. Greg argued that prostitution spread venereal disease and also that prostitution was so deeply rooted in and so much a part of conventional society that abolition was impossible. That venereal disease was a growing problem was shocking in itself; that prostitution was out of control in Britain was an admission unsuspected and unimagined. What was totally radical thinking for Britain, however, was Greg's opinion that venereal disease could only be controlled by the state regulation of prostitutes. He suggested that they only be allowed to operate if certified by the government, that they be imprisoned if they prostituted themselves without certification, and that certificates could only be obtained following regular medical inspections, with compulsory detention in a special hospital – called a Lock Hospital – if found to be diseased. This wasn't unique thinking, since many countries employed similar systems, and Greg did not push the point. That was left to William Acton.

William John Acton was a pioneering sexologist, author of a hugely influential book called *Functions and Disorders of the Reproductive System*,[6] and the recognised authority on venereal disease. Some of his ideas – that semen was a rare and valuable commodity, that women 'are not very much troubled by sexual feeling of any kind', and that male masturbation led to insanity[7] – have caused his reputation to suffer somewhat over time, but his books are extremely valuable historical sources because Acton supported his advocacy of state-regulated prostitution by providing facts and figures derived from police returns. In his book *Prostitution*[8] he states that in 1839 there were 6,371 prostitutes in the metropolitan area, in 1841 there were 9,409 and by the middle of 1857 8,600. And these figures, he pointed out, did not include casual prostitutes or women suspected, but not certainly known, to be prostitutes. If such women were included, he said, 'the estimates of the boldest who have preceded me would be thrown into the shade'.

But all this was relatively small beer. The call to action was an editorial in the *Lancet* in 1858 which observed that venereal disease was rife among the military – one-fifth of the fighting force of the country, it said, was in hospital being treated for venereal disease – and it suggested that since treating the men was almost a losing battle, it would make more sense to treat the women.

Cases of venereal disease had been increasing in the military since 1823 (in fact it was established in 1864 that a third of all sick cases among soldiers were venereal in origin) and in the wake of the disastrous performance of the British Army in the Crimean War (1853–56), when looking to blame something other than outrageous military incompetence and government parsimony, the authorities settled on venereal disease as the scapegoat and set up a Royal Commission to inquire into the health of the army. It reported in 1857, the same year in which Acton's *Prostitution* was published and the *Lancet* estimated that one house in 60 in the capital was a brothel and one woman in every 16 was a whore. Two views emerged: one posited that venereal disease among soldiers could be reduced if they were provided with improved recreational facilities and allowed to marry; the other advocated the regulation and enforced examination of prostitutes. The government took the view that improved recreational facilities were expensive[9] and that marriage would sap the fighting spirit, so elected to regulate prostitutes.

The result was the Contagious Diseases Act and the first of the three Contagious Diseases Acts was introduced to a poorly attended parliament as the last item of business on 20 June 1864, where, according to Gladstone, it was passed 'almost without the knowledge of anyone'[10] and thought by many of those who did notice it to have had something to do with cattle disease. A little over five weeks later it became law and was applied to the garrison and dockyard towns of Portsmouth, Plymouth, Woolwich, Chatham, Sheerness, Aldershot, Colchester, Shorncliffe, Cork, Queenstown and the Curragh. Two extensions to the Bill passed in 1866 and 1869 added Canterbury, Dover, Gravesend, Maidstone, Winchester, Windsor and Southampton. The Act allowed for a woman suspected by the police of being a prostitute to be brought before a magistrate and on his authority be subjected to medical examination. If found to be diseased she could be forcibly detained in a Lock Hospital for treatment for a period of up to nine months.

On the face of it the Contagious Diseases Act was very sensible. Being numerically fewer than the soldiers and sailors who were their customers, prostitutes were less expensive to treat and wouldn't deplete the available fighting force when locked away for treatment.

However, moralists and purity campaigners, among them quite a large number of religious fanatics, saw the Contagious Diseases Acts as the legalisation of prostitution and the first step on a downward path to moral degeneracy. Another and affiliate group perceived the Act as a dangerous infringement of personal liberty, an offence to women and, as Florence Nightingale wrote to Harriet Martineau – the 'deaf, eccentric economist with her famous ear trumpet beloved by Victorian reminiscers'[11] – 'any honest girl might be locked up all night by mistake'.

Nothing might have happened, however, had the Contagious Diseases Acts been restricted to docks and garrison towns, but their success in those places encouraged the supporters to advocate the application of the Acts to the country as a whole. Soon any woman, anywhere, could be stopped on suspicion of being a prostitute – itself enough to damage a woman's reputation – and be subjected to the humiliation of appearing before a magistrate and perhaps even being forcibly examined. It was undeniably a bad law, but no voice was raised against it because prostitution was the most unmentionable of unmentionable subjects and the objectors were far too discreet, prudish and respectable to discuss, let alone campaign about, anything so distasteful. If the opposition was to be heard, it needed to find a voice.

And it did – through Josephine Butler.

It began in a small way in 1869 when an obscure South Shields headmaster, Reverend Hoopell,[12] successfully challenged the extensionists (as those who wanted the Acts applied to the country as a whole were called) at a meeting in Newcastle. A press report of the meeting was read by a Nottingham doctor, Charles Bell Smith, who in turn organised a meeting of abolitionists at the Social Science Congress held in Bristol in October that year. This meeting was attended by Elizabeth Wolstenholme, who when it finished sent an urgent telegram which successfully solicited the support of her friend Josephine Butler.[13]

Josephine Elizabeth Butler, a second cousin to the former prime minister Lord Grey, was married to George Butler, the son of a former headmaster of Harrow who himself became vice principal of Cheltenham College and principal of Liverpool College. She was a mother of four[14] and an early feminist, inspired by what she believed was a divine call 'to the moral elevation of her sex'. In 1866 she moved with her husband and settled in Liverpool, where she became leader of the local branch of the North of England Council For Promoting the Higher Education of Women, which is where she met Elizabeth Wolstenholme, who was the leader based in Manchester. She also began to establish homes and refuges for homeless and troubled women, including prostitutes. In 1869 she was appointed secretary of the Ladies' National Association for Repeal of the Contagious Diseases Acts and her 14 year campaign to get the Acts repealed would turn her from a relatively quiet housewife into a national heroine. Thereafter she began to campaign on the continent, causing reforms in the law affecting the state regulation of vice. She visited France, Italy, Switzerland, Holland, Norway and Belgium – where in 1880 she revealed in the newspaper *Le National* how the *police des meurs* (the police department charged with regulating vice in Belgium) were involved with the illegal detention in brothels of under-age English girls. In 1886, the same year in which the Acts were repealed, the serious illness of her husband, who died in 1890, prevented further public activity. However, she continued her prolific writing, including her *Personal Reminiscences of a Great Crusade*,[15] and after her husband's death lived near her eldest son in Northumberland, where she died on 30 December 1906. Her work awakened Britain to the existence of prostitution, but more importantly did much to make it a subject that could be discussed. 'The agitation was important: first because it saved England from a bad system of vice-regulation . . .; secondly because it greatly advanced the idea of a single standard of virtue for men and women; and thirdly, because it powerfully stimulated the more general movement for women's rights'.[16]

The campaign to get the Contagious Diseases Acts repealed had kicked off in late 1869 with the first of four articles in the *Westminster Review* and the formation of two organisations, the National Anti-Contagious Diseases Acts Association and the Ladies' National Association for the Repeal of the Contagious Diseases Acts. Meanwhile, Harriet Martineau had drawn up an official protest against the Acts[17] which was signed by a number of influential women, among them Florence Nightingale, reformer Mary Carpenter, suffragist Lydia Becker[18] (co-founder with Elizabeth Wolstenholme and Emily Davies of the Manchester Women's Suffrage Committee) and Josephine Butler. This protest was published in full in the *Daily News*[19] and was greeted with severe criticism from those who thought it indecent that women should discuss such a delicate subject. Thereafter the media fell quiet, perhaps frowning on the campaign, hoping to kill it through silence, or not wishing to air such an unsavoury topic in their pages. In response Dr. Hoopell began publishing in March 1870 the campaign's own journal, *The Shield*.

The campaign moved into a full but curiously self-destructive gear in October 1870 with the death of Gordon Rebow, the Liberal MP for the Essex garrison town of Colchester. The Liberals chose Lieutenant General Sir Henry Storks as their candidate in the bi-election and victory was regarded as a foregone conclusion. His victory was also essential to the government, his support being needed for controversial reforms being pushed through Parliament by Viscount Cardwell, the Secretary for War. However, Storks was a fervent supporter of the Contagious Diseases Acts and had introduced such a system in Malta, where he had been Governor. It had been so successful that he advocated applying it to officers' wives! The National Association decided to oppose Storks with a rival candidate of their own. They chose Dr. J. Baxter Langley, who they all agreed had little chance of winning and who stood more or less as a publicity stunt. What happened was as extraordinary as it was outrageous. At a public meeting Dr. Langley was threatened and intimidated by crowds of roughs. They tried to shout him down, they hurled rotten vegetables, chairs, a sack of lime or plaster and lumps of mortar at Langley and other anti-CDA speakers. Josephine Butler was targeted by crowds who gathered outside the hotels where she stayed, in one case hurling stones through the windows and in another threatening to set fire to the place. Worse, Storks' committee members were seen to be organising and supporting the hired muscle. It became so dangerous that on one occasion Butler was strongly urged to cancel an engagement and felt alarmed enough to almost give in, but as she weakened 'it suddenly came over me that now was just the time to trust in God, and claim His loving care'. Thus fortified, she dressed as a working woman, managed to sneak into the hall and gave her talk, escaping afterwards through a back window. Unfortunately she and her companion got lost and found themselves in the midst of the mob on the High Street. Eventually the exhausted Josephine was given refuge,

> in a cheerfully lighted grocer's shop, where a very kind, stout grocer, whose name we knew – a Methodist – welcomed us, and seemed ready to give his life for me. He installed me among his bacon, soap and candles, having sent for a cab; and rubbing his hands, he said, 'Well, this is a capital thing; here you are, safe and sound!'[20]

From inside the shop Butler heard women in the street discussing the meeting and voicing their support. She would later wryly recall,

> I was walking down a by-street one evening after we had held several meetings with wives of electors, when I met an immense workingman, a stalwart man, trudging along to his home after work hours. By his side trotted his wife, a fragile woman, but with a fierce determination on her small thin face; and I heard her say, 'Now you know all about it; if you vote for that man Storks, Tom, *I'll kill ye!*' Tom seemed to think that there was some danger of her threat being put in execution. This incident did not represent exactly the kind of influence which we had entreated the working women to use with their husbands who had votes, but I confess it cheered me not a little.

Storks was unexpectedly and soundly defeated. *The Spectator* said that Storks had been 'defeated by Mrs. Josephine Butler'. The *Standard* said, 'Sir Henry Storks is much to be pitied. He has offended Harriet Martineau and Ursula Bright, and we fear he is a doomed man'.[21]

Two years later the same tactics were employed when future Home Secretary Hugh Childers was opposed by a National Association candidate at the Pontefract by-election in August 1872. Again there was violence – the most notorious incident being when Josephine Butler and a Mrs. Wilson were trapped in a hay loft by a gang who tried to smoke them out[22] – but Childers did everything he could to disassociate himself from it, apologising for the excesses of his supporters and offering to prosecute any who could be identified. This may have saved Childers, who was a popular candidate in an extremely safe seat, yet saw his majority of 233 cut to a mere 80.

Events such as these and the publicity that attended them gave the anti-CDA lobbies – 'Repealers' as they were popularly known – a very high public profile and put prostitution on the map, as it were. They were Pyrrhic victories, of course, because the Liberals were the only hope the Repealers had of getting the Acts repealed, and by splitting the Liberal vote and in some cases causing Liberal candidates to be defeated, they were playing into the hands of the staunchly anti-repeal Conservatives.

Eventually James Stansfield, the Repealers' parliamentary representative, created and dictated a policy of restricting anti-CDA agitation to the democratic process. He began by seizing opportunities to put forward the anti-CDA perspective in parliament, in particular during discussion of the annual army estimates. He debated them at such deliberate length and with such tedium that many MPs simply left the House. A Conservative MP named Henry Lucy bitchily defined an empty House as one in which 'Stansfield was on his legs delivering his annual speech on the rights of his fellow women'. Eventually, in March 1879, as Stansfield rose to his feet to begin yet another wearing debate, he was forestalled by an announcement that a select committee was about to be set up to investigate the workings of the Acts. It was a victory. The Acts were repealed.

The campaign against the Contagious Diseases Acts seems distant and unconnected with the Ripper crimes, but the campaign of Josephine Butler and her like played a huge part in awakening the public mind to the existence of social problems presented by prostitution. It focused attention on and enabled discussion of the subject. This in turn led to a couple of other campaigns that directly impacted on the East End and the public perception of Jack the Ripper.

Curiously, the first of these campaigns could have greater relevance than expected. One of the most shocking revelations of the 1880s was the white slave trade – the abduction into, or forcible detention in, brothels in England and abroad of girls and women. This was probably blown massively out of proportion, but did take place – and one of its victims may have been Mary Kelly, Jack the Ripper's final canonical victim. According to a story she told – which gained some independent support – she had arrived in London from Wales and been befriended by a French woman in Knightsbridge. She had entered a brothel run by the woman or her associates, had been presented with several fine dresses and been driven about in a carriage. A gentleman had then taken her to France, but she said that she didn't like it there and returned to England. But she did not return to the West End. Instead she went to the East End and an area noted for prostitution off the Ratcliffe Highway. The question, of course, is why? Why abandon the fine dresses and carriages and gentlemen of the West End for a notorious slum district of the East?

When the puritan lobby discovered that British women were being kept against their will in continental brothels they were outraged. The stories told, believed and perhaps in some cases even true, exposed a supposed scandal horrifying to a civilised country. It was also blown out of all proportion. Judith R. Walkowitz's research has suggested that 'the evidence for widespread involuntary prostitution of British girls at home or abroad is slim', and despite evidence of a small traffic, 'the women enticed into licensed brothels in Antwerp and Brussels were by no means the young innocents depicted in the sensational stories'.[23] This, however, was not the opinion of Alfred S. Dyer, a Quaker puritan activist who ran a small but successful publishing business in London producing all manner of religious literature and social commentary such as *A Manual for Mourners* and *The Menace of Opium*. Walking home one evening from the Friends' Meeting House in Clerkenwell, he was shocked and outraged by a story his companion related. Some weeks earlier a 'respectable' Englishman had visited a brothel in Brussels and there met a young English woman who said that she had been courted by a gentleman who had eventually proposed marriage and suggested that they marry in Brussels. They had travelled first to Calais, where her lover had unexpectedly announced that he had run out of money and needed to return to England to obtain more. He entrusted his bride-to-be to the care of a French friend who would take her on to Brussels, where he would rejoin her. Unhappy and protesting, she was nevertheless forced onto a train and taken by the Frenchman to Brussels, where she found herself placed on the register of prostitutes under a false name (taken from a false birth certificate obtained from Somerset House), violated and imprisoned in a brothel, 'as much a slave as was ever any negro upon Virginian soil'.[24]

Some friends put Dyer in touch with Pastor Leonard Anet in Brussels who investigated and confirmed that the story was true. He was able to rescue the young woman, whose name was Ellen Newland, and returned her to Britain in December 1879. The story of Ellen Newland and that of another young woman named Ada Higgleton who had also been forcibly detained in a Brussels brothel, received wide publicity in several newspapers, including the *Daily News, Daily Chronicle* and the *Standard*,[25] provoking a furious response from Edward Lenaers, chief of the Brussels *police des meurs*, who stated unequivocally that all women entering brothels had to state in their own language before a police officer that they were entering a brothel of their own free will, knew what a brothel was and also what would be expected of them. The British Consular official in Brussels, Thomas Jeffes, defended the Brussels police, writing, 'I can confidently assure the parents of all really virtuous girls that there is no fear whatever of finding their children in the same position as the girls referred to in Mr. Dyer's letter'.[26] Since this was contrary to his own experience, it is perhaps unsurprising that Mr. Dyer formed the view that he was not merely dealing with white slavers but with the conscious or unconscious collusion of the British and Belgian authorities. He therefore decided to go to Brussels and with his friend Charles Gillett, one of the most influential members of the Society of Friends, visit brothels and rescue any Englishwoman detained against her will. They discovered a woman in a brothel on the Rue St. Laurent named Louisa Bond who wanted her freedom, but who had no street clothes. The following morning Dyer and Gillette, along with a Brussels lawyer named Alexia Splingard, visited the Procureur du Roi, the official in charge of the morals police. He referred them to the commissioner of police, who referred them to the deputy commissioner, who visited the brothel and returned to say that Louisa was completely happy and did not want to leave. The three men then returned to the brothel and demanded to see Louisa, but were threatened with violence. They then went to see the Minister Plenipotentiary to Belgium, J.S. Lumley, who refused to see them and directed them to the vice-consul, whose office was closed. Dyer therefore went to the vice-consul's home, where he was passed onto the pro-consul, Thomas Jeffes, who wasn't particularly interested, having established to his own satisfaction that the Belgian authorities ensured that no women were held against their will.

Meanwhile, Dyer and Gillett found other women who wanted their freedom but were afraid to talk, and their fears were reinforced when the two men found a woman named Adeline Tanner being detained against her will in the prostitutes' wards of the Hôpital St. Pierre. Dyer confronted Thomas Jeffes, who quietly arranged for her to be sent home, but it turned out that she had signed the police register of prostitutes using a false name and had stated that she was over 21 when she was really only 19. The Belgian authorities therefore decided to prosecute her for making a false statement to the police. She was found guilty and sentenced to prison. It was a warning – fully appreciated by purity campaigners and the prostitutes themselves – of the treatment troublesome prostitutes could expect in future. Dyer managed to get Adeline Tanner back to England after she had been released, but would have been more convinced than ever that the authorities were on the side of the brothel keepers. Dyer busied himself forming the London Committee for the Exposure and Suppression of the Traffic in English Girls for the Purposes of Continental Prostitution and preparing for battle with the authorities.

What Dyer did not know was that the authorities actually shared his concern and on behalf of the Foreign Office, Chief Inspector Greenham of Scotland Yard had already begun a cautious investigation in Brussels. However, because they thought Dyer was a troublesome fanatic (which he probably was) they decided not to tell him anything and thereby created a garden ripe for the sowing of suspicion. Greenham reported that he had found nothing amiss in Brussels, where everything was 'tickety boo' as the Brussels officials had described it.

Meanwhile, on 1 May 1880 the formidable Josephine Butler published in *The Shield* an impassioned article in which she focused on the highly charged issue of child prostitution. As she would later write:

> In certain of the infamous houses in Brussels there are immured little children, English girls of from ten to fourteen years of age, who have been stolen, kidnapped, betrayed, carried off from English country villages by every artifice, and sold to these human shambles. The presence of these children is unknown to the ordinary visitors; it is secretly known only to the wealthy men who are able to pay large sums of money for the sacrifice of these innocents.[27]

Armed with a sworn statement by a Belgian detective alleging police corruption and collusion between the police and the Brussels brothel owners, Butler led a private prosecution in Brussels in December 1880 which resulted in the conviction of 12 brothel keepers for prostituting girls under the age of 21. A Belgian newspaper, *La Nationale*, used information supplied by Josephine Butler and named names. Stupidly, but perhaps with no alternative, Edward Lenares, chief of the *police des meurs*, and Schroeder, his second-in-command, accused the newspaper of libel, which served only to produce evidence of their collusion with the brothel owners and both policemen were dismissed. Back in England the carefully composed report by Chief Inspector Greenham was buried without ceremony and the Foreign Office undertook another investigation, run by a Middle Temple barrister named Thomas W. Snagge who in early December 1880 brilliantly broke through the façade to expose the corruption of the Brussels police. He concluded:

> Young English girls are a form of merchandise to be acquired by industry and disposed of at market prices per package. 'Three hundred francs per colis' appears to be the ordinary tariff. From the point of view of the brothel keepers the girls form a costly portion of their stock-in-trade; they are like stock in a farm, kept in good condition more or less, and prevented from straying or escaping.[28]

The Foreign Office set up a select committee that the Earl of Dalhousie brought before the House of Lords on 30 May 1881, saying:

It is no longer a matter of doubt that for many years past large numbers of English girls, some of whom were perfectly innocent, have been annually exported to supply the demand of foreign brothels ... there can be no doubt that, during the last 15 years, many Englishwomen have, against their will, endured a life worse than living death, from which there was no escape, within the walls of a foreign brothel.[29]

The select committee published its recommendations on 10 July 1882, advocating changes to the law that raised the age of consent to 16, made it illegal for anyone to allow a girl under 16 to use their home for sexual intercourse, gave police magistrates the power to issue a warrant permitting a police officer to search a house in which it was suspected that a girl under 16 was used for the purposes of sexual intercourse, and which made attempts to solicit or to procure English girls to leave their homes in order to enter foreign brothels (regardless of the girls' willingness) a serious misdemeanour.

These recommendations were then embodied in a piece of proposed legislation called the Criminal Law Amendment Bill, which the Earl of Rosebery introduced to the Lords on 31 May 1883. It received its second reading on 18 June, immediately ran into opposition and the government killed it. Having undergone some revisions, it was re-introduced to the Lords in 1884, got through the necessary three readings and was introduced to the House of Commons on 3 July 1884. A week later it was killed again, which meant it had to go back to the Lords, where it was introduced for a third time in the spring of 1885. It quickly passed through the Lords and was introduced to the Commons on 22 May 1885. That was the day before the Whitsun break, most MPs had already left for their holiday and Cavendish Bentinck, who opposed the Bill, talked until the Speaker seized the opportunity of Cavendish Bentinck drawing breath to adjourn the debate. As W.T. Stead, editor of the *Pall Mall Gazette*, noted:

> Once more we regret to see that the protection of our young girls has been sacrificed to the loquacity of our legislators. Mr. Bentinck talked out the Criminal Law Amendment Act yesterday, and we fear that the chances of proceeding with this measure before the General Election are the slightest ...[30]

Meanwhile, another scandal had been brewing. On 11 April 1882 a Metropolitan policeman named Jeremiah Minahan was promoted to Inspector and transferred from 'E' Division (Holborn) to 'T' Division (Kensington). After a short while he encountered a brothel keeper named Mrs. Jeffries who attempted to bribe him. This Mrs. Jeffries had four brothels, at 125, 127, 129 and 155 Church Street (Old Church Street), Chelsea, and also, according to Charles Terrot, a flogging house at Rose Cottage in Hampstead, a house catering for assorted perversions in or near the Gray's Inn Road, and a white slave clearing house for the Continent on the river near Kew Gardens. Her brothels catered for the rich and famous, had made Mrs. Jeffries very wealthy and apparently operated through the widespread use of bribery. Minahan – 'a narrow and puritanical figure in the Dyer and Scott mould. An honest man with principles, he worked with unwavering zeal and a remarkable lack of tact'[31] – complained to his superior, Superintendent Fisher, but was ignored. Minahan then kept a special watch on Mrs. Jeffries' houses and in April 1883 submitted an official report. He was almost immediately demoted to sergeant, apparently for making unfounded allegations against brother officers. Minahan protested and the MP for Chelsea, Charles Dilke, took up his case. Home Secretary Sir William Harcourt investigated and replied on 28 January 1884 that, 'After the most careful enquiry by the Assistant Commissioner and District Superintendent into a series of charges which he (Minahan) brought against the Superintendent of the Division and other officers, all of which were proved to be without foundation, I see no ground to review the decision of the Commissioners'.[32] Minahan resigned, sent a copy of his investigations to three newspapers, none of which paid him any attention, and in utter frustration decided to explore the possibility of publication. He knocked upon the door of publisher Alfred S. Dyer. Dyer, who believed the police and government were in collusion with the brothel keepers and white slavers, not unnaturally saw Minahan's charges as the proof he needed to blow the scandal wide open and with assistance from Benjamin Scott's London Committee for the Suppression of Traffic in English Girls, Minahan was hired as a private detective to gather evidence against Mrs. Jeffries. Neither white slavery nor catering for sexual perversions was illegal, so Minahan had to prove that Mrs. Jeffries ran brothels, and he was soon able to obtain evidence from former servants and neighbours that included a list of aristocratic clients: Lord Fife, Lord Douglas Gordon, Lord Lennox, Lord Hailford, Leopold, King of the Belgians,[33] and Edward, Prince of Wales.[34] Charges were brought against Mrs. Jeffries, she was arrested and Minahan presented his evidence at the magistrates' court. 'This alleged encouragement of vice and connivance in bribery on the part of highly-placed officers of police must be probed to the bottom', proclaimed the campaigning W.T. Stead the next day.[35] The trial, which opened on 5 May 1885, was a disappointing farce. On the instruction of her defence council, Montagu Williams, Mrs. Jeffries pleaded 'guilty' and thereby saved herself and her clients the embarrassment of being asked difficult questions. Mrs. Jeffries was fined £200, which she paid with cash.

It was on the day after the trial that the Criminal Law Amendment Bill received its second reading in the House of Commons, the debate being adjourned for the Whitsun break. Benjamin Scott, Chairman of the London Committee for the Suppression of Traffic in English Girls, realised that the Act would probably wither and die unless it received some support. On 23 May 1885 Scott visited W.T. Stead at the offices of the *Pall Mall Gazette* and told him all about how children and young women were abducted into brothels, some of them kidnapped from the very street, and how government and police alike turned their backs. Stead would write:

> everyone admitted that juvenile prostitution had increased to a terrible extent. All agreed that the law as it stood was powerless to deal with the evil. The Bill amending the law had been twice through the House of Lords but it had always been held up by the House of Commons. 'All our work', said the Chamberlain [Scott], 'will be wasted unless you can raise public opinion and compel the new Government to take up the Bill and pass it into law'.
>
> I naturally wanted to try, but every instinct of prudence and self-preservation restrained me. The subject was tabooed by the Press. The very horror of the crime was the chief secret of its persistence. The task was almost hopeless. No ordinary means could overcome the obstacles which were presented by the political situation.[36]

Stead visited Bramwell Booth, the son of Salvation Army founder William Booth. The Salvation Army had been reclaiming prostitutes since 1884 and their first refuge for 'fallen women' was in Hanbury Street in the East End where Jack the Ripper's second canonical victim would be found. Booth showed him three street children who had been used for prostitution. Moved but unpersuaded, Stead turned to Howard Vincent of the CID:

> 'Do you mean to tell me', said Stead, 'that actual violation, in the legal sense of the word, is constantly being perpetrated in London, on unwilling virgins, purveyed and procured to rich men at so much a head by brothel-keepers?' 'Certainly', replied the chief of the department, 'there is no

doubt of it'. 'Why', exclaimed Stead, 'the very thought is enough to raise hell'. 'It is true', said the officer, 'and although it ought to raise hell it does not even rouse the neighbours'. 'Then *I* will raise hell', said Stead, and set himself to arouse the nation. 'Be the results what they may', he wrote, 'no nobler work could a man ever be privileged to take. Even a humble part in it is enough to make one grateful for the privilege of life'.[37]

Shocked and angered, Stead then visited Benjamin Waugh, Honorary Secretary of the London Society for the Prevention of Cruelty, founded in 1884, who in 1889 would found the National Society for the Prevention of Cruelty to Children. Waugh had been a Congregational minister in the slums of East London and had there witnessed the cruelty and deprivation that children suffered. Waugh introduced him to two little girls who were in his care. One, aged 7, had been abducted to a fashionable brothel where she had been raped, the other, aged 4½, had been lured into a brothel and raped 12 times in succession. As the burly and bearded Stead approached her, she began to scream hysterically and plead with him not to hurt her. Stead broke down as emotion overwhelmed him: 'I'll turn my paper into a tub! I'll turn stump orator! I'll damn, and damn, and damn!'[38]

Stead realised that he didn't have much time. On 8 June 1885 Gladstone had resigned and Lord Salisbury formed a minority government. There not being a general election meant that the Criminal Law Amendment Bill still breathed – just! A general election would have cancelled all Bills not passed by parliament, so there was still a chance that it could get through the Commons and become law. But it was inevitable that Salisbury would soon have to call an election, so Stead and the campaigners didn't know how long they would have – Salisbury's administration in fact lasted seven months. It was self-evident that they needed to do something sensational.

Stead did it. He decided to prove that children could be bought and sent into enforced prostitution by doing it himself.

Having taken necessary precautions and secured legal advice, Stead set about finding a child to buy and was introduced to a woman named Rebecca Jarrett,[39] a reformed prostitute, brothel keeper and procuress, who was ideally suited to the task but very reluctant to do as Stead asked. 'She demurred, she shrank from it. I was very, very hard upon her. I think I may have done wrong; but when a woman tells you that she has taken young girls at the age of thirteen and beguiled them away ... administered sleeping potions, and then turned loose her good customer upon them unsuspectingly, a man may be pardoned if he does feel somewhat hot. I insisted; I was as ruthless as death'.[40]

Born on 3 March 1846, Rebecca Jarrett was probably prostituted by her mother at a young age. By 15 or 16 she was living with a succession of men, had begun drinking very heavily and had eventually become the manager of several brothels and specialised in procuring young virgins. There was a demand for child prostitutes, both by perverts and by men who paid for virgins because they were not diseased. Rebecca Jarrett once said of a young virgin she procured, 'A gentleman paid me £13 for the first of her'. This was a substantial sum of money, estimated by one source to be the equivalent of about £900 today. Child prostitution was the subject of somewhat chilling humour, as with Oscar Wilde's distasteful remark that Leonard Smithers, Aubrey Beardsley's publisher, 'loves first editions, especially of women: little girls are his passion'. In 1884, aged 38, a chronic alcoholic, suffering from severe bronchitis and badly lame from a diseased hip, Rebecca Jarrett met a Salvationist and underwent her own conversion. She was taken to the Salvation Army refuge in Hanbury Street, Spitalfields. Ten weeks later, after treatment and 'drying out' at the London Hospital, she went to a rescue home in Winchester run by Josephine Butler and enthusiastically set about rescuing other 'fallen women', eventually becoming matron of her own home, Hope Cottage. Hers was quite a remarkable conversion and achievement and it is understandable that she should have drawn back at Stead's request. However, browbeaten by him, she returned to her old haunts in London, met an old friend from her former life named Nancy Broughton and settled on a bright, dark-haired 13-year-old named Eliza Armstrong as suitable for Stead's plan.

The subsequent story is a little complicated: Jarrett and Broughton bought Eliza from her mother for £5. They maintained that they told the mother that Eliza would be entering a brothel and that she knew what this meant. The mother later said that she thought Eliza was going into service, which is what Eliza was told. Eliza then went through the procedure that she would have gone through if genuinely procured: she was examined and confirmed a virgin, taken to an accommodation house where Stead briefly entered her bedroom masquerading as a ravisher, examined by a doctor who confirmed that her virginity was still intact, then taken to France. Meanwhile, Eliza's stepfather Charles Armstrong, locally known as 'Basher', had come home to discover Eliza gone and his wife unable to say where she was, with whom she had gone or how she could be contacted. There was an argument, Basher lived up to his nickname, and Mrs. Armstrong fled for solace to the Marquis of Anglesey, where her £5 purchased so much solace that the police were called and she was arrested. News of the row and its cause became common knowledge in the slum community around the Armstrong home in Charles Street, Marylebone, and public opinion sided with Basher.

On 4 July 1885 the front page of the *Pall Mall Gazette* carried a warning to its readers:

> All those who are squeamish, and all those who are prudish, and all those who prefer to live in a fool's paradise of imaginary innocence and purity, selfishly oblivious of the horrible realities which torment those whose lives are passed in the London inferno, <u>will do well not to read the *Pall Mall Gazette* of Monday and the following days.</u>

For the first time a national newspaper exposed with unsparing detail to its complacent, hypocritical, self-satisfied and hitherto indifferent readership, the sordid sink of immorality and vice that had spread its corruption through the highest levels of society. Stead called the four articles 'the Maiden Tribute to Modern Babylon', alluding to young men and maidens sent from Athens to be sacrificed on Crete to the Minotaur – in this case the children of the poor being the men and maidens and the blood-sated creature of the mythical Labyrinth the profligate rich and influential:

> If the daughters of the people must be served up as dainty morsels to the passions of the rich, let them at least attain an age when they can understand the nature of the sacrifice which they are asked to make. And if we must cast maidens ... nightly into the jaws of vice, let us at least see to it that they consent to their own immolation, and are not unwilling sacrifices procured by force or fraud. That is not too much to ask from the dissolute rich.

Stead's articles made it clear that the rich and influential cared only about themselves and would mercilessly exploit the poor and underprivileged, even to the point of stealing their children so that they could uncaringly indulge their perverse lusts and passions:

> In all the annals of crime can there be found a more shameful abuse of the power of wealth than that by which ... princes and dukes and ministers and judges and the rich of all classes are purchasing for damnation the as yet uncorrupted daughters of the poor?

It is difficult to appreciate the sensation the articles caused. People clamoured to buy copies of the paper and when the chain of newsagents W.H. Smith declined to stock it, impromptu vendors took copies into the streets. A famous story of uncertain veracity has it that George Bernard Shaw took a pitch in the Strand and told Stead, 'I am quite willing to take as many quires of the paper as I can carry and sell them'.[41]

By the time the third article appeared the offices of the *Pall Mall Gazette* in Northumberland Street were under siege, the crowd over-spilling into the Strand, halting traffic and becoming a serious threat to public order. A riot even broke out, possibly caused by bullies hired by the brothel keepers, and the staff had to barricade doors with desks and cabinets. Stead, learning that the government was considering prosecuting him, challenged them to do it, ominously observing that 'Mrs. Jeffries pleaded guilty in order to save her noble and Royal patrons from exposure. There would be no such abrupt termination to any proceedings that might be commenced against us ... We await the commencement of those talked of proceedings with a composure that most certainly is not shared by those whom ... we should be compelled to expose in the witness box'. It was no idle threat.

On 9 July, Home Secretary Cross rose in the Commons to move the second reading of the Criminal Law Amendment Bill[42] and the ensuing debate was casual and unremarkable and the bill went to committee. The bill passed through the Commons and the Lords and received the royal assent on 14 August. Stead had won.

Stead also lost.

The *Pall Mall Gazette* had called Eliza Armstrong 'Lily', but otherwise published enough information for locals to identify her. A crowd descended on the Armstrong house and Mrs. Armstrong, who was fiercely maintaining that she had let Eliza go with extraordinary reluctance and only because she thought she would have a better life entering the service of respectable people, applied to the Marylebone magistrates' court for help in securing the return of her daughter. The court instructed the police to investigate and Inspector Borner set about the task of tracking Eliza down. He soon picked up the trail that led to Mrs. Broughton, who in turn directed him to Josephine Butler in Winchester, who sent him off to see Bramwell Booth, who said Eliza was safe but her whereabouts not known to him and that he'd make some enquiries and pass her address to Assistant Commissioner Monro. Borner told Mrs. Armstrong that Eliza was well and to drop the matter, and set about arranging his holiday. Mrs. Armstrong returned to the magistrates' court, the police were told to find the child, Borner set aside his holiday plans, retraced his steps, played the heavy here and there and eventually Eliza was handed over to her mother.

A week later warrants were issued for the arrest of W.T. Stead, Rebecca Jarrett, Bramwell Booth and others involved in the abduction of Eliza Armstrong. The issue that would prove their downfall was that a child's father possessed sole authority to make decisions on the child's behalf.[43] The mother had no rights. By not getting Basher's permission, Stead and his associates were indeed guilty of abduction. The prosecution seemed hypocritical when compared to the release of Mrs. Jefferies. As the *Methodist Times* observed:

> Do the government intend to prosecute the Pall Mall Commission and nobody else? Are public money and all the resources of the state to be used in attacking those who have exposed an infamous traffic, while those who engage in the traffic, and find their base pleasures in it, are to go scot-free? . . . Why did they not take the brave advice of Mr. Cavendish-Bentinck and prosecute the *Pall Mall Gazette* as an obscene publication? Was it because in that case Mr. Stead would have been able to place in the witness box those whom Mrs. Jeffries calls 'persons in the highest ranks of life', and to confront them with their obscure victims?[44]

Stead really had no defence. The best he could hope for was that the jury would believe Rebecca Jarrett's claim that Eliza's mother knew she was going to enter a brothel – but Rebecca Jarrett was disastrous in the witness box, tried hard not to implicate other people, lied and became confused. Left with no real defence except nobility of motive, Stead finally addressed the jury:

> Mr. Attorney said, 'We must protect the children of the poor'. Was not this the object which I did all this for? . . . You KNOW it was! You know that was why Rebecca did it – and Jacques did it – and Booth did it – and we ALL did it! It was not in order to abduct a girl, but to rescue a girl from what we believed to be her inevitable doom. And, gentlemen, if in the exercise of your judgement, you come to the conclusion that you can take NO note of motive, NO note of interest, NO note of the scope of the operations – all I have to say, gentlemen, is that when you return your verdict I shall make no appeal to any other tribunal . . . If in the opinion of twelve men – twelve Englishmen born of English mothers – with English fathers – and possibly fathers of English girls – if they say to me you are guilty, I take my punishment and do not flinch.[45]

Stead's closing speech was the work of genius and won him a spontaneous round of applause, but there was a final dramatic twist when the
jury, unable to agree, sought advice from the judge, saying through
the foreman: 'Our difficulty is this; that if Jarrett obtained the child by
false pretences, we feel it was directly contrary to Stead's intentions.
We find it therefore, difficult as businessmen to hold him criminally
responsible for that which, if he had known it, he would have repudi-
ated'. Judge Lopez dismissed this as irrelevant and insisted that the
only relevant question was whether Stead and Jarrett, individually or
together, had taken Eliza Armstrong out of the possession of the
father and against his will. After retiring for further discussion the jury
returned and through the foreman issued the following statement:
'We find that Stead did not have the consent of the father to use the
child for the use to which he put her, but that Stead was misled by
Jarrett. There's a further recommendation, m'lord, and that is this –
"That the jury trust that the Government will secure the efficient
administration of the Act recently passed for the protection of
children"'.[46]

The judge interpreted this as a guilty verdict against Stead and
Jarrett. Booth and the other defendants were acquitted. Stead faced a
further trial on the assault charge, was found guilty and sentenced to
three months' imprisonment without hard labour. Jarrett got six
months without hard labour, and Madame Mourey, another of Stead's
group, received six months with hard labour and died in prison.

Stead's professional reputation – and in some quarters his personal
stature – was sacrificed on the 'Maiden Tribute' altar. In getting the
Criminal Law Amendment Act passed he had achieved the impossible.[47] He was manipulative, scheming, bullying, emotionally
involved and committed to a unhealthy degree, and although the story
he told was broadly true, he served several helpings of fiction along
with the fact, in particular portraying the child's mother and father as
'indifferent to anything but drink', and saying that they had virtually
forced their daughter onto the procuress for the drink the offered
money could buy. He also failed to state that he had been the purchaser. Saying – and saying sensationally – that Eliza Armstrong had
been sold into vice carried a lot of impact; saying that a child *could
have been* sold into prostitution carried considerably less. People felt
duped. George Bernard Shaw said 'nobody ever trusted him [Stead]
after the discovery that the case of Eliza Armstrong was a put up job
and that he put it up himself'. Even the Judge, Mr Justice Lopez artic-

ulated these feelings when he said, 'It appears to me that you made statements which, when challenged, you were unable to verify. You then determined to verify the truth of your assertions by an experiment upon a child ... An irreparable injury has been done to the parents of this child. They have been subject to the unutterable scandal and ignominy of having been charged with having sold their child for violation'.[48] Even *The Times* wrote in an editorial, 'It is a matter for rejoicing that a test case has shown that one of the gravest charges against the English perpetrators – the charge of selling their children for infamous purposes – cannot be substantiated'.

The Times and Justice Lopez's 'generally bogus point about the Armstrong's damaged reputation'[49] all managed to miss the point that Mrs. Armstrong *did* sell her child for £5 and, whether she was told that the child was going to enter a brothel or told that she was entering service, she had no idea where the child had gone or to whom she had gone or how she could be contacted, and Eliza's ultimate fate was completely unknown to her. Mrs. Armstrong's sense of responsibility and concern was obviously seriously deficient and social welfare and legal protection obviously needed. The failure of Stead, who was to die in 1912 aboard the *Titanic*, was ultimately a 'failure to understand the law – which allowed a man to buy a child if he obtained the consent of *both* her parents'.[50]

Rebecca Jarrett worked for the Salvation Army following her release and died in 1928. As for Eliza Armstrong, 'shortly after the trial she was more or less adopted by the Salvation Army and did not see her parents again. She grew up into a fine young woman and married happily'.[51]

As far as the Jack the Ripper murders are concerned the Maiden Tribute may seem rather far removed, although the series did conclude with a blistering attack accusing the police of corruption and complicity in white slaving. It was based on hearsay, the only direct evidence of attempted bribery being that of Minahan, but an unnamed prison chaplain had told Stead that all prostitutes affirmed that they had to tip the police with money or sex or both, and brothels also paid the constable on his beat, one old brothel keeper telling Stead that he paid '£3 a week year in and year out' and that an East End brothel paid the Metropolitan Police £500 a year for protection.[52] However, the influence of the Maiden Tribute articles is incalculable, first because they highlighted the levels of depravity to which abject poverty could reduce someone, thus focusing attention on areas of poverty such as the East End, and second because they gave open air acknowledgement to the existence of the clearly visible but taboo subject of prostitution. But there was a third and far more long-term reason. Stead alleged that poor people were being exploited by the rich and privileged and that the most prurient and disgusting crimes were being suppressed and in some cases abetted by the influence of the rich and with the assistance of the authorities. In short, Stead alleged that the authorities were not interested in and did not care about the poor. This echoed and consequently attracted the support of the fledgling socialist movement and such diverse groups as Fabian intellectuals, socialists, the Marxist Democratic Federation and the working-class radical paper *Reynold's News* (all of whom had their own fears and doubts but for the moment rallied behind Stead). Convinced that although the bill had been passed it would not be implemented, these various and diverse groups maintained their pressure and found that they had enormous working-class support. A meeting in Hyde Park on 22 August attracted an estimated 100,000 to 150,000 people,[53] including a very substantial contingent from the East End. The exploitation of the poor by the upper classes would soon shift from white slavery and prostitution to focus on unemployment, but was very quickly revived when it became apparent that the police couldn't catch Jack the Ripper. It was then claimed that the authorities cared little about the women sacrificed to the Minotaur that was Jack the Ripper because they came from the poorest and most helpless strata of society. The police would soon have had the murderer behind bars, they said, if his victims were middle-class women from the West End. This view emerged very early, the foreman of the jury at an adjournment of the murder of Nichols stating that he thought the murder would not have happened if a substantial reward had been offered by the Home Secretary in the case of the murder in George Yard, adding that he believed a substantial one would have been offered had a rich person been murdered.[54]

And perversely, the passage of the Criminal Law Amendment Act may have made life easier for Jack the Ripper. The new law offered a reward to any private citizen reporting to the police a house operating as a brothel. This meant that the police were obliged to investigate any such house so accused and, if the accusation was correct, to prosecute. Frederick Charrington, heir to the huge brewing fortune, but himself a teetotaller and temperance activist, set out to use the law as a means of closing brothels. Charrington and some companions would seek out at night these sinks of iniquity and although they were frequently set upon and beaten up they proved so successful that a claimed 200 brothels in many notorious areas of Tower Hamlets were closed by his actions alone; 'the bullies, the keepers of evil houses, the horrible folk who battened on shame and enriched themselves with the wages of sin, feared Frederick Charrington as they feared no policeman, no inspector, no other living being ...'.[55] As far as Jack the Ripper was concerned, this may have helped: 'The Police commissioner pointed out to Charrington that he had forced the women to exercise their calling in the streets' where as a result they were horrifically butchered.[56] Charrington was not deterred. As the Ripper terror abated, he redoubled his efforts.[57]

Notes

1. Ensor, Sir Robert (1936) *England 1870–1914.* Oxford: Oxford University Press, p.170.
2. Strachey, Lytton (1921) *Queen Victoria.* London: Chatto and Windus, p.141.
3. Writing of his experiences of the East End of 1902, Jack London explained how he had encountered great difficulty finding anyone who knew about the East End. He visited the Cheapside branch of travel agent Thomas Cook, who, he said, could send him 'to Darkest Africa or Innermost Thibet' but of the East End, 'barely a stone's throw away', they admitted: 'we know nothing whatsoever about the place at all'. (London, Jack (1903) *The People of the Abyss.* London: Macmillan.)
4. Thomas, Christopher, Sloane, Barney and Phillpott, Christopher (1997) *Excavations at the Priory and Hospital of St. Mary Spital, London.* London: Museum of London Archaeology Service, p.43.
5. Mayhew, Henry (1983) *London's Underworld.* London: Braken Books (originally published with an introduction by Peter Quennell in 1950 and in numerous editions since then), is the fourth volume of Mayhew's *London Labour and The London Poor*, was orginally called *London Labour and The London Poor – Those That Will Not Work* and was published in London by Griffin, Bohn in 1862, years after the previous three.
6. Acton, William (1865) *The Functions and Disorders of the Reproductive Organs in Childhood, Youth, Adult Age and Advanced Life, Considered in their Physiological, Social and Moral Relations.* Philadelphia: Lindsay and Blakiston.
7. See the arguments surrounding the suspect Aaron Kosminski, the cause of whose insanity was given in his medical papers as 'self-abuse', otherwise masturbation.
8. Acton, William (1857) *Prostitution, Considered in Its Moral, Social, &*

Sanitary Aspects, In London and Other Large Cities. With Proposals for the Mitigation and Prevention of Its Attendant Evils. London: John Churchill.

9. The British soldier was rarely treated as more than cannon fodder. The pay was low, punishment savage, conditions appalling and the barracks were diseased and overcrowded – men in prison were allotted a minimum of 1,000 cu. ft. each; in barracks soldiers were given 300–400 cu. ft. – and the death rate in 1857 in barracks was higher than in the worst slums. (Ereira, Alan (1981) *The People's England.* London: Routledge and Keegan Paul, p.79.

10. *Hansard*, 7 May 1883 – but not without Gladstone's knowledge, given that he had concluded the 'debate' on the second reading of the 1866 bill. That the Act passed with such little attention was probably due to the absence of real interest in the welfare of either group, soldiers or prostitutes, both of whom fell into the category of 'outcasts'.

11. Pearsall, Ronald (1969) *The Worm in the Bud: The World of Victorian Sexuality.* London: Weidenfeld and Nicolson, p.100. For more information see Chapman, Maria Weston (1877) *Harriet Martineau's Autobiography, with Memorials.* Boston, Mass.: James R. Osgood and Co.

12. At meetings of working class men, Rev. Dr. Hoopell was in the habit of displaying the instruments used in the examination of women and describing minutely their use, which Josephine Butler described to Henry J. Wilson, 26 August 1872 as 'needlessly & grossly indecent'.

13. 1828–1906.

14. Josephine Butler suffered an early tragedy when before her eyes she witnessed her youngest child and only daughter fall to her death as she over-excitedly rushed from an upstairs room to welcome her home.

15. London: Horace Marshall and Son, 1898.

16. Ensor, Sir Robert, *op. cit.*, p.171.

17. Published in full in Johnson, George W. and Lucy A. (1909) *Josephine E. Butler.* Bristol: J.W. Arrowsmith, pp.94–7.

18. The unmarried Becker fell out with the married Emmeline Pankhurst when she supported – as a temporary measure – the proposal that Parliament grant single women the vote. Although forced to resign from the Married Women's Committee, she continued in the editorship of the *Women's Suffrage Journal* and in 1887 was elected as president of National Union of Women's Suffrage Societies (NUWSS). She died in 1890.

19. Published in full in Johnson, George W. and Lucy A., *op. cit.*

20. Josephine Butler in a letter to her husband in November 1870.

21. *The Shield*, 12 November 1870, p.292.

22. Butler, Josephine (1898) *Personal Reminiscences.* London: Horace Marshall and Son, pp.85–98.

23. Walkowitz, Judith R. (1980) *Prostitution and Victorian Society. Women, Class and the State.* Cambridge: Cambridge University Press, p.247.

24. Dyer, Alfred S. (1880) *The European Slave Trade in English Girls. A Narrative of Facts.* London: Dyer Bros., p.7.

25. Terrot, Charles (1959) *The Maiden Tribute: A Study of the White Slave Traffic of the Nineteenth Century*. London: Frederick Muller, p.68.

26. Pearson, Michael (1972) *The Age of Consent*. Newton Abbot: David and Charles, p.41.

27. Butler, Josephine, *op. cit.*

28. Terrot, Charles, *op. cit.*, p.116.

29. *Hansard*, 30 May 1881, cols.1608–9.

30. *Pall Mall Gazette*, 23 May 1885.

31. Fisher, Trevor (1995) *Scandal: The Sexual Politics of Late Victorian Britain*. Stroud, Gloucestershire: Sutton, p.58.

32. *Hansard*, 21 May 1885, col. 1024.

33. At the trial of Mrs. Jeffries Leopold was revealed as a purchaser and trafficker in under-age girls and was alleged to purchase as many as 100 under-age English virgins a year, paying as much as £800 annually. (See Railton, G.S. (ed.) (1885) *The Truth About the Armstrong Case and the Salvation Army*. London: Salvation Army Bookstores, p.8.)

34. Mrs. Jeffries consistently denied that he was one of her clients.

35. Stead, W.T. (1885) *The Armstrong Case: Mr Stead's Defence in Full*. London, p.6.

36. Scott, J.W. Robertson (1952) *The Life and Death of a Newspaper: An Account of the Temprements, Peturbations and Achievements of John Morley, W.T. Stead, E.T. Cook, Harry Cust, J.L. Garvin and three other Editors of the Pall Mall Gazette*. London: Methuen, pp.125–6.

37. Snell, Lord (1936) *Men, Movements, and Myself*. London: J.M. Dent.

38. Petrie, Glen (1971) *A Singular Iniquity, the Campaigns of Josephine Butler*. London: Macmillan.

39. There are several versions of Rebecca Jarrett's life. The archives at the Salvation Army Heritage Centre, Queen Victoria Street, London, contain four versions. One is handwritten by Rebecca Jarrett herself, another was typed by a Salvation Army officer who interviewed her. The two others are a typed version that more or less follows the former and a set of supplementary notes. Rebecca Jarrett also wrote a memoir specifically for Josephine Butler, who wrote a biography *Rebecca Jarrett* (London: Morgan and Scott, 1886).

40. Railton, G.S. (ed.) (1885) *The Truth About the Armstrong Case and the Salvation Army*. London: Salvation Army Bookstores.

41. Holroyd, Michael (1990) *Bernard Shaw Vol. 1: The Search For Love 1856–1898*. Harmondsworth, Middlesex: Penguin, p.290.

42. Cross had previously supported an amendment to lower the age of consent from a proposed 14 to 13!

43. Only much later was it discovered that 'Basher' Armstrong was the child's step-father and that his permission wasn't required.

44. Terrot, Charles, *op. cit.*, pp.190–1.

45. *The Times*, 5 November 1885.

46. *The Times*, 9 November 1885.

47. The Criminal Law Amendment Act of 1885, officially entitled 'An Act to

make provision for the Protection of Women and Girls, the suppression of brothels, and other purposes' (48 and 49 Victoria, Chapter 69), raised the age of consent from 14 to 16 and comprehensively protected women under 18 from 'white slavery'. It also contained Henry Labouchere's notorious Clause 11 measure against male homosexuality.

48. *The Times*, 11 November 1885.
49. Hattersley, Roy (1999) *Blood & Fire: William and Catherine Booth and Their Salvation Army*. London: Little, Brown, p.322.
50. *Ibid.*, p.321.
51. Terrot, Charles, *op. cit.*, p.221.
52. *Pall Mall Gazette*, 10 July 1888. It rather delightfully called the police 'the truncheoned custodians of public order' and spoke of them as being converted 'into a set of "ponces" in uniform, levying a disgraceful tribute on the fallen maidens of modern Babylon'.
53. *Pall Mall Gazette*, 24 August 1885.
54. *The Times*, 18 September 1888.
55. Thorne, Guy (1913) *The Great Acceptance: The Life Story of F.N. Charrington*. London: Hodder and Stoughton.
56. Bristow, Edward J. (1977) *Vice and Vigilance*. Dublin: Gill and Macmillan, p.167.
57. Fisher, Trevor *op.cit.*, p.163.

chapter eight

'AT THE CRATER OF A VOLCANO'

'The year 1880 opened in the midst of a fog unparalleled in our annals, which almost without intermission brooded over London from November 1879 to the following February. This gloom – bad for the health, depressing to the spirits, obscuring the outlook – might well have been the emanation of the feelings of Englishmen ...'.[1] Trade was struggling with falling prices, a soaking summer had caused a complete failure of the harvest, and in Hyde Park gatherings of the unemployed were beginning to bring public attention to the severity of the problem. A depression had hit Britain in the 1870s and the nation was just struggling out of it when another ushered in the new decade. 'The word "unemployed" used as a noun is first recorded by the *Oxford English Dictionary* from the year 1882; the word "unemployment" from 1888.'[2] The depression would begin to lift by the end of 1887, but by this time the effects would have changed Britain for ever.

Early in January 1885 3,000–4,000 men in Birmingham, 'orderly, quiet, but near starvation',[3] marched to petition the Mayor for employment. Similar marches took place in other cities, including London, as they had taken place in previous years, but the winter of 1884–85 had been harsh, unemployment severe, the distress appalling. And the men in consequence exhibited a new and menacing frame of mind. The Government, proclaimed the men who marched on the Local Government Board on 16 February, would be responsible for the deaths brought on by destitution. The Government, they said, was 'responsible for murder'.

Public demonstrations of this kind had become popular during the second half of the nineteenth century. In fact, the word 'demonstration', in the sense of a meeting showing public support, was first coined in the 1860s. By 1872 *The Times* was complaining that organising demonstrations 'appears to be becoming a recognised branch of industry in this country',[4] and by the 1880s 'Henry Matthews characterised its popularity as a national mania'.[5] Of all the things that had by 1888 focused public and media attention on the East End of London, perhaps nothing was more significant than the increasing militancy of the working classes and the various socialist groups associated with them. Demonstration by the unemployed, significant numbers of whom came from the East End, awakened or fed fears of revolution.

'The year 1886 was a terrible one for labour, everywhere reductions of wages, everywhere increase of the numbers of the unemployed.'[6] Desperation was great and revolution was in the air, as an outbreak of rioting by followers of the Social Democratic Federation would quickly bring home to the government and public alike, focusing eyes more firmly on the East End than ever before.

In 1880 a sometime *Pall Mall Gazette* journalist named Henry Mayers Hyndman (the son of barrister John Beckles Hyndman, sometime Liberal benefactor to East End churches) boarded a ship bound for the United States where he was to conduct some business. He had taken with him as a little light reading, Karl Marx's *Das Kapital*, and by the time he stepped onto American soil was a convert to socialism and determined to form a Marxist political group when he arrived back in England. The following year he founded the Democratic Federation, which became the Social Democratic Federation in 1884 and is regarded as the first important socialist body in England. Members included Tom Mann, John Burns, Ben Tillet, Eleanor Marx (Karl Marx's youngest daughter), William Morris, George Lansbury (future MP for Bow and Bromley), Edward Aveling, H.H. Champion and the remarkable Annie Besant. Hyndman and his organisation became deeply committed to resolving the plight of the unemployed.

Hyndman's Social Democratic Federation, the newly formed Social Democratic League (founded in 1884 by William Morris when he dropped out of the SDF) and the Fabian Society – whose most distinguished members were George Bernard Shaw, Sidney and Beatrice Webb (founders of the London School of Economics), H.G. Wells and Leonard Woolf – were all strongly opposed to an organisation called the Free Trade Movement, an anti-socialist organisation that believed the economic difficulties were a consequence of 'unfair' foreign competition. Although supported by manufacturers, it sought working class support and sponsored the London United Workmen's Committee that orchestrated rallies and demonstrations targeting the unemployed. The socialist groups thought fair traders were pawns of the capitalists and traitors to the labouring classes. Lambeth-born John Burns,[7] founder of the Battersea branch of the SDF, thought the fair traders were 'the most infamous scoundrels that ever wore boot-leather in the streets of London'. When the fair traders planned a mass demonstration of and for the unemployed in Trafalgar Square on 8 February 1886, the Social Democratic Federation decided to sabotage the meeting by getting to Trafalgar Square first. The fair traders got wind of the plan and at a meeting with Chief Inspector Charles Cutbush,[8] head of Scotland Yard's Executive Branch,[9] they warned that any interference by the SDF would inevitably lead to disturbances and suggested that their own force of 500 Stewards and 50 Marshals be augmented by additional police as a precaution.

On 5 February Metropolitan Police Commissioner Sir Edmund Henderson reviewed police preparations with the Home Secretary, Richard Cross. It was Cross's last day in office, Lord Salisbury's Conservative government having lost the election to a short-lived Gladstonian third term and Cross would be replaced by Hugh Childers. Demonstrations in London had been relatively orderly for several years and neither Henderson nor Cross thought that this one was likely to be different. Later that day Henderson, Cutbush and Assistant Commissioner Pearson agreed that they needed only to aug-ment the routine patrols by 260 police reserves. Henderson increased this reserve to 500 men on the morning of the demonstration. One hundred men were deployed at St. George's Barracks adjacent to the square, 60 more were at King Street Station to protect the Houses of Parliament, 20 at Vine Street Station and 320 were held in reserve at Scotland Yard, to be deployed wherever there may be trouble. In charge of these forces were District superintendents Dunlop, Hume and Walker, 10 inspectors and 50 sergeants, and four plainclothes detectives under Chief Inspector Shore.

Crowds were gathering in Trafalgar Square by noon on Monday 8 February. Childers made his first visit to his office and met with Henderson and Pearson, who assured him that sufficient policemen were available to handle any contingency. When riots proved them all wrong, Childers wrote complainingly to his son:

I took over this department between eleven and twelve, and the heads of the police told me that all necessary preparations had been made, and, of course, I could not have made any change even had I wished. But all the trouble of inquiry falls on me, and the Police are greatly discredited, part of this discredit being reflected on the Home Office.[10]

At about 2.30 in the afternoon District Superintendent Robert Walker, who was 74 years old and had overall responsibility for the police presence in Trafalgar Square, arrived there singularly ill-informed about what to expect. He knew only about the fair traders' demonstration, had no idea the SDF would turn up, had no special instructions about what to do if there was trouble, had no idea where the reserves were deployed, and in the course of the afternoon he would get lost in the crowd, see absolutely nothing of interest and would have his pockets picked clean.

The fair traders arrived at 3.00pm and conducted a very orderly meeting. Then the SDF arrived, John Burns brandishing a red flag – which he later claimed to be a worker's red handkerchief tied to a stick (the 'worker's flag'; Burns knew how to elaborate a good story when he saw one) – which he said he carried so that his followers and the police would know where he was. According to a freelance journalist named Joseph Burgess:

> Burns, in opening the meeting, declared that he and his friends of the Revolutionary Social Democratic League were not there to oppose the agitation for the unemployed, but they were there to prevent the people being made the tools of the paid agitators who were working in the interests of the Fair Trade League.
>
> He went on to denounce the House of Commons as composed of capitalists who had fattened on the labour of the working men, and in this category he included landlords, railway directors, and employers, who, he said, were no more likely to legislate in the interests of the working men than were the wolves to labour for the lambs.
>
> To hang these people, he said, would be to waste good rope, and as no good to the people was to be expected from these 'representatives', there must be a revolution to alter the present state of things.
>
> The people who were out of work, he continued, did not want relief, but justice. From whom should they get justice? From such as the Duke of Westminster and his class, or the capitalists in the House of Commons and their class?
>
> No relief or justice would come from them.
>
> The working men had now the vote conferred upon them. What for? To turn one party out and put the other in? Were they going to be content with that while their wives and children wanted food?
>
> When the people of France demanded food, the rich laughed at those

they called the 'men in blouses', but the heads of those who laughed soon decorated the lamp-posts.

Here the leaders of the Revolutionary Democratic League wanted to settle affairs peaceably if they could; but if not, they would not shrink from revolution.[11]

According to Burgess, Hyndman then pointed towards club-lined Pall Mall, asked what their members thought of the distress suffered by the unemployed and said they cared not a jot. The only hope left lay in revolution, he said, and proclaimed that the next time they met it would be to take the wealth of which they had been robbed. Inflamed by these revolution-preaching speeches, the SDF's followers overturned the fair traders' platforms and then at an apparently spontaneous suggestion Burns with his red flag, Hyndman, and two other SDF leaders led maybe as many as 3,000 men out of Trafalgar Square to march through the West End to Hyde Park. Nobody in authority saw them leave and Commissioner Henderson, who had been in Trafalgar Square, heard none of the speakers and having not seen the overturning of the fair traders' platforms, remarked to Pearson that 'it was the quietest meeting he had seen for a long time'.

Burns led his group of demonstrators into Pall Mall, lined by prestigious gentlemen's clubs and businesses. At 3.50pm someone threw a stone at and shattered the window of a wine merchants near the United Service Club. They passed the Athenaeum, the Travellers' Club and the Reform Club, then reached the mid-century Italian façade of the predominantly Conservative Carlton, where according to Burns a member at a window made a derisory gesture as the procession passed.[12] This infuriated the marchers who rushed the doors and hurled whatever they could find at the windows, including war medals. The march continued along Pall Mall. Stones were thrown indiscriminately: The Reform Club, the Beaconsfield, the Marlborough and the aristocratic White's and Boodles escaped damage, but the Service Club, Brooks's, the radical Devonshire and the New University Club[13] were badly stoned. Continuing to smash windows as it went, the mob moved along St. James Street and Piccadilly and began looting from shops. The crowd reached Hyde Park and split into two groups, following Burns into the park where the men listened to speeches before dispersing; the other, estimated at between 400 and 1,000 men, continued to loot and smash windows in the West End finally meeting opposition from the police – an Inspector Cuthbert and 15 constables from the Marylebone Police Station. There was a bit of a scuffle in which one of the constables received a severe cut on his head, but the mob dispersed quickly and three rioters were taken into custody. They were two painters and a labourer from East London. Damages reached as high as £50,000, mostly from broken windows, and businesses filed 281 claims for riot compensation.

It was later realised that the rioting could have been prevented. Commissioner Henderson idly thought as the demonstration in Trafalgar Square broke up – most of the men noticeably heading back to the East End – that some of the demonstrators could drift into Pall Mall. He issued instructions to inform Superintendent Hume to take his reserves there. This message passed down the chain until entrusted to PC William Hull, who unfortunately told Hume to take his men to The Mall. Other failures of communication compounded the problem, police scattered around London having taken no action whatsoever, 150 of the reserves never leaving Scotland Yard, and most of the police in general unaware that anything untoward had happened. Superintendent Walker, for example, was directing traffic in Trafalgar Square until almost 7.00pm without any notion of what had happened. It was hugely embarrassing.[14]

But this wasn't the end of it. The next day many shopkeepers anticipated further troubles and shuttered or barricaded their shops. The police entertained similar expectations and reinforced their patrols. Troops were put on standby at Chelsea, Wellington and Knightsbridge Barracks.

Nothing happened.

But on Wednesday an unusually dense fog descended over the city and it was rumoured that 75,000 unemployed from Deptford and Greenwich were using it to assemble unobserved before marching on the West End. The Police took the precaution of recommending shopkeepers to shutter their shops and factory owners to barricade their gates. 'One firm's engineers made preparations to defend the premises by means of fire hoses attached to cauldrons of boiling water. The Bank of England maintained a special guard throughout the day. The Houses of Parliament shut down and the huge iron gates at Charing Cross were closed.'[15] It was all probably very sensible in light of Monday's events, but the rumours proved to be untrue and the precautions looked like scare-mongering over-reaction. Home Secretary Childers formed a Parliamentary Committee of Inquiry and after four days of hearing testimony the blame was firmly laid on Commissioner Henderson's shoulders. By this time, however, he had tendered his resignation and it had been accepted. Childers ordered the arrest of the four SDF leaders and they were tried but acquitted.

Although most socialists, among them William Morris and Frederick Engels, condemned or otherwise deplored the rioting, the spontaneous outbreak of violence – preceded by all the ranting about the heads of capitalists hanging from French lampposts – made people, among them the workers themselves, realise that they had muscles to flex. Whether from a genuine desire to help the poor or a fear of revolution, the Mansion House Fund for poor relief in the City apparently doubled. Those in the City could afford such largesse. East London could not.

In August 1887, an 18-year-old girl accused of fighting in Covent Garden was brought before the Bow Street magistrates and in the course of the proceedings was asked where she lived. She replied, 'Nowhere'. Asked where she slept, she replied 'Trafalgar Square'. In his Utopian novel *News From Nowhere* William Morris portrays the disbelief with which a far-future generation greeted a story about a long-past disturbance in Trafalgar Square in which unarmed men were bludgeoned.

> The old man looked at me keenly, and said: "You seem to know a great deal about it, neighbour! And is it really true that nothing came of it?"
>
> 'This came of it', said I, 'that a good many people were sent to prison because of it'.
>
> 'What, of the bludgeoners?' said the old man. 'Poor devils!'
>
> 'No, no', said I, of the bludgeoned'.
>
> Said the old man rather severely: 'Friend, I expect that you have been reading some rotten collection of lies, and have been taken in by it too easily'.
>
> 'I assure you', said I, 'what I have been saying is true'.
>
> 'Well, well, I am sure you think so, neighbour', said the old man, 'but I don't see why you should be so cocksure'.[16]

Morris was referring to the events of 1887 in Trafalgar Square, which in his romance are followed by a general strike and the collapse of the Government, the Square itself being, as it was in reality, a national symbol of Britain and the Empire. At night it was extremely popular with vagrants and one of those who used to sleep there was Mary Ann Nichols, the first canonical victim of Jack the Ripper. It became a popular place for 'slummers' to visit, some of whom brought money and gifts, and charitable organisations brought meals. This generosity made Trafalgar Square even more attractive to the destitute, who arrived in greater numbers, used the fountain for bathing and washing their clothes[17] and lingered throughout the day, whereas before they had drifted away about dawn.

Throughout the second half of 1888 the socialists used Trafalgar Square almost daily for assorted events ranging from meetings and speeches to spectacles like a fife and drum band and as the starting place for demonstrations, such as a march by 2,000 unemployed to the Mansion House on 14 October. Speakers who appeared there included William Morris, George Bernard Shaw, Annie Besant, Henry George and the Russian anarchists Kropotkin and Stepniak.

By the end of October the marches were increasingly disorderly affairs, and there were occasional clashes with the police. The public, offended by the sight of vagrants and the unemployed, complained to the police, as did tradesmen who suffered loss of business, and a knock-on effect of the crowds and the marches was traffic congestion, which in turn added to the noise. All in all people got fed up with the whole thing and the complaints increased. For the new incumbent at the Home Office, a general election having installed Henry Matthews in the troubled chair of Secretary of State, the Trafalgar Square problem was one of several civil liberty cases to land on his desk. One was the Cass case, another the murder of Miriam Angel by Israel Lipski.

On Jubilee night, 21 June 1887, PC Bowden Endacott had arrested 23-year-old Elizabeth Cass for soliciting in Regent Street. Miss Cass, who had only recently arrived in London from Stockton-on-Tees, and her friends declared with considerable outrage that she was not a prostitute but a respectable woman. PC Endacott, however, maintained that he had observed her previously and that his decision to arrest her was neither spontaneous nor ill-considered. At the Marlborough Street Magistrates' Court the magistrate, Mr. Newton, found the charges against her unsupportable and the case was dismissed, but the magistrate concluded by saying to Miss Cass, 'If you are a respectable girl, as you say you are, do not walk Regent Street or stop gentlemen at ten o'clock at night. If you do you will be fined or sent to prison'.[18] Newton clearly believed PC Endacott, but should not have spoken as if the charges had been proven. There was a major public outcry, even a big debate in the Commons, and Henry Matthews was formally censured for having failed to set up an inquiry. Matthews tendered his resignation, but Lord Salisbury refused to accept it. The case did not put either Henry Matthews or the police in a good light.[19]

A few days later a murder in the East End of London became the focus of considerable press attention. On 28 June a young woman named Miriam Angel was found dead in her bedroom at 16 Batty Street, off the Commercial Road, nitric acid having been poured down her throat. A 22-year-old Polish immigrant named Israel Lipski was found beneath her bed, traces of nitric acid in his mouth. He was charged with her murder, but protested his innocence, claiming that two workmen named Rosenbloom and Schmuss had killed her. His story was not believed and he was sentenced to death, but there was immediate controversy about the verdict because the judge, James Fitzjames Stephen, had suggested to the jury that Lipski's motive for killing Miss Angel was lust. In fact no motive had ever been suggested by the prosecution, no evidence of lust had been presented and the defence had had no opportunity to refute the suggestion.

The *Pall Mall Gazette* came to the defence of Lipski, as it had Miss Cass, and campaigned vigorously for his reprieve:

> Stead had inflamed the public until a mob were demanding Lippski's [*sic*] reprieve at Buckingham Palace, and people might have believed the Home Secretary was the criminal. Lippski [*sic*] was to be hung on Monday and Matthews and Stephen spent both Friday and Saturday in fruitless consultation. Matthews even examined witnesses in their native Yiddish. On Sunday they met at five and carried their council into the night, their investigation being only illuminated by bursts of lightning from a thunderstorm, which had made applicable the proverb, *Ruat Coelum fiat justitia!*[20] Matthews used to describe the agony of that session. The last effort was being made to find reason for a reprieve and Matthews' whole reputation was at stake ... and, exhausted as he was, his ears suddenly caught the sound of a voice crying 'Extra!' in the night. Nearer and nearer it came and he distinguished the magic word 'Confession!' At nine o'clock word of Lippski's [*sic*] confession was brought from the prison. A few hours later he was executed and Matthews sank back, feeling as if an answer had come from God.[21]

British justice and the Home Secretary were triumphantly vindicated, but for W.T. Stead the confession was an utter disaster and the press turned on him like ravenous hounds, only the socialist weekly *The Commonweal* voicing a note of restraint, reminding its readers that pressures could have been brought upon Lipski to confess: 'it is well to remember that the witches who were burnt in the seventeenth century almost always confessed their guilt, and "admitted the justice of their sentence", or were said to have done so'.[22] Certainly Lipski's

confession probably saved Matthews' political career,[23] though in retrospect it's questionable that it was in itself worth saving. What is
important, however, is the observation made by author Martin L.
Friedland:

> Moreover, it is possible that if Matthews, the only Catholic in the Cabinet,
> had resigned, the Government would have fallen and Home Rule for
> Ireland would have been introduced. Incredible as it is, then, the confes-
> sion of a poor immigrant Jew, who could not even speak English, may have
> been a factor in the future of the United Kingdom, having repercussions
> even today in the troubles of Northern Ireland.[24]

This perhaps oversimplifies the complex issues involved, but it is certainly true that Salisbury wanted Matthews in office, as his refusal of
Matthews' tendered resignation after the Cass case demonstrates, and
the huge publicity campaign against the government during the
Ripper scare would have added to the anxiety about whether or not
Matthews would resign as a result of the negative criticism he was
receiving.

There are several links between Lipski and the Ripper case. Mr
'Injustice' Stephen, as W.T. Stead rather Rumpolianly described James
Fitzjames Stephen, would later preside over the much disputed trial of
Florence Maybrick, accused of poisoning her husband James, who has
subsequently been identified as the Ripper following the discovery of
a 'diary' supposedly written by him and confessing to the Ripper
crimes. Stephen's son, James Kenneth Stephen, has also been identified as the Ripper. But perhaps the strongest link is that at one of the
murder scenes someone who could have been Jack the Ripper was
addressed as, or could himself have called out, 'Lipski!'.

As Matthews lurched from the disastrous case of Miss Cass to the
career-saving confession of Israel Lipski, he hardly had time to breathe
easy before Trafalgar Square erupted in his face. Had he known that
Jack the Ripper waited in the wings, he would probably have felt like
resigning. As it was Sir Edmund Henderson *had* resigned and had
been succeeded in office by Sir Charles Warren, who took a close and
personal interest in the demonstrations, processions and other activities of the socialists and the unemployed in and around Trafalgar
Square, concluding that they were potentially very dangerous. But
they did not contravene the law and there was little either he or
Matthews could do about them. But as complaints and the pressure
on police resources increased Warren decided to take action. On

Monday 17 October 1887 he declared a temporary but unconditional ban on all meetings in Trafalgar Square. Two days later, on 19 October, Matthews, concerned about the legal issues, reversed the decision. Troops were put on standby. As they waited for legal opinion, Warren became increasingly concerned, telling Matthews that,

> the mob, which at first was disorganised is now beginning to obtain a certain amount of cohesion ... I think it more than probable that they will get out of hand in a very short time if they are not dispersed ... they appear to be able to get together now to the number of 2 or 3,000 in two or three minutes ...[25]

On 1 November the legal advice came through that it was not acceptable to close Trafalgar Square. Meanwhile, as Lord Mayor's Day (9 November) was approaching, the socialist orators were becoming increasingly inflammatory and on 3 November Warren, with Matthews' approval, instructed the police to arrest any person who used threatening language.

Over the next few days there were several meetings in Trafalgar Square and several arrests were made, but it was quite clear that the socialists intended a very disruptive Lord Mayor's Parade Day meeting and procession. On the eve of Lord Mayor's Day Warren obtained Home Office permission to exploit a loophole in the law that enabled him to order a general ban on all further Trafalgar Square meetings or demonstrations because the area was Crown property. By 8.00am the following morning 4,000 placards were posted around Trafalgar Square and its approaches:

> In consequence of the disorderly scenes which have recently occurred in Trafalgar Square ... and with a view to preventing such disorderly proceedings and to preserve the public peace, I, Charles Warren, the Commissioner of the Police of the Metropolis, do hereby give notice, with the sanction of the Secretary of State, and concurrence of the Commissioners of Her Majesty's Works and Public Buildings that ... until further intimation, no public meetings will be allowed to assemble in Trafalgar Square, nor will speeches be allowed to be delivered therein.[26]

Instead of explaining the reasons for this on-off attitude towards demonstrations, the authorities kept the public – and the would-be demonstrators – in the dark. The redoubtable Annie Besant no doubt reflected the opinion of many when she claimed that it was a deliberate trap. The delegates from various clubs met and decided to go ahead with the march to Trafalgar Square, formally protest 'against the illegal interference' and then break up the gathering. That this on-off policy was Warren's procrastination, or Matthews', is even reflected by Sir Robert Ensor, who suggests that it contributed to the irritation and anger of the demonstrators and gave publicity to them.[27]

As it happened it rained badly on Lord Mayor's Day, dampening the spirits of everyone, including the protestors, and it passed without incident, as did the rest of the rain-soaked week. But an announcement on Friday 11 November by the Metropolitan Radical Association of plans to stage a mammoth demonstration the following Sunday in Trafalgar Square won immediate support from a wide variety of other groups, including the Social Democratic Federation and the Socialist League, but also the Home Rule Union and assorted anarchist and radical clubs, groups and organisations. No doubt with the previous year's disorders in Pall Mall in mind, Sir Charles Warren put 5,000 constables on duty, positioning 2,000 in and around Trafalgar Square. The rest were distributed around the approaches. A battalion of Grenadier Guards and a regiment of Life Guards were put on standby. A magistrate was readied to read the Riot Act. Warren went to the Square himself and remained there from early morning until the middle of the afternoon.

Meanwhile groups gathered in various parts of London to be addressed by William Morris, George Bernard Shaw and Annie Besant. At various times they then set off to converge on Trafalgar Square.

The first conflict with the police was in Bloomsbury Street, when marchers were charged and dispersed by mounted and infantry police. At Westminster Bridge there was a conflict in which 26 marchers were injured sufficiently badly to be taken to St. Thomas's Hospital. At a second battle at Parliament Street a stonemason named George Harrison struck a policeman with an iron gas pipe and stabbed another with an oyster knife. An estimated 5,000 men marched from East London and they assaulted numerous policeman *en route* to the Square. But the police managed to break up the cohesion of the marchers, so that they arrived in small groups and were unable to unite. *The Times* estimated the size of the crowd by mid-afternoon at 20,000; the police estimated the numbers at 40,000–50,000.[28]

Annie Besant later described her own experiences:

> As we were moving slowly and quietly along one of the narrow streets debouching on Trafalgar Square, wondering whether we should be challenged, there was a sudden charge, and without word the police were upon

us with uplifted truncheons; the banner was struck down, and men and women were falling under a hail of blows. There was no attempt at resistance, the people were too much astounded at the unprepared attack. They scattered, leaving some of their number on the ground too much injured to move ...[29]

Burns, Hyndman and Cunninghame Graham (the well-to-do son of a Scottish laird, world traveller, author and since 1886 a Member of Parliament for N.W. Lanarkshire) reached the corner of the Square. Hyndman was separated from the others. Burns and Graham launched an attack on the police fronting the square. Graham struck a constable in the face, split his lip and knocked off his helmet. Arrested, he wasn't treated with gentleness when taken into custody:

I was seized by the police. Two constables seized me, one by each shoulder. Another pulled me by the ear from behind, and a fourth struck me on the head with his truncheon. Other blows were struck on various parts of my body, and the policeman who cut my head was making a second blow when Burns raised his folded arms above his head and rushed between us to ward off the blow.[30]

The police, who also arrested Burns, were ultimately able to stop the advance and the 200 Life Guards who were called in weren't really needed, but as they divided into two groups and trotted around the police cordon three or four times, their glittering cuirasses and plumed helmets made a magnificent and quelling sight. A short while later a battalion of Grenadier Guards marched into the Square, bayonets fixed, and cleared the entire area. According to George Bernard Shaw:

You should have seen that high-hearted host run. Running hardly expresses our collective action. We *skedaddled,* and never drew rein until we were safe on Hampstead Heath or thereabouts. Tarleton found me paralysed with terror, and brought me on to the square, the police kindly letting me through in consideration of my genteel appearance. On the whole I think it was the most abjectly disgraceful defeat ever suffered by a band of heroes outnumbering their foes a thousand to one ... It all comes from people trying to live down to fiction instead of up to facts.[31]

Annie Besant remarked:

The soldiers were ready to fire, the people unarmed; it would have been but a massacre.[32]

In the course of the afternoon 200 people were sent with injuries to hospital and two men subsequently died. Seventy-seven constables were injured. Forty rioters were arrested. Most received sentences of up to eight months with hard labour. George Harrison was sentenced to five years' imprisonment for stabbing the policeman. Burns and Graham, who were tried in January 1888, were convicted on one count of unlawful assembly – but acquitted of riot and assault – and sentenced to six months' imprisonment without hard labour. Seventy-five charges of brutality were lodged against the police. The day would go down in history, thanks to the *Pall Mall Gazette*, as 'Bloody Sunday' and the general consensus of opinion seems to have been that the police were at fault and heavy-handed in the extreme. Stead told Gladstone the police were '. . . characterised by a brutality which I have never before seen in the whole of my life; and the sentences of three and six months, which have been passed upon men who provoked beyond endurance, struck back at their lawless assailants in uniform are simply infamous'. Hamilton, whilst questioning whether the events deserved to be called 'Bloody Sunday', agreed that the police were open to criticism: 'There were no doubt a good many heads broken and the police appeared to have conducted themselves with some brutality, but nothing occurred to warrant the appellation "Bloody Sunday"'. And a spectator named Edward Carpenter wrote:

> Indeed, though a large crowd it was of a most good-humoured and peaceable kind; but the way in which it was 'worked up', provoked and irritated by the police, was a caution; and gave me the strongest impression that this was done purposely, with the intention of leading to a collision.[33]

The socialists' cause lost a lot of popular support and most newspapers deplored the demonstration. The following Sunday the plans for another meeting in Trafalgar Square were abandoned in favour of Hyde Park, where no disturbances were recorded. An attempt to hold a meeting on 28 November led to another conflict in which a man named Alfred Linnell suffered injuries from which several days later he died. His funeral on 18 December was matched for size only by that of the Duke of Wellington, with a procession stretching one and a half miles. Pall-bearers included Cunninghame Graham, W.T. Stead, William Morris and Annie Besant, who gave an indication of the depth of feeling in the East End when she remarked that 'at Aldgate the procession took three-quarters of an hour to pass one spot'.[34]

Sir Charles Warren came to be roundly blamed for initiating the violence of Bloody Sunday by closing off Trafalgar Square, and when the dust had cleared the police were severely criticised for their heavy-

handedness. It is curious, therefore, that the far more repressive poli-
cies of his successor, James Monro, have gone relatively unnoticed.
Monro banned almost all demonstrations! Matthews defended him in
public, but protested privately and so frequently over-ruled Monro
that it strained relations. When Monro banned a Friendly Societies'
parade in May 1890, Matthews wrote:

> These men are the pick of the working classes, perfectly orderly, with an
> excellent object in view. It would be disastrous to get the police into colli-
> sion with them. Processions are *not* necessarily illegal ... I am quite aware
> how troublesome to the police these demonstrations are, but it will not do
> to go beyond the law in dealing with them. In the case of Trafalgar Square
> the law was strained to the utmost; but public safety and public opinion
> supported the action of the Police. That would not be so in this instance.[35]

But, as Sir Robert Ensor remarks, 'Bitter memories of it [Bloody
Sunday] lasted in the working class districts for over twenty years.
Much odium fell on Warren, who was indeed largely to blame; and
much on the home secretary, Matthews, who was already unpopular
in parliament'.[36] Bloody Sunday 'ended in such a decisive victory for
the authorities that it marked the end of revolutionary heroics based
on the plight of the East End poor'.[37] It was a defeat for socialism.
Lord Salisbury observed that 'by October 1892 socialist quackeries
will either have been dropped or they will have been exposed by
experience'. As one biographer wryly observed, 'It is fortunate for
Lord Salisbury that history judges him for his governance rather than
his sooth-saying'.[38]

As the economy improved and unemployment decreased at the end
of 1887 and into 1888, enthusiasm for the demonstrations called by
the socialist organisations diminished considerably and the unity of the
groups and those within them began to fall apart. Eventually Herbert
Asquith, the Home Secretary during Gladstone's final term as Prime
Minister and a future Prime Minister himself, issued new regulations
which permitted daylight meetings on Saturdays, Sundays and Bank
Holidays provided police were given notice and approach routes
approved. The limited right of meeting in Trafalgar Square met with
approval from virtually all sides. The rules instituted by Asquith have
remained in force ever since.

As said, the events of 1887 lingered on in the minds of those on
both sides of the dispute. The demonstration was shocking, the brutality of the police frightening, the aftermath prosecutions, described

by Morris in *News From Nowhere*, disgusted the working man. There were rowdies and roughs among the demonstrators, even among their leaders if Cunninghame Graham's assault on the police officer is to be believed, but the memory of the working class was of 'peaceable, law-abiding workmen, who had never dreamed of rioting, were left with broken legs, broken arms, wounds of every description ... [and afterwards] men dazed with their wounds, decent workmen of unblemished character who had never been charged in a police-court before, sentenced to imprisonment without chance of defence'.[39] And although the demonstrators had gathered from all parts of London, a particularly large contingent had come from the East End, which was an area distinguished by being predominantly working class and home to the poorest among them, where unemployment was rife and destitution widespread and ever-present. Those who knew the East End poor and those who didn't alike recognised that a time bomb was ticking on the doorstep of 'respectable' society and wondered what it would take for the impoverished masses to spontaneously rise in hurt and anger and desperation. Suddenly the spectre of 2 or 3 million destitute, hopeless and desperate men rising *en masse* from the slums of London to overwhelm respectable society became a very real, and often talked about, possibility:

> ... men and their families are hovering on the brink of starvation, and there is grave reason to fear that a social revolution is impending.[40]

In the eyes of some, Jack the Ripper heralded that revolution. Rev. W.E. Kendall preached a sermon at the Harley Street Chapel in September 1888 called 'Moral and Social Aspects of the Murders' in which he referred to the centenary of the French Revolution:

> Unless something was done and done soon, for the destitute masses of London and other great cities of this Empire, we should have, not a centenary of revolution, but a revolution itself. It was all very easy to drive 10,000 men and boys before you; but when half a million or a million people spring up, there would be another kind of reckoning. We must see that those in high authority dealt with this matter, and that the people are not driven to excesses in their despair.[41]

The Rev. F.W. Newlands preached apropos of Jack the Ripper:

> we are living at the crater of a volcano which at any moment may overwhelm the community as with a torrent.[42]

Strong stuff, but not merely the outpouring of alarmist ecclesiastics.

Justice reported that the police had been ordered to break up any attempted procession by the unemployed and with distaste observed:

> Of what consequences are a few murders more or less in Whitechapel so long as polite society is secure from the denunciation of the Socialists? The unemployed are clubbed into silence, and the Red Flag is dragged from the hands of starving men lest it should offend the susceptibilities of the well-to-do.[43]

If one thing distinguishes the Jack the Ripper murders from other similar crimes it is their politicisation. The 1880s was indeed a decade of radical change, of old ideas being overthrown, of the seeds of the new thinking being planted, of people flexing their muscles and demanding their rights, be it Josephine Butler and her group campaigning for women's rights, or the likes of Burns and Shaw and Besant defending the working classes. Strangely, whilst these campaigns were nationwide, the focus was the East End and would be given shape and form and substance by a lone and mysterious figure to be called Jack the Ripper.

Notes

1. Gretton, R.H. (1930) *A Modern History of the English People 1880–1922*. London: Martin Secker, p.15.
2. Ensor, Sir Robert (1936) *England 1870–1914*. Oxford: Oxford University Press, p.112.
3. Gretton, R.H., *op. cit.*, p.158.
4. *The Times*, 9 August 1872.
5. Richter, Donald C. (1981) *Riotous Victorians*. Athens, Ohio: Ohio University Press, p.87.
6. Besant, Annie (1893) *An Autobiography*. London: T. Fisher Unwin, p.316.
7. John Burns enjoyed a remarkable career. He left the Social Democratic Federation in June 1889, after a fierce disagreement with H. Hyndman, but joined with Ben Tillett to lead the extraordinarily successful London Dock Strike in August 1889. Elected as the representative of Battersea in the newly created London County Council, he was elected as Battersea's MP in 1892, but refused to join the forerunner of the Labour Party. In 1906 Liberal Prime Minister Henry Campbell-Bannerman appointed Burns President of the Local Government Board, making him the first member of the working class to become a government minister. Appointed President of the Board of Trade in 1914, he resigned from the government in opposition to Britain's entry into World War I and played no further role in politics, spending the rest of his life on his hobbies: the history of London, book collecting and cricket. John Burns died on 24 January 1943.

8. Cutbush shot himself in front of his daughter in 1896 following several years of depression and mild paranoid delusions. His nephew, Thomas Hayne Cutbush, was named by the *Sun* newspaper on 13 February 1894 and on following dates as Jack the Ripper, having been arrested for stabbing young women and committed to Broadmoor, where he died in 1903. The police seem to have investigated the allegations seriously, but absolved him of guilt.

9. Responsible for supplies and pay.

10. Childers, E.S.E. (1901) *The Life and Correspondence of the Rt. Hon. Hugh Culling Eardley Childers*. London, Vol. II, p.240.

11. Burgess, Joseph (1911) *John Burns: The Rise and Progress of a Right Honourable*. Glasgow: The Reformers' Bookstall, p.54.

12. The secretary of the Carlton would give testimony that the crowd wasn't ugly until addressed by a man carrying a red handkerchief or flag, after a few minutes of which they obtained stones from some nearby construction work and began to throw them at the windows.

13. Hyndman had recently been expelled for socialist ideas. That it suffered particularly badly was a mere coincidence, he said.

14. Numerous commentators, among them Burns and the journalist Joseph Burgess, maintained that an adequate police presence would have stopped the riot before it began.

15. Richter, Donald C. (1981) *Riotous Victorians*. Athens, Ohio: Ohio University Press, p.121.

16. Morris, William (1891) *News From Nowhere, or An Epoch of Rest, being some chapters from a Utopian Romance*. London: Reeves and Turner.

17. Booth, General William (1890) *In Darkest England and the Way Out*. London: Salvation Army, p.100. He says 'In Trafalgar Square, in 1887, there were few things that scandalised the public more than the spectacle of poor people camped in the Square, washing their shirts in the early morning at the fountains'.

18. Begg, Paul and Skinner, Keith (1992) *The Scotland Yard Files*. 150 Years of the CID. London: Headline, p.113.

19. There was an inquiry and the police could not corroborate the charge against Miss Cass, although they played very dirty by producing evidence supplied by a Superintendent Ball of the Stockton police that Miss Cass enjoyed the company of several men and had once spent some time alone in a hotel room with a married man who had given her a diamond ring. This evidence suggested that Miss Cass was not the innocent flower she and her friends represented her as being, but was irrelevant as to whether she had been soliciting in Regent Street. The case ultimately rested on PC Endacott's claim that he had witnessed her soliciting in Regent Street in the past, but he could not prove this and Miss Cass's legal advisors brought a case of perjury against him which led to his suspension and appearance at the Old Bailey. Since nobody could prove that Endacott had not previously seen Miss Cass in Regent Street, the judge felt that there was insufficient evidence to sustain the charge.

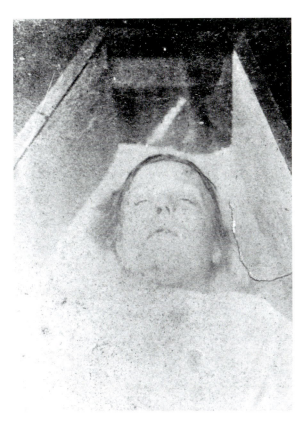

Mary Ann Nichols

Buck's Row

Annie Chapman in life with John Chapman, probably
taken at the time of their marriage in 1869. c. Annie
Chapman's family and Neal Shelden.

Mortuary phohograph of
Annie Chapman

Rear of Hanbury Street

Hanbury Street

Elizabeth Stride

Berner Street

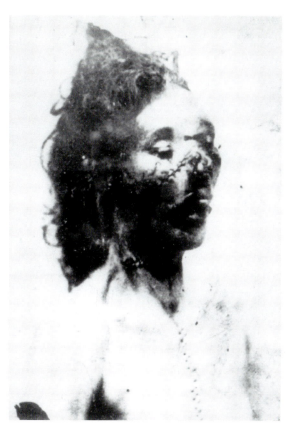

Catharine Eddowes

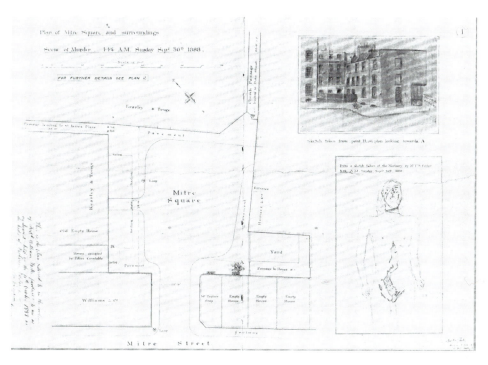

Contemporary drawing of Mitre Square

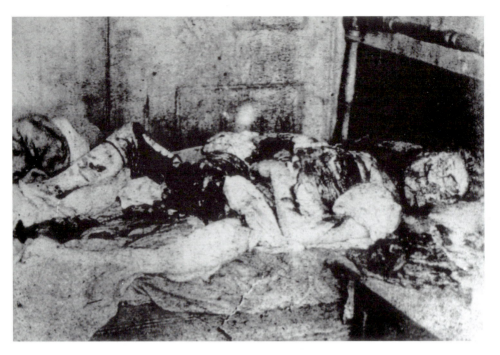

Mary Jane Kelly

Dorset Street and the arched entrance leading into Miller's Court

Sir Charles Warren

Home Secretary Henry Matthews

James Monro

Sir Robert Anderson

Chief Inspector Donald Sutherland Swanson

Sir Melville Macnaghten

Annie Besant

Josephine Butler

PC Endacott was reinstated and spent the rest of his career on special duty at the British Museum.

20. 'Let justice be done though the heavens fall' – meaning that the law must be followed precisely, no matter what the circumstances and eventualities.
21. Leslie, Shane (1921) 'Henry Matthews Lord Llandaff', *Dublin Review*, vol. 168, January, p.10.
22. *The Commonweal*, 22 August 1887.
23. Sir Edward Troup wrote 'In the famous case of Lipski ... a storm of protest was raised which would almost certainly have driven him [Matthews] from office had not Lipski confessed on the eve of his execution'. (Troup, Sir Edward (1925) *The Home Office*. London: G.P. Putnam and Sons, p.59.)
24. Friedland, Martin L. (1984) *The Trials of Israel Lipski. A True Story of Victorian Murder in the East End of London*. New York: Beaufort Books, p.187.
25. MEPO 2/182 Warren to Matthews, 31 October 1887.
26. This ban remained in force until October 1892.
27. Ensor, Sir Robert, *op. cit.*, p.180. 'Warren alternately permitted and prohibited them [the meetings]; but the more the police interfered, the larger the meetings became'.
28. Richter, Donald C. (1981) *Riotous Victorians*. Athens, Ohio: Ohio University Press, p.145.
29. Besant, Annie (1893) *An Autobiography*. London: T. Fisher Unwin, p.324.
30. Burgess, Joseph (1911) *John Burns: The Rise and Progress of a Right Honourable*. Glasgow: The Reformers' Bookstall, p.201.
31. Quoted in Kent, William (1950) *John Burns. Labour's Lost Leader*. London: Williams and Norgate, p.10.
32. Besant, Annie, *op. cit.*, p.325.
33. Carpenter, Edward (1916) *My Days and Dreams, Being Autobiographical Notes*. London: George Allen and Unwin.
34. Besant, Annie, *op. cit.*, p.327.
35. Matthews to Monro, 3 May 1890, PRO MEPO/2/248.
36. Ensor, Sir Robert, *op. cit.*, p.181.
37. Roberts, Andrew (1999) *Salisbury Victorian Titan*. London: Weidenfeld and Nicolson, p.471.
38. *Ibid.*, p.471.
39. Besant, Annie, *op. cit.*, pp.325–6.
40. *East London Observer*, letter from R.J.W. to Editor.
41. *East London News*, 21 September 1888.
42. *East End News*, 18 October 1888.
43. *Justice*, 22 September 1888.

chapter nine

ANNIE CHAPMAN

29 Hanbury Street was an uninspiring single-fronted house, three storeys high and two rooms deep, probably built by a carpenter named Daniel Marsillat who had leased the land in October 1740 from the owner Granville Wheler.[1] In 1888 its eight rooms provided homes for 17 people, among them John Davis, who lived with his wife and three sons in the front room on the third floor. At about 5.45am he got up and made himself a cup of tea. At about 6.00am he went downstairs and into the rear yard:

> I saw a female lying down, her clothing up to her knees, and her face covered with blood . . . What was lying beside her I cannot describe – it was part of her body. I did not examine the woman, I was too frightened at the dreadful sight.

The body was that of Annie Chapman.

The first of several children born to a soldier named George Smith and his wife Ruth Chapman, Annie Eliza Smith opened her eyes on the world in September 1841. She grew up, probably receiving an acceptable standard of education, and on 1 May 1869 married a coachman named John Chapman. A photograph of Annie Chapman at this time – the only photograph of one of Jack the Ripper's victims in life, shows a somewhat stern-faced couple, smartly dressed and obviously enjoying a degree of prosperity. They had three children, two daughters born in 1870 and 1873, and the third, a boy, in November 1880. During most of this time John Chapman had worked for a nobleman who lived in Bond Street, but Annie's character seems to have been doubtful even then, at least if her friend Mrs. Pearcer is to be believed, because she said John Chapman had been forced to resign the position because of his wife's dishonesty.[2] He managed to get a job as a coachman and domestic servant with Josiah Weeks, but again her character seems to have let her down, it later being said of her that 'her dissolute habits made it imperatively neces-sary that she should reside elsewhere than on the gentleman's grounds'.[3] A police report says they parted because of 'her drunken and immoral ways'[4] and she was both known to and had been arrested by the Windsor police for drunkenness.[5] In or about 1884 the couple formally separated, John Chapman thereafter regularly paying his wife a weekly allowance of 10s, made payable at the Commercial Road Post Office. These payments continued until his death on Christmas Day 1886.

By this time Annie Chapman had taken up with a sieve-maker named Jack Sivvey and was living with him in a lodging house at 30 Dorset Street. A little while later she formed a relationship with a bricklayer's labourer named Edward Stanley, nicknamed 'The Pensioner', who had known her when she lived in Windsor. By May or June 1888 Annie Chapman had taken to living at Crossingham's lodging house at 35 Dorset Street.

According to those who knew her, Annie Chapman had a taste for rum, drank to excess at times – as her arrest for drunkenness in Windsor testifies – and was said to get drunk regularly on Saturday nights (as many people did and still do), but to be sober the rest of the week. She does not appear to have resorted to prostitution prior to the death of her husband and the cessation of the money he provided, and had tried thereafter to support herself by doing some crochet work, selling flowers or selling matches.

Annie Chapman was also dying, she was far advanced in a disease of the lungs and the membranes of the brain.

Described as 5ft in height, with dark brown wavy hair, blue eyes and a thick nose, she was by 1888 stout and well proportioned. The police report states that she had two teeth missing in the lower jaw, but the teeth were not missing from the front. The doctor who examined Chapman's body and gave evidence at the inquest stated that Chapman was not missing any front teeth; the front teeth were perfect as far as the first molar and were very fine teeth indeed.

During the first week of September Chapman complained to friends of feeling unwell and she probably spent two days in the casual ward, being given a bottle of medicine which was found in her Dorset Street lodging house. Her friend Amelia Farmer saw Chapman about 5.00pm on 7 September in Dorset Street. Chapman complained of feeling unwell, too ill to do anything, but said: 'It's no use my giving way. I must pull myself together and go out and get some money or I shall have no lodgings'. At 11.30pm she had no money, but asked the lodging house keeper, Timothy Donovan, if she could enter the kitchen. William Stevens saw her there just after midnight. She took a box of pills from her pocket but the box broke and she wrapped the pills in a torn piece of envelope that she took from the mantelpiece over the fire. Chapman then left the kitchen and Stevens thought that she had gone to bed. In fact she had probably gone to the 'Ringers' (a corner pub called the Britannia but nicknamed the Ringers after the landlord) for a drink. Chapman returned to the lodging house about 1.35am and was seen by John Evans, the night watchman. She had not got enough money for a bed, but she would soon get it. She left the lodging house. Evans said that he saw her enter Paternoster Row and walk in the direction of Brushfield Street. That was the last time that Annie Chapman was definitely seen alive.

Mrs. Amelia Richardson was the landlady of 29 Hanbury Street and had occupied the first floor front room for 15 years. She now shared the room with her 14-year-old grandson. She also rented the cellar of the house and the rear yard, from where she ran a business manufacturing packing cases. Between 4.40 and 4.45am her son John Richardson stopped by the house on his way to work at Spitalfields Market. Several months earlier somebody had broken into their cellar and stolen some tools, since when he had made it a habit to check the cellar door. Having checked that the padlock was secure, Richardson pushed open the door leading into the yard and examined his boot, which had been hurting him, and cut off a strip of leather. He felt sure that he would have seen anything unusual, but didn't notice anything.

At 5.15am Albert Cadosch, who lived next door, went into the yard of his house and heard some people talking, apparently in the yard of number 29, but the only word he could catch was 'No'. He went into his house, but on returning to the yard a short time later he heard what sounded like something or someone falling against the fence. He did not take any notice, but went off to work. He did not see anybody in Hanbury Street. At 5.30am Elizabeth Long, who lived with her husband James Long, a park-keeper, at 32 Church Street, was walking down Hanbury Street on her way to Spitalfields Market. She was certain of the time because the brewer's clock had just struck. She was on the right hand side of the street – the same side as number 29 – and outside that house she saw a man and woman on the pavement talking, close against the shutters of number 29. Mrs. Long could not see the man's face, which was turned away from her, but she had a good view of the woman, whom she subsequently identified as Annie Chapman. She heard the man say, 'Will you?' and the woman reply, 'Yes'. Mrs. Long then passed on her way. Although she had not seen the man's face, Mrs. Long stated that he looked like a foreigner, a description which in those days usually meant a Jew. He was about 40 years old and she thought he was wearing a dark coat, a deerstalker hat, and that he was of a 'shabby genteel appearance'. He was a little taller than the woman, which, if the woman was Chapman, would make the man between 5ft and 5ft 5in.[6]

At 6.00am John Davis came down from his third floor room to the hallway that ran the 25 feet length of the house from the street door to the yard. Two steps led down from the hall to the yard, which was about 13–14 feet square and had a shed at the bottom but no exit. Between the steps and the old and rotten fence there was a recess. There lay the body of Annie Chapman.

Davis returned through the hallway to the street. He first attracted the attention of Henry John Holland, who was passing along the street on his way to work, and then shouted to two men, James Green and James Kent, who were standing outside the Black Swan Public House at 23 Hanbury Street. 'Men! Come here!' shouted Davis. 'Here's a sight. A woman must have been murdered!'. Footsteps in the passage woke a Mrs. Hardyman on the ground floor and she roused her son to go and see what was going on. He returned to say that a woman had been killed in the yard.

James Kent viewed the body, and then went to find a policeman but couldn't find one and went for a brandy instead, which he probably needed. He fetched a piece of canvas with which to cover the body. Henry John Holland also went in search of a policeman and found one in Spitalfields Market, but he was on fixed point duty – under no circumstances to leave his position – and told Holland to find another officer. Incensed, Holland that afternoon lodged a formal complaint against the constable at Commercial Street Police Station. By this time someone had conveyed the news up the road from the market to Inspector Chandler, H Division, at the Commercial Street Station. He went straight to the scene. There were lots of people in the passage, but none in the yard. Inspector Chandler sent for the Divisional Surgeon, Dr. George Bagster Phillips, whose surgery was at 2 Spital

Square, and an ambulance was brought from the Commercial Street Police Station, accompanied by other constables whom Chandler got clearing the area of bystanders. From a neighbour he acquired some sacking with which he covered the body.

Dr. Phillips arrived and viewed the body, which was then taken by Sergeant Edmund Berry to the mortuary in Old Montague Street in the same shell as that used to carry Mary Ann Nichols. Outside the house several hundred people had assembled and were described as very excitable. Inspector Chandler searched the yard. He found a piece of coarse muslin, a small pocket hair comb, a screwed up piece of paper containing two pills, and a portion of an envelope which on one side had the letter 'M' in a man's handwriting and a post office stamp 'London, 28 August 1888'. On the reverse was the seal of the Sussex Regiment.

At 7.00am Robert Mann, the pauper inmate of the Whitechapel Union who had charge of the mortuary and who received the body of Nichols, now received the body of Annie Chapman. Inspector Chandler arrived at the mortuary at about the same time and after checking that everything was secure, he left the body in the charge of PC Barnes. Two nurses from the infirmary, Mary Elizabeth Simonds and Frances Wright, were directed to undress the body (Mann left the mortuary whilst this was done). At the inquest Simonds said that she had been instructed by Inspector Chandler to do this. Chandler denied that he had ever issued any such instructions and the Coroner's Officer said that it had been done by order of the clerk of the Guardians. The nurses stripped the body and placed the clothes in a pile in the corner, though they left a handkerchief around the neck of Chapman. They then washed the body.

Meanwhile, Detective Sergeant Thicke, Sergeant Leach and other detective officers had arrived in Hanbury Street, and a telegram had been sent to Inspector Abberline at Scotland Yard. Sergeant Thicke went to the mortuary and took a description of the body, which was later circulated, and Acting Superintendent West, who was in charge of H Division reported to Scotland Yard that in the absence of Local Inspector Reid, who was on holiday, the enquiries had been entrusted to Inspector Chandler and Police Sergeants Thicke and Leach. He requested that Inspector Abberline 'who is well acquainted with H Division, be deputed to take up this enquiry as I believe he is already engaged in the case of the Buck's Row murder which would appear to have been committed by the same person as the one in Hanbury

Street'. Abberline discussed things with Acting Superintendent West and Inspector Helson over on J Division where Nichols had been found, and they agreed that the same man who had killed Mary Ann Nichols had murdered Annie Chapman.

Dr. George Bagster Phillips, the Divisional Surgeon for H Division, performed a post-mortem. He believed Chapman had first been strangled or suffocated, the lividity of the face, lips and hands consistent with asphyxia. A long incision had then been made through the neck, through which the blood had drained from the body. The post-mortem mutilation would therefore have been almost bloodless. The throat had been cut from the left side through to the spine, the murderer having apparently tried to remove Chapman's head. A portion of the small intestines and of the abdomen was lying on the ground over the right shoulder, but still attached to the body. Two other parts of the wall of the stomach were lying in a pool of blood above the left shoulder. Parts of the body had been removed, 'a certain portion of the abdominal wall, including the navel; two thirds of the bladder (posterior and upper portions); the upper third of the vagina and its connection with the uterus; and the whole of the uterus'.[7]

Dr. Phillips said that a sharp, thin, narrow blade 6 or 8 inches long had been used and he thought the murderer must have had anatomical knowledge. He said that he doubted that he could have performed all the mutilations in under a quarter of an hour, and that it would have taken him the best part of an hour had he been doing them professionally.[8]

The problem was in estimating the time of death. Dr. Phillips stated rigor mortis was commencing, which caused him to estimate death at about 4.30am. This meant the testimonies of Mr. Cadosch and Mrs. Long may be irrelevant to the murder. However, Dr. Phillips acknowledged that the coolness of the morning and the loss of blood meant that his timing of the murder could be less accurate than desired.

The newspapers had a field-day of indulgent prose:

London lies to-day under the spell of a great terror. A nameless reprobate – half beast, half man – is at large, who is daily gratifying his murderous instincts on the most miserable and defenceless classes of the community ... The ghoul-like creature who stalks through the streets of London, stalking down his victim like a Pawnee Indian, is simply drunk with blood, and he will have more.[9]

Not even during the riots and fog of February, 1886, have I seen London so thoroughly excited as it is to-night. The Whitechapel fiend murdered his fourth victim this morning and still continues undetected, unseen, and unknown. There is a panic in Whitechapel which will instantly extend to other districts should he change his locality, as the four murders are in everybody's mouth. The papers are full of them, and nothing else is talked of.[10]

One may search the ghastliest efforts of fiction and fail to find anything to surpass these crimes in diabolical audacity.[11]

Throughout that Sunday large numbers – the newspapers spoke of thousands – of well-dressed people visited both the murder scene in Hanbury Street – the people living either side of number 29 making a small charge to anyone who wanted to view the yard and where costermongers set up stands and did a brisk trade selling fruit and other refreshments – and the lodging house in Dorset Street where Annie Chapman had lodged. Sometimes the road became so crowded that the police had to charge at the spectators.

According to the police report, they searched the rooms and questioned the residents of 29 Hanbury Street and their neighbours, enquired at all common lodging houses about any bloodstained or otherwise suspicious individuals, made enquiries in an attempt to find Chapman's rings, and investigated all people who behaved suspiciously in the street or who were the subject of letters received from members of the public.

The piece of envelope bearing the regimental seal of the Sussex Regiment was investigated by Inspector Chandler, who travelled down to Farnborough where the 1st Battalion was located, where he learned that stationery bearing the regimental seal was on sale in the canteen and to members of the public at the local Post Office. Chandler concluded that Chapman had picked up the envelope in the lodging, used part of it to wrap her pills, as witnessed by William Stevens, and that as the lodging house was used by a large transient population the envelope could have belonged to anyone and wasn't a clue to the identity of the killer.

Chapman had worn three brass rings on the middle finger of her left hand and these were missing when her body was found, an abrasion over the ring finger suggesting that they had been wrenched off. Some newspapers reported that the rings were laid out near the body, but in fact they were missing and the police made enquiries at all pawnbrokers, jewellers and dealers.

The police concentrated their search for the mysterious 'Leather Apron', although there was a growing feeling that he owed much of his notoriety to the imagination, the nickname more likely heard 'accompanied by a guffaw than whispered in a tone which would indicate any fear of the mysterious individual'.[12] However, Timothy Donovan, the keeper of the lodging house at 30 Dorset Street where Chapman slept, claimed to 'know him well' and to have once turned him out of the lodging house when he attacked a woman there'.[13] The police early on connected 'Leather Apron' with a man named John Pizer, Inspector Helson reporting that: 'Jack Pizer, alias Leather Apron, has for some considerable period been in the habit of ill-using prostitutes in this, and other parts of the Metropolis, and careful search has been and is continued to be made to find this man in order that his movements may be accounted for on the night in question, although, at present, there is no evidence whatever against him'.[14]

On 5 September 1888 *The Star* had published a major feature on 'Leather Apron'. On 6 September it reported that two Bethnal Green constables had arrested the 'crazy Jew' the previous Sunday (2 September). On the day *The Star* article appeared, 6 September, John Pizer returned to his home at 22 Mulberry Street, arriving there about 10.45pm. He chatted with his sister's 'young man', then went to bed. Pizer did not leave the house, except to go into the yard, until 8.00am on Monday 10 September 1888 when he answered a knock on the front door and opened it onto the burly form of Sergeant Thicke. Pizer was taken to Leman Street police station where he, his family and friends protested his innocence. Curiously, at the inquest Pizer explained that he had not left the house because his brother had advised him not to do so because it was feared he would 'have been torn to pieces'. If Pizer was not 'Leather Apron' and was not even nicknamed 'Leather Apron', why would anyone have thought that Pizer would have been torn to pieces? Especially as he was quickly able on his arrest to provide an alibi for his whereabouts on the night of the murder of Nichols, which included the testimony of a police constable that he was at a lodging house in the Holloway Road.[15]

Before leaving 'Leather Apron', a figure who achieved some notoriety in the Ripper story in later years was L. Forbes Winslow, a noted authority on mental illness. He may have given birth to – or perhaps reflected – the idea that Jack the Ripper was a 'toff':

> I think that the murderer is not of the class of which 'Leather Apron' belongs, but is of the upper class of society, and I still think that my opinion given to the authorities is the correct one – *viz.*, that the murders have been committed by a lunatic lately discharged from some asylum, or by one who has escaped. If the former, doubtless one who, though suffering

from the effects of homicidal mania, is apparently sane on the surface, and consequently has been liberated, and is following out the inclinations of his morbid imaginations by wholesale homicide. I think the advice given by me a sound one – to apply for an immediate return from all asylums who have discharged such individuals, with a view of ascertaining their whereabouts. I am your obedient servant,

L. Forbes Winslow, M.B. Camb., D.C.L. Oxon. 70, Wimpole-street, Cavendish-square, W., Sept. 11.[16]

Several strange characters came to the attention of the police, among the main ones a man who drank a half pint of beer suspiciously quickly at the Prince Albert Tavern (known locally as the Clean House) at the corner of Brushfield Street and Stewart Street, and who was noticed by the landlady, Mrs. Fiddymont, to have blood spots on the back of his right hand, dried blood between his fingers and a narrow streak of blood below his right ear. This was on 8 September at 7.00am. The police appear to have taken Mrs. Fiddymont reasonably seriously and asked her to view a man called William Henry Pigott to see if he was her half-pint quaffing customer. Pigott had been arrested in Gravesend in the Pope's Head tavern where his conversation had betrayed a great hatred of women and had attracted attention. A PC Vollensworth was unable to obtain a satisfactory account from Pigott and arrested him. Inspector Abberline was summoned to Gravesend on Monday morning and returned with Pigott to London where he was one of 17 men placed in an identity parade before Mrs. Fiddymont, who declared he was not her customer. The police held on to Pigott, whose behaviour had become increasingly strange, and eventually he was removed to the workhouse lunatic yard preparatory to being committed to an asylum.

Another suspect was Joseph Issenschmidt, reported as a lunatic to the police on 11 September by two doctors. A butcher who became depressed and mentally unstable following the collapse of his business, he had spent ten weeks at Colney Hatch Asylum at the end of 1887. He was committed again in September 1888, this time to the asylum at Bow. In a report submitted by Inspector Abberline it was stated that Issenschmidt was 'identical with the man seen in the Prince Albert' and it was hoped that arrangements could be made for him to be seen by Mrs. Fiddymont. We possess no further reports on the matter and the press quickly lost interest in Mrs. Fiddymont, so it is quite possible that Issenschmidt was the man she saw.

Pigott and Issenschmidt indicate something of the dangerous sort of people who were wandering around the streets at that time.

The police also put a lot of effort into trying to trace the whereabouts of three insane medical students who had attended London Hospital. Two were traced and one apparently went abroad, but a Home Office file contains an interesting question from someone who signed himself 'W.T.B.', who asked Charles Murdoch, a senior Home Office Clerk, if information should be sought about what became of the third student, 'about whom there is a good deal of gossip in circulation'. Inspector Abberline replied:

> With regard to the latter portion of your letter I have to state that searching enquiries were made by an officer in Aberdeen Place, St. John's Wood, the last known address of the insane medical student named 'John Sanders', but the only information that could be obtained was that a lady named Sanders did reside with her son at number 20, but left that address to go abroad about two years ago.[17]

Nobody named Sanders lived at 20 Aberdeen Place in 1888 or in 1886 (or, indeed, prior to that date). John Sanders lived with his family at 20 Abercorn Place, St. John's Wood, and the Post Office London directories list Mrs. Laura T. Sanders, the widow of an Army Surgeon, as living there from 1874 to 1896 inclusive. She was the mother of six children, one of them, John W. Sanders, having entered the London Hospital Medical College on 22 April 1879 and who, according to the Examination Book, 'Retired because of ill health'. Who he was and what fate ultimately befell him is currently unknown, but he was evidently treated as a serious suspect and not merely just one of the many about whom enquiries were made. Curiously, the reference to John Sanders being the subject of 'a good deal of gossip' is interesting because it does not appear to have reached the press and may have been circulating at a high level.

One clue to the reason why the police took an interest in these medical students is possibly given by Sir Henry Smith, Chief Superintendent of the City Police at the time of the Ripper investigations, who wrote in his reminiscences, *From Constable to Commissioner*:

> After the second crime I sent word to Sir Charles Warren that I had discovered a man very likely to be the man wanted. He certainly had all the qualifications requisite. He had been a medical student; he had been in a lunatic asylum; he spent all his time with women of loose character, whom he bilked by giving them polished farthings instead of sovereigns, two of those farthings having been found in the pocket of the murdered woman.

Sir Charles failed to find him. I thought he was likely to be in Rupert Street, Haymarket. I sent up two men, and there he was, polished farthings and all, but he proved an alibi without shadow of doubt.[18]

Finally, soon after the discovery of Annie Chapman's body an unnamed woman reported that she had been accosted in Spitalfields by a man who struck her several times and ran off when she started to scream. She said that the man had given her two brass medals, passing them off as sovereigns. It was reported that the police were investigating. Whether or not this had the slightest bearing on the subject under discussion remains to be seen.

On 10 September the inquest was opened by Wynne Baxter and the Deputy Coroner George Collier at the Working Lads' Institute. The room was crowded and a large number of people gathered inside and outside the room. The jury was empanelled and went to view the body at the mortuary.

Criticism of the police – as well as the Home Secretary, the Coroner, and even Dr. George Bagster Phillips – mounted as the month progressed.

> It is clear that the Detective Department at Scotland Yard is in an utterly hopeless and worthless condition; that if there were a capable Director of criminal investigations, the scandalous exhibition of stupidity and ineptitude revealed at the East End inquests, and immunity enjoyed by criminals, murder after murder, would not have angered and disgusted the public feelings as it has done.[19]

> ... the detectives have no clue. The London police and detective force is probably the stupidest in the world.[20]

Sir Charles Warren came in for particular opprobrium, especially from the *Pall Mall Gazette*, which perhaps expectedly raised the point that the police had denied thousands of unemployed men the right to demonstrate in Trafalgar Square but were unable to detect a lone killer of prostitutes.[21] Otherwise Warren was accused of militarising the police, restricting the speed and movement of the detectives, and creating a system whereby the local police lacked local knowledge.

> the sooner the police make up their minds to catch him the better for their own reputation ... the Whitechapel tragedies open up the whole question of our police organisation ... We are militarising our police ... Sir Charles Warren, a martinet of apparently a somewhat inefficient type ... Nothing, indeed, has been more characteristic of the hunt after the Whitechapel

murderer than the want of local knowledge displayed by the police ... if Whitechapel had had a properly organised local force it would long ago have been rid of the ghoul whose midnight murders have roused all London and frightened decent citizens in their beds.[22]

Home Secretary Henry Matthews, distinctly unloved and having to take the blame for decisions that were not his own, was equally pilloried, which must have been a cause of considerable concern for Lord Salisbury, who would almost certainly have feared Matthews' resignation as a consequence:

We have had enough of Mr. Home Secretary Matthews, who knows nothing, has heard nothing, and does not intend to do anything in matters concerning which he ought to be fully informed, and prepared to act with energy and despatch. It is high time that this hapless Minister should be promoted out of the way of some more competent man.[23]

Wynne Baxter was criticised by a correspondent in *The Times* for prolonging the inquest:

Is it not time that the inquest on Annie Chapman should close ... The discovery of the murderer or murderers is the duty of the police, and if it is to be accomplished it is not desirable that the information they obtain should be announced publicly in the newspapers day by day through the medium of the coroner's inquiry.[24]

George Bagster Phillips received censure for not giving a full account of the injuries suffered by Annie Chapman, the former deputy coroner of Crickhowell in Breconshire pointing out that,

by the Statute de Coronatere, the coroner is bound to inquire the nature, character and size of every wound on a dead body ... Originally this was done *super visum corpus* ... the object of the inquest is to preserve the evidence of the crime, if any ...[25]

Samuel Barnett wrote to *The Times*:

Whitechapel horrors will not be in vain if 'at last' the public conscience awakes to consider the life which these horrors reveal. The murders were, it may almost be said, bound to come; generation could not follow generation in lawless intercourse, children could not be familiarised with scenes of degradation, community in crime could not be the bond of society and the end of all be peace.

He advocated 'efficient police supervision ... Adequate lighting and cleaning ... The removal of the slaughter-houses ... and sights are

common which tend to brutalise ignorant natures ... [and] The
control of tenement houses by responsible landlords'.[26]

People also sought to place the blame for the murders not merely
on the corrupting influences of slum dwelling, but also on the media,
be it blood-curdling stories or the posters advertising penny-dreadfuls.
Accounts of blood were sure to stir the feeble-minded, claimed the *St.
James Budget*, citing as an example 'the negro Bruce ... [who, when-
ever he] saw blood he "went mad", and performed an amount of mis-
cellaneous killing which would have done honour to one of Mr. Rider
Haggard's heroes'. The 'ghastly story' had recently been told 'with an
over-abundance of gory minuteness ... which it is greatly to be hoped
is wildly exaggerated' by W.B. Churchward in his book *Blackbirding
in the South Pacific*.[27] This unexpectedly free publicity no doubt
increased Mr. Churchward's sales handsomely.

The *Eastern Argus* complained of 'pictures of murders and assassi-
nations' that had been pasted to various walls in the parish and asked
if the Vestry had 'no control over this frightful method of inflaming
the minds of weak and passionate men?'.[28]

Others firmly laid the blame on serials in cheap magazines:

> It is only those whose duties cause them to be mixed up with the lower and
> criminal classes who can really appreciate how great is the evil influence of
> this pernicious literature ... It is, to my mind, quite possible that the
> Whitechapel murders may be the fruit of such pernicious seed falling upon
> a morbid and deranged mind.[29]

By 15 September newspapers were beginning to remark on the way in
which the murders had shed a terrible light on the depredation and
degradation of the area. In the florid prose typical of the period a journalist for the *East and West Ham Gazette* barely paused for breath as
he drew attention to what he felt was this neglected aspect:

> The Whitechapel tragedies have an aspect which should not be disregarded,
> though only of the nature of a side sight. The veil has been drawn aside that
> covered the hideous condition in which thousands, tens of thousands of
> our fellow creatures live in this boasted nineteenth century. In the heart of
> the wealthiest, healthiest and most civilised city in the world we have all
> known for years that terrible misery, cruel crime and unspeakable vice –
> mixed and matted together – lie just off the main thoroughfares that lead
> through the industrial quarters of the metropolis. The daily sin, the nightly
> agonies, and hourly sorrows that haunt and poison and corrupt the ill-fated
> sojourners in these dens of shocking degradation and vice have again and
> again been described by our popular writers. But it is when crime of this

terrible nature, or accident more than usually painful has given vividness and reality to the previously unrealised picture that we are brought to face – what our keenest powers failed adequately to perceive before – how parts of our great capital are honeycombed with cells hidden from the sight of day, where men are brutalised, women are demonised, and children are brought into the world only to become full of corruption, reared in terror, and trained in sin, till punishment and shame overtakes them too and thrusts them down to the black depth where their parents lie already lost or dead to all hope of moral recovery and social rescue.[30]

A lot of criticism was levelled at Henry Matthews in particular and at the government and the police in general for the refusal to offer a reward, but this had been official Home Office policy for several years. Matthews was not personally opposed to rewards, but he had to shoulder the brunt of the criticism. Such is the lot of a politician. Inevitably the newspapers drew parallels between the West and East End, notably *The Star* proclaiming that large sums would have been raised if the women had been murdered in the West End.

Very early on the *Daily Star* had advocated the creation of a Vigilance Committee:

> The people of the East-end must become their own police. They must form themselves at once into Vigilance Committees. There should be a central committee, which should map out the neighbourhood into districts, and appoint the smaller committees. These again should at once devote themselves to volunteer patrol work at night, as well as to general detective service.[31]

On 10 September, the day the inquest opened, there was a meeting of 16 local tradesmen who formed a vigilance association with a view to offering a reward for the capture of the murderer or for information leading to his arrest. The Committee included: Mr. J. Aarons, landlord of The Crown, 74 Mile End Road, who was appointed Chairman; a Mr. B. Harris, the hon. sec.; and Mr. George Lusk. Others included Messrs. Cohen, Houghton, H.A. Harris, Laughton, Lord, Isaacs, Rogers, Mitchell, Barnett, Hodgkins, Lindsay, Reeves and Jacobs. In the course of the proceedings a long list of subscriptions towards the reward fund for the apprehension of the murderer was read, including £5 from Mr. Spencer Charrington, £5 from Lusk and £5 from Aarons. It led to all sorts of questions about the government offering a reward, which as was made clear to the vigilance committee in a letter from E. Leigh Pemberton and widely published in the press, 'the practice of offering rewards for the discovery of criminals was discontinued some years ago, because experience showed that such offers of reward tended to produce more harm than good'.[32] The vigilance committee complained with considerable irritation that in consequence they had difficulty raising funds themselves, many otherwise generous and charitable people refusing to give money because they believed it to be the responsibility of the government. Other organisations were formed at various working, political and social clubs.[33]

The final sensation came when Wynne Baxter concluded the inquest on Wednesday 26 September 1888. During his summing up he proposed a theory about the motive of the murderer:

> The body had not been dissected, but the injuries had been made by someone who had considerable anatomical skill and knowledge. There were no meaningless cuts. The organ had been taken by one who knew where to find it, what difficulties he would have to contend against, and how he should use his knife so as to abstract the organ without injury to it. No unskilled person could have known where to find it or have recognised it when found. For instance, no mere slaughterer of animals could have carried out these operations. It must have been someone accustomed to the *post-mortem* room. The conclusion that the desire was to possess the missing abdominal organ seemed overwhelming.[34]

Baxter was saying that Annie Chapman had been murdered by a surgically skilled person for the specific purpose of obtaining the uterus,

> ... but the object of the murderer appears palpably shown by the facts, and it is not necessary to assume lunacy, for it is clear that there is a market for the object of the murder. To show you this, I must mention a fact which at the same time proves the assistance which publicity and the newspaper press afford in the detection of crime. Within a few hours of the issue of the morning papers containing a report of the medical evidence given at the last sitting of the Court, I received a communication from an officer of one of our great medical schools, that they had information which might or might not have a distinct bearing on our inquiry. I attended at the first opportunity, and was told by the sub-curator of the Pathological Museum that some months ago an American had called on him, and asked him to procure a number of specimens of that organ that was missing in the deceased. He stated his willingness to give £20 for each and explained that his object was to issue an actual specimen with each copy of a publication on which he was then engaged. Although he was told that his wish was impossible to be complied with, he still urged his request. He desired them preserved, not in spirits of wine, the usual medium, but in glycerine, in order to preserve them in a flaccid condition, and he wished them sent to America direct. It is known that request was repeated to another institution

of a similar character. Now, is it not possible that the knowledge of this demand may have incited some abandoned wretch to possess himself of a specimen? It seems beyond belief that such inhuman wickedness could enter into the mind of any man, but unfortunately our criminal annals prove that every crime is possible. I need hardly say that I at once communicated my information to the Detective Department at Scotland-yard.

The theory gained immediate acceptance in the press, but the response of the medical press was distinctly dismissive until investigations by the *British Medical Journal* found that some 18 months or more earlier a foreign physician had enquired as to the possibility of acquiring specimens of the uterus,[35] but Baxter or his informant had misunderstood or misreported much of what had been said.

The theory has attracted considerable interest in recent years, particularly as a result of interest in a suspect called Dr. Tumblety, but it should be noted that Wynne Baxter did not suggest that the doctor seeking uteri was responsible for the murders, only that on learning of the request some warped entrepreneur had sought to fulfill the request. The *Chicago Tribune* London correspondent expanded a little on the story:

> I learned today from a Scotland Yard man working on the case that the mysterious American who was here a few months ago offering money for specimens of the parts taken from the bodies of the victims has been discovered. He is a reputable physician in Philadelphia with a large practice, who was over here preparing a medical work on specific diseases. He went to King's College and Middlesex Hospitals and asked for specimens, and merely said he was willing to pay well if he could not get them otherwise.[36]

The police received hundreds of letters from all parts of the country offering suggestions of various kinds for the capture of the murderer, though 'it is almost needless to say that none of the communications help in any way to elucidate the mystery'[37] and one in particular was about to deepen it even further. The Central News Agency would receive a letter dated 25 September 1888 that began 'Dear Boss' and was signed 'Jack the Ripper'.

Before that, however, the nation would be shocked to its core by two murders on the same night.

Notes

1. Sheppard, F.H.W. (1979) *Survey of London. Vol. XXVII. Spitalfields and Mile End New Town. The Parishes of Christ Church and All Saints and the liberties*

of Norton Folgate and the Old Artillery Ground. London: The Athlone Press, University of London. L.C.C., p.192.

2. *Yorkshire Post,* 11 September 1888.

3. *Windsor and Eton Gazette,* 15 September 1888.

4. HO 144/221/a4930/1c sub.8a and MEPO 3/140 fol.16 18–20.

5. Various newspapers, but see *Woodford Times,* 14 September 1888.

6. Another woman, named Darrell or Durrell (who was not called to give evidence at the inquest and whose account may be a duplicate of that of Mrs. Long and falsely attributed) also claimed to have been walking along Hanbury Street at 5.30am and to have seen the couple standing outside number 29. It was initially reported that she was very doubtful if she could recognise the woman again, but after a visit to the mortuary she maintained that the woman had been Annie Chapman.

7. *British Medical Journal,* 22 September 1888.

8. *The Times,* 20 September 1888.

9. *The Star,* 8 September 1888.

10. *New York Times,* 9 September 1888.

11. *The Times,* 10 September 1888.

12. *Manchester Guardian,* 12 September 1888.

13. *Manchester Guardian,* 10 September 1888.

14. Report by Inspector Helson dated 7 September 1888, MEPO 3/140 fol. 238.

15. Pizer apparently threatened to sue *The Star* for defamation, but Ernest Parke – later the editor – invited him to the newspaper's offices. He was able to knock Pizer down from the £100 he demanded to £50. (See O'Connor, T.P. (1929) *Memoirs of an Old Parliamentarian.* London: Ernest Benn, vol.2, p.257.)

16. *The Times,* 12 September 1888.

17. HO 144/221/A49301C sub.8a.

18. Smith, Lieut.-Col. Sir Henry (1910) *From Constable to Commissioner: The Story of Sixty Years, Most of Them Misspent.* London: Chatto and Windus.

19. *East London Observer,* 22 September 1888.

20. *New York Times,* 9 September 1888.

21. *Pall Mall Gazette,* 8 September 1888.

22. *East London Advertiser,* 15 September 1888.

23. *East London Observer,* 22 September 1888.

24. Letter from J.P. to *The Times,* 19 September 1888.

25. Letter from Roland Adams Williams to *The Times,* 26 September 1888.

26. *The Times,* 19 September 1888.

27. *St. James Budget,* 15 September 1888; Churchward, W.B. (1888) *Blackbirding in the South Pacific; or, the First White Man on the Beach.* London: Swan Sonnenschein & Co. Churchward was an official in the British consular service in the South Pacific and his narrative described his travels in the South Seas.

28. *Eastern Argus,* 8 September 1888.

29. Letter from E.T.A. in *The Times*, 22 September 1888.
30. *East and West Ham Gazette*, 15 September 1888.
31. *The Star*, 8 September 1888.
32. *East London Advertiser*, 22 September 1888.
33. *The Times*, 11 September 1888.
34. *East London Observer*, 29 September 1888.
35. *British Medical Journal*, 6 October 1888.
36. *Tribune*, 7 October 1888. (My thanks to Michael Conlon for bringing this to my attention.) See George, Christopher (2002) 'The Philadelphia Doctor', *Ripperologist*, Issue 43, October.
37. *The Times*, 12 September 1888.

chapter ten

THE DOUBLE EVENT –
ELIZABETH STRIDE

The small village of Stora Tumlehead lies in the parish of Hisingen, north of the seaport of Gothenburg on the west coast of Sweden. Gustaf Ericson and his wife Beata Carlsdotter had a small farmstead there and on 27 November 1843 Beata gave birth to her second child, who was baptised Elizabeth in nearby Torslanda on 5 December. Her elder sister was named Anna Christina and two brothers would also be born, Carl in 1848 and Svante in 1861.

On 14 October 1860 Elizabeth moved to the parish of Carl Johan in Gothenburg, where she worked as a maid, looking after widower Lars Fredrik Olofsson and his children. After a few years she moved to Central Gothenburg but something had gone very wrong with her life, for in March 1865 she was registered by the police as a professional prostitute. Being on the prostitutes' register meant that she was the victim of a system not far removed from the one Josephine Butler fought so hard to have repealed in Britain – branded for life and forced in a life of sexual slavery, 'caught in a pitiless web of brothel madams, police inspections or medical checks, and the infirmary ... terrorised by inspectors, fines and prison'.[1]

In April 1865 Elizabeth gave birth to a stillborn girl and towards the end of the year was treated at the Holtermanska infirmary for venereal disease. Almost a month later she was discharged from the police record. This was no easy achievement and seems rather suspicious. It appears that a lady named Maria Wejsner took Elizabeth into service and vouched for her good behaviour. Although it is by no means certain, the possibility is that Maria Wejsner was a brothel keeper. If so, a tragedy brought with it a small amount of hope: Elizabeth's mother died and left her a small but acceptable inheritance. In due course Elizabeth applied for and was granted permission to go to London, where she arrived in 1866, according to one story entering the service of a foreign gentleman and to another as a servant to a family who lived in Hyde Park.[2]

By 7 March 1869 she had met and married John Thomas Stride and for 12 years the relationship was strong enough to survive several moves and changes of circumstance, but in 1881 they finally separated, Elizabeth Stride's heavy drinking reportedly one of the main causes. Three years later, on 24 October 1884, John Thomas Stride died at the sick asylum, Bromley.

One interesting story that Elizabeth Stride told for the rest of her life was that her husband and children had perished in the *Princess Alice* tragedy of 1878. The *Princess Alice* was a paddle steamer named after Queen Victoria's third daughter, Princess Alice, Grand Duchess of Hesse-Darmstadt, and it took passengers on pleasure cruises along the Thames from London Bridge to Sheerness. At about 7.45pm on Tuesday 3 September 1878, as dusk was falling on what had been a warm, sunny day, the band packing away their instruments and the 700 passengers gathering their belongings in preparation for disembarking, the *Princess Alice* rounded Tripcock point into Galleons reach, 11 miles below London Bridge, and came face to face with a giant steel collier named the *Bywell Castle*.[3] The collier threw its engines into reverse at full speed, but nothing could avert the inevitable collision. The *Princess Alice* was struck just forward of the starboard paddle box and sheared in half. The resulting scenes were from the worst imaginable nightmare. *The Times* called it 'one of the most fearful disasters of modern times'.[4] Only 69 people were pulled from the Thames alive. The exact number of dead was never established.[5]

Several newspapers on 8 October 1888 carried the following news agency story:

With reference to the identity of Elizabeth Stride, the Woolwich newspapers of the time of the Princess Alice disaster have been referred to, and it has been found that a woman of that name was a witness at the inquest and identified the body of a man as her husband, and of two children then lying in Woolwich Dockyard. She said she was on board and saw them drowned, her husband picking up one of the children, and being drowned with it in his arms. She was saved by climbing the funnel, where she was accidentally kicked in the mouth by a retired arsenal police inspector, who was also clinging to the funnel. The husband and two children are buried in Woolwich Cemetery.[6]

The Woolwich newspaper that carried this story has never been traced. Wynne Baxter, the coroner at Stride's inquest, said that the records of the subscription fund raised for the relatives of those who had died in the disaster had been checked and that Stride had not made an application. Of course, Elizabeth Stride had no children and John Thomas Stride was alive at the time of the accident. Curiously, however, the mortuary photograph of Elizabeth Stride shows a slight swelling or deformity of some kind on the side of her mouth and above her lip, which if not an injury caused at or shortly before her death, could have been the consequence of being kicked in the face.

How or why she ended up in Spitalfields is not known. By December 1881 she was living in Brick Lane and she spent Christmas and New Year in the Whitechapel Workhouse infirmary suffering from bronchitis. From there she moved to 32 Flower and Dean Street in Spitalfields[7] and had probably returned to prostitution. On 13 November 1884 she was sentenced for being drunk, disorderly, and soliciting. The following year she met and began a stormy relationship with a waterside labourer named Michael Kidney and the couple lived at 33 Dorset Street. They often separated, Stride going off for days or weeks at a time. Kidney estimated that five months of the three years they lived together had been spent apart.[8] They had parted company in Commercial Street on 25 September, apparently on good terms, although a woman named Catherine Lane claimed that Stride had told her that she'd left Kidney following a row,[9] but Kidney denied this and said he expected Stride to be at home when he returned from work. Where Stride went is not known, but on Thursday 27 September she returned to her old lodging at 32 Flower and Dean Street.[10]

The lodging house keeper, Elizabeth Tanner, who only knew Stride by the nickname 'Long Liz', described her as a very quiet woman who sometimes stayed out late at night, who did cleaning work for the Jews and who would sometimes clean the lodging house rooms, as she had done during the afternoon of Saturday 29 September, for which she had been paid 6d. A Mrs. Ann Mill, a bedmaker at the lodging house, said of Stride that 'a better hearted, more good natured cleaner woman never lived'.[11] But people would hardly have given bad testimonials to someone who had died in such tragic and shocking circumstances. The records of the Thames Police Court tell a different story, showing that between 1887 and her death she had appeared there at least eight times on charges of being drunk, disorderly and using obscene language. She also appeared in court in April 1887, having turned in Michael Kidney on a charge of assault. She didn't pursue the prosecution and the case was discharged.

At 6.30 that evening Stride visited the Queen's Head at 74 Commercial Street, almost opposite the entrance to Dorset Street. The building was converted in 1927 from a public house into a wholesale confectioners and in 1957 into warehousing. Stride did not stay there long and returned with Elizabeth Tanner to the lodging house. At 32 Flower and Dean Street she began preparing to go out and in one of those moments of pathos, such as Polly Nichols' pride in her jolly new bonnet, Elizabeth Stride borrowed a clothes brush in an effort to make her poor clothing look respectable. Looking cheerful, she set out for a Saturday night.

Berner Street, now called Henriques Street,[12] is a short, narrow street running north to south off Commercial Road. It was here, just inside some gates leading to the yard of number 40, that Elizabeth Stride would be found murdered.

40 Berner Street is historically the most interesting of all the murder scenes because it was the home of the International Workingmen's Educational Association, commonly referred to as the Berner Street Club.[13] At its rear were the printing and editorial offices of a radical socialist newspaper, *Arbeter Fraint* ('Worker's Friend'), founded in 1885 by Morris Winchevsky, one of the great names in the history of Jewish radicalism. He was known as the 'grandfather of Yiddish socialism' and, with Morris Rosenfeld, regarded as one of the great Ghetto poets (sometimes called 'sweatshop poets' or 'worker poets') whose work reflected the lives of working class immigrant Jews. The nonpartisan socialist *Arbeter Fraint*, 'open to all radicals ... social democrats, collectivists, communists and anarchists'[14] was first published as a monthly on 15 July 1885, from 29a Fort Street, which ran off Brushfield Street. It proved to be a particularly inspirational journal and became associated with a variety of other organisations, including the Society of Jewish Socialists, which in 1884 had inaugurated an International Workers' Educational Club and in February 1885 had acquired 40 Berner Street as a base for their radical and trades union activities. The founders of the Society allied themselves with *Arbeter Fraint* and in June 1886 became its sponsors. From July 1886 the newspaper became a weekly. The take-over,

marked a dramatic change in the tone of the paper. An earlier stilted dog-matism was replaced by the more popular vernacular and the circulation soared. The result was twofold. It helped to stimulate the drive towards unionisation both in London and the provinces. Small trade unions under workers' leadership sprang into existence in the major tailoring and shoe-making trades as well as among the smaller cigarette, cabinet and stick making industries. In Leeds the Jewish Socialists responded by forming a Workers' Educational Union, which generated the largest and strongest trade union in the clothing industry. Willing or not, Socialist and trade union forces were merging into a common front and moving in the same direction. Socialist societies proliferated in Glasgow, Liverpool and overseas in Paris, where a group of immigrant activists were involved in radical agi-tation. All owed their inception to the teachings of the *Arbeter Fraint*.[15]

Arbeter Fraint and the club enjoyed a national and international repu-tation, were highly controversial and regarded by the leaders of Anglo-Jewry as distinctly dangerous. Efforts were made to prevent publication. A compositor was bribed to change the traditional last page message, 'Workers, do your duty. Spread the *Arbeter Fraint!*', to 'Workers, do your duty. *Destroy the Arbeter Fraint!*' Later the printer succumbed to the taint of gelt and refused to print the paper. It was widely believed that the money for these efforts was supplied by Sir Samuel Montagu,[16] the Liberal MP for Whitechapel. Whether it was or not, some particu-larly weighty pressure must have been placed on the local printers because it took three months for a replacement to be found. Once news of *Arbeter Fraint*'s problems became known, readers and supporters from as far afield as New York gave money enough for the club to buy its own printing press, which, with the editorial office, was housed in a brick-built printing and editorial office in the yard behind the club.

Arbeter Fraint was edited by Philip Krantz, who arrived in London early in 1888 and of whom, 'it can be said about him, "no finer man wore shoe leather . . ." ',[17] it was heavily influenced by the anti-religion obsessed Benjamin Feigenbaum. Whilst this opened the newspaper and the club to a broader spectrum of people, it alienated many of the orthodox Jews and gave the club something of an unsavoury repu-tation among locals. Barnett Kentorrich, of 38 Berner Street, which adjoined the club, told a journalist reporting Elizabeth Stride's murder, 'The club is a nasty place', a young man in the surrounding crowd explaining, 'You see, the members are "bad" Jews – Jews who don't hold their religion – and they annoy those who do in order to show their contempt for the religion'.

40 Berner Street

was an old wooden[18] two-storey[19] building [and had] a spacious room with a capacity of over 200 people and contained a stage. Here were performed by amateurs mostly in Russian language plays by well known Russian revolutionists – Tchaikovsky (not the famous composer), Volchovsky, Stepniak, Winchevsky, Gallop; later came Simon Kahn, Krantz, Feigenbaum, Yanovsky, and others ... Invariably, on Saturday and Sunday evenings, there was a truly international gathering of Russian, Jewish, British, French, Italian, Czech, Polish, and radicals of other nationalities ... Quite often the renowned radical poet, William Morris was seen there reading his splendid verses. It may be said that there, in Berner Street, was laid the foundation for true International Brotherhood of Mankind ... Like Faneuil Hall in Boston, Berner Street Club was the 'Cradle of Liberty', for the workers' emancipation from economic slavery, in London.[20]

Saturday 29 September was no different to the weekends described above. The Chair was taken that evening by a young man named Morris Eagle, who opened the discussion, 'Why Jews Should Be Socialists'. About 100 people attended and the discussion finished at about 11.30pm. Most people left the club by the street door before midnight, including Morris Eagle who walked his sweetheart home and then returned to the club to get some dinner. The 20–30 people who remained behind were either upstairs, where they were talking, singing or dancing, or in the downstairs rooms.

The first floor was the room used for entertainments. 'It was of medium size and held hardly more than a hundred and fifty persons. Plain benches without backs stretched through it crosswise and along the walls. Everywhere extreme poverty, but everywhere also the endeavour to overcome poverty. On the walls hung a number of portraits: Marx, Proudhon, Lassalle overthrowing the golden calf of capitalism ... At the front the room was enclosed by a small stage ...'. [21] The room had three windows, all looking out on the rear yard. A third storey provided accommodation for the Steward, his wife and guests.

The house had a door and single window at the front. At the side, running the length of the house, was a passage entered through a 9–12 feet wide entrance with two wooden gates folding backwards from the street, one with a small door in it. A side-door, opposite which there were two lavatories, gave access to the rear room of the house.

The yard, known as Dutfield's Yard because a man named Arthur Dutfield carried on his business as a van and cart manufacturer there, contained a house on the left-hand side occupied by two or three tenants. A workshop facing the gates was used by a sack manufacturer named Walter Hindley and adjoining it was an unused stable. Next to it, built onto the rear of the club, was *Arbeter Fraint*'s two-roomed stone office.

Louis Diemschutz was a trader of cheap jewellery and had for the previous six months been Steward of the Berner Street club. He had, as usual, spent the day at Westow Market in Crystal Palace. He drove his pony down Commercial Road and as he turned into Berner Street glanced at the clock outside the baker's shop on the corner, noticing that it was 1.00pm. He intended to drop some goods off with his wife at the club before taking his pony and cart on to his stabling in George Yard:

> My pony is rather shy and as I turned into the yard it struck me that he bore too much towards the left hand side against the wall. I bent my head to see what it was shying at, and I noticed that the ground was not level. I saw a little heap which I thought might be some mud. I touched the heap with the handle of my whip, and then I found that it was not mud. I jumped off the trap and struck a match. When I saw that it was the body of a woman I ran indoors.[22]

Elizabeth Stride was laying on her back, almost against the wall near the gates, her head towards the rear of the building. Her face was turned towards the wall, mud on the left side and matting her hair. Her right arm was over her stomach, the hand and wrist covered with blood; the left was extended and the hand clutched a packet of cachous, several of which tumbled into the gutter when a doctor prized her fingers apart. According to the medical examiners, Stride's throat had been cut, the incision being 6 inches in length, commencing 2½ inches in a straight line below the angle of the jaw, and ¾ inch deep over an undivided muscle, then becoming deeper. The cut was very clean and deviated a little downwards. Death had resulted from the severance of the left carotid artery.

Over both shoulders there was a bluish discoloration that in the opinion of Dr. Frederick Blackwell had been caused 'by two hands pressing on the shoulders'. Dr. Phillips, who had charge of the post-mortem, gave it as his opinion that Stride had been seized by the shoulders and forced onto the ground, the murderer having then cut her throat from left to right. He thought that the murderer had 'a knowledge of where to cut the throat' and said that as the blood would have flowed away from the murderer and into the gutter the murderer would not necessarily have been bloodstained. That Stride was lying down when her throat was cut did not account for her bloodstained right hand and wrist, for which Dr. Phillips was unable to suggest an explanation. Dr. Blackwell, however, suggested that the murderer had been standing behind Stride and had grasped the back of the scarf Stride was wearing around her neck, pulling back her head. Stride would have instinctively reached for the front of the scarf with her hand and thus it would have been covered with blood as the knife severed the windpipe and sliced her throat. But this didn't explain the shoulder bruising.

Most notably, of course, was a complete absence of post-mortem mutilation. Either Stride was not murdered by Jack the Ripper, or, if she was, the killer had left the scene – perhaps disturbed by Diemschutz's pony and trap.

Having discovered the body, Diemschutz ran into the club looking for his wife:

> I did this because I knew she had rather a weak constitution. I saw my wife was sitting downstairs, and I at once informed the members that something had happened in the yard. I did not tell them whether the woman was murdered or drunk, because I did not then know. A member named Isaacs went down to the yard with me, and we struck a match. We saw blood right from the gate up the yard ... The woman seemed to be about twenty-seven or twenty-eight years old. She was a little bit better dressed, I should say, than the woman who was last murdered. Her clothes were not disarranged. She had a flower in the bosom of her dress. In one hand she had some grapes, and in the other some sweets. She was grasping them tightly. I had never seen her before.[23]

Diemschutz went into the yard with Isaac M. Kozebrodsky, familiarly known as Isaacs, followed by Morris Eagle, who recalled, 'As soon as I saw the blood I got very excited and ran away for the police. I did not touch the body'.[24] He returned to the yard with PC Lamb and PC Collins. Diemschutz, meanwhile, had run off with another man in search of a policeman and couldn't find one. They returned to the club followed by a man named Edward Spooner, who had been attracted by their commotion and asked what was happening. There were about 15 people in the yard. Somebody struck a match and Spooner lifted the chin of the woman. He said that she had a piece of paper doubled up in her hand (the packet of cachous) and that there was a white and red flower pinned to her jacket. He thought that maybe five minutes had passed between his arrival and the return of Morris Eagle with the two policemen, who viewed the body. PC Collins then went to fetch the doctor whilst Morris Eagle was despatched to fetch assistance from the police station.

PC Collins reached the residence of Drs Kay and Blackwell at 100 Commercial Road. Dr. Blackwell was asleep, but was roused by his assistant Edward Johnston and informed of what had been discovered. Johnston returned with Collins to Berner Street, followed by Dr. Blackwell, who arrived at Berner Street at precisely 1.16am. Dr. Blackwell estimated that Stride had been dead for 20–30 minutes by the time he arrived – placing death between 12.45am and 1.00am.

A rapid succession of people now descended on Berner Street, among them Dr. George Bagster Phillips and assorted senior police-men. Over the next few hours various premises were searched, people questioned and clothes examined. At 4.30am the body of Elizabeth Stride was removed to the mortuary. By 5.00am the police had con-cluded their initial enquiries. At 5.30am PC Collins washed away all traces of blood.

From 7.00pm on Saturday night – when dressed up and looking cheerful, she left Flower and Dean Street – until shortly after 1.00am on Sunday morning, when her body was found lying in the mud and dirt of a Berner Street passage, Elizabeth Stride's movements are unknown. Four hours, from 7.00pm to 11.00pm, are a complete blank. It was raining heavily and Stride may have stayed indoors, but no publican or pub customers are known to have come forward to say they had seen her or spent time with her. We know that it was prob-ably during this time that she had a meal of cheese and potato, the remains of which were found in her stomach. But from 11.00pm onwards there are several sightings of varying reliability.

She may have spent some time before 11.00pm drinking with a man in a pub called the Bricklayer's Arms in nearby Settles Street. A jour-nalist for *The Evening News* met three men at the mortuary who had gone there to view the body, believing that Stride was the woman they had seen with a man in or just outside the Bricklayer's Arms in Settles Street. One of them, J. Best, told the journalist:

> I was in the Bricklayer's Arms, Settles Street, about two hundred yards from the scene of the murder on Saturday night, shortly before eleven, and

saw a man and a woman in the doorway. They had been served in the public house, and went out when me and my friends came in. It was raining very fast, and they did not appear willing to go out. He was hugging her and kissing her, and as he seemed a respectably dressed man, we were rather astonished at the way he was going on with the woman, who was poorly dressed. We 'chipped' him, but he paid no attention. As he stood in the doorway he always threw sidelong glances into the bar, but would look nobody in the face. I said to him 'Why don't you bring the woman in and treat her?' but he made no answer. If he had been a straight fellow he would have told us to mind our own business, or he would have gone away. I was so certain there was something up that I would have charged him if I could have seen a policeman. When the man could not stand the chaffing any longer he and the woman went off like a shot soon after eleven.

I have been to the mortuary, and I am almost certain the woman there is the one we saw at the Bricklayer's Arms. She is the same slight woman, and seems the same height. The face looks the same, but a little paler, and the bridge of the nose does not look so prominent.

The man was about 5ft 5in in height. He was well-dressed in a black morning suit with a morning coat. He had rather weak eyes. I mean he had sore eyes without any eyelashes. I should know the man again amongst a hundred. He had a thick black moustache and no beard. He wore a black billycock hat, rather tall, and he had on a collar. I don't know the colour of his tie. I said to the woman 'that's Leather Apron getting round you'. The man was no foreigner; he was English right enough.[25]

Best was supported by a fellow drinker, John Gardner, who commented on a flower pinned to the woman's jacket and said 'Well, I have been to the mortuary and there she was with the dahlias on the right side of her jacket'.[26]

Whether the woman was Elizabeth Stride or not is uncertain.

Another unreliable sighting of Elizabeth Stride is that of a fruit-seller named Matthew Packer who claimed to have sold grapes to Elizabeth Stride, but he changed his story frequently and a recent analysis of the available evidence suggests that his story is a fabrication.[27]

The first reasonably reliable sighting of Elizabeth Stride we possess is therefore at about 11.45pm when labourer William Marshall went to the front door of his lodging at 64 Berner Street and saw outside number 63 a woman he identified as Elizabeth Stride with a man who kissed her and said, before walking off down the street, 'You would say anything but your prayers'. The man, said Marshall, was about

5ft 6in, middle aged, stout, clean shaven, and dressed in a small black coat, dark trousers and a round cap with a peak like sailors wear.[28]

Saturday slipped into Sunday and the heavy rain moved inland, which probably cheered PC William Smith as he turned into Berner Street from Commercial Road and began his weary beat along the same side of the road as the club. It was about 12.30 or 12.35am and as he drew near to the club he noticed a man and a woman talking on the opposite side of the road. The woman had a red flower pinned to her jacket. He felt certain the woman was Elizabeth Stride, he later said, having viewed the body in the mortuary. Her companion, to whom he paid little attention ('I didn't notice him much', he told the inquest) was aged about 28, was 5ft 7in, tall with a dark complexion and a small dark moustache. He was wearing a black diagonal coat, hard felt deerstalker's hat, white collar and tie.[29] PC Smith walked on.

Mrs. Fanny Mortimer, who lived with her husband at 36 Berner Street, told a reporter for *The Evening News*, 'that shortly before a quarter to one o'clock she heard the measured heavy tramp of a policeman passing the house on his beat. Immediately afterwards she went to the street door with the intention of shooting the bolts, though she remained standing there ten minutes before she did so'.[30] The only man she saw in Berner Street 'was a young man carrying a black shiny bag who walked very fast down the street from the Commercial Road. He looked up at the club, and then went round the corner by the board school ...'. We know who this man was, which means that we know Mrs. Mortimer's story is true. He was named Leon Goldstein and he visited Leman Street Police Station the day after the murder, identifying himself as the man who had walked down Berner Street shortly before Stride's body was discovered, that his bag contained empty cigarette boxes and that he had left a coffee house in Spectacle Alley a short time before. Mrs. Mortimer went back inside her house and five or six minutes later heard Louis Diemschutz's pony and cart pass by. A short time later she also heard the commotion following the discovery of Elizabeth Stride's body.[31]

Several other people were in the yard of the Berner Street club, in the passage running alongside the house, or in the street. Charles Letchford, who lived at 30 Berner Street, walked up the road at about 12.30am: 'Everything seemed to me to be going on as usual, and my sister was standing at the door at ten minutes to one, but did not see anyone pass by. I heard the commotion when the body was found, and heard the policeman's whistle, but did not take any notice of the matter, as disturbances are very frequent at the club, and I thought it was only another row'.[32] William West, overseer of the *Arbeter Fraint* printing office, left the club at about 12.30am by the side entrance and went into the printing office to return some literature. The editor, Philip Krantz, was there reading. West returned to the club, again by the side entrance, and looked towards the gates. He saw nothing unusual, but admitted that he was short-sighted and might not have noticed the body if it was there.[33] At 12.35am Morris Eagle, having accompanied his young lady home, returned to the club, found the front door locked and went down the passage to the rear door. He didn't see anything, although it was very dark and it was possible that he might not have seen the body if it was there. Joseph Lave, at about 12.40am, went into the yard for a breath of fresh air and 'walked for five minutes or more'. He went 'as far as the street. Everything was very quiet at the time, and I noticed nothing wrong'. Five minutes later Israel Schwartz turned into Berner Street from Commercial Road. According to a police report by Chief Inspector Donald Swanson:

> 12.45am 30th Israel Schwartz of 22 Helen Street,[34] Backchurch Lane stated that at that hour on turning into Berner St. from Commercial Road & having got as far as the gateway where the murder was committed he saw a man stop & speak to a woman, who was standing in the gateway. The man tried to pull the woman into the street, but he turned her round & threw her down on the footway & the woman screamed three times, but not very loudly. On crossing to the opposite side of the street, he saw a second man standing lighting his pipe. The man who threw the woman down called out apparently to the man on the opposite side of the road 'Lipski' & then Schwartz walked away, but finding that he was followed by the second man he ran as far as the railway arch but the man did not follow so far. Schwartz cannot say whether the two men were together or known to each other. Upon being taken to the mortuary Schwartz identified the body as that of the woman he had seen & he thus describes the first man who threw the woman down: age about 30 ht. 5 ft. 5in. comp. fair, hair dark, small brown moustache, full face, broad shouldered, dress, dark jacket & trousers black cap with peak, had nothing in his hands. Second man age 35 ht. 5ft. 11 in. comp. fresh, hair light brown, moustache brown, dress dark overcoat, old black hard felt hat wide brim, had a clay pipe in his hand . . .
>
> On the evening of 30th the man Schwartz gave the description of the man he had seen ten minutes later than the PC and it was circulated by wire. It will be observed that allowing for differences of opinion between

the PC and Schwartz as to apparent age & height of the man each saw with the woman whose body they both identified there are serious differences in the description of dress: thus the PC describes the dress of the man whom he saw as black diagonal coat, hard felt hat, while Schwartz describes the dress of the man he saw as dark jacket black cap with peak, so that it is at least rendered doubtful whether they are describing the same man.

If Schwartz is to be believed, and the police report of his statement casts no doubt upon it, it follows if they are describing different men that the man Schwartz saw & described is the more probable of the two to be the murderer, for a quarter of an hour afterwards the body is found murdered. At the same time account must be taken of the fact that the throat only of the victim was cut in this instance which measured by time, considering meeting (if with a man other than Schwartz saw) the time for the agreement & the murderous action would I think be a question of so many minutes, five at least, ten at most, so that I respectfully submit it is not clearly proved that the man that Schwartz saw is the murderer, although it is clearly the more probable of the two.[35]

Henry Matthews made an interesting marginal comment: 'The police apparently do not suspect the 2nd man whom Schwartz saw on the other side of the street & who followed Schwartz'. He also enquired as to the meaning of 'Lipski' and Inspector Abberline replied that,

since a Jew named Lipski was hanged for the murder of a Jewess in 1887 the name has very frequently been used by persons as mere ejaculation by way of endeavouring to insult the Jew to whom it has been addressed.[36]

It is to be doubted that Henry Matthews really needed reminding who Lipski was. Indeed, reading the name should have brought him out in a cold sweat as he recalled the whole ghastly episode of the year before, so he presumably wanted to know the context in which it was used. The importance of the question hasn't diminished over the years.

Was the word 'Lipski' directed at Schwartz or the second man, now commonly referred to as 'the pipeman'? If it was addressed at Schwartz, would this mean that the man assaulting the woman was not a Jew? Or was the man assaulting the woman trying to divert attention from himself to Schwartz, perhaps attempting to suggest that Schwartz had assaulted the woman? Or did 'the pipeman' call out 'Lipski', and if so was he addressing Schwartz or the man assaulting the woman? And since 'Lipski' on its own doesn't seem a sensible thing for anyone to have said, were there other words that Schwartz either didn't hear or didn't understand?

Inspector Abberline said that Israel Schwartz had 'a strong Jewish appearance' and that the insult 'was addressed to him as he stopped to look at the man he saw ill-using the deceased woman'. Confusingly, however, he also reported:

I questioned Israel Schwartz very closely at the time he made the statement as to whom the man addressed when he called Lipski, but he was unable to say. There was only one other person to be seen in the street, and that was a man on the opposite side of the road in the act of lighting a pipe.

On 1 October 1888 *The Star* picked up the Schwartz story and secured an interview:

Information which may be important was given to the Leman Street police yesterday by an Hungarian concerning this murder. This foreigner was well-dressed, and had the appearance of being in the theatrical line. He could not speak a word of English, but came to the police station accompanied by a friend, who acted as interpreter. He gave his name and address, but the police have not disclosed them. A *Star* man, however, got wind of his call, and ran him to earth in Backchurch Lane. The reporter's Hungarian was quite as imperfect as the foreigner's English, but an interpreter was at hand, and the man's story was retold just as he had given it to the police. It is, in fact, to the effect that he saw the whole thing.

It seems that he had gone out for the day, and his wife had expected to move, during his absence, from their lodgings in Berner Street to others in Backchurch Lane. When he came homewards about a quarter before one he first walked down Berner Street to see if his wife had moved. As he turned the corner from Commercial Road he noticed some distance in front of him a man walking as if partially intoxicated. He walked on behind him, and presently he noticed a woman standing in the entrance to the alleyway where the body was found. The half-tipsy man halted and spoke to her. The Hungarian saw him put his hand on her shoulder and push her back into the passage, but feeling rather timid of getting mixed up in quarrels, he crossed to the other side of the street. Before he had gone many yards, however, he heard the sound of a quarrel, and turned back to learn what was the matter, but just as he stepped from the kerb a second man came out of the doorway of the public house[37] a few doors off, and shouting out some sort of warning to the man who was with the woman, rushed forward as if to attack the intruder. The Hungarian states positively that he saw a knife in the second man's hand, but he waited to see no more. He fled incontinently, to his new lodgings.

He described the man with the woman as about 30 years of age, rather stoutly built, and wearing a brown moustache. He was dressed respectably in dark clothes and felt hat. The man who came at him with a knife he also describes, but not in detail. He says he was taller than the other, but not so stout, and that his moustaches were red. Both men seem to belong to the same grade of society. The police have arrested one man answering the description the Hungarian furnishes. This prisoner has not been charged, but is held for inquiries to be made. The truth of the man's statement is not wholly accepted.

The Star reported a slightly different version of Schwartz's story to that given in the police reports. The man is reported to have pushed Stride *into* the passage, not to have thrown her onto the pavement. It reports a quarrel between the woman and the man. Very significantly it is 'the pipeman' who is said to have shouted first – in which case 'the pipeman' addressed the man assaulting the woman as 'Lipski' – and to have produced a knife as Schwartz approached. No mention is made of the second man pursuing Schwartz.

Schwartz did not give evidence to the inquest, or if he did it was given *in camera*. A draft letter from Sir Robert Anderson to the Home Office contained in the files suggests that the latter is possible. Anderson wrote,

> 'With ref. to yr letter &c. I have to state that the opinion arrived at in this Dept. upon the evidence of *Schwartz at the inquest in Eliz. Stride's case* is that . . .' [my italics]

Any suggestion that Schwartz didn't appear at the inquest because the police had ceased to place credence in his story is dashed by the fact that the reports between Scotland Yard and the Home Office were written after the conclusion of the inquest. It is clear, therefore, that the story was believed throughout that time and the only reasonable explanation for his testimony not being reported in the newspapers is that Schwartz testified in private and was, one assumes, considered a very important witness.

It seems highly unlikely that two different women could have been assaulted in the same place or that the same woman could be assaulted twice in the same spot within fifteen minutes, therefore the probability is that the woman seen by Israel Schwartz *was* Elizabeth Stride and that the man who assaulted her *was* her murderer. The only reasonable alternative is that the assault was a common domestic, that the man who assaulted Stride left the scene and that another man, probably 'the pipeman', killed Stride. The surviving police documents don't mention 'the pipeman' as a suspect, and as was noted in the margin of Chief Inspector Swanson's report, the police did not appear to suspect him. Did the police therefore know who he was? We have no idea, but in later years Sir Robert Anderson would state that an eyewitness positively identified a Jack the Ripper suspect. Israel Schwartz and 'the pipeman' are two of the possible candidates.

It is a remote possibility that the woman was not Elizabeth Stride, but a dock labourer named James Brown was returning home about 12.45am when he saw a man and a woman standing outside the board school in Fairclough Street. Brown, who was almost certain that the woman was Elizabeth Stride, heard her say, 'No. Not tonight. Some other night', and he turned to look. The man was about 5ft 7in, stout

Witness	Time	Description
J. Best and John Gardner	11.00pm	5ft 5in, thick black moustache, no beard, weak, sore eyes, no eyelashes, wearing a black morning suit with a morning coat, a collar and tie, and a billycock hat. He was English in appearance.
William Marshall	11.45pm	Middle aged, 5ft 6in, stout, clean shaven, small, black cutaway coat, dark trousers, round cap with a peak like sailors wear.
Matthew Packer	12.00 – 12.30pm	Aged 25–30, 5ft 7in, black frock coat buttoned, soft felt hawker hat.
PC William Smith	12.30am	Aged 28, 5ft 7in, clean shaven, dark clothes, hard dark felt deerstalker hat.
James Brown	12.45am	5ft 7in, stout, long black diagonal coat which reached almost to his heels.
Israel Schwartz	12.45am	First man: aged 30, 5ft 5in, small brown moustache, brown hair, fair complexion, dark jacket and trousers, black cap with peak. Second man: aged 35, 5ft 11in, light brown hair, dark overcoat, old black hard felt hat with a wide brim.

and wearing a long coat that very nearly reached his heels. He walked on and about 15 or 20 minutes later he heard cries of 'Police!' and 'Murder!'.[38] Brown almost certainly didn't see Elizabeth Stride. His description of the woman doesn't mention a flower, the man doesn't fit other descriptions of a man seen with a woman presumed to be Stride, and *The Evening News* of 1 October 1888 briefly mentioned that an unnamed young girl was standing with her boyfriend in an unspecified 'bisecting thoroughfare' for about 20 minutes from about 12.40am. It is reasonable to assume that this was the couple seen by Brown. The reported descriptions of all possible suspects are outlined above.

It is noticeable that William Marshall, PC Smith and Israel Schwartz all saw a man wearing a hat with a peak. Marshall and Smith's man was clean shaven, but Schwartz's had a moustache.

Notes

1. Leufstadius, Birgitta (1994) *Jack the Rippers Tredje Offer*. Partille: Warne Förlag. My appreciation to Birgitta Leufstadius and translator Edwin R. Nye. This biography of Elizabeth Stride deserves publication in English.
2. According to inquest testimony given by Charles Preston, who lodged at the same lodging house, and Michael Kidney, with whom she lived for several years. *The Times*, 4 October 1888.
3. The *Bywell Castle* sank without trace in the Mediterranean five years later.
4. *The Times*, 4 September 1878.
5. For a full account of the disaster see Thurston, Gavin (1965) *The Great Thames Disaster*. London: George Allen and Unwin.
6. *Manchester Guardian*, *The Evening News*, 8 October 1888.
7. Elizabeth Tanner, in her inquest testimony, said Elizabeth Stride had lodged there on and off for six years. *Daily Telegraph*, 4 October 1888.
8. *The Times*, 4 October 1888.
9. *The Times*, 4 October 1888.
10. Dr. Thomas Barnardo, who drew attention to the 'myriads of young people' forced to live in the common lodging houses 'abodes of poverty and of crime', wrote to *The Times* on 6 October (published in *The Times*, 9 October under the heading 'The Children of the Common Lodging Houses') recalled: 'Only four days before the recent murders I visited No. 32, Flower and Dean-street, the house in which the unhappy woman Stride occasionally lodged. I had been examining many of the common lodging-houses in Bethnal-green that night, endeavouring to elicit from the inmates their opinions upon a certain aspect of the subject. In the kitchen of No. 32 there were many persons, some of them being girls and women of the same unhappy class as that to which poor Elizabeth Stride belonged. The company soon recognised me, and the conversation turned upon the previous murders. The female inmates

of the kitchen seemed thoroughly frightened at the dangers to which they were presumably exposed ... One poor creature, who had evidently been drinking, exclaimed somewhat bitterly to the following effect: "We're all up to no good, and no one cares what becomes of us. Perhaps some of us will be killed next!" And then she added, "If anybody had helped the likes of us long ago we would never have come to this!" ... I have since visited the mortuary in which were lying the remains of the poor woman Stride, and I at once recognised her as one of those who stood around me in the kitchen of the common lodging-house on the occasion of my visit last Wednesday week'. If the woman who spoke thus was Elizabeth Stride, then she had gone to 32 Flower and Dean Street on 26 September, but the deputy there said specifically that Stride had stayed there 'only on Thursday and Friday nights' (*Daily Telegraph*, 4 October 1888).

11. *Manchester Guardian*, 2 October 1888.
12. Named Henriques Street after Sir Basil Lucas Quixano Henriques (1890–1961), who for a time lived in Toynbee Hall and in 1914 opened the Oxford and St. George's Club, which in 1930 moved from its original location in Cannon Street Road to the Bernhard Baron Settlement in Berner Street. He wrote his autobiography *The Indiscretions of a Warden* (London: Methuen, 1937) and is the subject of a biography: Lowe, L.L. (1976) *Basil Henriques*. London: Routledge and Kegan Paul.
13. Eyges, Thomas B. (1944) *Beond The Horizon*. Boston, Massachusetts: Group Free Society. An unusual autobiography written in a singularly modest and pleasing style. Well worth reading.
14. *Arbeter Fraint*, no. 1, 15 July 1885, editorial.
15. Fishman, William J. (1975) *East End Jewish Radicals 1875–1914*. London: Duckworth, p.154. Professor Fishman's singular book is a highly recommended account of this fascinating and little appreciated subject.
16. Sir Samuel Montagu, later Baron Swathling, was a radical Liberal MP and determinedly orthodox, who was widely known for his charity: he gave 26 acres of land in Tottenham to the London County Council to build homes to ease overcrowding in Whitechapel; was co-founder of the Jewish Board of Guardians; founder in 1876 of the Jewish Working Men's Club 'for Anglicising the Jews of the East End ...'; was an authority on immigration and a member of the Commons Select Committee on Alien Immigration in 1888. And as if that wasn't enough he was a skilled fly-fisherman.
17. Eyges, Thomas B., *op. cit.*, p.81. Eyges described Philip Krantz, whose real name was Jacob Rombro, as 'a highly educated man, a linguist and a fine journalist'. He was born in Podolia in 1858 and left Russia during the pogroms of 1881, coming to London by way of Paris. He emigrated to the United States in 1889, where he edited *Arbeter Zeitung* in New York. For a fuller account of Rombro/Krantz see Zinna, Eduardo (2002) 'A Passion for Justice and the Berner Street Club', *Ripperologist*, 39.
18. It wasn't wooden.
19. It was in fact three storeys.

20. Eyges, Thomas B., *op. cit.*, pp.79–83.
21. Mackay, John Henry (1891) *The Anarchists: A Picture of Civilisation at the Close of the 19th Century*. Boston: Benj. R. Tucker. New York: Autonomedia, 1999, p.113.
22. *Manchester Guardian*, 1 October 1888; *The Times*, 2 October 1888.
23. *Daily Telegraph*, 1 October 1888.
24. *Manchester Guardian*, 1 October 1888.
25. *The Evening News*, 1 October 1888.
26. *The Evening News*, 1 October 1888.
27. It seems that the Vigilance Committee and several newspapers had hired two private detectives, a man calling himself Le Grand and a J.H. Batchelor, who had offices at 283 Strand. They interviewed two ladies, a Mrs. Rosenfield and her sister Miss Eva Harstein of 14 Berner Street, who claimed that they had seen a blood-caked grape stalk and some white flower petals in the passage before the police had washed it down. The detectives had probed the drain in the yard and among the gunge had found a grape stalk. Le Grand and Batchelor then questioned Packer, who told them his story about selling grapes to a man and a woman and who, on being taken to the mortuary, identified the woman as Elizabeth Stride. Packer proceeded to recite the story, but gave different details, particularly regarding the time he sold the grapes.

The facts, however, are that Sergeant Stephen White interviewed Packer about 9.00am on the morning of the murder, 30 September, and Packer told him that he wasn't doing any business because of the rain and had shut up shop early, about 11.30pm. 'I saw no one standing about, neither did I see anyone go up the yard. I never saw anything suspicious or heard the slightest noise. And I knew nothing about the murder until I heard of it this morning'. The sudden heavy rain had come on about 9.05pm and continued until after midnight, but we know that it rained very little on Whitechapel after 11.00pm, Stride, if it was Stride, having sheltered from the end of it when leaving the Bricklayer's Arms. None of those leaving the Berner Street club from 11.30pm onwards mentioned that it was raining – and significantly, Packer never mentioned seeing any of them leave – and Dr. Blackwell noted that Stride's clothes were not wet from the rain. From all of which it seems evident that Packer shut up shop because of the rain, which would in fact be before 11.00pm. In addition, Stride's clothes were not wet. They would have been if she'd bought grapes from Packer whilst it was raining.

As for Stride having been holding grapes or grape stalks when she was found, although the man who would find the body, Louis Deimschutz, told a journalist (see *Daily Telegraph* and *The Evening News*, 1 October 1888) that Stride's tightly clenched hands held sweets in one and grapes in the other. Two men who were among the first on the scene, Abraham Heahbury and Edward Spooner respectively, said, 'In her hand there was a little piece of paper containing five or six cachous' and Stride had only a 'piece of paper doubled up in her right hand'. And at the inquest Dr. Phillips said that 'neither on the hands nor about the body did I find any grapes, or connection with them. I am convinced the deceased had not swallowed either the skin or seed of grape within many hours of death'. However, he did say that on the larger of two handkerchiefs found on the body he found stains that he believed to be of fruit.

Perhaps the clearest indication that the whole story is a fabrication is that Le Grand was a crook. In 1877 he had been convicted for a series of thefts (he was an inveterate shoplifter) and was sentenced to a remarkably stiff eight years in prison. By 1888 he had reinvented himself as Le Grand and set up business in the Strand, but by June 1889 was again in trouble with the law, this time for sending threatening letters demanding money from a Harley Street surgeon named A. Malcolm Morris. He received a sentence of two years with hard labour. In 1891 he was again charged, this time under the name of Charles Grant, of sending letters to various wealthy women threatening to kill them if they did not pay him substantial sums of money. Le Grand appears in reality to have been a Dane named Christian Briscony, possibly the son of a Danish diplomat or someone connected with the Danish diplomatic service, and who variously called himself Nelson, Le Grand, Grant, 'French Colonel' and Captain Anderson. He was, it would seem, suffering from a mental illness since he did not need money when he made the threats.

An excellent analysis of the Packer story by Dave Yost is to be found in Chisholm, Alex, DiGrazia, Christopher Michael and Yost, Dave (2002) *The News From Whitechapel: The Whitechapel Murders in the Daily Telegraph*. Jefferson, North Carolina: McFarland and Company. For an account of Le Grand, see Nixon, Gerry (1998) 'Le Grand of the Strand', *Ripperologist*, issue 18, August, who provides full sourcing.

28. *The Times,* 6 October 1888.
29. *The Times,* 6 October 1888; HO 144/A49301C 8a.
30. *The Evening News,* 1 October 1888.
31. *The Evening News,* 1 October 1888; Report by Chief Inspector Donald Swanson, 19 October 1888, HO/144/221/A49301C 8a. Mrs. Mortimer's story has been the subject of some confusion because it was reported that she had been at her door for half an hour, this error resulting from her claim that she had gone to her door shortly after hearing the measured tread of a policeman passing by. As the only policeman known to have passed up Berner Street was PC William Smith at or shortly after 12.30am, it was assumed that Mrs. Mortimer must have gone to the door at that time. But had she done so then she would have seen other people in the street: the couple seen by PC Smith, Charles Letchford, who passed through the street at 12.30am, Morris Eagle returning to the club at 12.35am, Joseph Lave on his stroll at or about 12.40am, and the assault on a woman outside the club at 12.45am. That she saw none of these people – and none of these people said they saw her – suggests that her original timings were correct and that either PC Smith walked up the street later than he thought or that the footfalls heard by Mrs. Mortimer were not those of a policeman. Goldstein's statement puts

Mrs. Mortimer in the street for ten minutes immediately prior to 1.00am and corroboration might be provided by Charles Letchford if Mrs. Mortimer was his sister (although her maiden name, Skipp, suggests that she wasn't; if she wasn't then we would have two women at their front doors for ten minutes prior to 1.00am).

32. *Illustrated Police News*, 6 October 1888.

33. *The Times*, 2 October 1888.

34. Should read Ellen Street.

35. Report by Chief Inspector Donald Swanson, 19 October 1888; HO 144/221/A49301C 8a.

36. Report by Inspector Abberline, 1 November 1888; MEPO 3/140 fol. 204–6.

37. This was the Nelson at 26 Berner Street at the junction between Berner Street and Fairclough Street, owned by Louis Hagens, who is listed in the Trade Directory as a 'beer retailer', meaning that he was not licensed to sell spirits. In one version of the story the man had been standing in the pub doorway; in *The Star* he had come out of the pub.

38. *The Times*, 6 October 1888.

chapter eleven

CATHARINE EDDOWES

He was aged about 30, 5ft 7in or 5ft 8in, tall with a fair complexion and a fair moustache. He was wearing a pepper-and-salt loose jacket, red neckerchief and grey cloth cap with a peak. He had the appearance of a sailor.[1]

This was how Joseph Lawende described a man he saw talking with Catharine Eddowes shortly before her horribly mutilated body was found in the a corner of Mitre Square and it bears such a striking similarity to the description of the man seen by Israel Schwartz assaulting Elizabeth Stride that it is difficult not to believe the men are not one and the same. Schwartz described the man he saw as aged 30, 5ft 5in, small brown moustache, brown hair, a fair complexion, and wearing a dark jacket and trousers and a black cap with a peak.

Catharine Eddowes was born on 14 April 1842 at Graisley Green, Wolverhampton, the daughter of a tinplate worker named George Eddowes and his wife Catharine (née Evans), and she went to London the following year with her parents, brothers and sisters. In 1855 her mother died. Her father died just before Christmas two years later. Catharine, the younger of what had grown to be a family of 11 was admitted as an orphan to Bermondsey Workhouse. In due course she returned to Wolverhampton, where her Aunt Elizabeth had secured her a job, but soon had to leave the job, apparently for stealing. Thereafter she split her time between a job in Birmingham and living with a relative in Wolverhampton. At some point she took up with a man named Thomas Conway and lived with him as his common law wife. Two children were born, then they moved to London and a third child was born. But Catharine's heavy drinking had become alcoholism, which no doubt fed what was described as her fiery temperament, and the relationship began to deteriorate. From the black eyes and bruises Catharine sometimes bore it was obviously violent. Her daughter, Annie, said that 'before they actually left each other she was never with him for twelve months at a time, but would go away for two or three months ...'.[2] Annie also said that she had fallen out with her mother because of the latter's drinking. By 1880 the relationship had collapsed completely and the couple parted company in 1881.

It seems that by 1881 Catharine Eddowes was living at Cooney's Lodging House at 55 Flower and Dean Street, almost immediately forming a relationship with a man she met there. He was named John Kelly and for about 12 years had enjoyed fairly regular employment by a fruit salesman named Lander at the market. Kelly seems to have been a thoroughly decent sort, 'quiet and inoffensive ... [with] sharp and intelligent eyes', but he was suffering with a kidney complaint and had a bad cough.

Catharine, variously described as an intelligent and scholarly woman, 'was not often in drink and was a very jolly woman, often singing'. She was not known to be in the habit of walking the streets or known to have been intimate with anybody but John Kelly.[3] Kelly said that he did not know that Eddowes engaged in prostitution, and whilst admitting that she sometimes drank to excess, he said she was not in the habit of doing so. This said, Catharine had been charged at the Thames Magistrates' Court with being drunk, disorderly and using bad language (she was discharged without a fine) and several of her children refused to have anything to do with her because she persistently demanded money from them. Her daughter Annie had moved several times, never leaving a forwarding address, in the apparent hope of escaping Catharine.

Every year Eddowes and Kelly joined the traditional East End pilgrimage to Kent to pick hops. In the 1880s something in the region of 66,000 acres was given over to growing hops and the picking season – when the hop farmers hired casual labour – was an opportunity for thousands of city-dwellers to enjoy a paid 'holiday' in the countryside. It was estimated that between 50,000 and 60,000 people went to pick hops in a good season.[4] In 1888 Kelly and Eddowes went to Hunton – 'We didn't get on any too well and started to hoof it home. We came along in company with another man and woman who had worked in the same fields, but who parted with us to go to Chatham when we turned off towards London. The woman said to Kate, "I have got a pawn ticket for a flannel shirt. I wish you'd take it since you're going up to town. It is only for 2d, and it may fit your old man". So Kate took it and we trudged along ...'. They stopped off in

Maidstone. Kelly bought a pair of boots from Arthur Pash in the bustling High Street and Eddowes bought a jacket from a nearby shop.[5] She would be wearing it when she encountered Jack the Ripper. These purchases exhausted their funds – 'We did not have money enough to keep us going till we got to town, but we did get there, and came straight to this house. Luck was dead against us . . . we were both done up for cash. . .'.[6]

They reached London on the afternoon of Thursday 27 September 1888, and slept that night in the casual ward. The next day John Kelly got some work and earned 6d. He gave Eddowes 4d and told her to get a bed at their lodging house at 55 Flower and Dean Street, but Eddowes insisted that he take the money and she would get a bed in the casual ward in Shoe Lane. They parted company between 3.00pm and 4.00pm and Eddowes went to the casual ward. The Superintendent there later told a remarkable story to the *East London Observer*, saying that Eddowes was well known there but had not stayed there for some time. Eddowes had said that she'd been hopping in the country, but said, 'I have come back to earn the reward offered for the apprehension of the Whitechapel murderer. I think I know him'. The Superintendent cautioned Eddowes to take care that he did not murder her. 'Oh, no fear of that', replied Eddowes.[7] Eddowes left the casual ward very early the following morning, apparently having been turned out following some unspecified trouble there. By 8.00am she was back at 55 Flower and Dean Street. Without money they decided to pawn Kelly's new boots and Eddowes did so for 2s 6d with a broker named Smith in Church Street in the name of 'Jane Kelly', giving her address as Dorset Street. With this money Kelly and Eddowes bought some food, tea and sugar. Between 10.00am and 11.00am they were seen eating breakfast in the lodging house kitchen by Wilkinson, the deputy lodging housekeeper. They then went drinking, Kelly barefoot. By the end of lunchtime they were broke again and Eddowes decided to see if she could scrounge some money from her daughter in Bermondsey. At 2.00pm she and Kelly parted company in Houndsditch, Eddowes promising to be back home no later than 4.00pm. 'I never knew if she went to her daughter's at all', said Kelly, 'I only wish to God she had, for we had lived together for a long while, and never had a quarrel'.[8]

The daughter in Bermondsey was Annie. Annie told the inquest that she had last seen her mother two years and one month ago (during her last confinement), but added that she had moved a couple of times and purposefully left no forwarding address, and had done so because her mother was a persistent scrounger. If Eddowes was indeed a persistent scrounger then presumably she would have tried to contact her daughter sometime in the past two years and discovered that she no longer lived in Bermondsey. So was Eddowes really planning to visit Annie that afternoon? And if not, where did she intend going? And where, indeed, did she go? Did she have reasons of her own for being away from Kelly for a few hours? Did she really have an idea about the identity of Jack the Ripper?

We don't know what Catharine Eddowes did after she left Kelly at 2.00pm, other than that she drank a lot of alcohol. We don't know who she drank it with, where she drank it or where she got the money to buy it, but we know that at 8.30pm she was found incapably drunk by a City of London policeman, PC Louis Robinson, on his beat in Aldgate High Street. With the assistance of a fellow constable, PC Simmons, he managed to get Eddowes to the Bishopsgate Police Station, where nothing sensible could be got from her and she was placed in a cell by the Station Sergeant, James Byfield, to sleep it off. It possibly says something for Eddowes' constitution as far as alcohol was concerned that at 12.55am she was deemed sober enough to be brought from the cells and released, having first given her name as 'Mary Ann Kelly' and given her address as 6 Fashion Street.

As with Mary Ann Nichols' 'jolly bonnet' and Elizabeth Stride's borrowed clothes brush, Catharine Eddowes has a moment of pathos which came as she left the police station, precisely at 1.00am, just when Stride's body was being discovered in Berner Street. Heading towards the swing door opening onto the passage leading to the street, Eddowes remarked, 'I shall get a damned fine hiding when I get home'.

'And serve you right. You had no right to get drunk', said PC George Hutt, opening the swing door. 'This way, missus', he said, and as Eddowes headed towards the street door, 'Please pull it to'.

'All right', replied Eddowes, 'Good night, old cock'. Eddowes pulled the door almost closed.

Curiously she was seen to turn left, apparently heading for Houndsditch, the opposite direction to Flower and Dean Street. Her body would be found in Mitre Square, no more than a ten minute walk away, at 1.45am. Where did she spend those 45 minutes? PC Edward Watkins passed through Mitre Square on his beat at 1.30am and was absolutely positive Eddowes' body was not there at that time.

At 1.35am Joseph Lawende, Joseph Hyam Levy and Harry Harris left the Imperial Club at 16–17 Duke Street and, passing the entrance to Mitre Square, felt certain they had seen a women they identified as Eddowes standing there with a man. Coincidentally Joseph Levy had earlier remarked that Mitre Square should be watched, and with this in mind Joseph Lawende, a little ahead of the others, glanced at the couple as he passed by. The man and woman were about 9 or 10 feet away, the woman standing with her face towards the man, so that Lawende only saw her back. She had one hand on the man's breast. The man was taller than the woman, 'looked rather rough and shabby', and was wearing a cloth cap with a peak of the same material. The woman was wearing a black jacket and bonnet. He heard no conversation and although he took note of the couple, nothing about them aroused his interest enough to cause him to break his stride or look back.[9]

At the inquest Lawende was prevented from giving a full description of the man he'd seen, but the police had already issued a brief description:

> He was described as of shabby appearance, about 30 years of age and 5ft 9ins. in height, of fair complexion, having a small fair moustache and a cap with a peak.[10]

Detective Chief Inspector Donald Swanson added a note to the description held on Home Office files: 'For the purpose of comparison, this description is nearer to that given by Schwartz than to that given by the PC' [i.e. PC Smith in Berner Street].[11]

Lawende did not see the woman's face and could identify her as Catharine Eddowes only by her clothing, so the possibility remains that the woman was not Catharine Eddowes – and although he was able to give a fairly good description of the man, Lawende repeatedly stated that he would not be able to identify him again.

Joseph Hyam Levy and Harry Harris paid no attention to the couple, Levy thinking only that a couple standing at that time in the morning in a dark passage were not up to much good and remarking to Harry Harris, 'I don't like going home by myself when I see these sorts of characters about. I'm off'. He was unable to describe either of them.

There is a suspicion that Levy was being evasive. Questioned about what it was that prompted this remark, he wasn't able to say. Joseph Lawende had said he paid attention to the man and the woman because Joseph Hyam Levy had remarked that the passage and square should be watched. Yet Levy, who had made this remark, apparently hurried past without taking note of either the woman or the man. He also seemed sufficiently alarmed by the couple to comment on them unfavourably to Harry Harris, yet they were doing nothing to attract attention or cause concern. Perhaps Levy simply found their presence there disturbing or he was offended by what he supposed them to be up to. Nevertheless, there is a distinct feeling that something was going on behind the scenes. Even the newspapers picked up on it, *The Evening News* commenting about Lawende and Levy:

> They [the police] have no doubt themselves that this was the murdered woman and her murderer. And on the first blush of it the fact is borne out by the police having taken exclusive care of Mr. Joseph Levander [sic], to a certain extent having sequestrated him and having imposed a pledge on him of secrecy. They are paying all his expenses, and one if not two detectives are taking him about. One of the two detectives is Foster. Mr. Henry Harris [sic], of the two gentlemen our representative interviewed, is the more communicative. He is of the opinion that neither Mr. Levander nor Mr. Levy saw anything more than he did, and that was only the back of the man. Mr. Joseph Levy is absolutely obstinate and refuses to give the slightest information. He leaves one to infer that he knows something, but he is afraid to be called on the inquest. Hence he assumes a knowing air.[12]

In the immediate aftermath of the inquiry the police were very uncooperative, to the point at which several newspapers commented on it. *The Evening News* remarked: 'The police are extraordinarily reticent with reference to the Mitre Square tragedy'; the *Yorkshire Post* reported, 'The police apparently have strict orders to close all channels of information to members of the press'; and even the distant *New York Times* complained that the police 'devote their entire energies to preventing the press from getting at the facts. They deny to reporters a sight of the scene or bodies, and give them no information whatever'.[13] Then all of a sudden the silence was lifted. The *Manchester Guardian* reported, 'the barrier of reticence which has been set up on all occasions when the representatives of the newspaper press have been brought into contact with the police authorities for the purpose of obtaining information for the use of the public has been suddenly withdrawn, and instead of the customary stereotyped negatives and disclaimers of the officials, there has ensued a marked disposition to afford all necessary facilities for the publication of details and an increased courtesy towards the members of the press concerned'.[14]

At 1.40am PC James Harvey went down Duke Street, turned into Church Passage and went as far as the entrance to Mitre Square. He told the inquest, 'I saw no one. I heard no cry or noise'. Whoever the couple may have been that Lawende, Levy and Harris had seen, they had moved on soon afterwards. Had they gone off together? Was it Eddowes and her murderer and were they shrouded by the night in Mitre Square as PC Harvey stood at the entrance?

At 1.45am PC Watkins entered Mitre Square, where he discovered the body of Catharine Eddowes in a dark corner. Without touching the body he ran across to some warehouses and roused George Morris, a former policeman who was now night watchman there.

'For God's sake mate, come out and assist me', shouted Watkins.

Morris grabbed a lamp and went outside. 'What's the matter?' he asked.

'Another woman has been cut to pieces.'

Morris went over to the body, shone his lamp on it and ran off for assistance, bumping into PC Harvey in Aldgate. Harvey summoned PC Holland who was across the street and they returned to Mitre Square. PC Holland then dashed off to nearby Jewry Street to fetch Dr. George William Sequeira who arrived at 1.55am. About that time Inspector Edward Collard at Bishopsgate Police Station received news of the murder and headed for Mitre Square, first sending a constable to fetch the police surgeon, Dr. Frederick Gordon Brown. Collard arrived at the Square at 2.03am, Dr. Brown arrived a few minutes later. Various bigwigs descended on the area thereafter, among them Superintendent McWilliam, Superintendent Foster and Major Henry Smith, who wrote in his autobiography:

> The night of Saturday September 29, found me tossing about in my bed at Cloak Lane Station, close to the river and adjoining Southwark Bridge ... Suddenly the bell at my head rang violently. 'What is it?' I asked, putting my ear to the tube. 'Another murder sir, this time in the City.' Jumping up, I was dressed and in the street in a couple of minutes.[15]

Catharine Eddowes' throat had been cut through to the bone, death being immediate and caused by a haemorrhage following severance of the left common carotid artery. Post-mortem mutilation was extraordinary. Her face was terribly mutilated, her eyes, nose, lips and cheek ferociously attacked, the lobe and the auricle of the right ear cut obliquely through – a piece of ear dropped from her clothing when she was undressed at the mortuary – and the tip of the nose cut off.

There were two curious inverted 'v' cuts under each eye. The intestines had been pulled from the body and placed over the right shoulder, about two feet cut away completely and placed between the body and the left arm, apparently by design. The left kidney and some of the womb were missing. Dr. Frederick Gordon Brown commented, 'I should say that someone who knew the position of the kidney must have done it'. He went on to say that the killer must have possessed 'a good deal of knowledge as to the position of the organs in the abdominal cavity and the way of removing them'. He acknowledged that the required knowledge would have been possessed by a person accustomed to cutting up animals. This agreed pretty much with the professional opinion of Dr. George Bagster Phillips, who according to a police report said that there was 'no evidence of anatomical knowledge in the sense it so far evidenced the hand of a qualified surgeon ... the murder could have been committed by a person who had been a hunter, a butcher, a slaughterman, as well as a student in surgery or a properly qualified surgeon'. Drs Saunders and Sequeira said they didn't think the injuries indicated that the killer possessed great anatomical skill.

A distinction is made between anatomical knowledge and surgical skill. The murderer apparently had a good working knowledge of the former but exhibited little or no evidence of the latter, although it is uncertain how much allowance was made for the speed and conditions under which the killer was working.

Meanwhile another important incident in the Ripper story had unfolded in nearby Goulston Street. At 2.20am PC Alfred Long, one of the many policeman drafted into the East End to help the police, had walked along Goulston Street and noticed nothing to excite his attention. At 2.55am his beat brought him back into Goulston Street and this time he noticed a piece of apron on a common stairway leading to 118–119 Wentworth Model Dwellings. On the wall above where the apron lay there was a message written in white chalk. The apron looked to be stained with blood and it would later be positively shown to be a piece of the apron worn by Catharine Eddowes. The murderer had evidently torn or cut away the piece and taken it with him when he left Mitre Square and had used it to wipe his hands or his knife, discarding it in Goulston Street as he (apparently) headed back into the East End.

The white chalked message was on the black brickwork of the stairway. What it actually said is disputed[16] but the generally accepted reading is, 'The Juwes are the men that will not be blamed for nothing'. The meaning is uncertain, but seems to mean that the Jews were not the people who would tolerate being blamed for something they didn't do. If written by the murderer he may have intended it to indicate that he was responding to some real or imagined offence to his race or religion – i.e., that the murders were being committed in response to false accusations.

Superintendent Thomas Arnold of the Metropolitan Police explained in a report:

> Knowing in consequence of suspicion having fallen upon a Jew named John Pizer alias 'Leather Apron', having committed a murder in Hanbury Street a short time previously, a strong feeling existed against the Jews generally, and as the building upon which the writing was found was situated in the midst of a locality inhabited principally by that sect, I was apprehensive that if the writing were left it would be the means of causing a riot and therefore considered it desirable that it should be removed having in view the fact that it was in such a position that it would have been rubbed by the shoulders of persons passing in & out of the Building. Had only a portion of the writing been removed the context would have remained. An Inspector was present by my instructions with a sponge for the purpose of removing the writing when the Commissioner arrived on the scene.[17]

Commissioner Sir Charles Warren duly arrived at the scene and ordered the removal of the writing. City Police representatives protested, but Warren insisted and subsequently explained,

> A discussion took place whether the writing could be left covered up or otherwise or whether any portion of it could be left for an hour until it could be photographed, but after taking into consideration the excited state of the population in London generally at the time the strong feeling which had been excited against the Jews, and the fact that in a short time there would be a large concourse of the people in the streets and having before me the Report that if it was left there the house was likely to be wrecked (in which from my own observation I entirely concurred) I considered it desirable to obliterate the writing at once, having taken a copy of which I enclose a duplicate.[18]

It was never established that this piece of graffito was the work of the murderer. It was probably just one of the many pieces of graffiti that we're told adorned the streets.

> It was soon after the Hanbury Street murder that strange messages began to be chalked up on the walls in the vicinity of the crime. On a wall in a

passage running off Hanbury Street this terrible prophecy was read with awe by thousands of people:

THIS IS THE FOURTH. I WILL MURDER 16 MORE AND THEN GIVE MYSELF UP.

The public, ready by this time to believe anything, assumed that the man who inspired their dread could have written this message and others similar.

They may have been, but I very much doubt it. Far more likely that the writing was the work of mischievous minded people who obtained some grim pleasure in adding to the fears of an already demented people.

Unfortunately, the 'Ripper' messages were read by children as well as adults. Many of them became so nervous that they were afraid to go to school. Jack the Ripper became the children's bogey man.[19]

Compton Mackenzie recalled that as a child he had been terrified by stories of the Ripper:

> It was Jack the Ripper who first made the prospect of going to bed almost unendurable ... It would have been bad enough if I had only heard the talk about him ... Talk about Jack the Ripper was small talk compared with the hoarse voices of men selling editions of the *Star* or *Echo* as half a dozen of them, with posters flapping in front of them like aprons, would come shouting along the street the news of another murder in Whitechapel. 'Murder! Murder! Another horrible murder in Whitechapel. Another woman cut up to pieces in Whitechapel!'
>
> Whitechapel became a word of dread, and I can recall the horror of reading 'Whitechapel' at the bottom of the list of fares at the far end inside an omnibus. Suppose the omnibus should refuse to stop at Kensington High Street and go on with its passengers to Whitechapel?[20]

But as far as chalked messages on walls were concerned, Dew went on to make the very reasonable observation,

> Why should he fool around chalking things on walls when his life was imperilled by every minute he loitered?[21]

On the other hand, it is remarkable that two of the murders that night should have been committed close to clubs largely frequented by Jews, that both victims are said to have done occasional cleaning work for Jews, that in the one case there was a cry of 'Lipski!' and in the other that a piece of the victim's apron should have been dropped below a piece of graffito concerning the Jews.[22]

Notes

1. Report by Chief Inspector Donald Swanson, 19 October 1888. HO 144/221/A49301C/8b.

2. Annie Philips, quoted in the *Wolverhampton Chronicle*, 10 October 1888.

3. Frederick William Wilkinson, the deputy of Cooney's lodging house. *The Times*, 5 October 1888. Coroner's Inquests (L) 1888, no. 135, Corporation of London Records Office.

4. See Ford, Colin and Harrison, Brian (1983) *A Hundred Years Ago: Britain in the 1880s in Words and Photographs*. Harmondsworth, Middlesex: Penguin Books, quoting Mitchel, B.R. and Deane, Phyllis (1962) *Abstract of British Historical Statistics*. Cambridge: Cambridge University Press, p.78; Whitehead, George (1890) *Journal of the Royal Agricultural Society of England*, 3rd series, I, pp.323, 366; and Collins, E.T.J. (1976) 'Migrant Labour in British Agriculture in the Nineteenth Century', *Economic History Review*, February, pp.41–5. On hop picking, two easily available and informed guides are Filmer, Richard (1998) *Hops and Hop Picking*. Princes Risborough, Buckinghamshire: Shire Publications; and O'Neill, Gilda (1990) *Pull No More Bines*. London: The Women's Press.

5. *Daily Telegraph*, 4 October 1888.

6. *The Star*, quoted by various newspapers, including the *Yorkshire Post*, 4 October 1888.

7. *East London Observer*, 13 October 1888.

8. *The Star*, quoted by various newspapers, including the *Yorkshire Post*, 4 October 1888.

9. Coroner's Inquests (L) 1888, no. 135, Corporation of London Records Office. *Daily News*, 12 October 1888.

10. *The Times*, 2 October 1888.

11. Report by Chief Inspector Donald Swanson dated 19 October 1888. HO 144/221/A49301C/8a.

12. *The Evening News*, 9 October 1888.

13. *The Evening News, Yorkshire Post, New York Times*, 1 October 1888.

14. *Manchester Guardian*, 2 October 1888.

15. Smith, Major Henry (1910) *From Constable to Commissioner: The Story of Sixty Years, Most of Them Misspent*. London: Chatto and Windus, pp.149–50.

16. For example: 'The Juwes are not the men that will be blamed for nothing' (Detective Halse); 'The Juws are not the men to be blamed for nothing' (Frederick Foster, City of London Surveyor); 'The Jews shall not be blamed for nothing'. (*Pall Mall Gazette*, 8 October 1888.)

17. Thomas Arnold, report dated 6 November 1888, HO 144/221/A49301C/8c.

18. Sir Charles Warren to the Home Office, 6 November 1888, HO 144/221/A49301C.

19. Dew, Walter (1938) *I Caught Crippen: Memoirs of Ex-Chief Inspector Walter Dew CID*. London: Blackie and Son, p.126.

20. Mackenzie, Compton (1963) *My Life and Times: Octave One 1883–1891*. London: Chatto and Windus, pp.164–5.
21. Dew, Walter, *op. cit.*, p.137.
22. In later years the author Stephen Knight maintained that the 'Juwes' was the collective name for Jubelo, Jubela and Jubelum. These men, who murdered Grand Master Hiram Abiff at the time of the building of Solomon's Temple, featured in British Masonic rituals until 1814, but they were dropped during the major revision of the ritual between 1814 and 1816 and it is doubtful if many British Masons would even have known their names in 1888. In the United States the names were and are used. However, it appears that they were and are known as 'the Ruffians', not 'the Juwes'. 'Juwes' is not and apparently never has been a Masonic word, nor has 'Juwes' or any word approximating to it ever appeared in British, Continental or American Masonic rituals.

chapter twelve

DEAR BOSS

The appearance of East London early on the Sunday morning so soon as the news of the murders was known – and, indeed, all day – almost baffles description. At ten o'clock, Aldgate and Leadenhall-street, Duke-street, St. James'-place, and Houndsditch were all literally packed with human beings – packed so thick that it was a matter of utter impossibility to pass through. The babel of tongues as each inquired of the other the latest particulars, or the exact locality of the Aldgate murder, or speculated on the character or whereabouts of the murder, was simply deafening. Every window of every inhabited room in the vicinity was thrown open, for the better view of the inmates; and seats at these windows were being openly sold and eagerly bought. On the outskirts of this vast chattering, excited assemblage of humanity, costermongers, who sold everything in the way of edibles, from fish and bread to fruits and sweets, and newspaper vendors whose hoarse cries only added to the confusion of sounds heard on every hand, were doing exceedingly large trades.[1]

Thousands of people had gathered about Berner Street. The police cordoned off the entrances and posted men along the street. Reinforcements were brought in to protect the mortuary, and the entrances to Mitre Square were closed. Yet even so, reported the *East London Observer*, the crowd 'seemed to derive a kind of morbid satisfaction in standing even so near the scene of the tragedy of a few hours before, and in gazing with a kind of awe upon so much of the dull flagstones of the square as they could see'. The newspaper added that the crowds 'considerably diminished between two and four o'clock', which coincided with a public meeting which began at 3.00pm in Victoria Park under the chairmanship of Mr. Edward Barrow of the Bethnal Green Road. There were several speeches regarding the conduct of Sir Charles Warren and Home Secretary Matthews and a resolution was unanimously passed that 'it was high time both men should resign and make way for some other officers who would leave

no stone unturned for the purpose of bringing the murderer to justice'.[2] Thousands of people attended the meeting, which was but one
of four held in London that day.

Criticism of the police and particularly of Home Secretary
Matthews mounted following the announcement on 1 October by the
City Police that a reward of £500 would be paid for 'such information
as shall lead to the discovery and conviction of the murderer or murderers'. The Lord Mayor then offered in the name of the Corporation
of London a further reward of £500. George Lusk, the Chairman of
the Whitechapel Vilgilance Committee, pounced on the apparent
inequality between rich and poor in the matter of rewards, pointing
out that the Government had offered a reward for the capture of the
murderer of Lord Cavendish in Phoenix Park but refused to offer a
reward for the murderer of helpless and destitute prostitutes, and he
argued that a reward 'would convince the poor and humble residents
of the East End that the Government authorities are as much anxious
to avenge the blood of these unfortunate victims'.

Soon the press was crying for blood:

> It is rather hard upon Mr. Matthews that he, who has never proposed legis-
> lation for the reform of the City, nor indeed done anything by personal
> initiation of a remarkably useful character, should now be placed in this dif-
> ficulty by that unreformed Corporation he has done his best to protect. But
> if the £500 reward offered by the City for the apprehension of the
> Whitechapel murderer should be claimed, it may go hard with Mr.
> Matthews in regard to his refusal.[3]

> The Home Secretary now in office is a source of miserable weakness and dis-
> credit to the present administration. In the House of Commons he has been
> nothing more nor less than a fantastic failure. In the provinces he is scarcely
> known, even by name; and when the provincials do become aware of him,
> it is only to mistrust him and to express disrespectful and indignant aston-
> ishment that a Government, otherwise so capable and so popular, should
> drag with it a dead weight of so much vacillation, so much ineptitude, and
> so many frankly naive confessions of crass ignorance concerning things of
> which the most commonplace Home Secretary ought to be fully cognisant.[4]

> Mr. Matthews is a feeble mountebank, who would pose and simper over
> the brink of a volcano.[5]

Criticism of the police could hardly be worse than it was when the
sequence of murders began, but what must have seemed impossible
proved only too possible and once again police deficiencies and ineffi-

ciencies were paraded through the newspaper columns and letters pages amid dire warnings of panic and revolution. A press agency report repeated by numerous provincial newspapers warned:

> With each fresh murder in the Whitechapel series public alarm has been accentuated and unless something can soon be done to restore confidence in the detective powers of the police panic will be the result.[6]

Ironically, neither Matthews nor Warren were opposed to offering a reward. Henry Matthews' decision not to offer one was following a precedent set by Sir William Harcourt, the Home Secretary in Gladstone's Liberal Government. As Matthews explained to his secretary,

> I have never myself shared to the full extent the HO prejudice against rewards; nor have I thought Harcourt's reasoning on the subject at all conclusive. I am disposed to regret now that in the first instance I did not sacrifice to popular feeling and offer a considerable reward. But in as much as I did yield to the official view and refuse to make an offer and subsequently repeated the refusal, I feel that my hands are tied.

And when, on 3 October, Matthews had had a meeting with both Sir Charles Warren and James Monro, neither had advocated offering a reward, Warren having declared that, 'a reward was of no practical use; – that it would serve as 'eye-wash' for the public and nothing else'. It therefore came as something of a shock when Warren privately began to advocate a reward of £5,000 – a staggering amount. Matthews observed of Warren,

> For his own credit and that of the force it is imperative that some visible evidence of effort – of ingenuity – of vigorous and intelligent exertion – should be on record. Anybody can offer a reward and it is the first idea of ignorant people. But more is expected of the CID. Sir C.W. will not save himself, or put himself right with the public, by merely suggesting that.[7]

For his part Warren attributed his change of heart to the reward offered by the City and observed that, 'if other murders of a similar nature take place shortly, and I see no reason to suppose that they will not, the omission of the offer of a reward on the part of the Government may exercise a very serious effect upon the stability of the Government itself'.[8]

Warren's advocacy of a substantial reward may genuinely have been as a palliative to public feeling, but Matthews clearly thought the knives were out and that Warren was protecting his own back at Matthews' expense. It can hardly have helped the already strained relations between the two men. It is nevertheless interesting that Warren believed, as did the press, that Jack the Ripper could end Matthews' political career and even bring down the Government – an achievement that cannot be seriously laid at the door of many killers and an indication of just how serious these crimes really were.

Sir Robert Anderson, newly-appointed and absent head of the CID finally returned to England on 6 October. In his autobiography he commented that after the Chapman murder,

> The newspapers soon began to comment on my absence.[9] And letters from Whitehall decided me to spend the last week of my holiday in Paris, that I might be in touch with my office. On the night of my arrival in the French capital two more victims fell to the knife of the murder fiend; and the next day's post brought an urgent appeal from Mr. Matthews to return to London; and of course I complied.[10]

It is a slight mystery, perhaps capable of a simple solution, that if Anderson curtailed his holiday in the Alps in response to 'letters from Whitehall', why did he stop off in Paris for a week rather than return to London immediately? And if he received 'an urgent appeal from Mr. Matthews' on 1 October, why did he wait until 4 October before leaving? As has been remarked elsewhere,[11] in Paris at the same time as Anderson was a man named Richard Pigott, the central figure in a judicial Royal Commission due to open at the end of the month. To all intents and purposes this was set up to inquire into allegations in *The Times* that Irish Nationalist MP Charles Stewart Parnell was in league with Fenian terrorists. Anderson was somewhat involved in this entire debacle and it is interesting to speculate that he may have been in Paris for reasons other than health and holiday.[12]

Anderson writes that, arriving back in London,

> I found the Jack-the-Ripper scare in full swing. When the stolid English go in for a scare they take leave of all moderation and common sense. If nonsense were solid, the nonsense that was talked and written about those murders would sink a *Dreadnought*. The subject is an unsavoury one, and I must write about it with reserve.

He went on to explain,

> I spent the day of my return to town, and half the following night, in rein-vestigating the whole case, and next day I had a long conference on the subject with the Secretary of State and the Chief Commissioner of Police. 'We hold you responsible to find the murderer', was Mr. Matthews' greeting to me. My answer was to decline the responsibility. 'I hold myself responsible',

I said, 'to take all legitimate means to find him'. But I went on to say that the measures I found in operation were, in my opinion, wholly indefensible and scandalous; for these wretched women were plying their trade under definite Police protection. Let the Police of that district, I urged, receive orders to arrest every known 'street woman' found on the prowl after midnight, or else let us warn them that the Police will not protect them. Though the former course would have been merciful to the very small class of woman affected by it, it was deemed too drastic, and I fell back on the second.[13]

There is no evidence that any formal instruction was issued that prostitutes were no longer subject to police protection, but some, now lost, may well have been issued to the effect that they could not be protected if they walked the streets and took customers – any one of whom could have been the Ripper – into dark, secluded and lonely spots. If any such order was issued, it is the only action Anderson is known to have taken. And it is one he thought successful: 'However the fact may be explained, it is a fact that no other street murder in the "Jack the Ripper" series . . .'. Anderson specified 'street murder', the last of the crimes having been committed indoors.

In Anderson's absence Sir Charles Warren had appointed Chief Inspector Donald Swanson to oversee the Ripper inquiry. He was intelligent (a Greek and Latin scholar) and for a short time was a teacher before joining the Metropolitan Police. He was a very capable detective described as 'One of the best class of officers'[14] and 'a very capable officer with a synthetical turn of mind'.[15] In a report to the Home Office, Swanson described the efforts thus far taken by the police to find the murderer:

> 80,000 pamphlets to occupier were issued and a house to house enquiry made not only involving the result of enquiries from the occupiers but also a search by police & with a few exceptions – but not such as to convey suspicion – covered the area bounded by the City Police boundary on the one hand, Lamb St. Commercial St. Great Eastern Railway & Buxton St. then by Albert St. Dunk St. Chicksand St. & Great Garden St. to Whitechapel Rd. and then to the City boundary, under this head also Common Lodging Houses were visited & over 2000 lodgers were examined.
>
> Enquiry was also made by Thames Police as to sailors on board ships in Docks or river & extended enquiry as to asiatics present in London, about 80 persons have been detained at the different police stations in the Metropolis & their statements taken and verified by police & enquiry has been made into the movements of a number of persons estimated at upwards of 300 respecting whom communications were received by police & such enquiries are being continued.

Seventy six Butchers & Slaughterers have been visited & the characters of the men employed enquired into, this embraces all servants who had been employed for the past six months.

Enquiries have also been made as to the alleged presence in London of Greek Gipsies, but it was found that they had not been in London during the times of the previous murders.

Three of the persons calling themselves Cowboys[16] who belonged to the American Exhibition were traced & satisfactorily accounted for themselves.

Up to date although the number of letters daily is considerably lessened, the other enquiries respecting alleged suspicious persons continues as numerous.

There are now 994 Dockets besides police reports.

(sd) Donald S. Swanson

Ch. Inspr.[17]

Men were arrested for behaving suspiciously or when reported by members of the public – including a comical arrest of a journalist who attracted suspicion by being dressed in women's clothing. He hoped to attract Jack the Ripper's attention, but instead attracted the attention of a crowd in Lewisham (what was he doing trying to catch the East End murderer in Lewisham?) and had to be taken to the police station for his own protection.[18] Psychics and spiritualists offered such advice and assistance as they could, writing to the newspapers and even visiting the police. One group in Cardiff claimed to have been told by the spirit of Elizabeth Stride that a middle-aged man who lived off Commercial Street or Commercial Road and belonged to a gang consisting of 12 men had killed her.[19] At a séance in Bolton a medium described the Whitechapel murderer 'as having the appearance of a farmer, though dressed like a navvy, with a strap round his waist and peculiar pockets. He wears a dark moustache and bears scars behind the ear and in other places. He will, says the medium, be caught in the act of committing another murder'.[20] Robert James Lees, supposed Psychic by Appointment to Queen Victoria (which he certainly wasn't[21] – and who in recent years has popped up in some wilder theories about the Ripper's identity) apparently offered his services to the police, recording in his diary with disarming candour that he was variously called 'a fool and a lunatic', a 'madman and a fool', and on a third and final attempt received the 'same result' but did manage to obtain a promise that he would be contacted if his services were required. With much the same level of success, Sir Charles Warren investigated the possibility of using bloodhounds, which gave the press the opportunity to enjoy some humour at his expense and gave birth to some canards that have dogged Ripper studies ever since.

Elizabeth Stride was buried 'quietly and at the parish's expense' on the day of Anderson's return and on 8 October Catharine Eddowes was buried in a manner that she could never have anticipated in life. Eddowes made her last journey in a polished elm coffin with oak mouldings, borne in an open-glass hearse drawn by a pair of horses, followed by mourning coaches. The route was thronged with crowds of people and the cortège was conducted to the cemetery by the police. A Mr. Hawks, an undertaker, met all the expenses.[22]

The press were playing a very significant part in the 'creation' of the Ripper case.[23] It is almost impossible to fully appreciate how insular life was for most people in the 1880s. Obviously people did not have the Internet, telephone, television, radio and all the numerous means of communication and news dissemination we possess today. The average person was poorly educated and barely literate. By 1819 most of the population was 'certainly basically literate, including even women and the very poor'[24] but didn't travel abroad, rarely travelled out of their immediate community – except, perhaps, on their annual pilgrimage to the hop fields of Kent – and had little comprehension of anything beyond their immediate surroundings. Poverty was even more restrictive. As an example of what the poorer end of the population knew, Henry Mayhew questioned a lively and spirited boy on general and religious knowledge:

> Yes, he has 'eered of God, who made the world. Couldn't exactly recollec' when he'd heer'd of him. Didn't know when the world was made or how anybody could do it. It was afore his time, 'or your'n either, sir'. Knew there was a book called the Bible; didn't know what it was about ... Had never heer'd of France, but had heer'd of Frenchmen ... Had heer'd of Ireland. Didn't know where it was ... thought he had heer'd of Shakespeare, but didn't know whether he was alive or dead, and didn't care ... Had seen the Queen but didn't recollec' her *name* just at the minute ... Had no notion what the Queen had to do.[25]

The boy was far from unique and Mayhew cited numerous other examples of profound ignorance. Such ignorance had increasingly concerned the authorities as the nineteenth century progressed, not, of course, because people were being denied the right to education but because it was weakening military and business superiority. It was believed that the North's victory over the South in the American Civil War and Prussia's defeat of Austria was due to the victors' soldiers being better educated. Improved schooling among Britain's commercial competitors also caused the government to reconsider its opposition to primary education. Government reforms led to the passing of the Education Act in April 1870, which enabled local authorities to set up locally-elected school boards to oversee the building of schools financed from the rates. These were called board schools. One such was the imposing structure at the end of Buck's Row where the first murder occurred. The Act was for children aged under 13 (secondary education would not be reformed until 1902), but by the 1880s education had improved considerably and in the election year of 1885 it was estimated that only 4 per cent of the electorate were illiterate.

Better education and improved literacy created a new and hungry market for newspapers, and the abolition of various taxes[26] that had made newspapers expensive and beyond the reach of ordinary people, coupled with improvements in newspaper production and distribution, meant that newspaper proprietors could target a whole new market and create publications directed wholly at their needs and interests. There was a boom in both the number of daily and evening newspapers and also in the circulation of existing and new titles. For example, there were 14 daily newspapers in the United Kingdom in 1846, and 158 by 1880. Newspaper distribution also improved. In 1876 W.H. Smith managed to arrange for newspapers to go to press in time to be delivered to 'newspaper trains' which left London before dawn and arrived, even in distant places like Liverpool, before midday. As a consequence the number of newsagents almost doubled during the 1880s.

The press also began to acquire a new power. Some politicians recognised the influence of the press. Lord Randolph Churchill, a 'genius for vulgarisation',[27] almost obsessively cultivated links with the press, so much so that when he impulsively resigned as Chancellor of the Exchequer in the middle of the night in December 1886, Lord Salisbury observed to his wife, 'if I know my man, it will be in *The Times* this morning'. It was.[28] But politicians also began to appreciate how intrusive the press was and how it moulded public opinion – be it the influential and campaigning *Pall Mall Gazette* or Henry Labouchere's weekly *Truth*, which peered into murky corners for political scandals and financial swindles. There is a subtle irony in that it was politician W.H. Smith (the son of the newsagent) who, fed up when journalists disturbed a business meeting at the home of Lord Salisbury, observed of journalists, 'these vermin are omnipresent and it is hopeless to attempt to escape observation ... it is really quite intolerable'.[29] Gladstone, like Churchill, rather liked publicity at first,[30] but complained to Lord Hartington in December 1885 that 'the whole stream of public excitement is now turned upon me, and I am pestered with incessant telegrams which there is no defence against, but either suicide or Parnell's method of self-concealment ... [he was] so battered with telegrams that I hardly know whether I stand on my head or my heels'.[31]

The telegraph made it possible to gather and disseminate news very quickly, and the immediacy of reporting, so familiar today but revolutionary then, considerably heightened public awareness of the world at large and increased interest in foreign affairs. It also meant that provincial newspapers – which grew from two dailies in 1846 to 88 by 1880[32] – were able, through the services of London correspondents and press agencies, to report London news almost as it happened, and also to influence London-based decision-making. The Liberal agitation against Disraeli's foreign policy in the latter years of the 1870s began in the provincial press – much to Queen Victoria's disgust; she disliked Gladstone even more as a result.

Newspapers took on a new role. Instead of simply reporting, some newspapers saw themselves as having a pre-Reithian responsibility to educate as well as inform; not just educating their readers in the intricacies of national and international politics, economics, and social concerns, but in educating the ruling elite in the opinion of the people. With a readership of hundreds of thousands, the newspaper could accurately test public opinion, and the newspaper 'would be a great secular or civic church and democratic university ... the very soul of our national unity', as Stead put it.[33] But it was 'investigative journalism' – 'new journalism' – for which the latter part of the 1800s is best remembered.

Victorian newspapers were extraordinary beasts. Typified magisterially by *The Times*, they had no headlines or cross-heads, just row after row, column after column of densely packed blocks of tiny type. The content catered almost exclusively for the upper and middle classes and was overwhelmingly political. Parliamentary reports alone occupied about a quarter of *The Times*'s editorial content and a fifth of the *Daily Telegraph*'s. Speeches in and out of parliament were often printed in full. The 'papers otherwise covered business and religious news, sports like racing and cricket, and sensational law cases. Editorial opinion was almost non-existent and where it existed it was in the leader or thrashed out in the letters columns. Newspapers themselves were not primarily commercial and their owners 'were usually well-educated, middle class people, cautious rather than ambitious, seeking no new worlds to conquer, valuing their papers chiefly for the political and social influence which accrued through them, and disposed in most instances to view the proper exercise of this influence very seriously as a sort of personal trust'. But it was a quiet and ordered world under threat: 'This dignified phase of English journalism reigned unchallenged till 1886 and indeed beyond. Yet the seed of its destruction was already germinating'.[34] And, 'in a few short years it was rivalled, defeated and eventually almost driven out of the field, by the meteoric rise of another type, but far more widely sold'.[35]

It sounds horribly dramatic and in many respects it was – the newspaper revolution has been described as 'one of the turning points in national evolution'[36] – but the 'new journalism' was almost single-handedly responsible for creating the enduring legend of Jack the Ripper. 'New journalism' was a term coined in 1887 by Matthew Arnold, in an article expressing a thinly veiled but profound distrust of the unintelligent masses, 'the new voters, the *democracy*':

> We have had opportunities of observing a New Journalism which a clever and energetic man has lately invented. It has much to recommend it; it is full of ability, novelty, variety, sensation, sympathy, generous instincts; its one great fault is that it is featherbrained.[37]

The 'new journalism' was criticised, even by a standard work such as Sir Robert Ensor's *England 1870–1940*, where it is described as having replaced 'dignified journalism', compared to which it was 'far less responsible and far less intellectual' and catered for 'people who had been taught to decipher print without learning much else, and for whom the existing newspapers, with their long articles, long paragraphs, and all-round demands on the intelligence and imagination, were quite unsuited.[38]

The 'clever and energetic man' referred to by Matthew Arnold was W.T. Stead, and the 'new journalism' was his campaigning, investigative journalism. But whether or not Stead was deserving of the accolade and whether or not his journalism was the 'new journalism' has been fiercely debated. As L. Perry Curtis, Jnr, has observed,

> If this term is confined to the shock-provoking and crusading journalism associated with William T. Stead's famous exposé of child prostitution in 1885, then the accolade of innovator should fall on the *Pall Mall Gazette*.

But if we extend the term to include a heavier emphasis on crime, scandal, disaster, and sports along with bolder and more lurid headlines and sub-heads, then the Sunday and evening press of the 1860s and 1870s deserves most of the credit for this development.[39]

As far as Sir Robert Ensor was concerned, 'The key feature of the new journalism was not sensation but commercialism. It ran its sensations, as it ran everything else, to make money, and measured them solely by the sales they brought'.[40] Ensor had Alfred Harmsworth and the *Daily Mail* in mind, but Frank Harris'[41] earlier editorship of *The Evening News* had been dependent on his ability to increase the circulation, which he did from 7,000 to 70,000. In the process he pioneered the human interest story, the success of which he is said to have once explained to Henry Labouchere:

> I edited the *Evening News* first as a scholar and man of the world of twenty-eight; nobody wanted my opinions but as I went downwards and began to edit as I felt at twenty, then at eighteen, then at sixteen, I was more successful; but when I got to my tastes at fourteen years of age I found instantaneous response. Kissing and fighting were the only things I cared for at thirteen or fourteen and these are the things the British public desires and enjoys today ... when I got one or other or both of these interests into every column, the circulation of the paper increased steadily.[42]

But the 'new journalism' wasn't an adoption of commercialism. Commercialism was thrust upon it by the competition for readers. T.P. O'Connor, founder in 1888 of the radical *The Star*, thought the 'new journalism' consisted of stories that hit the reader 'right between the eyes'. Edward Dicey, the *Daily Telegraph*'s leader writer, thought the 'new journalism' delivered the news in 'minces and snippets' rather than 'in chops and joints', which for an accomplished leader writer seems a rather tortured metaphor.

The 'new journalism' was a combination of racier journalism (shorter sentences, shorter paragraphs, emphasis on the human angle, providing summaries instead of verbatim reports); investigative journalism (digging out the story behind the story); making the news (campaigns highlighting scandals, inefficiencies and inadequacies, and news analysis); sensationalism (exaggerated reporting, perhaps what Gladstone in 1885 described as a 'prevailing disposition to make a luxury of panics'[43]); and general presentation (headlines, cross-heads, large typeface – emphasised by the *Pall Mall Gazette*'s 'smaller size, larger type, more readable format and gossipy style'[44]). The 'new journalism' was looking for a sensation. It had found a few. Jack the Ripper rolled them all into one.

As innovative as the *Pall Mall Gazette* was, it was a traditional newspaper in the sense that it directed its campaigns at the upper middle classes. Its campaigns, like the Maiden Tribute, weren't produced for the titillation of the readers, but to shock and spur the powers that be into action. The readership – the '*democracy*' – were the people who could influence the ruling elite. They were not primarily the new voters, the newly literate. The first newspaper to cater specifically for this new market was *Tit-bits*, founded in 1880 by a schoolfellow of Stead's named George Newness. The manager of the northern branch of a London-based fancy goods business, he conceived the idea of a journal that would be a digest of material culled from all available sources and on 2 October 1881 produced the first edition of the weekly *Tit-bits*. Within two hours 5,000 copies were sold. He would go on to launch numerous publications, including the *Strand* magazine in 1891, which if nothing else provided a permanent home for one of the greatest literary creations of all time – Sherlock Holmes, who had debuted in 1887 in Mrs. Beetons' Christmas Annual. Among those employed by Newness was Alfred Harmsworth, who in 1888 started his own newspaper, a weekly rival to *Tit-bits* called *Answers to Correspondents*. It would achieve an unheard of circulation of 250,000 and by 1896 would provide Harmsworth with the money to launch the *Daily Mail*, the first true newspaper for the masses – 'written by office boys for office boys' was how Lord Salisbury famously described it – which within three years reached a circulation of 543,000, untouched by the competition.

But Harmsworth was a different animal to W.T. Stead. Stead was a newspaperman who recognised that newspapers were a business. Harmsworth – albeit that his brother was the financial genius – was a businessman whose business was newspapers. Stead saw the newspaper as a means for evoking change; Harmsworth saw the newspaper as a way of making money. Stead knew his newspaper could and did influence people and therefore had a responsibility to those people; Harmsworth did not. As a friend and admirer put it, Harmsworth's 'conviction [was] that whatever benefits them [his publications] is justifiable, and that it is not his business to consider the effect of their contents on the public mind'.[45] As Sir Robert Ensor observed, Harmsworth appreciated newspapers brought power but 'he never appreciated they brought responsibility'. Harmsworth's was a development of 'new journalism' and goodness knows what the *Daily Mail* would have done with the Ripper murders. As it happens, it was Jack the Ripper who nearly killed the *Daily Mail* before it had even been conceived. *Answers To Correspondents* was not an immediate success and Harmsworth was reduced to utter despair when the circulation began to fall and he could do nothing to revive it, blaming 'the heavy fog that was blanketing London; this plus the Jack the Ripper scare then at its height'.[46]

Ironically, whilst Jack the Ripper nearly killed *Answers to Correspondents*, he was instrumental in the success of another newspaper launched in 1888 – *The Star*. *The Star* was founded by staunch radical T.P. O'Connor – Tay Pay, as he was nicknamed, who 'survived until 1936, but his mind never advanced beyond the year 1865'[47] – for the express purpose of providing the pro-Home Rule movement with a voice in the London evening press. *The Star* saw itself from its first issue as a 'people's' newspaper – not necessarily *for* the people, but reflecting the view of the people and the effect of policy on the people. As such it was a pioneer of 'new journalism'. As O'Connor observed in his first editorial, complete with a reference to Whitechapel:

> The charwoman that lives in St. Giles, the seamstress that is sweated in Whitechapel, the labourer that stands begging for work outside the dockyard gate in St. George's-in-the-East – these are the persons by whose condition we shall judge the policy of the different political parties, and as it relieves or injures or leaves unhelped their position, shall that policy by us be praised or condemned, helped or resisted.

O'Connor hired 'a young, flossy-haired man, with a keen face' named Ernest Parke, who was an excellent journalist and future renowned editor of the newspaper. 'He might be trusted to work up any sensational news of the day, and he helped, with "Jack the Ripper", to make gigantic circulations hitherto unparalleled in evening journalism'.[48]

A few years later H.W. Massingham, O'Connor's assistant editor, recalled that *The Evening News*, *The Star* and the *Echo* had their presses running 'around the clock' during the sensation of the Ripper crimes.[49] The Sunday newspaper, the *People*, sold more copies than it had ever done. Crime always boosted sales, of course, but a sensational series of horrific crimes unfolding like a serial in a penny dreadful was 'a journalistic windfall' as far as Fleet Street was concerned – opportunistically happening at a time when the competition for readers was becoming fierce enough to cause several investors qualms.

The press drew its battle-lines according to its political colours. The liberal and radical press launched an assault on the police and the government, the *Pall Mall Gazette* and the new kid on the block, *The Star*, unsurprisingly singling out Matthews and Warren, and accusing them of not caring about the victims because they were destitute and immoral women. The *Pall Mall Gazette*, *The Star* and the *Daily Chronicle* reminded their readers that Warren had been active enough when brutally repressing the legitimate right of starving workers to hold meetings in Trafalgar Square. The conservative press tried to defend both Matthews and Warren, and *The Times* at one point tried to shift the responsibility to the victims themselves. As time passed, particularly during the long murder-free month of October, the press struggled to keep the story going, despite the long and detailed coroner's inquiry. One distinguished journalist, J. Hall Richardson, recalled that covering the inquiry

> ... was a time of great nightmares ... It involved the most unpleasant work, long hours of vigil in the streets of the East End, contact with repulsive people, constantly 'up against' the inventions and fictitious stories of competitors in journalism.[50]

The 'inventions and fictitious stories' spoken of by J. Hall Richardson may be those mentioned by a fantasist, novelist and journalist for the *Globe*, William Le Queux, who rather more breezily wrote of how he played 'a three-handed game' with Charles Hands[51] and Lincoln Springfield[52] of *The Star*:

> We practically lived as a trio in Whitechapel, and as each murder was committed we wrote up picturesque and lurid details while we stood on the very spot where the tragedy had occurred. One evening Springfield of the *Star* would publish a theory as to how the murders had been done . . .; next night Charlie Hands would have a far better theory in the *Pall Mall*, and then I would weigh in with another theory in the *Globe*.[53]

One of the reasons why the journalists were forced to scratch around for stories was that the police were not particularly forthcoming with information. Complaints about police reticence were voiced particularly after the 'double event', but also in a book, *Police!*, published in 1889 and co-authored by the same J. Hall Richardson who spent 'long hours of vigil in the streets of the East End' and was an intimate of many policemen. Both the police and the coroner, he wrote, 'distrusted the newspapers', and he blamed 'the police by their reticence' for the 'Leather Apron'/John Pizer scare, after which, he said, under pain of dismissal, the detectives refused information even to the accredited representatives of London papers. But there was a suspicion that there was favouritism exercised.

There has always been a rule to the effect that information is not to be given to the press, Mr. Vincent having enjoined: 'Police must not on any account give any information whatever to gentlemen connected with the press relative to matters within police knowledge, or relative to duties to be performed or orders received, or communicate in any manner, either directly or indirectly, with editors or reporters of newspapers on any matter connected with the public service, without express and special authority. The slightest deviation from this rule may completely frustrate the ends of justice, and defeat the endeavour of superior officers to advance the welfare of the public service. Individual merit will be invariably recognised in due course, but officers who without authority give publicity to discoveries, tending to produce sensation and alarm, show themselves wholly unworthy of their posts.[54]

Not that the rule was always observed. As the authors observed, 'there was a suspicion that there was favouritism exercised' and they singled out James Monro as one who used the *Daily Telegraph* to thwart crimes, notably the Fenian plot to assassinate Queen Victoria during her Jubilee celebrations in 1887. It is difficult not to think that Richardson didn't have his tongue in cheek when he wrote about favouritism, however, as he worked for the *Daily Telegraph* and was 'a great personal friend' of Monro.[55]

The news agencies also 'served as conduits for information that Scotland Yard wanted to divulge'.[56]

Prior to the Telegraph Act of 1868 there were several private tele-graph companies and, under the collective name of the Magnetic and Electric Companies, they exercised a monopoly over distributing news to the provincial press. The news was mainly political and commercial, not always pertinent and sometimes inaccurate, but complaints were greeted by the charges being increased and a cessa-tion of the service to those who refused to pay. The Telegraph Act nationalised the private telegraph companies and as passage of the Act approached, several provincial newspaper bosses got together and decided to form their own press agency to provide news 'unvar-nished and unspun'. Thus was the Press Association born. It quickly formed an alliance with the international press agency founded in London in 1851 by Paul Julius de Reuter, and was then able to pro-vide London news to the world and world news to London and the provinces.

The Press Association was not the first such organisation serving the provincial press. William Saunders (1823–95),[57] who had started the *Plymouth Western Morning News* in 1860 and other newspapers in Newcastle and Hull, had launched the first news-distributing agency, Central Press, in 1863 with his brother-in-law Edward Spender. In 1870–71 it became the Central News Agency and went into direct competition with the Press Association, 'and unofficial war was declared in the battle for business'. The battle was a bloody one and Central News developed a reputation both for delivering scoops and for playing dirty: 'During the 1880s there was a suspicious series of incidents that caused the Press Association to fear there was an element of corruption, possibly bribery, at work' when PA reports didn't arrive in newspaper offices until after Central News reports, even though the PA handed their reports to the Post Office before Central News. The implication was that somebody was delaying the PA text. Complaints were lodged, but nothing could be established. Not that the Press Association always played clean!

By 1887 the war had degenerated into a cost-cutting battle, 'the Central News slashed its charge for special reporting – such as major political speeches – from fifteen shillings to ten shillings a column. The P.A. followed suit at a cost of £3,000 a year'. Throughout 1888 the agencies battled one another, Central News supplying less stodgy copy, 'was more lively, colourful and, as it sometimes seemed, much faster. Its correspondents did not feel so diffident about using their imaginations when the facts were unexciting'. And this was by no means a recent phenomenon – *Judy, or the London Serio-Comic Journal* in October 1883 having castigated Central News for spreading a false story about a plot to murder the new Governor-General of the Dominion of Canada:

> What is to be done with the concoctors of false news and those who, without the expense of verification, disseminate for pecuniary gain? , .. Were the bogus telegram agency forced to return the money received for the falsehood, and the newspapers reproducing it fined, more care might perhaps be taken in announcing one moment what has to be contradicted the next.[58]

Central News developed something of a reputation for underhand practices and supplying stories of dubious veracity, particularly in its overseas operation, and in 1895 *The Times* printed a highly critical article accusing Central News of embellishments in its reports.[59]

It was to the Central News agency that a letter would be sent, purporting to be from the Whitechapel murderer, being signed and for the first time giving the name 'Jack the Ripper'.

On 25 September 1888 the penman wrote and dated a letter which he posted to: The Boss, Central News Office, London City. It was posted on 27 September and received by Central News the same day. It read:

25 September 1888
Dear Boss

I keep on hearing the police have caught me but they won't fix me just yet. I have laughed when they look so clever and talk about being on the right track. That joke about Leather Apron gave me real fits. I am down on whores and I shant quit ripping them till I do get buckled. Grand work the last job was. I gave the lady no time to squeal. How can they catch me now. I love my work and want to start again. You will soon hear of me with my funny little games. I saved some of the proper *red* stuff in a ginger beer bottle over the last job to write with but it went thick like glue and I can't use it. Red ink is fit enough I hope *ha. ha*. The next job I do I shall clip the lady s ears off and send to the Police officers just for jolly wouldn't you. Keep this letter back till I do a bit more work . then give it out straight. My knife's so nice and sharp I want to get to work right away if I get a chance. Good luck.

Yours truly
Jack the Ripper
Don't mind me giving my trade name

Wasn't good enough to post this before I got all the red ink off my hands curse it. No luck yet. They say I am a doctor now *ha. ha.*

At first the agency treated it as a joke, but decided on 29 September to send it to Scotland Yard, which it did with a short covering letter:

The Editor sends his compliments to Mr. Williamson & begs to inform him the enclosed was sent to the Central News two days ago, & was treated as a joke.

The 'Jack the Ripper' letter with its strange scatterings of Americanisms such as 'the boss' and 'quit', well written with a neat, copperplate hand, was intriguing. On 1 October Central News received a second communication, a postcard that read:

I was not codding dear old Boss when I gave you the tip, you'll hear about saucy Jacky s work tomorrow double event this time number one squealed

a bit couldn't finish straight off. Had not time to get ears for police thanks
for keeping last letter back till I got to work again.
Jack the Ripper

These communications were almost certainly written by the same
person, although the possibility that the postcard was an imitative
hoax certainly exists. If so it was written by a hoaxer who must have
had access to good information at an early stage in the police
enquiries, especially as the postcard said that the first 'one squealed
bit', which seems to be a reference to the largely unpublished testimony of Israel Schwartz who said the woman he saw assaulted had
'screamed three times but not very loudly'. The press largely regarded
the communications as a hoax, however, *The Star* reporting on 1
October 1888 that, 'A practical joker, who signed himself "Jack the
Ripper", wrote to the Central News last week ...'. The *Daily
Telegraph*, which published a facsimile of part of the letter on
4 October, stated that the police 'do not attach any great importance
to them, still they thought it well to have *facsimiles* prepared, and to
send them to the Press, in the possibility that the handwriting may be
recognised by some one'. *The Star*, in a front page editorial on 4
October criticised the *Daily Telegraph* for publishing the facsimile,
interestingly adding, 'We were offered them by "Central News", and
declined to print them. They were clearly written in red pencil, not in
blood, the obvious reason being that the writer was one of those fool-
ish but bad people who delight in unholy notoriety. Now, the murderer is not a man of this kind ...'. The police certainly regarded the
letter and postcard as a hoax, as a letter from Sir Charles Warren to
Godfrey Lushington dated 10 October shows. He said, 'At present I
think the whole thing is a hoax'. But as Warren observed, the police
were 'bound to try & ascertain the writer in any case'.[60]

We cannot say why the police seem to have paid more attention to
the 'Jack the Ripper' correspondence than to the hundreds of other
letters, although the content as already noted may explain it in part,
which made it necessary for the police to try to identify the author.
But the chilling soubriquet was a fortuitous stroke of genius and
bestowed upon the unknown murderer an immortality among the
greatest villains of fact and faction. In this respect – and others, not the
least being that they spawned hundreds of further hoax letters – the
distribution of the facsimiles was a mistake:

The fame of 'Jack the Ripper' spread far and wide. It is probable that nothing would have been heard of this cognomen had it not been for the indiscretion of Scotland Yard in publishing a facsimile of sensational letters sent to a news agency, which thereby gave to these interesting documents the stamp of official authority.[61]

Finally, on Friday 5 October Central News received a third missive from 'Jack the Ripper' and informed Scotland Yard, though curiously the agency this time only supplied a transcript:

Dear Mr. Williamson

At 5 minutes to 9 o'clock tonight we received the following letter the envelope of which I enclose by which you will see it is in the same hand-writing as the previous communications

'5 Oct 1888
Dear Friend
In the name of God hear me I swear I did not kill the female whose body was found at Whitehall. If she was an honest woman I will hunt down and destroy her murderer. If she ['was an honest woman' deleted] was a whore God will bless the hand that slew her, for the women of of [*sic*] Moab and Midian shall die and their blood shall mingle with the dust I never harm any others or the Divine power that protects and helps me in my grand work would quit for ever. Do as I do and the light of glory shall shine upon you. I must get to work tomorrow treble event this time yes yes three must be ripped. will send you a bit of face by post I promise this dear old Boss. The police now reckon my work a practical joke well well Jacky's a very practical joker ha ha ha. Keep this back till three are wiped out and you can show the cold meat

Yours truly
Jack the Ripper'

Yours truly
T.J. Bulling

The police, at least at a senior level, seem not only to have regarded the 'Jack the Ripper' correspondence as bogus, they apparently knew – or thought they knew – the identity of the hoaxer. Writing in 1910 in a serialisation of his memoirs that would be published in book form later in the year, the now-retired Sir Robert Anderson wrote,

I will only add here that the 'Jack-the-Ripper' letter which is preserved in the Police Museum at New Scotland Yard is the creation of an enterprising London journalist.

And, as a footnote, added,

> I should almost be tempted to disclose the identity of the murderer and of
> the pressman who wrote the letter above referred to ...[62]

A correspondent to the *East London Observer* at the time of
Anderson's revelations about the author of the 'Jack the Ripper' correspondence, as well as the identity of the murderer (of which more
later), wrote to say that the letter and postcard had been written by 'an
enterprising local penny-a-liner' – meaning a journalist who was paid
a penny a line. The correspondent signed himself 'A Wide-Awake
East-Ender'.

An anonymous contributor to *Crime and Detection* in August 1966
recalled,

> In 1931, working on an outline for a life of William Palmer, the Rugeley
> poisoner, a friend mentioned an ex-jockey who was living not far from my
> home (then Henley-on-Thames). Through several introductions, to reach
> this character, I finally arrived at a man named Best, an ex-journalist. He
> was spry and very clear-minded, though well past 70. He knew the jockey,
> and arranged a meeting at the house of a friend in a small place called
> Culham, on the Oxon-Berks border.
>
> I met the ex-jockey, a vigorous old gentleman of, he claimed, 95. Known
> as Jack, or John, Faulkener, he had ridden a number of races for William
> Palmer, and his fund of reminiscences was large.
>
> Returning homewards with me, Best discussed murders, the
> Whitechapel murders in particular. With much amplifying detail he talked
> of his days as a penny-a-liner on the *Star* newspaper. As a freelance he had
> covered the Whitechapel murders from the discovery of the woman,
> Tabram. He claimed that he, and a provincial colleague, were responsible
> for *all* the 'Ripper' letters, to 'keep the business alive ... in those days it
> was far easier to get details, and facts from the police, than today'. Best
> did not mind me having these facts so many years later, and said a close
> reading of the *Star* of the time might be informative, and that an experi-
> enced graphologist with an open mind would be able to find in the orig-
> inal letters 'numerous earmarks' of an experienced journalist at work; the
> pen used was called a 'Waverley Nib' and was deliberately battered to
> achieve an impression of semi-illiteracy and 'National School' training!
> Best scoffed at the notion that the 'Ripper' had written a single word
> about his crimes.
>
> Some years before this the late Edgar Wallace mentioned that in his
> reporting days the better informed Fleet Street men were satisfied that a
> newspaperman was 'behind' the letters.

This story, with its lack of detail about 'Best', the battered pen nib to give the impression of 'semi-illiteracy and "National School" training!' (which doesn't fit the Dear Boss and Saucy Jacky correspondence, but could fit the Lusk letter discussed shortly), is intriguing. A reading of *The Star* does suggest that it was determinedly not taken in by the correspondence, which is interesting. Best, of course, wasn't necessarily talking about what are today known as the Dear Boss letter and Saucy Jacky postcard. The police had received hundreds of letters from all parts of the country offering suggestions of various kinds for the capture of the murderer, advancing suspects and even claiming to be the murderer, and 'it is almost needless to say that none of the communications help in any way to elucidate the mystery'.[63] Best, assuming he existed, could have meant any of these. On the other hand, hardly any of the correspondence achieved any notoriety or were worthy of note or discussion, and Best could hardly have meant that he wrote all of it.

R. Thurston Hopkins, in his book *Life and Death at the Old Bailey*, also pointed the finger of guilt at a journalist:

But it was in a letter, received by a well-known News Agency and forwarded to the Yard, that the name first appeared ... It was perhaps a fortunate thing that the handwriting of this famous letter was not identified, for it would have led to the arrest of a harmless Fleet Street journalist. This poor fellow had a breakdown and became a whimsical figure in Fleet Street, only befriended by the staffs of newspapers and printing works. He would creep about the dark courts waving his hands furiously in the air, would utter stentorian 'Ha, ha, ha's', and then, meeting some pal, would buttonhole him and pour into his ear all the 'inner story' of the East End murders. Many old Fleet Streeters had very shrewd suspicions that this irresponsible fellow wrote the famous Jack the Ripper letter ...[64]

Sir Melville Macnaghten, who succeeded Anderson as Assistant Commissioner CID, also said he 'could discern the stained forefinger of the journalist' in the Ripper correspondence.[65] The ever-cautious Macnaghten didn't commit himself to actual knowledge of the identity of the perpetrator, but said 'I had shrewd suspicions as to the actual author!'. For a name we had to wait until the distinguished Ripper authority Stewart Evans purchased some correspondence once belonging to the journalist George R. Sims, a man famous in his day but now largely remembered, when he is remembered at all, for 'Christmas Day In The Workhouse'. Among the letters was one written in September 1913 by ex-Chief Inspector John Littlechild:

> With regard to the term 'Jack the Ripper' it was generally believed at the
> Yard that Tom Bullen of the Central News was the originator but it is prob-
> able Moore, who was his chief, was the inventor. It was a smart piece of
> journalistic work. No journalist of my time got such privileges from
> Scotland Yard as Bullen. Mr James Munro when Assistant Commissioner,
> and afterwards Commissioner, relied on his integrity. Poor Bullen
> occasionally took too much to drink, and I fail to see how he could help it
> knocking about so many hours and seeking favours from so many people
> to procure copy. One night when Bullen 'had taken a few too many' he got
> early information of the death of Prince Bismarck and instead of going to
> the office to report it sent a laconic telegram 'Bloody Bismarck is dead'. On
> this I believe Mr. Charles Moore fired him out.[66]

The names here are incorrect, Tom Bullen being Thomas John
Bulling and Charles Moore almost certainly John Moore, the Manager
of Central News.

As was recognised at the time, it was highly unlikely that a member
of the public would have sent correspondence to a news agency. It is
equally difficult to understand how, except in the broad general sense
of prolonging the story, any journalist, particularly a penny-a-liner,
would have hoped to benefit personally from the hoax. The same
question could be asked of Central News: what would they have
gained?

Perhaps the most extraordinary comment about the correspondence was published in radical MP and pro-Parnellite Henry
Labouchere's magazine, *Truth*, on 11 October:

> On the doctrine of possibilities, it is long odds against the murderer having
> written the 'Jack the Ripper' letters. He may have, and so may many thou-
> sands of others. But there is a coincidence in respect to these letters to
> which attention has not yet been drawn. The handwriting is remarkably like
> that of the forgeries which the *Times* published, and which they ascribed to
> Mr. Parnell and to Mr. Egan. I do not go so far as to suggest that the *Times*
> forger is the Whitechapel murderer, although this, of course is possible; but
> it may be that the forger takes pride in his work, and wishes to keep his
> hand in.

Parnell certainly knew by 11 October, when this article was published,
that Pigott was the author of the forged letters supposedly written by
Parnell and used in a series of articles alleging Parnell's involvement
with crime, and Labouchere may have known too. Anderson may have
met Pigott in Paris on 4 October, also obtaining a confession to the
authorship of the letters. Could Pigott have confessed to writing 'Dear

Boss'? He *was* a journalist ... At times the subject of Jack the Ripper provides rich seams from which to mine tempting speculation.

Probably the most significant event of the month took place shortly after 5.00pm on 16 October when a letter and a cardboard box were delivered to George Lusk, the Chairman of the Whitechapel Vigilance Committee. The letter read:

> From Hell
> Mr Lusk.
> Sor,
>
> I send you half the kidne I took from one woman prasarved it for you, tother piece I fried and ate; it was very nice. I may send you a bloody knif that I took it out if you only wate a while longer.
>
> [signed] 'Catch me when you can
> Mishter Lusk.'

At first Lusk thought it was a hoax but he was persuaded by other members of the Vigilance Committee to take the contents of the box to the nearby surgery of Dr. Reed at 56 Mile End Road. Reed examined the contents and recommended that they be taken to Dr. Thomas Openshaw of the London Hospital. Openshaw pronounced it to be a left human kidney (nothing more), and Mr. Lusk then took it to Inspector Abberline at the Leman Street Police Station. The Metropolitan Police in due course passed it to the City Police, where it was examined by Dr. Gordon Brown.

Lieutenant-Colonel Sir Henry Smith, Acting Commissioner of the City of London police, wrote with perhaps typical inaccuracy of the 'Lusk kidney' in his memoirs under a chapter heading, 'Of Kidneys, Not Devilled', which perhaps gives something of the flavour of these remembrances:[67]

> When the body was examined by the police surgeon, Mr. Gordon Brown, one kidney was found to be missing, and some days after the murder what purported to be that kidney was posted to the office of the Central News, together with a short note of rather a jocular character unfit for publications. Both kidney and note the manager at once forwarded to me. Unfortunately, as always happens, some clerk or assistant in the office was got at, and the whole affair was public property next morning. Right royally did the Solons of the metropolis enjoy themselves at the expense of my humble self and the City Police Force. 'The kidney was the kidney of a dog, anyone could see that', wrote one. 'Evidently from the dissecting-room', wrote another. 'Taken out of a corpse after a post-mortem', wrote a third.

'A transparent hoax', wrote a fourth. My readers shall judge between myself and the Solons in question.

I made over the kidney to the police surgeon, instructing him to consult with the most eminent men in the profession, and send me a report without delay. I give the substance of it. The renal artery is about three inches long. Two inches remained in the corpse, one inch was attached to the kidney. The kidney left in the corpse was in an advanced stage of Bright's Disease; the kidney sent me was in an exactly similar state. But what was of far more importance, Mr. Sutton, one of the senior surgeons of the London Hospital, whom Gordon Brown asked to meet him and another practitioner in consultation, and who was one of the greatest authorities living on the kidney and its diseases, said he would pledge his reputation that the kidney submitted to them had been put in spirits within a few hours of its removal from the body – thus effectually disposing of all hoaxes in connection with it. The body of anyone done to death by violence is not taken direct to the dissecting-room, but must await an inquest, never held before the following day at the soonest.[68]

The reality, of course, is that the kidney wasn't sent to Central News or passed by the Central News to Major Smith. No renal artery seems to have been attached to the piece of kidney, there was no evidence of Bright's Disease, and we don't know who Mr. Sutton was. In any event the kidney being preserved in spirits would suggest that it was removed during an autopsy or dissection, not, as Major Smith seems to have imagined, the reverse. Apart from this there is no immediate reason to doubt what's left of Major Smith's story – which isn't much.

A report submitted to the Home Office by Chief Inspector Swanson of the Metropolitan Police does throw doubt on Major Smith's belief that the kidney could not have come from a body used in a dissecting room:

The result of the combined medical opinion they have taken upon it, is, that it is the kidney of a human adult; not charged with a fluid, as it would have been in the case of a body handed over for the purpose of dissection to a hospital, but rather as it would be in the case where it was taken from the body not so destined. In other words similar kidneys might and could be obtained from any dead person whom a post mortem had been made from any cause by students or dissecting room porter.[69]

Dr. Gordon Brown told a journalist for *The Sunday Times*,

I cannot see that it is the left kidney. It must have been cut previously to its being immersed in the spirit which exercised a hardening process. It certainly had not been in spirit for more than a week. As has been stated, there is no portion of the renal artery adhering to it, it having been trimmed up, so, consequently, there could be no correspondence established between the portion of the body from which it was cut. As it exhibits no trace of decomposition, when we consider the length of time that has elapsed since the commission of the murder, we come to the conclusion that the probability is slight of its being a portion of the murdered woman of Mitre Square.

Mounting opinion, contrary to the view advanced by Major Smith, was that the kidney was a hoax. But the correspondence has lived on to intrigue and fascinate, and most recently a new so-called Ripper letter has generated a new round of theorising. On 29 October 1888 Dr. Openshaw received a letter himself. Addressed to 'Dr. Openshaw, Pathological curator, London Hospital, Whitechapel':

> Old boss you was rite it was the left kidny i was goin to hopperate agin close to your ospitle just as i was goin to dror mi nife along of er bloomin throte them cusses of coppers spoilt the game but i guess i wil be on the job soon and will send you another bit of innerds Jack the ripper
> O have you seen the devle with his mikerscope and scalpul a lookin at a Kidney with a slide cocked up.

The crime novelist Patricia Cornwell has discovered that this letter has the same watermark as paper used by the noted British Artist and sometime Jack the Ripper suspect Walter Sickert.[70]

It may not have seemed at the time that Jack the Ripper was changing the face of the press, but the 'new journalism', seeded in the Sunday press in the 1860s and finding root with the *Pall Mall Gazette* and 'Modern Babylon', flowered following 'Bloody Sunday' in 1887 and 'Jack the Ripper' in 1888. The world *was* changed. And in their own small way the murder of five helpless prostitutes in the warren of streets and alleys of London's East End, were instrumental in changing it. But the full horror had yet to be played. Jack the Ripper still had a curtain call.

Notes

1. *East London Observer*, 6 October 1888.
2. *The Times*, 1 October 1888.
3. *Manchester Guardian*, 2 October 1888.
4. *Daily Telegraph*, 2 October 1888.
5. *The Star*, 2 October 1888.

6. See the *Manchester Guardian* and the *Yorkshire Post*, 1 October 1888, as examples.

7. Matthews' comments are in a letter from Matthews to his private secretary, Sir Evelyn Ruggles-Brise, dated 5 October 1888. This is contained in the J.S. Sandars papers, MS. Eng. Hist. C.723 at the Bodleian Library, Department of Western Manuscripts, Oxford. The letter is reproduced in full in Begg, Paul (1988) *Jack the Ripper: The Uncensored Facts.* London: Robson Books, pp.132–5.

8. Letter from Sir Charles Warren to Henry Matthews dated 6 October 1888. HO 144/220/A49301B/sub.9.

9. The *Pall Mall Gazette*, 8 October 1888, for example: 'Strange, almost incredible, though it appears, it was in the very midst of the series of murders at Whitechapel that the internal disputes which for some time past paralysed the efficiency of the Metropolitan police came to a head, and in so doing decapitated the Criminal Investigation Department. Mr. Monro who for the last four years has acted as the chief of the detective force, resigned at the end of August, finding his position intolerable. His successor is Dr. Robert Anderson: a millenarian and writer of religious books was appointed in his place. But although Dr. Anderson is nominally at the head of the C.I.D. he is only there in spirit. At a time when all the world is ringing with outcries against the officials who allow murder to stalk unchecked through the most densely crowded quarter of the metropolis, the chief official who is responsible for the detection of the murderer is as invisible to Londoners as the murderer himself. You may seek for Dr. Anderson in Scotland-yard, you may look for him in Whitehall-place, but you will not find him, for he is not there. Dr. Anderson, with all the arduous duties of his office still to learn, is preparing himself for his apprenticeship by taking a pleasant holiday in Switzerland! No one grudges him this holiday. But just at present it does strike the uninstructed observer as a trifle off that the chief of London's intelligence department in the battle, the losing battle which the police are waging against crime, should find it possible to be idling in the Alps'.

10. Anderson, Sir Robert (1910) *The Lighter Side of My Official Life.* London: Hodder and Stoughton, p.135. In a letter to a London newspaper in April 1910 – erroneously quoted as being written in 1912 in Richardson, J. Hall (1927) *From The City To Fleet Street.* London: Stanley Paul & Co. Ltd, p.217 – Anderson stated that, 'The night on which the murder [the Double Event, as he makes clear when discussing the Goulston Street graffito] in question was committed I was on my way home from Paris...'. He had, as his memoirs make clear, just arrived in Paris from Switzerland.

11. Campbell, Christy (2002) *Fenian Fire: The British Government Plot to Assassinate Queen Victoria.* London: HarperCollins, p.309.

12. In December 1885 Richard Pigott, a journalist with a dubious reputation for honesty, approached Edward Caulfield Houston, secretary of the Irish Loyal and Patriotic Union and a former *Times* journalist, saying that he could lay hands on material confirming a direct connection between the pro-

Home Rule Parnellites and the Fenian terrorists who had planted bombs across London. In April 1886 he supplied Houston with copies of five letters allegedly written by Parnell, which Houston took to George Buckle, Editor of the staunchly anti-Parnell *Times*, who showed no interest. In June Pigott returned from a trip to Paris saying that for suitable financial remuneration he could get the original letters. Houston paid up, Pigott went back to Paris and in July returned to London with the originals. This time Buckle bought them. He sat on them until March 1878, when the paper began a series of articles charging Parnell and his party with murder and urging them to sue for libel if the accusations weren't true. Finally, on 18 April, *The Times* published the facsimile of a letter allegedly written by Parnell in which he condoned the Phoenix Park murders. Parnell treated the whole thing as beneath contempt, denied that the accusations and documents were genuine and professed apparently genuine disbelief that 'what used to be a respectable journal could have been so hoodwinked, so hoaxed, so bamboozled ... as to publish such a production as that as my signature'. But he did not sue *The Times*, as the newspaper and the anti-Parnell lobby wanted. Eventually the Salisbury administration set up a Royal Commission, which began sitting on 22 October 1888. By this time it was known in certain circles, and possibly to Anderson, that the documents sold to *The Times* had been forged by Pigott. On Saturday 23 February 1889, Pigott would confess to the radical MP and ardent Parnell supporter Henry Labouchere. On Monday he travelled to Paris and from there went to Madrid, where he checked into the Hotel des Ambassadeurs on the Thursday and shot himself on the Friday.

Richard Pigott was enobled by having a poem dedicated to him by William McGonagall. Too long to quote in full, a 'feel' for the merit of the poem is provided by the opening:

Richard Pigott, the forger, was a very bad man,
And to gainsay it there's nobody can,
Because for fifty years he pursued a career of deceit.
And as a forger few men with him could compete.
For by forged letters he tried to accuse Parnell
For the Phoenix Park murders, but mark what befel.
When his conscience smote him he confessed to the fraud,
And the thought thereof no doubt drove him mad.

Anderson, who was staunchly anti-Parnell, was involved in this debacle because following the *Times* articles he had anonymously written a series of anti-Parnell articles for the same newspaper, called 'Behind the Scenes in America'. These articles were based on letters received from his deep-cover spy in the Fenian movement, Henri Le Caron. If Anderson knew or strongly suspected that Pigott had forged the letters and knew or anticipated that *The Times* was walking into disaster by relying on Pigott's testimony at the Commission, he had Le Caron up his sleeve as a trump card to play on behalf of *The Times*. The possibility that Anderson met with Pigott in Paris at the beginning of October 1888 therefore opens up a world of possibilities. It also suggests that the Ripper crimes were not uppermost in his mind at that time.

13. Anderson, Sir Robert, *op. cit.*, pp.135–6.

14. Sweeney, John (1904) *At Scotland Yard*. London: Grant Richards, p.343.

15. Macnaghten, Sir Melville (1914) *Days of My Years*. London: Longmans, Green and Co., p.273.

16. These cowboys belonged to Buffalo Bill Cody's Wild West Show which had come to London as a part of Queen Victoria's Jubilee celebrations in 1887. They left for the United States in the spring of 1888, but some cowboys are known to have liked Britain and stayed behind.

17. Report by Chief Inspector Swanson to the Home Office dated 19 October 1888. HO/144/221/A49301C 8a.

18. *Yorkshire Post*, 8 October 1888.

19. *Yorkshire Post*, 8 October 1888.

20. *East London Advertiser*, 13 October 1888.

21. Longford, Elizabeth (1964) *Victoria R.I.* London: Weidenfeld and Nicolson. London: Abacus, 2000.

22. *Yorkshire Post*, 8 October 1888; *The Times*, 9 October 1888; *Wolverhampton Chronicle*, 10 October 1888.

23. An excellent specialist survey of the press coverage of the crimes is Curtis Jr, L. Perry (2001) *Jack the Ripper and the London Press*. New Haven and London: Yale University Press.

24. Rubinstein, W.D. (1998) *Britain's Century: A Political and Social History 1815–1905*. London: Arnold, p.13.

25. *London Labour and the London Poor*, 1851. London: Griffin, Bohn & Co., vol. 1, p.530.

26. These taxes were a tax on advertisements, abolished in 1853, a newspaper tax, abolished in 1855 and a duty on paper, abolished in 1861. They were collectively called, and condemned by radicals as, a 'tax of knowledge'. The abolition made newspapers more affordable, which meant they could target a new market of the middle and lower middle classes.

27. Foster, R.F. (1981) *Lord Randolph Churchill, A Political Life*. Oxford: Clarendon Press, p.76.

28. James, Robert Rhodes (1959) *Lord Randolph Churchill*. London: Weidenfeld and Nicolson, p.296.

29. Chilston, Viscount (1965) *W.H. Smith*. Routledge & Kegan Paul, p.212.

30. His Cabinet of 1880–85 leaked. Gladstone himself had used his influence with John Morley, W.T. Stead's predecessor at the *Pall Mall Gazette*.

31. Holland, Bernard (1911) *The Life of Spencer Compton: Eighth Duke of Devonshire*, London: Longmans, Green and Co., vol. II, pp.99–100.

32. Most remarkable was the growth of London suburban newspapers, which grew from one in 1846 to 104 in 1880.

33. *Contemporary Review*, November 1886, quoted in Ford, Colin and Harrison, Brian (1983) *A Hundred Years Ago: Britain in the 1880s in Words and Photographs*. Harmondsworth, Middlesex: Penguin Books.

34. Ensor, Sir Robert (1936) *England 1870–1914*. Oxford: Oxford University Press, pp.144–5.
35. *Ibid.*, p.310.
36. *Ibid.*, p.310.
37. Arnold Matthew (1887) 'Up To Easter', *Nineteenth Century*, May, pp.638–9.
38. Ensor, Sir Robert, *op. cit.*, p.145.
39. Curtis Jnr, L. Perry (2001) *Jack the Ripper and the London Press*. New Haven and London: Yale University Press, p.61.
40. Ensor, Sir Robert, *op. cit.*, p.310.
41. Described delightfully by George Bernard Shaw as 'neither first rate, nor second rate, nor tenth rate. He is just his horrible unique self'; and rather more deliciously by Oscar Wilde, who rightfully said, 'He has no feelings. It is the secret of his success'.
42. Harris, Frank (1969) *My Life and Loves*. London: W.H. Allen. Quoted in Brome, Vincent (1959) *Frank Harris*. London: Cassell, p.66.
43. Lynd, Helen Merrell (1945) *England in the Eighteen-Eighties. Toward A Social Basis For Freedom*. Oxford: Oxford University Press, p.225.
44. Curtis Jnr, L. Perry, *op. cit.*, p.61.
45. Fyfe, Hamilton (1930) *Northcliffe: An Intimate Biography*. London: George Allen and Unwin, p.106.
46. Taylor, S.J. (1996) *The Great Outsiders: Northcliffe, Rothermere and the Daily Mail*. London: Weidenfeld and Nicolson, p.16.
47. George Bernard Shaw quoted in Pope, Wilson (1938) *The Story of The Star 1888–1938*. London: The Star Publications Department, p.36.
48. O'Connor, T.P. (1929) *Memoirs of an Old Parliamentarian*. London: Ernest Benn, vol. II, pp.255–7.
49. Massingham, H.W. (1892) *The London Daily Press*. London: Religious Tract Society, p.182.
50. Richardson, J. Hall (1927) *From The City To Fleet Street*. London: Stanley Paul & Co. Ltd, p.216.
51. 'Hands was a genius ... He could write agreeably and wittily about anything – if he felt so disposed. If he did not feel like it, no editor in Fleet Street could make him write, but he had a charming and disarming way with him which saved him from the usual fate of the unreliable'. He worked for *The Star*, moved to the *Pall Mall Gazette* and finally to the *Daily Mail*. Blind in his later years, he died in 1919, hailed by *The Times* in an obituary as 'the Laughing Cavalier of the new journalism ...'. Pope, Wilson, *op. cit.*, pp.37–8.
52. Lincoln Springfield, 'a curly-haired youth who came from Brighton ... He was probably the best and keenest man of his day at the news story ...'. Pope, Wilson, *op. cit.*, pp.37–8. See also Springfield, Lincoln (1924) *Some Piquant People*. London: T. Fisher Unwin.
53. Le Queux, William (1923) *Things I Know About Kings, Celebrities and Crooks*. London: Eveleigh Nash and Grayson, p.165.

54. Clarkson, Charles Tempest and Richardson, J. Hall (1889) *Police!* London: Field and Tuer, pp.278–9.
55. Richardson, J. Hall, *op. cit.*, p.222.
56. Curtis Jnr, L. Perry, *op. cit.*, p.117.
57. Saunders was elected Liberal member for East Hull in 1885, but was defeated in the general election of 1886, in which year his interest in London politics took on a radical character as he joined with those groups campaigning to keep Trafalgar Square open for public meetings. He was elected to the first London County Council as the representative for Walworth in 1889 and wrote *A History of the First London County Council* in 1892. He entered Parliament as a Liberal for the same constituency in 1892, but by this time he was espousing socialist opinions that alienated many of his fellows.
58. Scott, George (1968) *Reporter Anonymous: The Story of the Press Association.* London: Hutchinson, pp.114–18.
59. Moncrieff, Chris (2001) *Living on a Deadline: A History of the Press Association.* London: Virgin, pp.53–8.
60. MEPO 1/48 quoted in Evans, Steward P. and Skinner, Keith (2001) *Jack the Ripper: Letters From Hell.* Stroud, Gloucestershire: Sutton, p.43.
61. Clarkson, Charles Tempest and Richardson, J. Hall, *op. cit.*, p.278.
62. Anderson, Sir Robert, *op. cit.*
63. *The Times*, 12 September 1888.
64. Hopkins, R. Thurston (1935) *Life and Death at the Old Bailey.* London: Herbert Jenkins, pp.202–3.
65 Macnaghten, Sir Melville, *op. cit.*, p.58.
66. Letter from ex-Chief Inspector John Littlechild to journalist George R. Sims, 23 September 1913. In the private collection of Ripper expert Stewart P. Evans.
67. Smith, Lieut.-Col. Sir Henry (1910) *From Constable to Commissioner: The Story of Sixty Years, Most of Them Misspent.* Chatto and Windus.
68. Smith, Lieut.-Col. Sir Henry, *op. cit.*, pp.154–5. George H. Edwards, Secretary of the Metropolitan Police 1925–27, presented his personal copy of Lieut.-Col. Smith's autobiography to the Scotland Yard Library on his death. It contains an interesting seven line comment on the page opposite the frontispiece, describing Smith as, 'A good raconteur and a good fellow, but not strictly veracious'. He went on to say that much of the book consisted of after dinner stories outside his personal experience and in his account of matters within his own knowledge 'he is often far from accurate'.
69. Report by Chief Inspector Swanson to the Home Office dated 6 November 1888. HO/221/A49301C/8c.
70. For a comprehensive account of all the Ripper correspondence see Evans, Stewart P. and Skinner, Keith, *op. cit.*

chapter thirteen

MARY JANE KELLY

The number of murders committed by Jack the Ripper is disputed. Sir Robert Anderson[1] and Sir Melville Macnaghten[2] state five, the series ending with Mary Jane Kelly.

Very little is known about Mary Kelly's life and hardly any of it has been substantiated. We are told that she was about 25 years old, 5ft 7in, stout, blonde haired[3] and blue eyed, with a fair complexion. Sir Melville Macnaghten reported that she was 'said to have been possessed of considerable personal attractions'.[4] Walter Dew, who was a young constable attached to Whitechapel at the time, wrote, 'I knew Marie quite well by sight. Often I had seen her parading along Commercial Street, between Flower and Dean Street and Aldgate, or along Whitechapel Road. She was usually in the company of two or three of her kind, fairly neatly dressed and invariably wearing a clean white apron, but no hat ... a pretty, buxom girl'.[5]

The story she told about herself was a tragic one. She said she had been born in Limerick, Ireland, though it isn't known whether she meant Limerick the town or County Limerick, but had moved with her family to Wales. Her boyfriend, Joseph Barnett, to whom she told this story wasn't sure whether it was Carnarvonshire or Carmarthenshire, but it was probably the latter because when a young girl she apparently met and married a collier named Davies – and the coal mines were in South Wales. Within a short time her husband was killed in a mining accident. Left without any means of support, Kelly joined a cousin in Cardiff who introduced her to prostitution and according to Joseph Barnett she 'was in an infirmary there for eight or nine months'. From Cardiff she went to London, where, again according to Joseph Barnett, she had worked in a high-class bordello in the West End. He said that she claimed to have accompanied a gentleman to Paris, but had not liked it there and had returned after about two weeks. Certainly she affected the name 'Marie', by which Walter Dew referred to her. Some independent support was unearthed for this part of her story: On 10 November a Mrs. Elizabeth Phoenix called at Leman Street police station and according to the Press Association 'made a statement as to the identity of the murdered woman':

> She states that about three years ago a woman, apparently deceased, judging from the published description, resided in Mrs. Phoenix's brother-in-law's house at Breezer's Hill, Pennington Street, near London Docks.

The Press Association reporter made enquiries in the area of Breezer's Hill[6] and wrote:

> It would appear that on her arrival in London she made the acquaintance of a French woman residing in the neighbourhood of Knightsbridge, who, she informed her friends, led her to pursue the degraded life which had now culminated in her untimely end. She made no secret of the fact that while she was with this woman she drove about in a carriage and made several journeys to the French capital, and, in fact, led a life which is described as that 'of a lady'. By some means, however, at present not exactly clear, she suddenly drifted into the East End. Here fortune failed her and a career which stands out in bold and sad contrast to her earlier experience was commenced. Her experience of the East End appears to have begun with a woman who resided in one of the thoroughfares off Ratcliffe Highway, now known as St. George's Street. This person seems to have received Kelly direct from the West End home, for she had not been there very long when, it is stated, both women went to the French 'lady's' residence and demanded the box which contained numerous dresses of a costly description.
>
> Kelly at last indulged in intoxicants, it is stated, to an extent which made her unwelcome. From St. George's Street she went to lodge with a Mrs. Carthy at Breezer's Hill (off Pennington Street). This place she left about 18 months or two years ago and from that time seems to have left Ratcliffe altogether.

According to Mrs. Carthy, Kelly left her house when she 'went to live with a man who was apparently in the building trade and who Mrs. Carthy believed would have married Kelly'.[7] This story seems to have confirmation from Joseph Barnett who at the inquest said that after she left Cardiff she 'was in a gay house in the West-end, but in what part she did not say. A gentleman came there to her and asked her if she would like to go to France'. Kelly went with him, 'but she did not remain long. She said she did not like the part, but whether it was the part or purpose I cannot say. She was not there more than a fortnight, and she returned to England, and went to Ratcliffe-highway'. And the crucial comment was that 'she described a man named Joseph Fleming, who came to Pennington-street, a bad house, where she stayed. I don't know when this was. She was very fond of him. He was a mason's plasterer, and lodged in the Bethnal-green-road'.[8]

As we have seen, Kelly's story is far from impossible, the cross-channel trade in women being quite well established, albeit not the huge trade suggested by the *Pall Mall Gazette* in its 'Maiden Tribute To Modern Babylon' articles. Girls destined for the brothels of Belgium and France had to make a formal declaration that they wished to enter a brothel and knew what would be expected of them, and they had to undergo a medical check. They may, however, have been seriously misled about how much money they would earn or the conditions in which they would live, apparently encouraged to believe that they would be living a luxurious lifestyle by being treated lavishly when in London. The procurer would have made a substantial investment by the time the woman reached France and would have been very displeased with any woman who did not go ahead with the arrangement. What we know happened certainly corresponds with Kelly's stories about fine dresses and being driven about in a coach, and Kelly would certainly have made some serious enemies if she had refused to stay in France.

From Mrs. Carthy's house she went to live with Joseph Fleming and lived somewhere in Bethnal Green. Even when she lived with Barnett, Fleming used to visit Kelly and Barnett said Kelly seemed very fond of him. A neighbour of Kelly's named Julia Venturney confirmed this, saying that Kelly was fond of a man other than Barnett whose name was also Joe. He was, she thought, a costermonger and sometimes visited and gave money to Kelly.[9] After Fleming she appears, according to Barnett, to have lived with a man named Morganstone – or Morgan Stone – opposite, or in the vicinity of, Stepney gasworks.

By 1886 Mary Jane Kelly was living at Cooley's lodging house in Thrawl Street, one of the streets in the dreaded Flower and Dean Street rookery, and it was while living there that she met Billingsgate Market fish porter and sometime fruit hawker Joseph Barnett in Commercial Street on Good Friday, 8 April 1887. The following day they met again and decided to live together. They lodged in various locations, finally moving to a single room, 13 Miller's Court. This was in fact the back room of 26 Dorset Street.

A 3 feet wide arched passage separated 26 and 27 Dorset Street and led to what in distant times would have been the rear yards of 26 and 27. Six houses had been built there, three on either side of the court-yard. The back room of 26 Dorset Street had been converted into a self-contained room, a false partition having been erected to cut it off from the rest of the house, and it was entered by a door at the end of the arched passage. The house was owned by John McCarthy, who ran a business from 27 Dorset Street.

As we saw in Chapter One, back in the mid-1600s the area had been 'a field of grass with cows feeding on it' and criss-crossed by several footpaths. When the owners wanted to close the footpaths they were obliged to build a road 40 feet long and 24 feet wide. That road was called Datchet Street, corrupted in due course to Dorset Street. By the time Mary Kelly moved there it was one of the most notorious and reputedly one of the most dangerous streets in the East End.[10] Years later a minor villain named Arthur Harding recalled Dorset Street and John McCarthy:

> Dorset Street had an even worse reputation than Flowery Dean Street. That's where Jack the Ripper done some of his murders. We just used to call it 'the street'. There was such a large number of doss-houses there that they called it 'Dossers' Street' and they abbreviated it again just to 'the street' which is what we called it. There were doss-houses on one side, fur-nished rooms on the other. McCarthy owned all the furnished rooms down there. He was an Irishman, a bully, a tough guy.
>
> Marie Lloyd used to see him, because there was a pub round the corner she used to go to. All his daughters were in show business on account of Marie Lloyd. They had plenty of money. McCarthy lived down there ...[11]

'Bully' could mean pimp and a 'bully boss' was the title of a landlord of a brothel or thieves' den. Inspector Reid told Charles Booth that the prostitutes of Pennington Street were not controlled by pimps: 'there are no bullies who live off the earnings of the women', and it is interesting in light of Arthur Harding's comment to note that several of the women living in Miller's Court were prostitutes. Harding's statement that McCarthy was a friend of the revered music hall enter-tainer Marie Lloyd is also true. His family entered showbusiness and McCarthy's son and daughter-in-law were major music hall per-formers. He was also the great-great grandfather of the actress Kay Kendall, possibly best known for her role in the movie *Genevieve* and as wife of Hollywood star Rex Harrison.[12]

Kelly's room was small and sparsely furnished. It was about 12 feet square, there was a fireplace opposite the door, two windows to the left of the door and to the right a bedside table so close that the door would bang against it when swung open. Kelly's bed was between the bedside table and the false partition. A journalist who visited the room with the inquest jurors noted in addition to the bed and bedside table 'a farthing dip in a bottle ... The only attempt at decoration were a couple of engravings, one "The Fisherman's Widow", stuck over the mantelpiece, while in the corner was an open cupboard containing a few bits of pottery, some ginger-beer bottles, and a bit of bread on a plate'.[13] Some sources mention another table and a chair. Kelly paid a weekly rent of 4s 6d and at the time of her death she was substantially in arrears, a debt that it is surprising McCarthy had allowed to accumulate.[14]

In late August or early September Joseph Barnett lost his job and Kelly returned to prostitution. Barnett did not like this and decided to leave her,[15] although he explained to various journalists and told the inquest the problem was that he objected when Kelly allowed prostitutes to stay in the room. 'She would never have gone wrong again', he told a reporter, 'and I shouldn't have left her if it had not been for the prostitutes stopping at the house. She only let them because she was good hearted and did not like to refuse them shelter on cold bitter nights'.[16] Barnett seems to have tried to publicly portray Kelly in a better light, generously offering her room to fellow prostitutes rather than bringing her own customers back to their room. The possibility that other prostitutes used Kelly's room has spawned several avenues of interesting conjecture over the years because Kelly was mutilated beyond recognition and this has allowed speculation that the victim in room 13 was not Mary Jane Kelly but a prostitute whom she allowed to stay the night in her room. Some support for this notion exists in the claim by several people to have seen Kelly alive several hours after the medical experts were of the opinion that she was dead (see below). Whatever the real reason, there was a fight and Barnett left Kelly between 5pm and 6pm on 30 October, going to Buller's boarding house in Bishopsgate and later moving in with his sister, who lived off Gray's Inn Road.

On Wednesday 7 November 1888, Kelly bought a halfpenny candle from John McCarthy's shop – the 'dip' seen by the journalist who toured Kelly's room – and was later seen in Miller's Court by Thomas Bowyer, a pensioned soldier nicknamed 'Indian Harry' employed by McCarthy:

Harry Bowyer [*sic*] states that on Wednesday night he saw a man speaking to Kelly who resembled the description given by the fruiterer of the supposed Berner Street murderer. He was, perhaps, 27 or 28 and had a dark moustache and very peculiar eyes. His appearance was rather smart and attention was drawn to him by showing very white cuffs and a rather long white collar, the ends of which came down in front over a black coat. He did not carry a bag.[17]

Given the notoriety of Dorset Street as a dangerous area and the fact that Miller's Court was a cul-de-sac accessed through a narrow passage into which nobody would likely have strayed by accident, the presence there of a 'rather smart' man warrants comment, especially as he resembled someone perhaps seen in the vicinity of the Berner Street murder.

The next day, Thursday 8 November, Mary Kelly went to the Ten Bells, where she met a friend called Elizabeth Foster, who said she had known Kelly for 18 months and found her to be 'as nice a woman as one could find'. Kelly left about 7.05pm and apparently returned to Miller's Court. She was joined in her room by a young woman named Lizzie Albrook. Between 7.30pm and 7.45pm Joseph Barnett called, as he had been in the habit of doing most days since they split up. Albrook left when Barnett arrived, but Barnett did not stay long and Mary Kelly's movements from this time onwards are uncertain.

Mary Kelly 'went out drinking in the local public-houses', said Walter Dew. 'This was unusual, for normally Marie was a sober girl'.[18] About 11.00pm John McCarthy (who may have been reporting what he had been told rather than what he had seen) said, 'she was seen in the Britannia public house [on the corner of Dorset Street and Commercial Street] ... with a young man with a dark moustache. She was then intoxicated. The young man appeared to be very respectable and well dressed'.[19]

At 11.45pm Mary Ann Cox, who lived at 5 Miller's Court and was a prostitute, entered Dorset Street from Commercial Street. Kelly, who was drunk, was walking just ahead of her with a stout man, shabbily dressed in a long overcoat and wearing a round billycock hat, aged about 35 or 36, with a blotchy face and sporting a full carroty moustache. He was carrying a pail of beer. The couple turned into the passage leading into Miller's Court and were standing outside the door to Kelly's room when Mrs. Cox passed.

'Goodnight', said Mrs. Cox.

'Goodnight', Kelly replied, 'I am going to sing'.

A minute or two later Kelly began singing, 'Only a Violet I Plucked from my Mother's Grave'. At midnight Mary Ann Cox returned to the streets. Kelly was still singing the same song.[20]

Catherine Picket, a neighbour, was becoming fed up with Kelly's singing but her husband stopped her from going across to Kelly's room to complain. At 1.00am it was starting to rain. Mary Ann Cox returned to her room for a few minutes warmth by her fire. Kelly was still singing. John McCarthy confirmed this: 'the last thing he had heard of her was at one o'clock Friday morning, when she was singing in her room, and appeared to be very happy'.[21] Elizabeth Prater, a prostitute who lived in the room above Kelly, returned home about 1.00am and she stood at the entrance to Miller's Court for about half an hour, except for ten minutes when she went into McCarthy's shop and chatted. She saw nobody enter or leave the Court. Curiously, she didn't hear any singing. Prater then went to her room, put two chairs in front of her door and without undressing lay on her bed and fell into a deep, drink-induced sleep.

At 2.00am George Hutchinson was walking along Commercial Street. Near the corner of Flower and Dean Street he met Mary Kelly, who asked him to lend her sixpence. Hutchinson said he had been to Romford and was spent out. 'I must go and look for some money', said Kelly, and walked towards Thrawl Street where there was a man standing. The man put his hand on Kelly's shoulder and must have said something because Kelly and the man laughed. Hutchinson heard Kelly say, 'All right' and the man say, 'You will be all right for what I have told you'. He then put his arm around Kelly's shoulders and they began to walk back towards Dorset Street. Hutchinson had now stopped beneath the lamp outside the Queen's Head, where a month earlier Elizabeth Stride had enjoyed a drink before setting off for her Saturday night out, and saw the man distinctly as he and Kelly passed him. He had a soft felt hat drawn down over his eyes, had a dark complexion – a Jewish appearance – and a heavy moustache turned up at the ends, dark eyes and bushy eyebrows. He was wearing a long dark coat trimmed with astrakhan and a white collar with a black necktie, in which was fixed a horseshoe pin. He wore dark spats and light button-over boots. A massive gold chain was displayed in his waistcoat. His watch chain had a large seal with a red stone hanging from it. He carried a pair of kid gloves in his right hand and in his left there was a small package. He was about 5ft 6in, tall, aged about 35 or 36.

It was a dramatic style of dress for Spitalfields, not to say a stupid one – a gold watch and chain on display in an area distinguished as one of the roughest in East London! – and one must inevitably question the accuracy of such a detailed description. However, according to Hutchinson, Kelly and the man crossed Commercial Street, turned into Dorset Street and for about three minutes stood talking outside the passage leading to Miller's Court. Hutchinson heard Kelly say 'All right, my dear. Come along. You will be comfortable', to which the man put his arm around Kelly and kissed her. Kelly said 'I've lost my handkerchief!', which seems about the most incongruous remark possible in the circumstances, but the man pulled a red handkerchief out of his pocket and gave it to her. The couple then went down Miller's Court. As the Christ Church clock struck 3.00am, Hutchinson, wandered off.[22]

A young woman named Sarah Lewis told the inquest into Kelly's death that she had passed Christ Church as the clock struck 2.30am, turned into Dorset Street and entered Miller's Court.

> When I went into the court, opposite the lodging-house I saw a man with a wideawake. There was no one talking to him. He was a stout-looking man, and not very tall. The hat was black. I did not take any notice of his clothes. The man was looking up the court; he seemed to be waiting or looking for some one. Further on there was a man and woman – the latter being in drink.[23]

This man was probably George Hutchinson. It is curious, however, that Hutchinson never mentioned seeing Sarah Lewis or the man and drunken woman further down the street.[24] George Hutchinson's testimony is hugely important as it is likely that he saw Kelly with her murderer. He has provided an excellent description of Jack the Ripper that shows him to have been the 'toff' of popular lore, rather than one of the poverty-stricken inhabitants of the East End or a poor immigrant Jew. On the other hand, it is tempting to dismiss George Hutchinson's testimony because his detailed description seems too good to be true, because he didn't see Sarah Lewis and the other people in the street and because he didn't give his story to the police until after the inquest had been concluded, which suggests that he may have been a publicity-seeker spinning a yarn safe in the knowledge that he wouldn't be contradicted by an army of witnesses attending the inquest proceedings. This said, Inspector Abberline, who said Hutchinson claimed to have known Kelly for three years and to have occasionally given her a few shillings, thought that Hutchinson had made 'an important statement' and gave it as his opinion that 'the statement is true'.[25]

By 3.00am it was raining hard and Hutchinson cannot have been gone long when Mrs. Cox returned to her room. Kelly's room was dark and quiet. Mrs. Cox went to bed and tried to get some sleep.

Between 3.30am and 4.00am Elizabeth Prater, in the room above Kelly's, was woken by her pet kitten Diddles walking across her neck. 'I heard a cry of "Oh! Murder!" as the cat came on me and I pushed her down, the voice was a faint voice – the noise seemed to come from close by – it is nothing uncommon to hear cries of murder, so I took no notice. I did not hear it a second time. I heard nothing else whatever'. Sarah Lewis also heard the cry, which to her was a loud shout: 'The sound seemed to come from the direction of the deceased's room; there was only one scream – I took no notice of it'.

Having grabbed a few hours sleep, Elizabeth Prater was awake by 5.00am and went to the Ten Bells for a glass of rum. She saw two or three men harnessing some horses in Dorset Street, but nothing aroused her suspicions. At 5.45am Mrs. Cox thought she heard a man's footsteps leaving Miller's Court. Catherine Picket, the flower seller, woke up at 7.30am and by 8.00am was on her way to market to buy some flowers. The morning was chilly and as it was also raining she thought she would borrow Kelly's shawl. There was no reply when she knocked on Kelly's door and she went off to her day's work. About the same time, 8.00am, a tailor named Maurice Lewis said he saw Kelly leave her room, then return to it a few moments later.[26]

Perhaps the most extraordinary and persistent testimony was that of Mrs. Caroline Maxwell. Caroline Maxwell, who lived at 14 Dorset Street and was the wife of a lodging house deputy, Henry Maxwell, said she had known Kelly for about four months, but had only spoken to her twice. She nevertheless knew her name, and Kelly knew hers.[27] She knew Kelly was a prostitute and although she had seen her 'in drink', she was not a notorious character. She kept herself to herself, and did not mix up with anybody. On Friday morning she came out of the lodging house and saw Kelly standing at the corner of the entry to Miller's Court. The time was between 8.00am and 8.30am, which she was able to fix because her husband had finished work, as he did about that time. It was unusual to see Kelly up so early. Mrs. Maxwell spoke across the street, 'What, Mary, brings you up so early?'

Kelly replied, 'Oh, Carrie, I do feel so bad. I've had a glass of beer, and I've brought it up again'. It was in the road. Mrs. Maxwell, who thought Kelly had been to the Britannia beer shop at the corner of the street, said, 'I can pity your feelings' and hurried off to Bishopsgate Street to get her husband's breakfast. About 8.45am she returned to Dorset Street and saw Kelly outside the Britannia, talking to a man. They were some distance away – Abberline estimated 25 yards – and although she was positive the woman was Kelly, the couple were too far away for her to give a description of the man, except that he was stout and dressed in dark clothes. The woman was wearing a dark skirt, a velvet body, a maroon shawl and no hat.

Mrs. Maxwell's story was completely contrary to the evidence of the doctors regarding time of death, but she was emphatic about the time, the day and the conversation, even in the imposing surroundings of the inquest when reminded by the Coroner, 'You must be very careful about your evidence, because it is different to other people's'. And *The Times* on 12 November reported corroboration of Mrs. Maxwell's story:

> When asked by the police how she could fix the time of the morning, Mrs. Maxwell replied, 'Because I went to the milkshop for some milk, and I had not before been there for a long time, and that she was wearing a woollen cross-over that I had not seen her wear for a considerable time'. On inquiries being made at the milkshop indicated by the woman her statement was found to be correct, and the cross-over was also found in Kelly's room.[28]

Walter Dew wrote of Mrs. Maxwell, 'She seemed a sane and sensible woman, and her reputation was excellent', and he added, 'In one way at least her version fitted into the facts as known. We know that Marie had been drinking the previous night, and, as this was not a habit of hers, illness the next morning was just what might have been expected'.[29]

On the face of it, Mrs. Maxwell was a woman of 'excellent' reputation who stuck to her story and whose story about the day was corroborated by the milk shop. In addition, it was, as Walter Dew pointed out, consistent with what emerged about Mary Kelly's movements the night before, and was also consistent with Kelly being unwell – if, as Dew believed, she was not given to drinking to excess. But it is also a story impossible to accept. If Kelly was the murdered and mutilated woman in 13 Miller's Court, then Caroline Maxwell did not see her that Friday morning and must have been recalling another day. The testimony of the milkshop does not support this idea, if *The Times* report that she had not visited the shop recently is to be believed, and whilst there is no corroboration from the Britannia or any local pub that Kelly was served or seen that morning, this assumes that somebody, journalist or policeman, sought corroboration; and that Kelly would have been remembered amid what may have been a brisk early morning trade with market staff finishing the night shift.[30]

At 10.45am John McCarthy called for his assistant, Thomas 'Indian Harry' Bowyer, and told him to go to 13 and try to get some rent from Kelly. Bowyer went to Kelly's room and knocked at the door, but did not get a reply. He tried the door, but it was locked. He knocked again. He looked through the keyhole. Sometime earlier a pane of glass in the window nearest the door had been smashed and left unrepaired, largely, it would seem, because Kelly and Barnett had some time earlier lost the key to the room 'and since it has been lost they have put their hands through the broken window, and moved back the catch. It is quite easy'.[31] Going to the window, Bowyer reached through the broken pane of glass and plucked back the muslin curtain. The horribly butchered mess that lay before his horrified gaze was barely recognisable as a human being.

Bowyer rushed back to McCarthy, spluttered his discovery and McCarthy rushed to the broken window and looked into the room. 'The sight we saw I cannot drive away from my mind', he said later, 'It looked more like the work of a devil than of a man. I had heard a great deal about the Whitechapel murders, but I declare to God I had never expected to see such a sight as this. The whole scene is more than I can describe. I hope I may never see such a sight as this again'.[32]

Bowyer fetched Inspector Beck and Sergeant Betham from the Commercial Street Police Station. Beck took one look and sent for police assistance and the divisional surgeon, Dr. George Bagster Phillips. The time was now about 11.00am and the police managed to very effectively close off Miller's Court, stopping anyone outside the Court from entering and anyone inside the Court from leaving. A veil of silence fell over the inquiry.

Newspaper reporters had to gather snippets of information wherever they could. Most of the initial reports are wrong, sometimes wildly so, and misleading. The early press coverage is a minefield for the incautious. However, it was quickly realised that a murder had been committed and according to the Press Association, 'Women rushed about the streets telling their neighbours the news and shouting their rage and indignation'.

Dr. George Bagster Phillips arrived at 11.15am, and viewed the body through the window. At 11.30am Inspector Abberline arrived, received a general report from Inspector Beck, and had a hurried conference with Dr. Phillips. A photographer took photographs of the murder scene. The weather was deteriorating, the leaden sky making it almost dark in Miller's Court, and there was an annoying drizzling rain. There were delays on account of it being thought that bloodhounds would be brought in, but they weren't and eventually McCarthy forced open the door with a pick-axe – which suggests that Kelly must have found the lost key, otherwise the police would have reached through the window to open the door, in the fashion Abberline described. The door swung open and hit against the bedside table.

Mary Kelly had been mutilated to an extraordinary degree. The surviving black and white photograph of the body *in situ* conveys the horrific and horrible sight that greeted the eyes of the policeman and other witnesses of whose consequent traumas we hear nothing. Walter Dew, who records that he was 'the first police officer on the scene', says that the scene he witnessed through the broken window 'was too harrowing to be described. It remains with me – and always will remain with me – as the most gruesome memory of the whole of my police career'.[33] The scalpel-cold post-mortem report by Dr. Thomas Bond is clinical and precise:

> The body was lying naked[34] in the middle of the bed, the shoulders flat, but the axis of the body inclined to the left side of the bed. The head was turned on the left cheek. The left arm was close to the body with the forearm flexed at a right angle & lying across the abdomen. the right arm was slightly abducted from the body & rested on the mattress, the elbow bent & the forearm supine with the fingers clenched. The legs were wide apart, the left thigh at right angles to the trunk & the right forming an obtuse angle with the pubes.
>
> The whole of the surface of the abdomen & thighs was removed & the abdominal Cavity emptied of its viscera. The breasts were cut off, the arms mutilated by several jagged wounds & the face hacked beyond recognition of the features. The tissues of the neck were severed all round down to the bone.
>
> The viscera were found in various parts viz: the uterus & Kidneys with

one breast under the head, the other breast by the Rt foot, the Liver between the feet, the intestines by the right side & the spleen by the left side of the body. The flaps removed from the abdomen and thighs were on a table.

The bed clothing at the right corner was saturated with blood, & on the floor beneath was a pool of blood covering about 2 feet square. The wall by the right side of the bed & in a line with the neck was marked by blood which had struck it in a number of separate splashes.

Postmortem examination

The face was gashed in all directions the nose, cheeks, eyebrows and ears being partly removed. The lips were blanched & cut by several incisions running obliquely down to the chin. There were also numerous cuts extending irregularly across all the features.

The neck was cut through the skin & other tissues right down to the vertebrae the 5th & 6th being deeply notched. The skin cuts in the front of the neck showed distinct ecchymosis.

The air passage was cut at the lower part of the larynx through the cricoid cartilage.

Both breasts were removed by more or less circular incisions, the muscles down to the ribs being attached to the breasts. The intercostals between the 4th, 5th & 6th ribs were cut through & the contents of the thorax visible through the openings.

The skin & tissues of the abdomen from the costal arch to the pubes were removed in three large flaps. The right thigh was denuded in front to the bone, the flap of skin, including the external organs of generation & part of the right buttock. The left thigh was stripped of skin, fascia & muscles as far as the knee.

The left calf showed a long gash through skin & tissues to the deep muscles & reaching from the knee to 5 ins above the ankle.

Both arms & forearms had extensive & jagged wounds.

The right thumb showed a small superficial incision about 1 in long, with extravasation of blood in the skin & there were several abrasions on the back of the hand moreover showing the same condition.

On opening the thorax it was found that the right lung was minimally adherent by old firm adhesions. The lower part of the lung was broken & torn away.

The left lung was intact: it was adherent at the apex & there were a few adhesions over the side. In the substances of the lung were several nodules of consolidation.

The Pericardium was open below & the Heart absent.

In the abdominal cavity was some partially digested food of fish & potatoes & similar food was found in the remains of the stomach attached to the intestines.

In another report Dr. Bond added:

> The body was laying on the bed at the time of my visit at two o'clock quite naked and mutilated ... Rigor Mortis had set in but increased during the progress of the examination. From this it is difficult to say with any certainty the exact time that had elapsed since death as the period varies from six to twelve hours before rigidity sets in. The body was comparatively cold at two o'clock and the remains of a recently taken meal were found in the stomach and scattered about over the intestines. It was therefore pretty certain that the woman must have been dead about twelve hours and the partly digested food would indicate that death took place about three or four hours after food was taken, so one or two o'clock in the morning would be the probable time of the murder.
>
> The corner of the sheet to the right of the woman's head was much cut and saturated with blood, indicating that the face may have been covered with the sheet at the time of the attack.

The police wrapped the Kelly murder as tight as a snare drum and the press had little or no reliable information. The carnage in the room was bad enough, but became exaggerated. It was a gruesome enough scene, 'blood was everywhere and pieces of flesh were scattered about the floor ...'.[35] Walter Dew recalled, 'I had slipped and fallen on the awfulness of that floor'.[36] There was considerable interest in and speculation about any missing body parts.

Central News reported:

> It is stated, upon authority which should be trustworthy, that the uturus, as in the case of the Mitre Square victim, has been removed and taken away by the fiend, but on this important point the police officers and surgeons refuse in the most emphatic manner to give the slightest information. It is almost self-evident, however, that had this particular organ not been removed the police would gladly have said so, if only to allay in some slight measure the panic which has again set in ...[37]

Whereas on the same day *The Times* reported,

> No portion of the murdered woman's body was taken away ... the post-mortem was of the most exhaustive character and the surgeons did not quit their work until every organ was accounted for and placed as closely as possible in its natural position.[38]

Speculation has continued to this day, it appearing that the murderer took away Mary Kelly's heart, which Dr. Bond says was 'absent'.

Dr. Bond also offered something of a psychological profile of the murderer, one of the first on record. A report submitted to the police and the Home Office on 10 November in part read:

> In each case [i.e. in all five murders from Nichols to Kelly] the mutilation was inflicted by a person who had no scientific or anatomical knowledge. In my opinion he does not even possess the technical knowledge of a butcher or horse slaughterer or any person accustomed to cut up dead animals.
>
> The murderer in external appearance is quite likely to be a quiet inoffensive looking man probably middle-aged and neatly and respectably dressed.
>
> Assuming the murderer to be such a person as I have just described, he would be solitary and eccentric in his habits, also he is most likely to be a man without regular occupation, but with some small income or pension. He is probably living among respectable persons who have some knowledge of his character and habits and who may have grounds for suspicion that he isn't quite right in his mind at times. Such persons would probably be unwilling to communicate suspicions to the Police for fear of trouble or notoriety, whereas if there were prospect of a reward it might overcome their scruples.

Bond's report is highly speculative, his deductions befitting Sherlock Holmes, and his view that the murderer exhibited no anatomical knowledge or surgical skill or even the basic dissecting knowledge of a slaughterer or butcher was at variance with the opinion of most of the other doctors who had viewed victims of Jack the Ripper. One possibly significant point did emerge from his report and from other details: Bond said that 'both arms & forearms had extensive & jagged wounds ... The right thumb showed a small superficial incision about 1 in long, with extravasation of blood in the skin & there were several abrasions on the back of the hand moreover showing the same condition'. This has suggested that Mary Kelly might have put up something of a struggle. Against this, however, is Dr. Bond's statement about the bed sheet, the corner of which 'was much cut and saturated with blood, indicating that the face may have been covered with the sheet at the time of the attack'. In other words, the cuts in the sheet suggest that it had been pulled up around her neck, wholly or partly covering her face, the reasonable inference being that Kelly had gone to sleep.

Did Kelly take a man back to her room and share her bed with him for the night? Or had she gone to bed alone and her murderer then entered her room? If the latter, was her murderer someone she knew or someone she had been with earlier that evening? The questions tumble out: if Kelly was asleep when attacked, would she have had an opportunity to cry out the words, 'Oh! Murder!', as heard by two neighbours? And even if she had had time to cry out, would she have cried out 'Oh! Murder!', instead of screaming or calling for help? Would 'Oh! Murder!' be more consistent with the discovery of the body than an exclamation on being attacked?

And why was the door to Kelly's room locked, as it must have been for McCarthy to take a pickaxe to it instead of opening it by reaching through the broken window, as Abberline said it was easy to do? Had Mary Kelly found the key to the room? Anyone studying the Jack the Ripper case is accustomed to questions. Sadly, answers are generally precious few!

Trying to calculate the time of death is equally problematic, but Dr. Bond's estimate of death about 2.00am is likely to be tolerably accurate. Unfortunately, this doesn't help to tie her time of death to the time when she suddenly stopped singing. Did she stop singing because she had fallen asleep? Did she go out? Did she die as George Hutchinson watched Miller's Court? Did George Hutchinson therefore describe her murderer? In death, as apparently in life, Mary Kelly remains an enigma.

The murder of Mary Jane Kelly was followed by a repeat of the procedures following each of the previous murders – a search of common lodging houses, the questioning of lodgers, a series of arrests and subsequent releases after questioning and investigation. The inquest was opened and closed on 12 November at the Shoreditch Town Hall under the direction of Dr. Roderick Macdonald, Coroner for northeast Middlesex. There was some initial dispute between Macdonald and a juryman, the latter maintaining that the body of Kelly had been found in Whitechapel and that the responsibility for conducting the inquest fell to Wynne E. Baxter, not to Macdonald and the parish of Shoreditch. Macdonald responded that the body had been taken to the mortuary within his district and that legally he was responsible for conducting the inquest. Apparently Macdonald was wrong. It was illegal to remove a body from one district to another and in December 1889 a man who died in a common lodging house in Heneage Street, Spitalfields, had to be left laid out for three days on the edge of a kitchen table – screened by a blanket from diners using the rest of the table – because there was no mortuary within the district to which he could be taken. As the *Pall Mall Gazette* reported, 'as the law stood it would not allow a body to be removed' to a mortuary in a neighbouring district.[39]

Macdonald also heard the testimony of no more than a handful of witnesses before instructing the jury that they had heard enough to establish the cause of death and to bring in a verdict. The jury naturally returned a verdict of 'wilful murder against some person or persons unknown'. The press expressed much surprise at the sudden termination and Rowland Adams Williams, the former Deputy Coroner of Crickhowell, was moved to write in *The Times* pointing out several deficiencies in the proceedings.

Mary Jane Kelly was buried on Monday 19 November 1888 at the exclusively Roman Catholic Leytonstone Cemetery.

The remains of the unfortunate woman, Marie Jeanette Kelly, who was murdered on November 9th, in Miller's-Court, Dorset-street, Spitalfields, were carried on Monday from the Shoreditch mortuary to the Roman Catholic Cemetery at Leytonstone, for interment, amidst a scene of turbulent excitement. On the afternoon of the murder the body of the murdered woman was conveyed to the mortuary attached to St. Leonard's Church, Shoreditch, and there it remained until on Monday. Since the inquest a great amount of sympathy for the fate of the unhappy creature has been created, but it remained for Mr. H. Wilton, the sexton attached to Shoreditch Church, to put sympathy into a practical form, and as no relatives have appeared he incurred the total cost of the funeral himself. Mr. Wilton has been sexton for over 50 years, and he provided the funeral as a mark of sincere sympathy with the poor people of the neighbourhood, in whose welfare he is deeply interested. The body was enclosed in a polished elm and oak coffin, with metal mounts. On the coffin plate were engraved the words: 'Marie Jeanette Kelly, died 9th Nov. 1888, aged 25 years'. Upon the coffin were two crowns of artificial flowers and a cross made up of heartsease. The coffin was carried in an open car drawn by two horses, and two coaches followed. An enormous crowd of people assembled at an early hour, completely blocking the thoroughfare, and a large number of police were engaged in keeping order. The bell of St. Leonard's began tolling at noon, and the signal appeared to draw all the residents in the neighbourhood together. There was an enormous preponderance of women in the crowd, and scarcely any had any covering to their heads. The wreaths upon the coffin bore cards inscribed with remembrances from friends using certain public-houses in common with the murdered woman. As the coffin appeared, borne on the shoulders of four men, at the principal gate of the church, the crowd appeared to be greatly affected. Round the open car in which it was to be placed men and women struggled desperately to get to touch the coffin. Women with faces streaming with tears cried out 'God forgive her!' and every man's head was bared in token of sympathy. The sight was quite remarkable, and the emotion natural and unconstrained. Two mourning coaches followed, one containing three, and the other five persons – mourners who had been fortifying themselves for the journey at a public house close to the church gates. Joe Barnett was amongst them, with someone from M'Carthy's, the landlord; and the others were women who had given evidence at the inquest. After a tremendous struggle, the car, with the coffin fully exposed to view, set out at a very slow pace, all the crowd appearing to move off simultaneously in attendance. The traffic was blocked, and the constables had great difficulty in obtaining free passage for the small procession through the mass of carts, vans and tramcars.[40]

The most extraordinary thing is that whilst one would have expected the murder of Mary Kelly, by far the most horrendous in the series, to have sparked the press and public into another outburst of outrage and panic and sensationalism, the reverse was the case. Press interest poured away like bathwater when the plug is pulled out. The abrupt termination of the inquest on 13 November combined with the police news blackout deprived the press of material and the long murder-free month of October had exhausted the permutations of press speculation. All that could be said had been said and the radical press such as *The Star* was finding news and sensation in the semi-judicial Commission into Parnell and the Pigott forgeries. In dramatically diminishing column inches the press continued to report the arrest of assorted oddballs such as Dr. Holt of Willesden who with blackened face had been wandering the streets in the hope of discovering Jack the Ripper. On 11 November he terrified a woman named Humphreys by appearing from the shadows of George Yard, where Martha Tabram was murdered. A crowd descended, among them the famous pugilist Wolf Bendoff,[41] and amid cries of 'Lynch him!' the police arrived and managed to get him to the safety of a police station, from where he was released a few hours later. He passed into Jack the Ripper lore through the imaginative pen of Edwin T. Woodhall[42] who described him as the 'painted menace' or 'white-eyed man' – a ghoulish creature with large white-painted circles around his eyes (in reality Dr. Holt's spectacles), white-painted nose, moustache and mouth, and who when arrested was taken to Scotland Yard, but during questioning grabbed a heavy ebony ruler and laid into two senior officials, escaped and vanished, three weeks later being pulled from beneath a paddle boat on the Thames near Hungerford Bridge, the burnt cork and white paint still clear on his decomposing features. As his authority for this story Woodhall cited Sir Melville Macnaghten, who in his autobiography does indeed express his belief that Jack the Ripper was pulled from the Thames 'after he had knocked out a Commissioner of Police and very nearly settled the hash of one of Her Majesty's principal Secretaries of State'.[43] However, Macnaghten was referring to the press condemnation of Henry Matthews, the resignation of Sir Charles Warren and the apparent suicide of a barrister named Druitt.

The day before the inquest, 10 November 1888, the government offered a pardon to any accomplice 'not being the person who contrived or actually committed the murder'. It was no more than a palliative to public feeling, and Henry Matthews, the Home Secretary, had already mooted it to Ruggles-Brise: 'You say nothing about the suggestion of my offering a free pardon to anyone not the actual perpetrator of the murders, I could do that more easily, and with less discredit, than would follow from offering a reward'.[44] On the same day Warren tendered his resignation and it was accepted. It had nothing to do with Jack the Ripper, but was in response to a reprimand by Matthews following the publication in the November issue of *Murray's Magazine* of an article by Warren in which he defended himself and the police in general against long-standing press criticism. The article was in contravention of a Home Office circular of 27 May 1879 that required Warren to obtain the permission of the Home Office before discussing police matters. He had obtained no such permission, and professed complete ignorance of the rule, but felt unable to stay in office if he was expected to carry the can for things that were not his responsibility and against which he could not defend himself. As Warren's grandson wrote, not unfairly:

It has been publicly stated, both at the time and also in more recent years, that Warren's resignation resulted from the failure of the police to discover the Whitechapel murderer. This statement is absolutely untrue. Others have said that it was the result of *pique* at the censure which his *Murray's Magazine* article received. This, although somewhat ungenerously phrased, is nearer the truth. The censure of his article provided the occasion, rather than the cause, of his resignation. The real cause lay in the increasing lack of *entente* between Scotland Yard and the Home Office, and in particular over the question of police pensions, since Warren's pleas for an improved pension scheme and a curtailment of other less necessary expenses had been systematically ignored. He had accepted the chief Commissioner-ship solely from a sense of duty, and for the special purpose of increasing the efficiency of the police and restoring order among the riotous elements in the Metropolis. He had had, from the start, no intention of remaining in office after that purpose had been achieved. In March 1888 he began to discuss the question of his resignation with Matthews: in the late summer he resigned, but the outbreak of murders in Whitechapel made it undesirable that his resignation should be accepted at that time. The *Murray's Magazine* affair, however, left him no alternative but to resign again, which he did on November 8th, and this time Matthews was disposed to accept his resignation. The appointment of Monro as his successor – a man who, as his sub-ordinate, had been instrumental in throwing obstacles in his way – did nothing to gild the pill that Warren was forced to swallow.[45]

The dearth of news is probably illustrated by two stories concerning John McCarthy and his wife. The latter received a Folkestone postmarked postcard saying, 'Don't be alarmed. I am going to do another; but this time it will be a mother and daughter', and signed 'Jack Sheridan, the Ripper'. It was handed to the police but treated as a hoax.[46] And John McCarthy was offered £25 by a showman for the use of Kelly's room for a month, and another showman offered to buy the few sticks of furniture in Kelly's room. McCarthy rejected both offers.[47]

The curious thing about the murder of Mary Jane Kelly is that she was a frightened woman. Joseph Barnett was asked at the inquest if Mary Kelly had ever expressed fear of anyone. Barnett replied, 'Yes; several times'. And he went on to say that she had asked him about the murders and that he had 'bought newspapers, and I read to her everything about the murders'.

Walter Dew remarked, 'There was no woman in the whole of Whitechapel more frightened of Jack the Ripper than Marie Kelly'.[48]

Notes

1. Anderson, Sir Robert (1910) *The Lighter Side of My Official Life*. London: Hodder and Stoughton, p.137. 'The last and most horrible of that maniac's crimes was committed in a house in Miller's Court on the 9 November.'
2. Report by Sir Melville Macnaghten dated 23 February 1894. MEPO 3/141 fol.178: 'Now the Whitechapel murderer had 5 victims and 5 victims only', the last being Mary Kelly.
3. Blonde – or perhaps not: Barnett 'at once identified the body as that of Kelly, or "Ginger", as she was called, owing to the colour of her hair' (*Western Mail*, 10 November 1888, citing a Press Association report); 'a blonde of medium height ...' (*East London Observer*, 17 November 1888), 'She was short and

stout and dark . . .' (Maurice Lewis reported in *The Illustrated Police News*, 17 November 1888).

4. Macnaghten, Sir Melville (1914) *Days of My Years*. London: Longmans, Green & Co., p.60.

5. Dew, Walter (1938) *I Caught Crippen: Memoirs of Ex-Chief Inspector Walter Dew CID*. London: Blackie & Son, pp.86, 146.

6. According to Charles Booth, Breezer's Hill and Pennington Street were noted for prostitutes, 'but the prostitution is of a sturdy kind and there are no bullies who live off the earnings of the women', said an Inspector Reid, Booth's guide.

7. *Western Mail*, 13 November 1888, quoting a Press Association report.

8. Joseph Barnett's inquest testimony reported in the *Daily Telegraph*, 13 November 1888.

9. Julia Venturney, quoted in *The Times*, 13 November 1888.

10. Dorset Street was noted also – as Charles Booth recorded in his notebook when taken on a tour through the street – for 'One very fat lady at a window. She has sat there for years. She is too fat to get out of the door!'.

11. Samuel, Raphael (1981) *East End Underworld: Chapters in the Life of Arthur Harding*. London: Routledge and Keegan Paul, p.100.

12. John McCarthy's son, John Joseph McCarthy, was an entertainer under the stage name of Steve McCarthy, and he married a top-billing music hall performer named Marie Kendall. They had two children, one of whom, Terrence Kendall-McCarthy married Gladys Drewery and was the father of Kim and Kay Kendall-McCarthy. See Aliffe, Andy (2002) 'The Kendall-McCarthy's: A Showbusiness Dynasty'. *Ripperologist*, 41, June, pp.5–6; Golden, Eve and Kendall, Kim (2002) *The Brief, Madcap Life of Kay Kendall*. Lexington, Kentucky: The University Press of Kentucky, pp.7–8.

13. *Pall Mall Gazette*, 12 November 1888.

14. It was common practice among brothel keepers to keep their 'girls' in debt, thereby ensuring that they had to keep working for them. Kelly's debt has therefore been seen by some commentators as further evidence that McCarthy was a pimp. However, it is tempting to speculate that there was a family relationship – oddly enough an American newspaper reported, 'About a year ago he [John McCarthy] rented it to a woman who looked about thirty. She was popular among the females of the neighborhood, shared her beer generously, as I have been tearfully informed, and went under the title of Mary Jane McCarthy. Her landlord knew that she had another name, Kelly, that of her husband, but her friends had not heard of it' (*Washington Evening Star*, 10 November 1888). Or perhaps Kelly knew McCarthy through his links with the stage, Lizzie Albrook having said that Kelly had spoken of a relative who was on the stage in London (reported in the *Western Mail*, 12 November 1888). Could that relative have known McCarthy?

15. Statement by Joseph Barnett to Inspector Abberline, MJ/SPC/NE 1888. Box 3, no. 19. Corporation of London, Greater London Archives. Coroner's Papers.

16. Joseph Barnett, *Western Mail*, 12 November 1888.
17. *Western Mail*, 12 November 1888.
18. Dew, Walter (1938) *I Caught Crippen: Memoirs of Ex-Chief Inspector Walter Dew CID*. London: Blackie & Son, p.151.
19. *Illustrated Police News*, 17 November 1888.
20. Mary Ann Cox, inquest testimony and statement to Inspector Abberline. MJ/SPC/ME. 1888. Box 3, no. 19. Corporation of London, Greater London Archives, Coroner's Papers.
21. *Illustrated Police News*, 17 November 1888.
22. George Hutchinson, statement dated 12 November 1888, signed by Hutchinson, Inspector Abberline, Sergeant E. Badham, Inspector C. Ellisdon and Supt. Arnold. MEPO 3/140 fol. 227–9.
23. *Daily Telegraph*, 13 November 1888.
24. 'One policeman went by the Commercial Street end of Dorset Street while I was standing there, but no one came down Dorset Street. I saw one man go into a lodging house in Dorset Street, and no one else'. George Hutchinson reported in *The Times*, 14 November 1888.
25. Report by Inspector Abberline dated 12 November 1888. MEPO 4/140 fol. 230–2.
26. *The Times*, 10 November 1888.
27. At the inquest she was questioned on this by the coroner: 'And yet you say you had only spoken to her twice previously; you knew her name and she knew yours?'. Maxwell replied, 'Oh, yes; by being about in the lodging-house'.
28. *The Times*, 12 November 1888.
29. Dew, Walter: *op. cit.*, pp.153–4.
30. See *Daily Telegraph*, 13 November 1888; *The Times*, 13 November 1888.
31. Inspector Abberline reported in *Reynold's Newspaper*, 18 November 1888.
32. John McCarthy, an interview given to Central News and reported in several newspapers.
33. Dew, Walter, *op. cit.*, p.86.
34. It wasn't naked, but was dressed in a chemise, clearly visible in the photograph.
35. *Western Mail*, quoting a Central News report, 10 November 1888.
36. Dew, Walter, *op. cit.*, p.148.
37. Central News report, quoted in various newspapers including *Western Mail*, 10 November 1888.
38. *The Times*, 10 November 1888.
39. *Pall Mall Gazette*, 27 December 1889.
40. *East London Advertiser*, 21 November 1888.
41. 27-year-old Wolf Bendoff fought J.R. Couper in Johannesburg in July 1889 for the world heavyweight boxing championship. Couper won. The fight lasted 30 minutes and went 26 rounds.
42. Woodhall, Edwin T. (1937) *Jack the Ripper or When London Walked in Terror*. London: Mellifont Press, p.79.

43. Macnaghten, Sir Melville, *op. cit.*, p.62.

44. Matthews' comments are in a letter from Matthews to his private secretary, Sir Evelyn Ruggles-Brise, dated 5 October 1888. It is contained in the J.S. Sandars papers, MS. Eng. Hist. C.723 at the Bodleian Library, Department of Western Manuscripts, Oxford. The letter is reproduced in full in Begg, Paul (1989) *Jack the Ripper: The Uncensored Facts.* London: Robson Books, pp.132–5.

45. Williams, Watkin Wynn (1941) *The Life of General Sir Charles Warren: By His Grandson.* Oxford: Blackwell, p.224.

46. *Daily Telegraph*, 13 November 1888.

47. *East London Observer* 24 November 1888.

48. Dew, Walter, *op. cit.*, p.150.

chapter fourteen

THE GREAT VICTORIAN MYSTERY: WHO WAS JACK THE RIPPER?

The American author and Ripperologist Christopher-Michael DiGrazia has called Jack the Ripper 'The Great Victorian Mystery'. This perhaps softens the fact that these crimes were the exceptionally brutal murders of women from the most vulnerable class of society and replaces it with images of carboniferous fogs, hansom cabs, flickering gas-lamps, people in fancy dress clothing, Sherlock Holmes with deerstalker and meerschaum pipe and Mrs. Hudson ready with tea and a roaring coal fire back at 22b. But for many people that image of Victorian London is what this subject is all about. It is an opportunity to mentally return to a different but not unrecognisable world to play armchair detective, assembling the evidence like the pieces in a jigsaw until a picture is produced. Some pictures are sufficiently persuasive to be advanced in books, others receive an airing in one of the several magazines devoted to the mystery. Some just get discussed in letters or on Internet message boards. Arguing for a favoured suspect with others is half the fun of being an armchair detective, although sticking to the facts is one of the rules of the game. The Great Victorian Mystery has all the attractions of a Sergeant Cribb or similar detective novel, but without a resolution, and for those who wish to leave their armchair, there is a chance to play the real detective, the tantalising pot of gold at the end of the rainbow being not a solution but the discovery of some new snippet of information.

But is it a mystery that will ever be solved? The disappointing answer is that it probably won't. In the absence of any firm evidence, you must choose the hypothesis you prefer. But as it is pretty much possible to make a case against almost anyone who was alive at the time, the most likely candidates must be those who were suspected by the most informed policemen of the day. There are five: Montague John Druitt, Michael Ostrog, 'Kosminski', Francis Tumblety and Severin Klosowski (otherwise known as George Chapman). We know the first three from a document known as the Macnaghten Memoranda.

The Macnaghten Memorandum

In 1959, when researching a television series called *Farson's Guide To The British*, television investigative journalist Daniel Farson made a programme about cats and interviewed the Dowager Lady Christabel Aberconway, noted cat-lover and author of *A Dictionary of Cat Lovers*.[1] He was also making a programme about Jack the Ripper[2] and in the course of talking with Lady Aberconway he discovered that she was the daughter of Sir Melville Macnaghten and possessed some of her father's papers. The papers were a copy – typewritten by Lady Aberconway's secretary, except for two pages, naming the three suspects, which Lady Aberconway had handwritten herself – of the original document inherited by Lady Aberconway's elder sister, Julia Donner. The original documents had passed from Julia Donner to her son, Gerald Melville Donner, who took them with him when he went to India and all trace of them was lost with his death in November 1968.[3]

A second version of the Memorandum was found in the Scotland Yard files. They differ in several important respects from the Aberconway version, which was almost certainly a draft of the Scotland Yard report. The purpose of the report and who had commissioned it is unknown, but it was prompted by a series of articles in the *Sun* newspaper which argued that Jack the Ripper was Thomas Cutbush, a young man sent to Broadmoor in 1891 after having stabbed two women – Florence Johnson and Isabelle Anderson – in Kennington. The Memorandum may have been written at the request of the Home Office, either for the information of the Home Secretary or in anticipation of questions being asked in the Commons. No questions appear to have been asked and as far as is known the Memorandum was never used. There are some differences between the two documents, the most obvious being the deletion from the Scotland Yard version of almost every personal comment. The result is that the report reads like informed police opinion, whereas from the notes it is clear that much was Macnaghten's own perception. Both versions also contain errors that suggest that Macnaghten was relying on his memory. Perhaps the most important error is in his account of the murder of Elizabeth Stride, where he suggests that the murderer was possibly disturbed when 'three Jews drove up to an Anarchist Club in Berners [*sic*] Street'. It will be recalled that the murderer was possibly disturbed by the arrival of Louis Diemschutz, whilst the three Jews Macnaghten had in mind were probably Lawende, Levy and Harris, the men believed to have seen Catharine Eddowes. This error has a further implication because in the Aberconway transcript Macnaghten wrote that the suspect Kosminski 'in appearance strongly resembled the individual seen by the City PC near Mitre Square'. We do not know of any City PC seeing a suspect in the vicinity of Mitre Square, but a Metropolitan policeman, PC Smith, did see a man talking to a woman who may have been Elizabeth Stride in Berner Street. If Macnaghten mentally transferred Lawende, Levy and Harris from Mitre Square to Berner Street, could he have transferred PC Smith from Berner Street to Mitre Square?

The document is most important because it names three suspects. The versions differ in what they say and are given opposite for comparison.

The general introduction shows the most difference. Macnaghten removes his personal conjectures. The official report makes no mention of the City PC, and he changes 'the police held very reasonable suspicion against' to 'more likely than Cutbush' (which with hindsight could have been said about almost anyone). This last change has suggested to some commentators that no particular significance should be attached to these suspects. However, given that in the draft Macnaghten felt 'inclined to exonerate the last 2' – which would have been a superfluous comment even in a draft document if they were just a few names chosen at random – that one of those named was Macnaghten's own preferred candidate and that another is believed to have been the favoured suspect of Sir Robert Anderson, it seems reasonable to suppose that these were the main suspects.

Montage John Druitt

Montague Druitt's body was pulled from the Thames at Thorneycroft's Wharf near Chiswick by a waterman named Henry Winslade just after midday on Monday 31 December 1888. Winslade pulled the body ashore and immediately fetched PC George Moulson,

Aberconway version	*Scotland Yard version*
No one ever saw the Whitechapel murderer (unless possibly it was the City PC who was a beat [*sic*] near Mitre Square) and no proof could in any way ever be brought against anyone, although very many homicidal maniacs were at one time, or another, *suspected*. I enumerate the cases of 3 men against whom Police held very reasonable suspicion. Personally, after much careful & deliberate consideration, I am inclined to exonerate the last *2*, but I have always held strong opinions regarding *no. 1*, and the more I think the matter over, the stronger do these opinions become. The *truth*, however, will never be known, and did indeed, at one time lie at the bottom of the Thames, if my conjections [*sic*] be correct.	No one ever saw the Whitechapel murderer, many homicidal maniacs were suspected, but no shadow of proof could be thrown on any one. I may mention the cases of 3 men, any one of whom would have been more likely than Cutbush to have committed this series of murders:–
No. 1. Mr. M.J. Druitt a doctor of about 41 years of age & of fairly good family, who disappeared at the time of the Miller's Court murder, and whose body was found floating in the Thames on 31st Dec: i.e. 7 weeks after the said murder. The body was said to have been in the water for a month, *or more* – on it was found a season ticket between Blackheath & London. From	(1) A Mr. M.J. Druitt, said to be a doctor & of good family, who disappeared at the time of the Miller's Court murder, & whose body (which was said to have been upwards of a month in the water) was found in the Thames on 31st. Decr., or about 7 weeks after that murder. He was sexually insane and from private inf. I have little

private information I have little doubt but that his own family suspected this man of being the Whitechapel murderer; it was *alleged* that he was sexually insane.

doubt but that his own family believed him to have been the murderer.

No. 2. Kosminski, a Polish Jew, who lived in the very heart of the district where the murders were committed. He had become insane owing to many years indulgence in solitary vices. He had a great hatred of women, with strong homicidal tendencies. He was (and I believe still is) detained in a lunatic asylum about March 1889. This man in appearance strongly resembled the individual seen by the City PC near Mitre Square.

(2) Kosminski, a Polish Jew, & resident in Whitechapel. This man became insane owing to many years indulgence in solitary vices. He had a great hatred of women, specially of the prostitute class, & had strong homicidal tendencies; he was removed to a lunatic asylum about March 1889. There were many circs connected with this man which made him a strong 'suspect'.

No. 3. Michael Ostrog, a mad Russian doctor & a convict & unquestionably a homicidal maniac. This man was said to have been habitually cruel to women, & for a long time was known to have carried about with him surgical knives & other instruments; his antecedents were of the very worst & his whereabouts at the time of the Whitchape [*sic*] murders could never be satisfactorily accounted for. He is still alive.

(3) Michael Ostrog, a Russian doctor, and a convict, who was subsequently detained in a lunatic asylum as a homicidal maniac. The man's antecedents were of the worst possible type, and his whereabouts at the time of the murders could never be ascertained.

---

who searched the body, finding: 'four large stones in each pocket in the top coat; £2.10s. in gold, 7s. in silver, 2d. in bronze; two cheques on the London and Provincial Bank (one for £50 and the other for £16), a first-class season ticket from Blackheath to London (South Western Railway), a second-half return Hammersmith to Charing Cross dated 1 December, a silver watch, gold chain with silver guinea attached, a pair of kid gloves and a white handkerchief. There were no papers or letters of any kind. There were no marks of injury on the body, but it was rather decomposed and was quickly removed to the mortuary'.

On 2 January 1889 Dr. Thomas Bramah Diplock opened the inquest at the Lamb Tap (it was common to hold inquests at pubs). A report in the *Acton, Chiswick and Turnham Green Gazette,* Saturday 5 January 1889, states that Montague's brother, William, told the inquest that Montague had stayed with him in Bournemouth for a night towards the end of October. On 11 December a friend told William that Montague had not been seen at his chambers for more than a week and William travelled to London to make enquiries, learning at the school where Montague had taught that he had got into serious trouble and been dismissed. Among Montague's things he found a paper addressed to him which 'was to the effect: – "Since Friday I felt that I was going to be like mother, and the best thing for me was to die" '.

Diligent research has unearthed a lot of information about Montague John Druitt. He was the son of William and Ann Druitt, born on 15 August 1857 at Westfield in Wimborne, Dorset. He was educated at Winchester and New College, Oxford, graduating with a 3rd class Honours degree in Classics. In 1881 he took a teaching job at a school at 9 Eliot Place, Blackheath, 'a highly successful educational establishment'[4] boarding boys destined for university, the army and the professions. Many of the pupils there achieved distinction in later life and the headmaster, George Valentine, was widely respected. The school itself was staffed with graduate teachers and servants. Druitt was a keen cricketer, began playing for the Morden Cricket Club, Blackheath, and was soon appointed Treasurer. In 1882 he was admitted to the Inner Temple and he was elected to the MCC on 26 May 1884.

On 29 April 1885 he was called to the Bar of the Inner Temple and had chambers at 9 Kings Bench Walk. The Law List entry of 1886 records that he was of the Western Circuit and of the Winchester Sessions. The entry for 1887 records that he was a special pleader for the Western Circuit and Hampshire, Portsmouth and Southampton Assizes.

In September 1885 Druitt's father died of a heart attack and his mother's precarious mental health began to deteriorate. She developed delusions (that she was being electrified, for example; she also exhibited an unreasonable refusal to spend money and refused to eat) and became melancholic, defined at the time as a form of clinical depression accompanied by strong suicidal urges. In July 1888 she was sent to the Brook Asylum in Clapton, London, where she was placed under care of Dr. Frederick William Pavy, then to an establishment in Brighton, where she was looked after by Dr. Joseph Raymond Gasquet; and in 1890 to the Manor House Asylum, Chiswick, where she would die from heart failure on 15 December that year. Mental instability seems to have been an inherited trait in the Druitt family: Ann's mother committed suicide whilst insane and her sister suffered a bout of mental illness.

We know the whereabouts of Montague Druitt around the time at which some of the murders were committed. At 11.00am on 8 September 1888, a few hours after the discovery of the body of Annie Chapman, he was playing cricket at Blackheath. Later in September he appears to have conducted the defence of a clerk named William Power, who was charged with malicious wounding and was found to be insane. On 1 October, only a few hours after the murder of Stride and Eddowes, he may have been active in court at an appeal in the West Country. On 19 November he was present at a board meeting of the cricket club, so only ten days after the murder of Mary Jane Kelly he was continuing to carry out his responsibilities. On 22 November he represented the family firm when the appeal was heard. On 21 December the minutes of the Blackheath Cricket, Football and Lawn Tennis Co. record: 'The Honorary Secretary and Treasurer, Mr. M.J. Druitt, having gone abroad, it was resolved that he be and he is hereby removed from the post of Honorary Secretary and Treasurer'. On 31 December his body was pulled from the Thames.

The most detailed account of the inquest into Montague Druitt's death was in the *Acton, Chiswick and Turnham Green Gazette*, 5 January 1889:

FOUND DROWNED. – Shortly after midday on Monday, a Waterman named Winslade, of Chiswick, found the body of a man, well-dressed, floating in the Thames off Thorneycroft's. He at once informed a constable, and without delay the body was conveyed on the ambulance to the mortuary. On Wednesday afternoon, Dr. Diplock, coroner, held the

inquest at the Lamb Tap, when the following evidence was adduced:–
William H. Druitt said he lived at Bournemouth, and that he was a solicitor. The deceased was his brother, who was 31 last birthday. He was a bar-
rister-at-law, and an assistant master in a school at Blackheath. He had
stayed with witness at Bournemouth for a night towards the end of
October. Witness heard from a friend on the 11th December that deceased
had not been heard of at his chambers for more than a week. Witness then
went to London to make inquiries, and at Blackheath he found that
deceased had got into serious trouble at the school, and had been dismissed. That was on 30 December. Witness had deceased's things searched
where he resided, and found a paper addressed to him (produced). The
coroner read this letter, which was to the effect:– 'Since Friday I felt that I
was going to be like mother, and the best thing for me was to die'.

Witness continuing, said deceased had never made any attempt on his
life before. His mother became insane in July last. He had no other relative. Henry Winslade was the next witness. He said that he lived at No. 4,
Shore Street, Paxton Road, and that he was a waterman. About one o'clock
on Monday he was on the river in a boat, when he saw the body floating.
The tide was at half flood running up. He brought the body ashore and
gave information to the police. PC George Moulson, 216 T 131, said he
searched the body, which was fully dressed, excepting the hat and collar.
He found four large stones in each pocket in the top coat; £2.10s. in gold,
7s. in silver, 2d. in bronze, two cheques on the London and Provincial
Bank (one for £50 and the other for £16), a first-class season ticket from
Blackheath to London (South Western Railway), a second-half return
Hammersmith to Charing Cross (dated 1 December), a silver watch, gold
chain with silver guinea attached, a pair of kid gloves, and a white handkerchief. There were no papers or letters of any kind. There were no marks
of injury on the body, but it was rather decomposed. A verdict of suicide
whilst in unsound mind was returned.

This report is deficient in certain areas and has the appearance of
having been written by an inexperienced and probably a trainee journalist. It does not name Montague Druitt, the subject of the inquest,
for example. Nor does it refer to any medical testimony which would
have been legally required to establish the cause and probable time of
death. It also contained several mistakes, not the least being the claim
that 'no papers or letters of any kind [were] found on the body',
whereas both the *County of Middlesex Independent* of 2 January 1889
and the *West London Observer* of 5 January 1889 say papers found on
the body led the authorities to contact relatives in Bournemouth.
There are assorted other problems. The first-class season ticket from
Blackheath to London would have been to Charing Cross – the

nearest railway station to the Inner Temple. The season ticket suggests that Druitt regularly visited his chambers, as indeed his noted absence from 11 December confirms. However, it was a journey provided by the South Eastern Railway, not South Western as the report states. At Charing Cross on Saturday 1 December, Druitt bought a return ticket to Hammersmith, which is slightly odd because the letter found at his lodgings – stating that since Friday he had felt that he was going to be like his mother – suggests that Druitt had contemplated suicide, whereas the purchase of a return ticket suggests that he intended to return from the journey. But, since people contemplating suicide often do what in retrospect is irrational, not too much emphasis should be placed on this. What isn't clear from any surviving reports is when Druitt committed suicide. The report records that William Druitt visited the school and discovered that Montague had got into trouble and been fired. The large cheques found on his body suggest that he had very recently been paid off, but we don't know whether he had been dismissed and immediately vacated the premises or had served a period of notice. The newspaper says that William Druitt visited the school on 30 December and there is no real reason why we should doubt this, but it is just possible that the date relates to when Druitt was dismissed and is a mistake for 30 November, which was a Friday. If so, Druitt's letter basically meant that he had developed fears for his sanity since being dismissed. He therefore bought the return ticket to Hammersmith on 1 December, which would have been the day he killed himself.

What doesn't emerge from anything discovered about Druitt is a single clue as to why suspicion ever fell on him. And Macnaghten gives no real clues either. In addition to what he wrote about Druitt in the Memorandum, he gave some details in his autobiography, *Days of My Years*:

> Although, as I shall endeavour to show in this chapter, the Whitechapel murderer, in all probability, put an end to himself soon after the Dorset Street affair in November 1888, certain facts, pointing to the conclusion, were not in possession of the police until some years after I became a detective officer.
>
> There can be no doubt that in the room at Miller's Court the madman found ample scope for the opportunities he had all along been seeking, and the probability is that, after his awful glut on this occasion, his brain gave way altogether and he committed suicide; otherwise the murders would not have ceased.

I do not think there was anything of religious mania about the real 'Simon Pure' nor do I believe that he had ever been detained in an asylum, nor lived in lodgings. I incline to the belief that the individual who held up London in terror resided with his own people; that he absented himself from home at certain times, and that he committed suicide on or about the 10 November 1888, after he had knocked out a Commissioner of Police and very nearly settled the hash of one of Her Majesty's principal Secretaries of State.[5]

The real problem with Macnaghten's account of Druitt is that it contains so much incorrect biographical detail. He says that Druitt was 'said to be a doctor', when he was a barrister/teacher, and Druitt's occupation was made clear at the inquest. In his autobiography he says that Druitt 'resided with his own people' and 'absented himself at certain times'. Neither is true, as again was made clear at the inquest. Macnaghten says that 'Druitt disappeared at the time of the Miller's Court murder' and he is even more precise in his autobiography, saying that Druitt 'committed suicide on or about 10 of November 1888'. This seems to be an assumption, probably based on the length of time the body had been in the water and the theory that Druitt's mental stability completely collapsed after the murder of Mary Jane Kelly and that he committed suicide within days. Neither assumption is true. The dichotomy, however, is that this ignorance is marginally offset by his knowledge of some details, such as the season ticket from Blackheath to London found on Druitt's body. Macnaghten evidently had a source that preceded the inquest, but obviously followed the discovery of the body, and the most likely source in this case would have been PC George Moulson's report of the discovery of the body.

Apart from his claim that Druitt was, or was alleged to be, sexually insane, Macnaghten gives no indication at all as to why Druitt should have been suspected by anyone of being the Ripper and no clues are provided in the detailed, albeit pretty general, account of his life that researchers have unearthed. The most damning evidence against Druitt is the suspicion or belief of the family that he was the Whitechapel murderer.

But Macnaghten did not know this for certain. In both versions of the Memorandum he wrote, 'I have little doubt but that his own family suspected/believed' Druitt to have been the murderer. Had his information been from a member of the family then he would probably have had no doubt at all about what they believed; more importantly, he would have had accurate biographical detail. On the other hand, the informant must have been close to the family even to have had any idea about what they thought.

It is often said that there is no evidence against Montague John Druitt and it is true that we don't have any evidence of the kind required in a court of law. But the court of history isn't quite so demanding of evidence. The fact that Sir Melville Macnaghten suspected him and favoured him above other suspects – persisting in that belief for the rest of his life (as far as we know) – suggests that he had a reason for doing so, and one must surely assume that it was rather more than simply because Druitt was found dead at a time coincident with the cessation of the crimes. The biggest objection to Druitt as the prime suspect, however, comes from a remark by Inspector Frederick Abberline in the *Pall Mall Gazette* on 31 March 1903 when he was asked about a recent newspaper article:

> Our representative called Mr. Abberline's attention to a statement made in a well-known Sunday paper, in which it was made out that the author was a young medical student who was found drowned in the Thames.
>
> 'Yes', said Mr. Abberline, 'I know all about that story. But what does it amount to? Simply this. Soon after the last murder in Whitechapel the body of a young doctor was found in the Thames, but there is nothing beyond the fact that he was found at that time to incriminate him. A report was made to the Home Office about the matter, but that it was "considered final and conclusive" is going altogether beyond the truth. Seeing that the same kind of murders began in America afterwards, there is much more reason to think the man emigrated. Then again, the fact that several months after December, 1888, when the student's body was found, the detectives were told still to hold themselves in readiness for further investigations seems to point to the conclusion that Scotland Yard did not in any way consider the evidence as final'.

In his autobiography Macnaghten states: 'Although, as I shall endeavour to show in this chapter, the Whitechapel murderer, in all probability, put an end to himself soon after the Dorset Street affair in November 1888, certain facts, pointing to the conclusion, *were not in possession of the police until some years after I became a detective officer*'. [my italics]

Sir Melville Macnaghten joined the Metropolitan Police in June 1889. Therefore the 'certain facts' indicating Druitt came into the possession of the police 'some years' after that date. Abberline, however, seems to think that the only evidence against Druitt – assuming his 'young doctor' was the same person as the well-known Sunday newspaper's 'young medical student', and assuming that one or the other or both referred to 31-year-old barrister/teacher Montague John Druitt – emerged at the time he was found drowned. Had the evidence emerged later than that then his comment about the detectives being told several months after December 1888 to prepare themselves for further investigations would have been completely irrelevant. The report to the Home Office therefore seems to have been a routine report prepared in the instance of any death in suspicious circumstances. There therefore seem to have been several years separating what Abberline knew about Druitt, assuming he knew anything, and Macnaghten's information.

It might also be worth observing that it is often assumed that the 'certain facts' that came into the possession of the police several years after Macnaghten joined the Metropolitan Police are the same as the 'private information' Macnaghten had about the suspicions or beliefs of Druitt's family. There is no real reason for supposing that this was the case. Indeed, unless 'the police' was a reference to himself, it would seem that the two pieces of information were distinct and that Macnaghten's opinion was based on private information.

Kosminski

A Polish Jew was also the suspect of Sir Robert Anderson, who made, or had attributed to him, a number of references to this suspect over the years.

> Or, again, take a notorious case of a different kind, 'the Whitechapel murders' of the autumn of 1888. At that time the sensation-mongers of the newspaper press fostered the belief that life in London was no longer safe, and that no woman ought to venture abroad in the streets after nightfall. And one enterprising journalist went so far as to impersonate the cause of all this terror as 'Jack the Ripper', a name by which he will probably go down to history. But all such silly hysterics could not alter the fact that these crimes were a cause of danger only to a particular section of a small and definite class of women, in a limited district of the East End; and that the inhabitants of the metropolis generally were just as secure during the weeks the fiend was on the prowl as they were before the mania seized him, or after he had been safely caged in an asylum.[6]

Here, in 1901, Anderson is saying that Jack the Ripper 'had been safely caged in an asylum'. He would repeat this assertion several times, most notably in *Blackwood's Magazine* and in his book.

It is important to note the differences between these two statements. Anderson adds in the book version that the Jews were low-class Polish Jews and omits the reference to the publisher accepting liability for libel and the reference to the identification having taken place when the suspect was caged in an asylum. He changed 'declined to swear to him' to the harder 'refused to give evidence against him', and he added the last three sentences stating that it was 'a definitely ascertained fact' that Jack the Ripper was a Polish Jew, that he was specifying race not religion, and that to have discussed the religion of the Ripper would have been an outrage to all religious sentiment.

> Detractors of the work of our British Police in bringing criminals to justice generally ignore the important distinction between moral proof and legal evidence of guilt. In not a few cases that are popularly classed with 'unsolved mysteries of crime', the offender is known, but evidence is wanting. If, for example, in a recent murder case of special notoriety and interest (Crippen), certain human remains had not been found in a cellar, a great crime would have been catalogued among 'Police failures'; and yet, even without the evidence which sent the murderer to the gallows, the moral proof of his guilt would have been full and clear. So again with the Whitechapel murders of 1888. Despite the lucubrations of many an amateur 'Sherlock Holmes', there was no doubt whatever as to the identity of the criminal, and if our London 'detectives' possessed the powers, and might have recourse to the methods, of Foreign Police Forces, he would have been brought to justice.[7]

> Robt. Anderson has assured the writer that the assassin was well known to the police, but unfortunately, in the absence of sufficient legal evidence to justify an arrest, they were unable to take him. It was a case of moral versus legal proof ... But the question still remains, who and what was Jack the Ripper? Sir Robt. Anderson states confidently that he was a low-class Jew, being shielded by his fraternity. Sir Hy. Smith pooh-poohs this, declaring with equal confidence that he was a Gentile ...[8]

At the end of 1987 the *Daily Telegraph* revealed the existence of a copy of Anderson's memoirs presented by Anderson to the retired ex-Superintendent Donald S. Swanson, into whose capable hands the Ripper investigation had been placed. It was one of several books presented by Anderson to his old friend, a copy of Anderson's *Criminals and Crime* having been given to Swanson as a New Year's Day gift in 1908. Swanson's copy of the book contains pencil notes in the margins and on the endpapers. At the bottom of page 138, where Anderson had written, 'I will merely add that the only person who had ever had a good view of the murderer unhesitatingly identified the

Blackwood's Magazine, March 1910

The Lighter Side of My Official Life, 1910

One did not need to be a Sherlock Holmes to discover that the criminal was a sexual maniac of a virulent type; that he was living in the immediate vicinity of the scenes of the murders; and that, if he was not living absolutely alone, his people knew of his guilt, and refused to give him up to justice. During my absence abroad the Police had made a house-to-house search for him, investigating the case of every man in the district whose circumstances were such that he could go and come and get rid of his blood-stains in secret. And the conclusion we came to was that he and his people were low-class Jews, for it is a remarkable fact that people of that class in the East End will not give up one of their number to Gentile justice. And the result proved that our diagnosis was right on every point. For I may say at once that 'undiscovered murders' are rare in London, and the 'Jack-the-Ripper' crimes are not within that category. And if the Police here had powers such as the French Police possess, the murderer would have been brought to justice. Scotland Yard can boast that

One did not need to be a Sherlock Holmes to discover that the criminal was a sexual maniac of a virulent type; that he was living in the immediate vicinity of the scenes of the murders; and that, if he was not living absolutely alone, his people knew of his guilt, and refused to give him up to justice. During my absence abroad the Police had made a house-to-house search for him, investigating the case of every man in the district whose circumstances were such that he could go and come and get rid of his blood-stains in secret. And the conclusion we came to was that he and his people were certain low-class Polish Jews; for it is a remarkable fact that people of that class in the East End will not give up one of their number to Gentile justice. And the result proved that our diagnosis was right on every point. For I may say at once that 'undiscovered murders' are rare in London, and the 'Jack-the-Ripper' crimes are not within that category. And if the Police here had powers such as the French Police possess, the murderer would have been brought to justice. Scotland Yard can boast that not even the subordinate officers of the department will tell tales out of school, and it would not even the subordinate officers of the department will tell tales out of school, and it would ill become me to violate the unwritten rule of the service. The subject will come up again, and I will only add here that the 'Jack-the-Ripper' letter which is preserved in the Police Museum at New Scotland Yard is the creation of an enterprising London journalist.

In a footnote he added:
Having regard to the interest attaching to this case, I should almost be tempted to disclose the identity of the murderer and of the pressman who wrote the letter above referred to, provided that the publishers would accept all responsibility in view of a possible libel action. But no public benefit would result from such a course, and the traditions of my old department would suffer. I will only add that when the individual whom we suspected was caged in an asylum, the only person who had ever had a good view of the murderer at once identified him, but when he learned that the suspect was a fellow Jew he declined to swear to him.

ill become me to violate the unwritten rule of the service. So I will only add here that the 'Jack-the-Ripper' letter which is preserved in the Police Museum at New Scotland Yard is the creation of an enterprising London journalist.
Having regard to the interest attaching to this case, I am almost tempted to disclose the identity of the murderer and of the pressman who wrote the letter above referred to. But no public benefit would result from such a course, and the traditions of my old department would suffer. I will merely add that the only person who had ever had a good view of the murderer unhesitatingly identified the suspect the instant he was confronted with him; but he refused to give evidence against him.
In saying that he was a Polish Jew I am merely stating a definitely ascertained fact. And my words are meant to specify race, not religion. For it would outrage all religious sentiment to talk of the religion of a loathsome creature whose utterly unmentionable vices reduced him to a lower level than that of the brute.

suspect the instant he was confronted with him . . .', Swanson added, 'and after this identification which suspect knew, no other murder of this kind took place in London'.

After 'but refused to give evidence against him', Swanson wrote, 'because the suspect was also a Jew and also because his evidence would convict the suspect, and witness would be the means of murderer being hanged which he did not wish to be left on his mind'. Swanson continued on the end-paper, 'Continuing from page 138, after the suspect had been identified at the Seaside Home where he had been sent by us with difficulty in order to subject him to identification, and he knew he was identified. On suspect's return to his brother's house in Whitechapel he was watched by police (City CID) by day & night. In a very short time the suspect with his hands tied behind his back, he was sent to Stepney Workhouse and then to Colney Hatch and died shortly afterwards – Kosminski was the suspect – DSS'.

Who was Kosminski? A search of asylum records by the author Martin Fido has revealed only one asylum inmate named Kosminski – a man named Aaron Kosminski. Martin Fido's findings have been supported as far as is possible by a comprehensive search of the death registers. Little is known about him, although considerable work has been done following up clues to identify his family. As yet none of this work has thrown any light on why he was suspected of being Jack the Ripper. Aaron Kosminski was born in 1864 or 1865 in Poland and entered England in 1882 when aged 17. He had a brother named Woolf and some sisters, and was a hairdresser by profession. On 12 July 1890 his brother Woolf had him admitted to the Mile End Old Town workhouse. At that time Aaron appears to have been living at 3 Sion Square,[9] which was located at the top of Mulberry Street (where John Pizer lived), and documents state that he was '2 years insane'. He was discharged on 15 July 1890 into the care of his brother, whose address is given as 16 Greenfield Street. However, Aaron's condition seems to have worsened considerably, because during the afternoon of 4 February 1891 his brother had Aaron re-admitted to the Mile End Old Town workhouse. Three days later, in the morning of 7 February 1891, Aaron was discharged to Colney Hatch, where the details entered onto the Register of Admissions provides much of the information given above, but adds: 'Education: R&W; Time insane: 6 years (i.e., since 1885); Physical disorder: self-abuse; Form of disorder: mania; Symptoms: incoherence; Bodily state: fair'. The Male Patients'

Day Book, New Series, no. 20, adds, 'If first attack: no; Previous treatment: Mile End Old Town Workhouse July 1890, Duration of existing attack: 6 months [somebody added in red ink '6 years']; Supposed cause: unknown [again, in red: self-abuse]; Subject to epilepsy: no; Suicidal: no; Dangerous to others: no; Any relative afflicted with insanity: not known; Nearest known relative: Woolf Kosminski, 8 Sion Square, Commercial Road East'. Additional information was apparently provided by the certifying medical officer, E.K. Houchin of 23 High Street, Stepney:

> He declares that he: is guided and his movements altogether controlled by an instinct that informs his mind, he says that he knows the movements of all mankind, he refuses food from others because he is told to do so, and he eats out of the gutter for the same reason.
>
> Jacob Cohen, 51 Carter Lane, St Paul's EC says that he goes about the streets and picks up his bits of bread out of the gutter and eats them, he drinks water from the tap and he refuses food at the hands of others. He took up a knife and threatened the life of his sister. He is very dirty and will not be washed. He has not attempted any kind of work for years.

On 19 April 1894 Aaron Kosminski was admitted to the Leavesden Asylum. Among some loose papers at the Greater London Record Office is a document which gives Aaron's nearest known relative at this time as his mother, Mrs. Kosminski, who was living at 63 New Street, New Road, Whitechapel.

It should be observed – and in assessing Aaron Kosminski it is a crucially important point that is frequently overlooked or unappreciated – that all we know about Aaron Kosminski's physical and mental condition relates to 1891 and later, not to 1888. Experts agree that mental collapse in some cases can be dramatically sudden, so it should not by any means be assumed that the shambling, unwashed wreck of a man we see in 1891 reflects in anyway the Aaron Kosminski of 1888. Also, we actually know very little about his mental condition even when admitted. We know that he suffered audio and visual hallucinations, but we don't know what form they took, and the surviving medical records are terse, often one-line bi-annual comments on his physical condition. For example, one series of reports states,

1.4.14	Patient has hallucinations of sight and hearing, is very excitable and troublesome at times, very untidy, bodily condition fair.
1.3.15	No improvement.
11.11.15	Patient has cut over left eye caused by knock on tap in washhouse.

8.7.16	No improvement.
5.4.17	No improvement.
26.5.18	Patient put to bed passing loose motions with blood and mucous.
27.5.18	Transferred to 8a.
3.6.18	Diarrhoea ceased. Ordered up by Dr. Reese.
28.1.19	Put to bed with swollen feet.
20.2.19	Put to bed with swollen feet and feeling unwell. Temp. 99°.
13.3.19	Hip broken down.
22.3.19	Taken little nourishment during day, but very noisy.
23.3.19	Appears very low. Partaken of very little nourishment during day.
24.3.19	Died in my presence at 5.05am. Marks on body, sore right hip and left leg. Signed: S. Bennett, night attendant.[10]

The Greater London Record Office possesses several documents relating to the arrangements for Aaron Kosminski's burial. One, dated 25 March 1919, was signed by H.W. Abrahams, 'The Dolphin', Whitechapel, E. London. Abraham's relationship to the deceased is given as 'brothers'. The letter was sent to Mr. Friedlander, Undertaker of Duke Street, United Synagogue, London. Another document is dated 30 March 1919, from G. Friedlander, Sexton, Officer of Burial Society, St. James Place, Aldgate EC3 to A.J. Freeman, Leavesden Asylum, acknowledging receipt of a certificate dated 28 March registering Aaron Kosminski's death.

And that is pretty much all we know.

The sources present an almost overwhelming number of problems. To begin with Anderson, in the *Blackwood*'s version of his memoirs, says that the identification took place in the asylum, whereas Swanson says it took place in 'the Seaside Home' *before* the suspect was committed. This isn't a major problem because Anderson was clearly in error when he wrote that the suspect was identified in the asylum. Once committed to an asylum the suspect would almost certainly have been deemed 'unfit to plead', in which case no court case would have been heard and it would have been irrelevant whether the witness had testified or not. Anderson's emphasis on the witness's behaviour, however, suggests that had he been willing to testify then proceedings would have been taken against the suspect. If so, the suspect had not been committed to an asylum when the identification took place.

Anderson provides very few details about the suspect. He was male, Polish, a Jew; he lived in the heart of the district where the murders were committed, and he had 'people' (presumably a family – not the entire Jewish population, as Major Smith rather stupidly suggested) who protected him. All of which fit Aaron Kosminski. And perhaps the clincher to the identification is Anderson's statement, 'For it would outrage all religious sentiment to talk of the religion of a loathsome creature whose utterly unmentionable vices reduced him to a lower level than that of the brute'.

The 'utterly unmentionable vices' almost unquestionably refers to masturbation and corresponds to Macnaghten's comment about Kosminski that, 'This man became insane owing to many years indulgence in solitary vices' – 'solitary vices' being the common euphemism for masturbation. This also corresponds with various documents relating to Aaron Kosminski's admissions to mental institutions which give the cause of his insanity as 'self-abuse'.

Masturbation doesn't cause insanity, of course, but it was widely believed to, as Kosminski's medical papers alone demonstrate. The sexologist William Acton described someone who masturbated:

> The frame is stunted and weak, the muscles undeveloped, the eye is sunken and heavy, the complexion is sallow, pasty, and covered with spots of acne, the hands are damp and cold, and the skin moist. The boy shuns the society of others, creeps about alone, joins with repugnance in the amusements of his schoolfellows. He cannot look anyone in the face, and becomes careless in dress and uncleanly in person. His intellect has become sluggish and enfeebled, and if his evil habits are persisted in, he may end in becoming a drivelling idiot or a peevish valetudinarian. Such boys are to be seen in all stages of degeneration, but what we have described is but the result towards which *they all* are tending.

One can only wonder at how many masturbators Acton had discovered and in whom these symptoms were observed. The terror associated with the first appearance of acne doesn't bear thinking about, but Acton's description fits Aaron Kosminski precisely. The point, however, is that masturbation links Aaron Kosminski with Macnaghten's 'Kosminski' and with Anderson's unnamed Polish Jew suspect who Swanson identifies as Kosminski. The sparse details that Anderson provides also fit Aaron Kosminski. This said, Swanson's account fits Aaron Kosminski in the main, but on two points there is disagreement: Swanson says the suspect was sent to Stepney Workhouse, whereas Aaron Kosminsky was sent to Mile End Old Town Workhouse. However, the expanding borough of Stepney absorbed Mile End Old Town in 1901, so that when Swanson wrote nine years later Mile End

Old Town Workhouse technically would have been Stepney Workhouse.

Swanson said that the murders ended with the suspect's identification, whereas commentators like Anderson and Macnaghten believed the murders ended in 1888. This is true of the 'Jack the Ripper' sequence, but other murders were included in the files because at the time they were thought to have been committed by the Ripper. The last of these was the murder on 13 February 1891 of Frances Coles, and among Swanson's private papers was a list of victims compiled at the time of Alice McKenzie's murder in Castle Alley in 1889 and to which was appended the name of Frances Coles. This was the last crime in the wider Whitechapel murders sequence, and it coincides with the committal of Aaron Kosminski, which may have been what Swanson meant.

However, no explanation seems available for Swanson's claim that the suspect died soon after committal. Aaron Kosminski lived on until 1919.[11] It is perhaps one small indication that Aaron Kosminski was not the 'Kosminski' named by Macnaghten – Aaron Kosminski is not known to have had a 'great hatred of women', a particular hatred 'of the prostitute class', 'strong homicidal tendencies' or to have been committed to an asylum 'about March 1889' – or the Kosminski named by Swanson. On the other hand Aaron Kosminski fits almost all the other details.

Swanson wrote: 'after the suspect had been identified at the Seaside Home where he had been sent by us with difficulty in order to subject him to identification, and he knew he was identified. On suspect's return to his brother's house in Whitechapel he was watched by police (City CID) by day & night. In a very short time the suspect with his hands tied behind his back, he was sent to Stepney Workhouse and then to Colney Hatch and died shortly afterwards – Kosminski was the suspect'.

This is an incredible story. A suspect taken 'with difficulty' for identification at a place called 'the Seaside Home', being positively identified by an eye-witness but allowed thereafter to return to his brother's house, where the City CID mount 24 hour surveillance. Informed commentators reject this story as contrary to acceptable police procedure and many questions spring up: Why did the police have difficulty taking someone suspected of committing a serious crime for identification? Why did the identification take place at the 'Seaside Home'? Why did the police release a positively identified suspect? Why wasn't pressure brought to bear on the witness to make him testify? Why did the City CID keep surveillance on a Metropolitan Police suspect in Metropolitan Police territory (assuming the suspect was Aaron Kosminski)? On the other hand, Swanson was an experienced policeman, as aware of police procedure as anyone and probably more so than a modern commentator, so why would he have told a story so alien to what was likely to have happened unless it was the truth?

Swanson's story is interesting. There is no good reason why the Metropolitan Police would have asked for the City CID to maintain surveillance on a positively identified suspect. The Met. would have done the job itself. It therefore seems reasonable to assume that the City CID were maintaining surveillance *before* the Met. took the suspect to be identified and Swanson's remark that the suspect was taken for identification 'with difficulty' may suggest that the Metropolitan Police managed to sneak the suspect away without the City CID's knowledge. The 'Seaside Home' is almost certainly the Convalescent Police Seaside Home opened at Clarendon Villas, West Brighton, in March 1890. The police had used other establishments, but they were not for the exclusive use of the police and whilst it is possible that Swanson could have meant one of these, he is elsewhere sufficiently precise in his details for us to suspect that he was describing a specific place.

Other interesting remarks in Swanson's account include the fact that the suspect 'knew he was identified' and 'after identification which suspect knew ...'. This seems a pretty fatuous statement to make and reiterate. It may mean, however, that the suspect reacted in some way to the witness.

If identifying the suspect is a problem, identifying the witness is more so.

There are two principle candidates: Joseph Lawende, who saw Catharine Eddowes with a man at the entrance to the passage leading into Mitre Square; and Israel Schwartz, who saw a man assault a woman he identified as Elizabeth Stride outside the gates of the Berner Street club, her body being found just within the gates. Other witnesses such as Mrs. Long and George Hutchinson have to be discounted because the witness was a Jew, also male. There is a possibility that a witness exists of whom we know nothing. We only know about Schwartz by good fortune and we should perhaps also consider the 'Pipeman', the second man seen by Schwartz at the scene of the Stride assault. But of the two principle candidates Schwartz tends to be given very short shrift by most commentators, who then assess Joseph Lawende and conclude that his testimony wouldn't have stood up in court for two seconds.[12]

Objections to 'Lipski' are that Macnaghten said that Kosminski 'in appearance strongly resembled the individual seen by the City PC near Mitre Square'; Swanson said that the City CID maintained surveillance on the suspect, which they would have had no business doing if the man in question was suspected of committing a Metropolitan Police crime; and if the murderer called out the derogatory term 'Lipski' at Schwartz then the attacker wasn't a Jew, as the suspect undoubtedly was.

We know of no City PC witness, so either there wasn't one and Macnaghten was completely adrift, or he wrote City PC when in fact he meant Joseph Lawende, a Jewish commercial traveller in the cigarette trade. The third possibility is that he confused the location and meant PC Smith in Berner Street, and we have evidence of a transposition in Macnaghten's claim that the Berner Street murderer had been disturbed by the arrival of three Jews. The three Jews were Lawende, Levy and Harris, thus he transferred the three witnesses of Mitre Square to Berner Street and could most reasonably have transferred the witness of Berner Street, PC William Smith, to Mitre Square. That the City CID would have had no business maintaining surveillance in Metropolitan Police territory on a suspect in a Metropolitan Police crime is a moot point, especially if they suspected the Metropolitan Police crime to have been committed by the same hand as a City Police crime. But the reverse is even more absurd, that the Met. should have taken a City suspect in a City crime to be identified by a City witness. And unfortunately there is such uncertainty about who shouted 'Lipski', and at whom, that one has to weigh it in the balance against the reasons for thinking that the witness was Schwartz.

Most commentators who prefer Lawende over Schwartz proceed to point out all the reasons that make him a bad suspect.[13] For example, that he merely glimpsed the man as he passed, that he persistently claimed thereafter that he would be unable to recognise the man again, that he paid the couple scant attention and it remains uncertain that the woman he saw was Eddowes, and that there was time after he had passed for the man to have left the woman and for her killer to have emerged from the shadows of Mitre Square. All reasons which in themselves don't argue in favour of Lawende being the witness in the first place.

Interestingly, Lawende *was* used in the identification of a man named Thomas Sadler who was suspected of murdering Frances Coles in February 1891. He couldn't identify him. He was used again, it would seem, in the spring of 1895, when he positively identified another man, William Grant Grainger, a man who serious assaulted a prostitute, as the man he had seen. The use of Lawende in these cases has been employed as evidence to suggest that he was also the witness who would have been used to identify Anderson's suspect, a corollary to which is the fact that if the witness was used twice after his identification then it is clear that the first identification was nowhere near conclusive. But the identifications of Sadler and Grainger took place *after* the positive identification of Aaron Kosminski would have taken place and the police are unlikely to have re-used a witness who had already positively identified a suspect – as it would devalue both the first identification and certainly devalue any further identifications. The fact that Lawende was used therefore strongly suggests that he wasn't Anderson's witness.

The most likely candidate to be the witness, despite the reservations already mentioned, is Israel Schwartz. He saw a man actually assault a woman whom he identified as Elizabeth Stride at the very place where her body was later discovered. Since it is highly improbable that Stride would have been attacked by different men in the same place within 15 minutes, or that two women would be assaulted in the same place within 15 minutes, it must be assumed that Schwartz did see Stride's murderer and therefore was indeed 'the only person who had ever had a good view of the *murderer*' [my emphasis], just as Anderson said. And even if Kosminski was under surveillance by the City CID under suspicion of having murdered Catharine Eddowes, the strong similarities between the man seen with Eddowes and the man seen with Stride would have made it worthwhile for the Metropolitan Police to have put the suspect before their own witness.

But whoever the suspect and the witness were, was Anderson right? Was his suspect Jack the Ripper? More energy seems to have been given to devising reasons why he was wrong. It has been suggested that he made the whole story up, that his belief in the suspect's guilt was geriatric wishful thinking, or that he confused the identification of someone else with the solution to the Whitechapel murders. He has been shown in later years to have suffered from a poor memory. Minor errors have been catalogued, a Parliamentary joke at Anderson's expense has been used to suggest that he was notably 'flighty with the truth', and his character has been torn apart to find evidence of dishonesty, boastfulness, inability to accept failure, ineptitude and other foibles and failings. But at the end of the day none of the arguments seem to hold together. He said as early as 1901 that the Ripper had been 'safely caged in an asylum'. It wasn't a matter of wishful thinking, confusion or a faulty memory. Unless someone can produce evidence that Anderson lied, there *was* a suspect, there *was* a witness and there *was* an identification; Anderson came away from it believing that the suspect was guilty.

Michael Ostrog

It is only in the last few years that anything at all has been known about Michael Ostrog and now we actually know quite a lot, although none of it sheds any light on why he was ever suspected of being Jack the Ripper. He was a petty thief and conman who had numerous aliases, among them Bertrand Ashley, Claude Clayton (Cayton), Dr. Grant, Max Grief, Gosslar, Ashley Nabokoff, Orloff, Count Sobieski and Max Sobiekski. He wasn't very successful, was mentally unstable and probably highly delusional. From 1863, when we first hear of him following his sentence to ten months in prison for a theft in August, until 1904, when he was released from prison and entered St. Giles Christian Mission in Holborn and vanishes from the historical record, it is obvious that he spent his life in and out of prison or hospital. Crucially, and thanks to the diligent research of Ripper scholar Philip Sugden,[14] on 26 July 1888 Ostrog was arrested by the French police in Paris. On 14 November 1888 – five days after the murder of Mary Kelly – he was charged under the name of Stanislas Lublinski, alias 'Grand Guidon', and convicted of the theft of a microscope belonging to Monsieur Legry in Paris. Taking previous convictions into account, and the fact that since 1866 he had been barred from entering the country, he received the harsh sentence of two years in prison as well as costs. This discovery has naturally shed doubt on the real value of the Macnaghten Memorandum: why should someone whose whereabouts were unknown, who therefore wasn't even known to be in London, let alone Whitechapel, be listed among the top three suspects? Sadly, the answer is that we don't know and it seems futile to guess.

Francis Tumblety

In February 1993 Stewart Evans, one of the country's leading Ripper experts and a collector of crime ephemera, purchased some documents from a Richmond-based antiquarian book-dealer named Eric Barton, among which was a letter written by ex-Chief Inspector John Littlechild to a well-known journalist and author named George R. Sims. This letter was typewritten, running to three pages and dated 23 September 1913. It was in reply to a letter written by Sims in which he appears to have asked Littlechild if he had ever heard of a Dr. D.:

8, The Chase,
Clapham Common, S.W.
23rd September 1913.
Dear Sir.,

I was pleased to receive your letter which I shall put away in 'good company' to read again, perhaps some day when old age overtakes me and when to revive memories of the past may be a solace.

Knowing the great interest you take in all matters crininal [*sic*], and abnormal, I am just going to inflict one more letter on you on the 'Ripper' subject. Letters as a rule are only a nuisance when they call for a reply but this does not need one. I will try and be brief.

I never heard of a Dr. D. in connection with the Whitechapel murders but amongst the suspects, and to my mind a very likely one, was a Dr. T. (which sounds much like D.). He was an American quack named Tumblety and was at one time a frequent visitor to London and on these occasions constantly brought under the notice of police, there being a large dossier concerning him at Scotland Yard. Although a 'Sycopathia Sexualis' subject he was not known as a 'Sadist' (which the murderer unquestionably was) but his feelings towards women were remarkable and bitter in the extreme, a fact on record. Tumblety was arrested at the time of the murders in connection with unnatural offences and charged at Marlborough Street, remanded on bail, jumped his bail, and got away to Boulogne. He shortly left Boulogne and was never heard of afterwards. It was believed he committed suicide but certain it is that from this time the 'Ripper' murders came to an end.

With regard to the term 'Jack the Ripper' it was generally believed at the Yard that Tom Bullen of the Central News was the originator but it is probable Moore, who was his chief, was the inventor. It was a smart piece of journalistic work. No journalist of my time got such privileges from Scotland Yard as Bullen. Mr James Munro when Assistant Commissioner, and afterwards Commissioner, relied on his integrity. Poor Bullen occasionally took too much to drink, and I fail to see how he could help it knocking about so many hours and seeking favours from so many people to procure copy. One night when Bullen 'had taken a few too many' he got early information of the death of Prince Bismarck and instead of going to the office to report it sent a laconic telegram 'Bloody Bismarck is dead'. On this I believe Mr. Charles Moore fired him out.

It is very strange how those given to 'Contrary sexual instinct and degenerates' are given to cruelty, even Wilde used to like to be punched about. It may interest you if I give you an example of this cruelty in the case of the man Harry Thaw and this is authentic as I have the boy's statement. Thaw was staying at the Carlton Hotel and one day laid out a lot of sovereigns on his dressing table, then rang for a call boy on pretence of sending out a telegram. He made some excuse and went out of the room and left the boy there and watched through the chink of the door. The unfortunate boy was tempted and took a sovereign from the pile and Thaw returning to the room charged him with stealing. The boy confessed when Thaw asked him whether he should send for the police or whether he should punish him himself. The boy scared to death consented to take his punishment from Thaw who then made him undress, strapped him to the foot of the bedstead, and thrashed him with a cane drawing blood. He then made the boy get into a bath in which he placed a quantity of salt. It seems incredible that such a thing could take place in any hotel but it is a fact. This was in 1906.

Now pardon me – It is finished. – Except that I knew Major Griffiths for many years. He probably got his information from Anderson who only 'thought he knew'[15] J.G. Littlechild.
George R. Sims Esq.,
12, Clarence Terrace,
Regents Park. N.W.

Francis Tumblety was a regular visitor to England and arrived at Liverpool in June 1888. We don't know what he did in the country between that time and 7 November, but on that date he was arrested and charged with homosexual activities with four men between 27 July and 2 November. On 12 November he was charged in connection with the Whitechapel murders. This would suggest that Tumblety was at liberty after 7 November and thus able to have murdered Kelly. He was bailed on 16 November, attended a hearing at the Old Bailey on 20 November, then fled the country on 24 November under the false name of 'Frank Townsend', going first to Boulogne and then taking the steamer *La Bretagne* to New York City.

American newspapers reported that Scotland Yard men had followed Tumblety across the Atlantic and we know that in December 1888 Inspector Walter Andrews, who had taken two criminals to

Montreal, then went to New York on business connected with the Ripper case, but it is not known that it had anything to do with Tumblety. Andrews gave a press interview in which he said that Scotland Yard had 20 detectives, 2 clerks and 1 inspector employed on the Ripper investigations, and this became garbled in the English press suggesting that these men were employed on the case in the United States. Meanwhile, Chief Inspector Byrnes of the New York City police, traced Tumblety to a lodging at 79 East Tenth Street and kept him under surveillance, but did not arrest him, saying that 'there is no proof of his complicity in the Whitechapel murders, and the crime for which he was under bond in London is not extraditable'. On 5 December Tumblety disappeared from his lodgings and vanished from the public gaze until 1893 when he lived with his sister in Rochester, New York. He died a wealthy man in 1903 in St. Louis.

Curiously Tumblety attracted no attention in the British press, either because the police kept his arrest a secret or because he was not really suspected of complicity in the Ripper crimes at all.

Tumblety is an extraordinarily attractive candidate for the mantle of Jack the Ripper, but unfortunately much of the evidence around him is speculative – albeit that the speculation is generally well-founded. He apparently hated women and prostitutes, it is probable that he possessed anatomical knowledge – and he had a curious anatomical collection that included uteri, he was charged in connection with the crimes (although we don't know the connection and should not assume that he was charged on suspicion of being the murderer), he fled England, and a senior Ripper investigator was detailed from Canada to New York when Tumblety was there.

Against Tumblety is the fact that contrary to what is sometimes asserted, Littlechild did not think Tumblety was Jack the Ripper and probably wouldn't ever have mentioned him had not G.R. Sims asked about Dr. D. Although Littlechild wrote, 'amongst the suspects, and to my mind a very likely one, was a Dr. T. (which sounds much like D.). He was an American quack named Tumblety', Littlechild also wrote of Tumblety that, 'Although a "Sycopathia Sexualis" subject he was not known as a "Sadist" (which the murderer unquestionably was) but his feelings towards women were remarkable and bitter in the extreme, a fact on record'. In other words, Tumblety had an exceptional dislike of women – which was probably what recommended him to Littlechild's mind as 'a very likely' candidate among the suspects – but he was not a sadist, which Littlechild believed Jack the Ripper 'unquestionably was'. Whether or not the Ripper was actually a sadist is irrelevant, of course; Littlechild believed he was, knew that Tumblety wasn't and accordingly wouldn't have believed that Tumblety was the Ripper. Littlechild did not say he thought Jack the Ripper was Francis Tumblety or say anything that allows us even to infer that he thought Tumblety was likely to be the Ripper. Indeed, though he describes Tumblety as a likely suspect, what he does say indicates that he probably did *not* think Tumblety was the Ripper.

Which doesn't mean that he wasn't Jack the Ripper. With Druitt and Kosminski he remains at the top of the tree of suspects.

George Chapman

Finally there is George Chapman, whose real name was Severin Klosowski, a Pole with surgical training who came to England in 1887 and worked for a hairdresser in the East End until going to America in 1890. He returned to England in 1895 and between 1895 and 1901 he poisoned three women, for which crime he was hanged in 1903. He was suspected by no greater authority on the Ripper crimes than Inspector Abberline, and as the man in charge of the investigation on the ground, Abberline's opinion deserves our attention. Unfortunately, it doesn't deserve our attention for very long. In *The Trial of George Chapman*, H.L. Adam wrote:

> Chief Inspector Abberline, who had charge of the investigations into the East End murders, thought that Chapman and Jack the Ripper were one and the same. He closely questioned the Polish woman, Lucy Baderski, about Chapman's nightly habits at the time of the murders. She said that he was often out until three or four o'clock in the morning, but she could throw no light on these absences. Both Inspector Abberline and Inspector Godley spent years in investigating the 'Ripper' murders. Abberline never wavered in his firm conviction that Chapman and Jack the Ripper were one and the same person. When Godley arrested Chapman Abberline said to his confrere 'You've got Jack the Ripper at last!'.[16]

Although H.L. Adam thanks Inspector Godley for his assistance in preparing his book, and therefore we must assume that some such comment was made, this story contains claims that seem untenable. Abberline is said to have closely questioned Lucy Baderski about George Chapman's nightly habits at the time of the murders, but at Klosowski's trial Lucy Baderski's brother, Stanislaus, said that Lucy had met Klosowski at a Polish club and had married him in August (or

October) 1889 after only having gone out with him for four to five weeks. Even allowing for quite a substantial margin of error in the estimate by Stanislaus of the duration of his sister's romance, Lucy Baderski would still have been in no position to speak with authority about Klosowski's nocturnal habits at the time of the Ripper murders in 1888. Furthermore, Inspector Abberline had retired from the Metropolitan Police in February 1892, just over ten years before the arrest of Severin Klosowski on 25 October 1902, so in what capacity would he have questioned Lucy Baderski so closely? Finally, a reporter for the *Pall Mall Gazette* visited Abberline on Monday 23 March 1903 and found him busy writing to Macnaghten and expressing his opinion that Chapman was Jack the Ripper. The *Pall Mall Gazette* reported Abberline as saying, 'I have been so struck with the remarkable coincidences in the two series of murders that I have not been able to think of anything else for several days past – not, in fact, since the Attorney-General made his opening statement at the recent trial, and traced the antecedents of Chapman before he came to this country in 1888'.[17] Therefore, by Abberline's own admission he did not have any opinions about Klosowski until March 1903, when 'the Attorney-General made his opening statement at the recent trial'. Abberline could not have said to Godley, 'You've got Jack the Ripper at last!' when, as H.L. Adam says, 'Godley arrested Chapman' in October 1902.

But Abberline did entertain suspicions about Severin Klosowski/George Chapman. His opinion, however, was based on nothing more substantial than a series of coincidences: Klosowski/Chapman had studied medicine and surgery in Russia, had first lodged in George Yard where Martha Tabram was murdered, and had attempted to murder his wife with a long knife. His arrival in London coincided with the beginning of the murders, and he then went to America where similar murders began. His height and the peaked cap he favoured 'quite tallies with the descriptions I got of him', and all the descriptions the police got of the Ripper described him as 'a foreign-looking man'.

The biggest objection to Abberline's theory then and now is the improbability of a murderer who eviscerated five women with the brutality displayed by Jack the Ripper turning to wife poisoning. Unfortunately, Abberline's answer to this objection, though seemingly sensible, isn't hugely inspiring. Referring back to the inquest, Abberline seized upon the story made public by Coroner Wynne

Baxter about an American doctor seeking to purchase anatomical organs. Baxter had suggested that someone had thus been inspired to collect the organs. Abberline thought that this might have accounted for Chapman's change of modus:

> 'As to the question of the dissimilarity of character in the crimes which one hears so much about', continued the expert, 'I cannot see why one man should not have done both, provided he had the professional knowledge, and this is admitted in Chapman's case. A man who could watch his wives being slowly tortured to death by poison, as he did, was capable of anything; and the fact that he should have attempted, in such a cold-blooded manner, to murder his first wife with a knife in New Jersey, makes one more inclined to believe in the theory that he was mixed up in the two series of crimes. What, indeed, is more likely than that a man to some extent skilled in medicine and surgery should discontinue the use of the knife when his commission – and I still believe Chapman had a commission from America – came to an end, and then for the remainder of his ghastly deeds put into practice his knowledge of poisons? Indeed, if the theory be accepted that a man who takes life on a wholesale scale never ceases his accursed habit until he is either arrested or dies, there is much to be said for Chapman's consistency. You see, incentive changes; but the fiendishness is not eradicated. The victims, too, you will notice, continue to be women; but they are of different classes, and obviously call for different methods of despatch'.

Abberline therefore supposed that Klosowski/Chapman had murderous instincts, channelled first into the collection of organs, then into the destruction of his wives when he tired of them. But nobody who looks at the photograph of Mary Kelly, or reads one of the medical reports, could ever seriously believe that she had been murdered by a coldly clinical seeker of body parts for sale. As the *Morning Advertiser* prophetically observed, 'Students of modern crime are not likely to pay much heed to Inspector Abberline's theory'.[18] Abberline's theory, though, has recently garnered some distinguished supporters.

So who was Jack the Ripper? The sad fact is that nobody knows and nobody is likely to know. Having said that, somewhere there may be a document – perhaps misfiled at the Public Record Office, in the archives of a library, or maybe sitting in a dusty box in someone's loft, that will reveal all. As things stand, I think Aaron Kosminski is the leading contender, not because I think he was Jack the Ripper, but because of all the policemen who expressed an opinion, Anderson is the only one to have expressed certainty. We need to find out why.

In the preceding chapters we have seen that many social issues came to a head or put down their roots during the 1880s, and focused attention on the East End of London. There is a lot more that could be said, much more that would give a fuller flavour to the crimes and the East End. This book has barely explored the Jewish East End, for example, but, although immigration was a dominant feature of the East End, it didn't significantly focus attention on the area in the way that other things did. Hopefully it will be the subject of a future book. What we have seen is how the 1880s were a time of profound change, and how, at the centre, was Jack the Ripper.

Notes

1. Aberconway, Christabel (1949) *A Dictionary of Cat Lovers*. London: Michael Joseph.
2. Broadcast on ITV at 10.45pm on 5 and 12 November 1969.
3. There is a possible third version of the Memorandum. In the early 1950s a friend of Gerald Donner, named Philip Loftus, spent Christmas with him and was shown Sir Melville's papers. In August 1972 he wrote to Lady Aberconway about the document he had seen and described the three named suspects as 'Michael John Druitt', 'a feeble-minded man [probably Thomas Cutbush]' and 'a Polish-Jew cobbler nicknamed Leather Apron'. (Philip Loftus to Lady Aberconway, 11 August 1972, private collection.) In October 1972 he wrote for the *Guardian* a review of a book written by Daniel Farson. He omitted Cutbush and 'Leather Apron', but added that the material he had seen was 'in Sir Melville's handwriting on official paper, rather untidy and in the nature of rough jottings'. (Philip Loftus, review of *Jack the Ripper* by Daniel Farson, 7 October 1972.) This version would seem to suggest that the 'Polish-Jew cobbler nicknamed Leather Apron' corresponds with the Polish Jew called 'Kosminski' in the extant versions, but there is no evidence that 'Kosminski' was either a cobbler or nicknamed Leather Apron. That Loftus' memory was at fault is indicated by the fact that he recalled that Thomas Cutbush was a suspect, when the charges against Cutbush were what Macnaghten wrote the report to refute. It seems likely that Loftus' memory had been contaminated by his acknowledged reading and earlier Druitt-naming Ripper book, Tom Cullen's *Autumn of Terror*.
4. Heard, Stawell (2000) 'Mr Valentine's School'. Maidstone: *Ripperologist*. No. 32, December.
5. Macnaghten, Sir Melville (1914) *Days of My Years*. London: Longmans, Green & Co, pp.54, 61–2.
6. Anderson, Robert (1901) 'Punishing Crime', *The Nineteenth Century*, February.
7. Anderson, Sir Robert, 'Preface' to Adam, H.L. (1911) *The Police Encyclopedia*, Vol. 1. London: Routledge.

8. Adam, Hargrave L. (1912) 'Scotland Yard and its Secrets', *The People*, 9 June.
9. As a child the famous artist Max Gertler would live in Sion Square.
10. Register of Patients, Leavesden [loose papers], 1894.
11. In 1986–87 Martin Fido undertook an exhaustive but as yet unduplicated search of asylum records in search of Macnaghten's 'Kosminski' whom he had concluded was Anderson's suspect. But misled by Macnaghten's claim that committal occurred 'about March 1889' he did not extend his search far enough and therefore missed Aaron Kosminski's committal in 1891. Concluding that Anderson would not have lied about the Polish Jew suspect, he assumed that the suspect must be in the records under another name. The most likely candidate was a man named 'David Cohen' – his real name turned out to be Aaron Davis Cohen – a 23-year-old Jew arrested in December 1888, apparently in a police raid on a brothel, and who was found to be insane, being committed first to Whitechapel Workhouse and then to Colney Hatch, where he died in October 1889. This man, who was apparently violent, who was committed as a result of police action, and at a time that would explain the sudden cessation of the crimes, was an attractive candidate. Martin Fido then discovered Aaron Kosminski, but dismissed him as Anderson's suspect on the grounds of date, and because his medical records – which describe him as non-violent and a danger to nobody – made him sound a very unlikely Ripper. This assumed that Anderson's suspect *was* Jack the Ripper and that he would therefore betray Ripper-like characteristics in the asylum (whatever those might be), but was otherwise a reasonable conclusion. The subsequent discovery of the Swanson marginalia created an additional problem in that it named Anderson's suspect as 'Kosminski'. Martin nevertheless noted details that could relate to Cohen, namely identification whilst in the asylum, which would apply to Cohen, and the death of the suspect soon after admission. Martin has suggested that somehow the two men were confused, hence the accounts by Swanson and Anderson containing some details pertaining to Kosminski and some to Cohen. Although the reasoning behind all this isn't terribly complex, it has nevertheless caused some eyes to glaze over with confusion. Essentially, if one rejects Aaron Kosminski as Anderson's suspect – and it has to be acknowledged that there is absolutely no reason from what is known about him to suspect that he was the Ripper – but believes that there was a Polish Jew suspect committed to an asylum, Martin Fido's research pushes Aaron Davis Cohen to the fore and forces some sort of explanation about why he and Kosminski were confused. Unfortunately, we don't really know enough about Aaron Kosminski to say whether or not he would have made a likely Ripper in 1888. There is also a lot of evidence available to suggest that the police suspected that the post-Kelly murders could have been the work of the Ripper. (Anderson himself wrote in *The Lighter Side of My Official Life*, 'I am here assuming that the murder of Alice McKenzie on the 17th of July 1889, was by another hand'. He would not have assumed this if he had known the Ripper had been caged in an asylum seven months earlier.) These

suspicions may not have lasted very long but the fact that they existed at all show that there was no belief that the Ripper was dead or locked away.

12. See Sugden, Philip (2002) *The Complete History of Jack the Ripper*. London: Robinson, pp. xiii–xv. Sugden writes, 'In light of the evidence we have the witness can only have been Joseph Lawende ...' then proceeds to explain 'why we have to discount Lawende. He saw the Ripper fleetingly in a dark street, and had no reason at the time to take particular note ...' etc.

13. Sugden, Philip (2002) *The Complete History of Jack the Ripper*. London: Robinson, 1994. London: Robinson, 1995 paperback; with new introduction. London: Robinson, 2002, pp. 409–10 for example.

14. Sugden, Philip, *op. cit.*, p. xx.

15. This is probably a mistake. Although Major Griffiths was a friend of Anderson, the source of his information looks to be Macnaghten. He gives details about the three suspects named by Macnaghten, though he doesn't name them of course, and he repeats 'errors' that were Macnaghten's – such as the fact that the only person to have glimpsed the murderer was a PC in Mitre Square. And, of course, whilst Anderson claimed that he knew the identity of the killer, Macnaghten did only ever claim that he thought he knew.

16. Adam, Hargrave Lee (1930) *The Trial of George Chapman*. London: Hodge.

17. *Pall Mall Gazette*, 24 March 1903.

18. *Morning Advertiser*, 24 March 1903.

chapter fifteen

OTHER RIPPER SUSPECTS

As observed in the opening chapter, the subject of Jack the Ripper bloomed in the 1960s following Daniel Farson's 'discovery' of the Macnaghten memoranda and the consequent hopes that the mystery of the Ripper's identity might be solvable. Those hopes have never diminished, but over the years the Ripper has achieved an international notoriety because of several sensational stories, undoubtedly the best known of which being that Jack the Ripper was a member of the royal family and a variation on the story now known as the Masonic Conspiracy – inspiration for at least four movies![1] – and the further variation or offshoot theory that Jack the Ripper was the famous artist Walter Sickert. Another tale that has attracted attention is that of the so-called Maybrick 'diary', a document in which the Liverpool cotton-broker James Maybrick claimed to have been driven to commit the Jack the Ripper murders by his wife's infidelity, and who in 1889 was a silent lead in cause célèbre when his wife Florence was accused of his murder and convicted after a highly questionable trial presided over by a mentally unstable judge.

Prince Albert Victor Christian Edward was born prematurely on 8 January 1864 at Frogmore, Buckinghamshire, the eldest son of Albert Edward, the future Edward VII, grandson of Queen Victoria, and heir-presumptive to the throne. Privately educated until 1877, he served aboard the training ship *Britannia* at Dartmouth, accompanied his younger brother George on a world cruise to British colonies aboard HMS *Bacchante*, a voyage distinguished by a sighting of the legendary ghost ship called the 'Flying Dutchman'.[2] Between 1882–83 he received some tuition from James Kenneth Stephen (himself advanced as a Jack the Ripper suspect[3]) and entered Trinity College, Cambridge in October 1883, went to Aldershot in 1886, became a lieutenant in the 19th Hussars in 1886, visited Ireland in

1887, received an honorary LL.D. from Cambridge in 1888, went to India in 1889–90,[4] was created Earl of Athlone and Duke of Clarence and Avondale in 1890 and died from pneumonia following influenza at Sandringham on 14 January 1892.

Prince Albert Victor – Eddy as he was known – was the typical upper-class twit of the type portrayed so skilfully by P.G. Wodehouse as a member of the Drones in the Bertie Wooster novels. Languid, interested in nothing, showing enthusiasm for little beyond 'every form of dissipation and amusement'.[5] 'Prince Eddy was certainly dear and good, kind and considerate. He was also backward and utterly list-less. He was self-indulgent and not punctual. He had been given no proper education, and as a result he was interested in nothing. He was heedless and as aimless as a gleaming goldfish in a crystal-bowl.'[6] He was, in short, lazy, dull, apathetic, irresponsible, and backward to the point of idiocy, was a problem for his family and as heir-presumptive he must have been a significant worry to those responsible for the stability of the Empire and consequently of the world as a whole. That he was also Jack the Ripper is an idea not traceable beyond a book by Philippe Jullian entitled *Edward and the Edwardians*:

> Before he died, poor Clarence was a great anxiety to his family. He was quite characterless and would soon have fallen a prey to some intriguer or group of roués, of which his regiment was full. They indulged in every form of debauchery, and on one occasion the police discovered the Duke in a *maison de rencontre* of a particularly equivocal nature during a raid. Fifty years before, the same thing had happened to Lord Castlereagh, and he had committed suicide.[7] The young man's evil reputation soon spread. The rumour gained ground that he was Jack the Ripper . . .[8]

Jullian intriguingly gives the impression that the rumours circulated during the lifetime of the Duke of Clarence, which Jullian may have believed, but the *maison de rencontre* or 'house of meeting' is a refer-ence to the Cleveland Street scandal of 1889 in which a number of prominent men were discovered to be clients of a homosexual brothel and Prince Albert Victor was rumoured to be among them.[9] Jullian therefore seems to be saying that the Prince's 'evil reputation' spread *after* 1889. The question is, how long after?

What is interesting is that Jullian's book was published in French in 1962, an English translation appearing in 1967, but his remarks about Prince Albert Victor passed largely unnoticed. Then, in 1970, a dis-tinguished doctor named Thomas Stowell published an article 'Jack the Ripper – A Solution?' in a relatively obscure magazine called *The*

Criminologist.[10] Basically, Stowell claimed that Jack the Ripper was an individual he called 'S', but provided sufficient detail to establish beyond question that he was talking about Prince Albert Victor.[11] According to Stowell, Caroline Acland, the daughter of the Royal physician Sir William Gull, had told him that Gull's diary contained an entry for November 1889: 'Informed Blank that his son was dying of syphilis of the brain.' We do not know, but the reasonable assumption is that the diary named the person and that 'blank' was Dr Stowell's discretion. This, it seems, provided the basis for Dr Stowell's theory. That the Prince suffered from syphilis is entirely possible. Prince Albert Victor regularly used a young doctor named Alfred Fripp – who would later become a famous surgeon – and a prescription found among his papers after his death by his biographer suggests that the Prince suffered from a gonorrhoeal infection.[12] Even if the diary entry was genuine, it seems extraordinary to extrapolate without more substantive argument that the Prince was Jack the Ripper, and Dr. Stowell was an eminent man who was executor to Theodore Dyke Acland, Caroline Acland's husband, and as such may have had access to additional information that had formed his belief.

A speculation advanced by Colin Kendall in *The Criminologist*[13] was that Dr. Stowell was 'playing a very artful game' and really pointing the finger of guilt at Sir William Gull while appearing to identify someone else. Stowell certainly introduced Sir William Gull in a rather awkward way; describing his suspect, then commenting that 'many false trails were laid', one of them being that the Ripper exhibited surgical skill. 'To support this fantasy,' wrote Stowell, 'it was not unnatural for the rumour mongers to pick on a most illustrious member of my profession of the time – perhaps of all time – Sir William Gull, Bt., M.D., F.R.C.P., F.R.S.'

Stowell doesn't say which rumour mongers he had in mind – Stowell was the first person to name Gull in connection with the Ripper crimes, although the Chicago *Sunday-Times Herald* back in 1895 had published a possibly spoof and factually inaccurate article based on a story allegedly told by an unnamed Chicago gentleman who had in turn heard it from a 'Dr. Howard of London'. This story was that the medium Robert James Lees had followed a psychic trail to the home of an eminent physician. The doctor had been questioned by a policeman who had accompanied Lees to the house, admitted that he sometimes suffered losses of memory and had once come round to discover his shirt bloodstained. On his house being searched, proofs of his guilt were discovered and he was committed to an asylum in Islington under the name Thomas Mason. The public were told that he had died and been buried in Kensal Green cemetery. The physician was evidently intended to be Sir William Gull, though his name was never mentioned in connection with the Lees story until Stowell referred to a version of the tale told by Fred Archer in his book *Ghost Detectives* and commented that it was 'a variation of one told to me by Sir William Gull's daughter, Caroline'. Stowell said that Caroline Acland told him that during the Ripper scare

> her mother Lady Gull, was greatly annoyed one night by an unappointed visit from a police officer, accompanied by a man who called himself a 'medium' and she was irritated by their impudence in asking her a number of questions which seemed to her impertinent, She answered their questions with non-committal replies such as 'I do not know,' 'I cannot tell you that,' 'I am afraid I cannot answer that question.'
>
> Later Sir William himself came down and in answer to the questions said he occasionally suffered from 'lapses of memory since he had a slight stroke in 1887'; he said that he once had discovered blood on his shirt. This is not surprising, if he had medically examined the Ripper after one of his murders.

Either Caroline Acland did tell Dr. Stowell this story, in which case it in some way supports the generally discredited Chicago *Sunday-Times Herald* story and stories implicating Dr. Gull may have been circulating in the early 1890s, or Dr. Stowell wittingly or otherwise attributed the account to Caroline Acland.

According to Colin Wilson, Stowell had learned that Prince Albert Victor was Jack the Ripper 'when Caroline Acland, daughter of the royal physician, Sir William Gull, had asked him to examine her father's papers in the 1930s'. Stowell, says Wilson, had sat on the story 'for thirty years' (Wilson, Colin and Odell, Robin: *Jack the Ripper Summing Up and Verdict*. London: Bantam Press, 1987. London: Corgi Books, 1988. p.200). Colin Kendall suggested that Dr. Stowell therefore developed his theory around 1930 and he observed that Gull's son-in-law Theodore Dyke Acland had died in 1931. But Caroline Acland had pre-deceased her husband, dying two years earlier, and therefore couldn't have asked Dr. Stowell to go through her father's papers in the 1930s. However *The Times* on 4 November 1970 says that Stowell, who had appeared on BBC Television news programme *24 Hours* two days earlier, 'says he has kept to himself for 50 years evidence about the identity of the killer'. Fifty years, not thirty years, would date the conception of Stowell's theory to 1920. So, did Caroline Acland seek Dr. Stowell's assistance in 1920 and did Dr. Stowell see something in Gull's papers that convinced him that Gull or Prince Albert Victor was Jack the Ripper? And if he did, what could he have seen?

Unfortunately, whatever the evidence on which Dr. Stowell's belief was based, Prince Albert Victor does not appear to have been in London at the time of any of the Jack the Ripper murders. He was in Yorkshire between 29 and 31 August staying with friends; between 7 and 9 September he was either at Danby Lodge in Yorkshire with Lord Downe or at the Cavalry Barracks in York where he was stationed with the 9th Lancers. He lunched with Queen Victoria at Balmoral on 10 September (as is recorded in Queen Victoria's journal), so could not have been very far from there on the evening of 9 September; on 29 September he was in Scotland and lunched with Queen Victoria on 30 September at Balmoral and he was at Sandringham for the Prince of Wales's birthday celebrations on 9–10 November. Pending evidence that he was definitely not in these places, it must be concluded that Prince Albert Victor was *not* Jack the Ripper.

The big mystery and most intriguing question, however, is how Philippe Jullian, who died in Paris in 1979, knew about the rumours connecting Prince Albert Victor and Jack the Ripper. He wrote in 1962, eight years before Dr. Stowell published his theory in *The Criminologist* in 1970. We know that Dr. Stowell's theory was not new to him because in 1960 the author Colin Wilson had written a series of articles for the *Evening Standard*[14] and Dr. Stowell, mistakenly thinking that he had also concluded the Prince was the Ripper, invited him to lunch at the Athenaeum, where he explained what subsequently appeared in his article. Had he therefore talked to other people? Was he ultimately Philippe Jullian's source? And if not, who was? Colin Wilson? We know he told the story to several people, among them German newspaper editor Frank Lynder, writers Daniel Farson and Donald McCormick, television journalist Kenneth Allsop and *The Criminologist* editor Nigel Morland.[15] Philippe Jullian may therefore have been repeating gossip acquired via one of these sources and ultimately traceable back to Dr. Stowell. But if the source wasn't Dr. Stowell . . .?

Dr. Stowell's revelations caused newspaper headlines around the world and the idea that a member of the Royal family was the murderer certainly did a great deal to awaken public interest in Jack the

Ripper. The next stage in the popularising of the story came in 1973 when the BBC made a television drama-documentary series which referred to a story the researchers had picked up that was being told by a man named Joseph Gorman, better known as Joseph Sickert, who claimed to be the illegitimate son of the artist Walter Sickert. The tale was subsequently investigated by a journalist named Stephen Knight, who wrote what is unquestionably the biggest and more sustained selling book on the subject, never out of print since it was published, *Jack the Ripper: The Final Solution.*

According to Joseph Gorman's story, Walter Sickert and Prince Albert Victor were friends and the latter would visit Sickert's studio in Cleveland Street, opposite which, at 6 Cleveland Street, was a tobacco shop where a young woman name Annie Crook worked. Annie Crook and Prince Albert Victor met, fell in love and were married, the marriage being witnessed by Mary Kelly. When the establishment discovered that the Prince had married they were horrified, partly because Annie Crook was a commoner and partly because she was a Catholic. The authorities staged a raid on the shop in Cleveland Street in April 1888, Prince Albert Victor was whisked away and in due course sent to India and Annie Crook was committed to an asylum, but Mary Kelly escaped with the baby, which she later gave into the care of Walter Sickert while she fled into the East End from where she and a group of friends tried to blackmail the government. This time Lord Salisbury turned to Freemason friends, who in their turn enlisted the assistance of Sir William Gull. Gull and a coachman named John Netley, together with Sir Robert Anderson who acted as lookout during the murders and helped to misdirect the investigation, commit the murders and Kelly and her friends are silenced.

Jack the Ripper: The Final Solution differed little from Joseph's original story, except that it argued that Walter Sickert, not Sir Robert Anderson, was the third man. A later variation on the theme would identify the third man as Lord Randolph Churchill. (Fairclough, Melvyn: *The Ripper and the Royals.* London: Duckworth, 1991. Second edition, London: Duckworth, 1992. London: Duckworth, 2002.)

Knight confirmed much of Joseph's story: Annie Elizabeth Crook was the daughter of William Crook (d.1891) and Sarah Ann Crook (1839–1916) and on 18 April 1885 she gave birth to an illegitimate daughter at St. Marylebone Workhouse and named her Alice Margaret. At that time Annie was living at 6 Cleveland Street and her occupation was given as 'confectionary assistant' (not a tobacconist, but confectioners often sold tobacco so it isn't a significant discrepancy). Knight was even able to show that John Netley existed. On the face of it the story looked good, very good in fact. The problem is that none of it fits what is known about the principal players. Walter Sickert isn't known to have had a studio in Cleveland Street. No.6 Cleveland Street was demolished in 1886 and Annie Elizabeth Crook wasn't living there when the supposed raid took place in April 1888 – by coincidence an Elizabeth Cook moved into one of the flats built on the site and lived there between 1888 and 1893. For a while some researchers thought Annie Elizabeth Crook and Elizabeth Cook were the same person. They weren't. Annie enjoyed her liberty for many years after 1888, living at various known addresses and workhouses before being committed to the lunacy ward of Fulham Road Workhouse. She wasn't a Roman Catholic. The secret marriage would have been illegal under the Royal Marriages Act of 1772 and the child just another Royal bastard, so no elaborate plot to rid the establishment of the blackmailing prostitutes would have been necessary. As for Mary Kelly, as we have seen, from 1886 she was living in the East End and from Easter 1887 had lived with Joseph Barnett, who said nothing about her working in a shop in Cleveland Street. Kelly wouldn't have been around to take care of Annie's child and wouldn't thereby have possessed information with which she could blackmail the Royal family.

If any part of the story is true, it happened in 1885, not 1888. In 1992 I met Ellen May Lackner, Joseph Sickert's cousin, and she confirmed that elements of Joseph's story circulated within the family during Joseph's infancy, so the story wasn't his invention, and she thought that Walter Sickert, not Prince Albert Victor, was the father of Alice Margaret, not Joseph. There was some connection with Royalty, she recalled, or at least with wealthy persons visiting the house, and there was some mysterious and frightening connection with Jack the Ripper, although my feeling was that this tale evolved as a way of frightening away too much inquisition.

As a footnote to the story one should mention *Prince Jack*, a book by the late Frank Spiering that has never been published in the United Kingdom and is basically a re-telling of Dr. Thomas Stowell's theory, with the added bonus of a claim to have found the material Dr. Stowell first saw. Attracted by Dr. Stowell's story, Frank Spiering had begun to research material for a proposed book of his own. According to Spiering, a friend who was a professor at Rutgers observed that Gull was a pioneer in internal medicine and recommended that Spiering visit the Academy of Medicine Library at 2 East 103rd Street in Manhattan, New York, because it has one of the most extensive collections of writings in the field and if anywhere outside the United Kingdom was bequeathed Gull's papers it would have been the Library.

In the card index Spiering found a single card

> S115 Acland, Theodore Dyke
> See:
> Gull, Sir William Withey
>   A collection of the public writings
> of ... Edited ... by Theodore Dyke Acland.
>   Medical Papers
> London, New Sydenham Soc, 1894 IX2
> p.3-609 p.19 p.80

This card was a reference to a published book, a collection of Sir William Gull's published writings arranged and edited by his son-in-law Theodore Dyke Acland and published in London by the New Sydenham Society in 1896. He ordered it and in due course it arrived from the basement, accompanied by a sheaf of 120 handwritten and unsigned pages in a brown stiff leather binding. Written in black ink in Sir William Gull's handwriting, they covered a variety of topics and about 30 pages in he read:

On 3 October I informed the Prince of Wales that his son was dying of syphilis of the brain. Under suggestion using the Nancy method my patient admitted to me the details of the murders he had committed in Whitechapel.

Patient related that the knife he used was taken from a horse slaughterhouse in Buck's Row.

An overwhelming ecstasy from watching butchers in Aldgate High Street caused him to add a leather apron to his accoutrements.

He tied a red bandanna around the second woman's throat which he used to half strangle her before he cut her throat back and forth until the blade touched bone. He said he felt extreme fear when he drove the knife into her chest but kept slashing until he had cut open her stomach.

Patient continued on as to how he later showed a kidney to James and James did not believe him. But James thought it would be funny to send it to the police.

Patient complained of headache over the forehead and vertex and intense pain down the back. His manner is quick and talkative with slight delirium . . .[16]

The notes abruptly ended, the next page being notes about another patient. Had the pages about Prince Albert Victor survived because they had become mixed up with papers relating to someone else? It's probably not worth asking that question. The notes sound too contrived to be true, particularly the reference to the leather apron, and Mr Spiering can be shown to elsewhere indulge in exaggeration. In 1994 the author Martin Fido visited the New York Academy of Medicine Library and checked the card index, finding it exactly as Frank Spiering had described, but there was no accompanying volume of handwritten notes and the library staff had no knowledge of any such volume.[17]

A more intriguing story along the same theme was told by writer Jean Overton Fuller in her book *Sickert and the Ripper Crimes*.[18]

Ms. Fuller relates a story told to her in 1948 by her mother, Violet Overton Fuller, and pieced together by her from various statements made by a friend, Florence Pash (1862–1951), an artist, friend and associate of Walter Sickert. Unfortunately, when writing her recollections of what she had been told, Jean Overton Fuller had already read Stephen Knight's book and there are reasons for thinking that her memory or interpretation of what she was told may have been contaminated by what she had read.

The way in which the story was received, information dribbled out over time by Florence Pash, related to Jean Overton Fuller at different times by her mother, and constructed and re-constructed at various times over the years with all the risk of external influences, makes the tale a difficult one to properly analyse. The core, however, is that Florence Pash knew that Walter Sickert had had an illegitimate son named Joseph and knew his mother very well. Sickert, she said, had a studio in a street where a few doors away there was a male brothel. A shopgirl, Mary Kelly, whom Florence Pash came to know quite well, was employed by Sickert as a nanny, but she left his employment when her pay was irregular and dependent on Sickert selling a picture. She drifted into prostitution, found her way to the East End and was murdered. Walter Sickert continued to look after the child, who one day Florence Pash took out and who was hurt in an accident when a coach drove straight at them. Walter Sickert had said it was a murder attempt and Florence Pash lived in fear for a long time thereafter. Mary Kelly started blackmailing Walter Sickert, possibly threatening to reveal details of Sickert's affairs with other women to his wife, and Sickert murdered Kelly and her friends. The only evidence presented for this, however, is Florence Pash's belief that Sickert had seen all the bodies *in situ*, which he could only have done if he had been the murderer.

On the face of it Jean Overton Fuller's story seems desperately thin and it is extremely easy to dismiss it as a tale blown out of all proportion.

But if one accepts Ms. Filler's claim that the basic details were known to her before she read Stephen Knight's *Jack the Ripper: The Final Solution*, and there seems no reason to suppose that her claim is untrue, then Florence Pash did tell Violet Overton Fuller that Walter Sickert looked after a child, Florence Pash did know a woman she called Mary Kelly and whom she said became an East End prostitute, and Walter Sickert did seem to think that the child entrusted to his care could have been the subject of a murder attempt. And Florence Pash did know that Joseph Sickert was the illegitimate son of Walter Sickert, which if true opens up the Joseph Sickert derived Stephen Knight story and suggests that it might have a factual foundation somewhere. But looking at the bodies of Jack the Ripper's victims, particularly the terrible photograph of Mary Kelly, or reading the accounts of what the Ripper did to his victims, it is impossible to believe that these murders were committed with any motive beyond the desire to inflict the horrible mutilations. The Ripper was clearly driven by personal demons to mutilate and destroy, not by a motive such as revenge or to silence a blackmailer. It is this that makes such theories difficult to accept. But stories like these often contain a kernel of truth, a small factual core around which has grown an accretion of elaboration, exaggeration and misunderstanding. The factual core is generally the purpose of the story, the reason why the story is told. There is probably something in Walter Sickert's early years concerning a child and Joseph, but how the Ripper links in, if he links in at all, remains deeply uncertain. As of writing, the best-selling author Patricia Cornwell is about to publish the results of her investigations which point the finger of guilt at Walter Sickert and which may lead the saga off in a completely new and interesting direction.

The story of the Maybrick diary is altogether different in that it depends on the authenticity of a document rather than stories based on old memories and rumours, and much of the interest in the story rests not in whether or not the document is genuine (because *prima facie* it is a forgery) but on the trials and tribulations involved in proving it a forgery.

On 9 March 1992 a man calling himself Michael Williams contacted Doreen Montgomery of the respected literary agency Rupert Crew Ltd, and told her that he possessed what purported to be the diary of Jack the Ripper. As unbelievable as his claim was, something about what he said or the way he said it made Doreen Montgomery listen rather more seriously than the claim seemingly warranted, and, whilst she felt that the story was probably untrue, she knew that turning it down could be turning away the publishing coup of the decade. She then turned to two clients, Shirley Harrison and her research partner Sally Evemy, who together make The Word Team, who she thought might be interested in taking the matter further if it should prove more than the suspected obvious hoax. They expressed interest and agreed to meet Mike. On 10 March Doreen wrote to 'Mike Williams' and invited him to bring the diary to her office. On Monday 13 April Michael Williams – who had in the meantime revealed that his real name was Mike Barrett (it has never been properly established why he called himself 'Williams') – arrived at Doreen Montgomery's office and produced the 'diary'. It was a Victorian 'scrapbook', a special book for pasting in postcards, photographs, theatre tickets, autographs and assorted mementoes (the pages had a divider between them so that the book would close flat even when items like postcards had been pasted in). The first 64 pages had been removed. There were 63 pages of handwritten text beginning mid-sentence and concluding with the signature 'Jack the Ripper, and the last 17 pages were blank.

The history – provenance – of the document was appalling. Mike Barrett had been in the habit of stopping off at a pub called The Saddle for a couple of pints before he collected his daughter from school. He there met 67-year-old Tony Devereux and they became casual friends. In March 1991 Tony Deverux had gone into hospital for a hip replacement and afterwards Mike would visit him at home, occasionally running small errands. On one visit in May 1991 Tony Devereux had the diary wrapped in brown paper waiting for him. He gave it to Mike and told him to do something with it. Mike took it home, unwrapped it, read it and disbelievingly pestered Tony Devereux for additional information. He was given none, except an assurance that the diary was genuine and that nobody else living knew it existed. The document mentioned few names and the author or supposed author wasn't immediately identifiable, but Mike Barrett eventually connected a place called Battlecrease in the diary with Battlecrease House, the home of James and Florence Maybrick, who in 1889 were at the centre of a cause célèbre when the latter was accused and convicted of poisoning the former. In August 1991 Tony Devereux died in Walton hospital, his death unanticipated, leaving Mike Barrett with a diary the origins of which were unknown and had died with Tony Devereux. Six months later, Mike Barrett contacted Doreen Montgomery.

With the identification of James Maybrick as the author of the diary the pieces of the story fell into place: James Maybrick, an ostensibly moneyed, upper middle class and middle-aged cotton broker had discovered that his young and beautiful wife Florence was having an affair and he saw her with her lover (who is not identified) in an area of Liverpool called Whitechapel. Tormented by a knowledge he could confide in no one, by an anger he could not release and by a strange excitement at the thought of his wife and her lover together, he vented his emotions on a prostitute in Manchester and having tasted blood settled on committing more murders, choosing Whitechapel, London. The diary continues with a rambling account of the murders, notably lacking any real detail, and concludes with a change of heart and a full confession to Florence. The diary ends: 'I give my name that all know of me, so history do tell, what love can do to a gentle man born. Yours truly, Jack the Ripper. Dated this third day of May 1889.'

The whole story sounded – and sounds – wildly improbable. Would anyone really murder and mutilate as Jack the Ripper had murdered and mutilated Mary Kelly simply because their wife had taken a lover? It didn't seem likely, but likely or not, if the diary was genuine then that is what happened. And thus was laid the problem that investigators would face for the next ten years. One could analyse the content of the diary and be impressed by it and dismiss it an obvious and amateurish bit of horror fiction, but personal opinion, gut reaction and even educated conclusions didn't determine when the ink went on the paper. From that day onwards the questions concerned *when* the diary was written.

Shirley Harrison first took the diary to the British Museum, then to the respected antiquarian bookdealers Jarndyce. Both gave the diary a cursory examination and concluded that nothing jumped up and screamed forgery, but both strongly recommended proper scientific analysis.

Numerous and sometimes conflicting scientific tests were conducted, but the results have been inconclusive, although almost every handwriting expert to have examined the document has stated that the handwriting does not match that of either James Maybrick or the Dear Boss letter and Saucy Jacky postcard, the diarist having claimed to have penned both – and this has alone been sufficient to persuade most people, the present author included, that the diary is definitely a forgery, but it has to be acknowledged that handwriting analysis may not be wholly reliable in this case. The problem is that an example of handwriting known to be by the person concerned, in this case James Maybrick, should be as similar as possible to the questioned writing – that is to say, written under the same physical and emotional conditions and hopefully containing the same words and letter combinations. This is relatively easy when comparing signatures, as on a cheque, but becomes increasingly difficult with long documents, and comparison between a formal document such as a business letter or a will (as was for a long time the only known example of Maybrick's handwriting) and a document such as the diary, written in an extreme and extraordinary emotional state and perhaps influenced by drugs (Maybrick was an arsenic addict, although it is questionable whether arsenic would influence handwriting) is obviously open to considerable imprecision. Nevertheless, all the examiners, distinct from graphologists (who seek to judge personality from handwriting), are agreed that the handwriting is not that of James Maybrick and the prudent must therefore conclude that the diary is a forgery.

But is it a modern forgery or an old forgery? And what was its purpose?

In June 1994 Mike Barrett confessed that he had written the diary to Liverpool journalist Harold Brough, who had been covering the story since it broke, but Brough was less than impressed by the confession, noting that Mike Barrett had been unable to answer simple questions such as where he'd bought the diary itself and the ink. Mr Barrett's marriage had broken up shortly before and it was believed that he blamed it on the diary and confessed in the hope that getting rid of it would encourage reconciliation. It didn't. The following month his estranged wife, Anne, told a story which led to a confession that her father had been bequeathed the diary among the possessions of his grandmother shortly before the outbreak of WWII, that he'd seen the diary when on leave in 1943 and had finally taken possession of it on 1950. Anne said Mike had been drinking consistently and too heavily, but knowing that he nurtured aspirations to be a writer she believed that the diary would prove inspirational. She had given the diary to Tony Devereux to give to Mike because she did not want Mike pestering her terminally ill father for more information.

Many people have doubted the story told by Anne Graham (she reverted to her maiden name after her divorce from Mike Barrett), but it was confirmed by her now deceased father and the tale hasn't advanced far since then, although a new dimension was given to the story in 1993 when Mr Albert Johnson reported that he had found scratched on the inner case of a gold watch made in 1846 and which he had recently purchased, initials matching the five canonical victims, the signature 'J. Maybrick' and the words 'I am Jack'. Reportedly a ladies watch, which has caused some people to question why James Maybrick would have carried a ladies watch (apparently dismissing the possibility that the watch would have belonged to Florence), two reputable and respected examiners have concluded that the scratches are old, Dr. S. Turgoose, of the University of Manchester Institute of Science and Technology's Corrosions and Protection Centre, giving it as his opinion that the scratches are likely to be tens of years old, are compatible with a date of 1888/89 and are not likely to be recent. The results of the tests have been disputed, as indeed the results of practically all the tests have been, but currently not definitively.

And so the story of the Maybrick diary has remained to taunt the investigator. Is it a modern forgery, as most people seem to believe, or an old forgery pre-dating 1950? Or is there just a remote chance that it could defy all the odds and be genuine?

Notes

1. *Murder By Decree* (1979) in which Sherlock Holmes and Dr. Watson, played by Christopher Plummer and James Mason penetrate the establishment; Sir William Gull is called Dr. Thomas Spivey. *Jack the Ripper* (1988) in which Chief Inspector Abberline and Sergeant George Godley, played by Michael Caine and Lewis Collins, repeat the act. *The Ripper* (1998), a seriously underrated movie that has Patrick Bergin as a fictional Inspector Jim Hansen discovering that Prince Eddy (Samuel West) is the Ripper. And *From Hell* (2001), a disappointing fourth re-working of the theme starring Johnny Depp and Robbie Coltrane as Abberline and Godley, again revealing Gull as the Ripper.
2. As recorded in two stout volumes Dalton, John N. (1886) *The Cruise of Her Majesty's Ship "Bacchante" 1879–1882. Compiled from the Private Journals, Letters, and Note-Books of Prince Albert Victor and Prince George of Wales.* London: Macmillan & Co. (2 vols).
3. Stephen was proposed as a suspect by Michael Harrison, who admitted in an interview in the *Listener* (17 August 1972) that he didn't agree with the theory

that the Ripper was Prince Albert Victor, but felt compelled to suggest an alternative candidate and settled on Stephen, speculating that he and the Prince had become homosexual lovers and was driven to murder prostitutes – according to Harrison evidence of sadistic tendencies being found in Stephen's poetry – on dates having some sort of significance. Dr David Abrahamson suggested that J.K. Stephen *and* Prince Albert Victor committed the murders together, whilst John Wilding has argued that J.K. Stephen committed the murders with Montague Druitt. The arguments lack evidential support. See: Harrison, Michael (1972) *Clarence: The Life of H.R.H. The Duke of Clarence and Avondale 1864–1892*. London: W.H. Allen. Published as *Clarence. Was He Jack the Ripper?* New York: Drake, 1974. Abrahamson, Dr. David (1992) *Murder & Madness. The Secret Life of Jack the Ripper*. New York: Donald I. Fine with new appendices, London: Robson Books, 1992. New York: Avon Books, 1993. Wilding, John (1993) *Jack the Ripper Revealed*. London: Constable.

4. A contemporary account of which was published, see Rees, J. D. (1891) *H.R.H. The Duke of Clarence & Avondale in Southern India, with a Narrative of Elephant Catching in Mysore by G. P. Sanderson*. London, Kegan Paul.

5. Pope-Hennessy, James (1959) *Queen Mary*. London: George Allen and Unwin.

6. Pope-Hennessy, James (1950) *Queen Mary*. London: George Allen and Unwin, p.190.

7. Castlereagh cut his throat with a penknife in his dressing-room at North Cray Place in Kent and died almost immediately on 12 August 1822. He believed he was about to be exposed as a homosexual, but the true facts are obscure. The most likely truth is that Castlereagh did accompany prostitutes who accosted him on his walk home from Parliament and that on one occasion he was recognised by a group of roughs. A short time later he accompanied a young woman to her rooms and where to his horror he discovered 'she' was a young man. At that moment roughs burst into the room. Castlereagh handed over the money he had on him and paid up when he received a blackmail letter. Three years later, the receipt of a second blackmail letter at a time when he was under considerable strain, turned Castlereagh's mind and he killed himself. See: Hyde, H. Montgomery (1959) *The Strange Death of Lord Castlereagh*. London: Heinemann.

8. Jullian, Philippe (1962) *Edouard VII*. Paris: Librarie Hachette. Published as *Edward and the Edwardians*, translated by Peter Dawney, London: Sidgwick and Jackson, 1967.

9. For what is probably the best account see Hyde, H. Montgomery (1976) *The Cleveland Street Scandal*. London: W.H. Allen. ch.2. Mr. Hyde says that there is no evidence that Prince Albert Victor was homosexual, but is nevertheless persuaded that he visited the brothel, perhaps in the mistaken belief that it provided striptease or was innocently taken there.

10. Stowell, Thomas E.A. (1970) 'Jack the Ripper' – A Solution?' Vol.5, No. 18 pp.40–51.

11. In November 1970 he would write to *The Times* saying, 'I have at no time associated His Royal Highness, the late Duke of Clarence, with the Whitechapel murders or suggested that the murderer was of Royal blood.' (Stowell, Thomas (1970) 'Letters to the Editor: Jack the Ripper'. London: *The Times*, November 9.) Technically true, because he hadn't actually named anyone or said that 'S' was a royal, there is no doubt that Prince Albert Victor was 'S' and Dr. Stowell had told Colin Wilson that Prince Albert Victor was his suspect.

12. Roberts, Cecil (1932) *Alfred Fripp*. London: Hutchinson.

13. Kendall, Colin (1990) 'The Intentions of Thomas Eldon Stowell'. *The Criminologist*, Vol.14, No.2, Summer, pp.113–20.

14. Wilson, Colin (1960) 'My Search For Jack the Ripper'. London: *Evening Standard*, 8–12 August.

15. Wilson, Colin and Odell, Robin (1987) *Jack the Ripper Summing Up and Verdict*. London: Bantam Press. London: Corgi Books, 1988. p.200.

16. Taken from an unpublished article by Frank Spiering found among papers purchased by writer Paul Feldman in 1993.

17. Spiering, Frank (1975) *Prince Jack: The True Story of Jack the Ripper*. New York: Doubleday. New York: Jove Books, 1980. Also see Begg, Paul, Fido, Martin and Skinner, Keith (1991) *The Jack the Ripper A to Z*. London: Headline. Revised editions, London: Headline, 1992, 1994, 1996.

18. Fuller, Jean Overton (1990) *Sickert & the Ripper Crimes*. Oxford: Mandrake. Oxford: Mandrake, 2001.

INDEX

INDEX